100 Trailblazers

Other books by Richard Lapchick

100 Trailblazers

GREAT WOMEN ATHLETES
Who Opened Doors for Future Generations

Richard Lapchick

with

Jessica Bartter
Sara Jane Baker
Catherine Lahey
Stacy Martin-Tenney
Horacio Ruiz
Ryan Sleeper

FiT

FITNESS INFORMATION TECHNOLOGY
A Division of the International Center
for Performance Excellence
West Virginia University
262 Coliseum, WVU-PASS
PO Box 6116
Morgantown, WV 26506-6116

Library of Congress Card Catalog Number: 2009923998

ISBN: 978-1-885693-86-0

Cover photographs (wrapping around from back cover): Tracy Caulkins, courtesy of University of Florida Athletic Association Communications; Michelle Akers, courtesy of UCF Athletics Communications; Annika Sorenstam, courtesy of Arizona Athletics Media Relations; Lyn St. James, courtesy of Lyn St. James; Venus Williams, courtesy of IMG; Lisa Leslie, courtesy of the University of Southern California; Lisa Fernandez, Courtesy of UCLA Sports Information; film strip courtesy of Nicola Gavin, bigstockphoto.com; race track courtesy of Evangelos Thomaidis, bigstockphoto.com

Cover Design: Bellerophon Productions
Typesetter: Bellerophon Productions
Copyeditor: Maria denBoer
Proofreader: Berkeley Bentley
Printed by United Book Press, Inc.

10   9   8   7   6   5   4   3   2   1

Fitness Information Technology
A Division of the International Center for Performance Excellence
West Virginia University
262 Coliseum, WVU-PASS
PO Box 6116
Morgantown, WV 26506-6116
800.477.4348 (toll free)
304.293.6888 (phone)
304.293.6658 (fax)
Email: fitcustomerservice@mail.wvu.edu
Website: www.fitinfotech.com

To Rich and Helen DeVos, whose generosity has created the DeVos Sport Business Management Program and The Institute for Diversity and Ethics in Sport at the University of Central Florida and has enriched the existing programs of the National Consortium for Academics and Sports. Rich and Helen have become heroes to me and enabled all three programs to help use sport as a powerful vehicle for social change.

—*Richard Lapchick*

Contents

CHAPTER 6 • Female Swimmers and Divers: Lapping Expectations in the Pool   221

CHAPTER 9 • The Explosion of Women's Soccer   361

CHAPTER 10 • Women's Softball and Women in Baseball: Standing Tall for Females for Decades   377

CHAPTER 11 • Women Basketball Players: Leaving Footprints on the Hardwood   407

Foreword

It is my great pleasure to introduce you to this new work by Dr. Richard Lapchick. I have long admired Dr. Lapchick for his integrity, his courage, and his determination to bring justice throughout society. He has chosen the vehicle of sport for his work. He has dedicated his life to promoting a better understanding of sport and through that, developing a pathway to social justice.

Dr. Lapchick was introduced to sport as the son of the great professional basketball coach, Joe Lapchick. While it would seem to be the best of all worlds to have a dad coaching the fabled New York Knicks basketball team, he was living through a turbulent time as the color of one's skin defined the role one would play in life. While many would use the color of skin to define a person, Lapchick's father, Joe, was interested in the skill and ability of the athlete and considered the color of skin as merely an ancillary descriptor.

Richard, Joe's son, has taken the strength of his father's conviction to help us all understand the limitations our society through the amazing prism of sport. He has written of his own frightening and enlightening experiences at the hand of some racist terrorists who expressed their anger and ignorance by cutting words onto his body. Dr. Lapchick has chronicled the injustices found throughout sport and most recently in the hiring patterns of the leadership of sports, especially the coaches and managers of professional sports.

Now, he has turned the light of his investigation to illuminate the field of women's sports. Yes, folks, women have been a part of the history of sports. Sadly, we are still in the era of introduction to these great leaders who should be household names. It is well past time to learn about the hundreds of women who have helped form the world of sport. Richard Lapchick has provided us with an extraordinary opportunity to meet *100 Trailblazers: Great Women Athletes Who Opened Doors for Future Generations*. This book will not only introduce the reader to these women, but it will also encourage the reader to learn more about the role that each woman has played in furthering sport and a just society through sport.

Sit back and get comfortable as you enter the classroom of Dr. Richard Lapchick. You are about to meet 100 women who have made life choices to support sport. Learn from those who endeavor to be the best on the field of play and to provide the best for our game of life.

—Anita L. DeFrantz

February 2009

Acknowledgments

It is with a deep sense of appreciation that I acknowledge the individuals who helped turn *100 Trailblazers* from a dream into a reality. We have been a team of writers who share a passion for equality in sport and society. My teammates are students in the DeVos Sports Business Management Program at the University of Central Florida who are my graduate assistants in The Institute for Diversity and Ethics in Sport. Their skills and commitment assure me that the leaders of the next generation can, and will, make a difference. It is with great respect and love that I acknowledge the team members: Horacio Ruiz, Sara Jane Baker, Catherine Lahey, Stacey Martin-Tenney, and Ryan Sleeper. The team leader, as she has been on all three books in the series, is Jessica Bartter, who is the assistant director for communications and marketing for the National Consortium for Academics and Sports (NCAS). She does amazing work and her efforts here are no exception. Without Jessica, there would be no series of books.

I must also mention Catherine Elkins, who handled the arduous process of editing each and every story.

Dr. Bill Sutton, my colleague and dear friend at DeVos, wrote the story of Effa Manley, which adds so much to the book.

Above all, we have to acknowledge the 100 trailblazers whose lives collectively form the tapestry of this work. Each of their stories could be required reading in American history classes. It was a privilege and great honor that our team of writers told their stories in hopes of inspiring others to do more. To all of the 100 trailblazers, thank you for the differences you made.

Finally, I would like to thank everyone associated with the NCAS and the DeVos Program. My colleagues Keith Lee, Tom Miller, Robert Weathers, Jessica Bartter, Jeff O'Brien, Shannon Spriggs, and Shantina Gordon at the NCAS and Bill Sutton, Keith Harrison, Philomena Pirolo, and Maria Molina at DeVos inspire me with their never-ending commitment to social justice.

But for me, number one will always be family, so I thank them for their support, which did not waver when I undertook this book after vowing to take a long break after I had completed my 11th book. My family fills me with strength and courage, and my heart with love and happiness each day. My wife, Ann, our children Joe, Emily, Chamy and her husband, Michael, and grandchildren, Taylor and Emma, provide the type of encouragement and understanding that makes me motivated each morning. Their spirits brighten each day and keep me striving to leave this world better than how I found it.

I

AN INTRODUCTION

GREAT WOMEN ATHLETES WHO OPENED DOORS FOR FUTURE GENERATIONS

Richard Lapchick

As with all history these days, many people know the stories of a few important figures, often without much of the rich detail of their lives. Too frequently the people we know best are white men. Historically, racism and sexism have meant that the stories of people of color and women are far less well known. Sometimes when racism and sexism combine, they totally obscure the lives of women of color. This is true in society and in sport.

This is why I have undertaken, along with Jessica Bartter, Horacio Ruiz, Sara Jane Baker, Catherine Lahey, Stacey Martin-Tenney, and Ryan Sleeper, to write this book about 100 women in sport who have been trailblazers for others. It is the third book in a series devoted to shedding light on the lives of people whose life stories are important but are not well known.

A revolution for women in sport started in the 1970s when, within 15 months of each other, Title IX of the Education Amendment Act was signed by President Richard M. Nixon on June 23, 1972, and tennis-great Billie Jean King defeated Bobby Riggs on September 23, 1973. The world of sports was never the same again.

In 1970, one in 27 high school girls played a varsity sport compared to two out of five in 2008. In 1971 the 294,015 girls competing in high school sports accounted for 7 percent of all high school varsity athletes. In 2007–08, the 3,057,266 girls competing accounted for 41.5 percent of all high school varsity athletes, reflecting a more than 900 percent increase since the Act's enactment.

At the college level, in 1971 there were 29,977 women competing compared to 170,384 men. In 2006–07, there were 172,534 women and 233,830 men competing. Women had 42.46 percent of the college team slots in 2006–07.

Before Title IX, female collegiate athletics received 2 percent of overall athletic budgets compared to approximately 40 percent today. A school with a football program is more likely to have a bigger disproportion than those without a costly football program. In 1970, there was an average of 2.5 women's teams per college. Today, the average is 9.28 women's teams per institution. In 1972, 90 percent of women's teams were coached by women, while in 2007–08, 42.8 percent of women's teams were coached by men.

In 2007, we published *100 Pioneers: African-Americans Who Broke Color Barriers in Sport.* We recognized that almost everyone knew the story of Jackie Robinson and how his joining the Brooklyn Dodgers in 1947 began to change the face of American sports. We celebrate Jackie Robinson in every ballpark, his number has been retired, and there are regular ceremonies in his honor. When Americans are asked who the greatest racial pioneer in sport is, they most often mention Jackie Robinson's name.

Yet, few know names of the people who broke the barriers in the American League just a few months later, or in the National Football League (NFL), the National Basketball Association (NBA), or the National Hockey League (NHL), or who were the first African-American athletes to break down the barriers of segregation at the Southeastern, Atlantic Coast, Big Ten, Big 8/Big 12, and Ivy League conference schools.

Some know about Arthur Ashe and Althea Gibson in tennis, but few know the names of those who led the way in other sports. Many who know Muhammad Ali do not know Jack Johnson.

100 Pioneers was designed as the second book in a series to tell readers just that.

The series began at the National Consortium for Academics and Sports (NCAS). Because of the work that we do in the NCAS and the DeVos Sport Business Management Program, we have become all too aware of the problems that exist in sport. Each day we seem to read about a rule being violated, an athlete getting in trouble with drugs, an athlete arrested for sexual assault, steroid use in baseball, the NFL, or track and field, the threat that gambling poses to college sports, or agents recruiting young athletes with illegal monetary inducements. The list goes on and on. That is why it was so joyous for me when Dr. Taylor Ellis, the dean of undergraduate education in the College of Business Administration at the University of Central Florida, came to my office February 2005.

I had just finished a book called *New Game Plan for College Sport* and was frankly tired of writing. I vowed that I would not take up another book project for several years. Taylor changed all of that on the morning after the 2005 NCAS banquet. He came in, sat down, and said, "When I was a boy, I wasn't focused and wasn't living up to my potential." He said, "Then someone gave me this book." Taylor placed a well-worn copy of Barlow Meyers's *Real Life Stories: Champions All the Way*, published 45 years earlier, on my desk. He said, "Somebody gave me this book about seven athletes and the obstacles they overcame to do great things in life. This book transformed my life and gave me a sense of direction and hope." Taylor said, "Every year you honor five or six such athletes at the Consortium's award banquet. You have to write a book about them." So came the idea for *100 Heroes: People in Sport Who Make This a Better World*.

I had to undertake the project in spite of my vow to the contrary. This book could be, I thought, a real celebration of sport. It could portray the power of sport to transform not only individuals, but their impact on the broader society. I ran through my head the names of all the award winners I could recall and knew that their stories would inspire people collectively who could not be in the presence of these people in the halls when we honored them.

With the 20th anniversary of the Consortium exactly a year away, I knew that we would have to work hard to get this project done. I enlisted the support of Jessica Bartter, who is the assistant director for communications and marketing of the NCAS. We began to draw all of the names and addresses together and contact the previous award winners who were still alive. Their support for the project was overwhelmingly positive. We began to collect the biographical materials and stories that were the basis for the awards. We also asked Drew Tyler, Stacy Martin, Jennifer Brenden, and Brian Wright, all graduate students in the DeVos Sport Business Management Program, to help write the individual stories.

100 Heroes was published in February 2006. I knew there was more to do.

For *100 Pioneers* we included the stories of the first African-American players, coaches, general managers, and team presidents in the various professional sports. We hoped to have the first African-American male and female student-athletes to compete in each of the Southeastern Conference (SEC), Atlantic Coast Conference (ACC), Big 10, Big 8/Big 12, and Ivy League schools as well as the first African-American coaches and athletic directors in those conferences. We have John Thompson and Carolyn Peck, the first African-American coaches to win the National Collegiate Athletic Association (NCAA) men's and women's basketball championships, respectively, and Ty Willingham, the first to coach in a Bowl Championship Series (BCS) Bowl Game. Included is Willie Jefferies, the first African-American Division I football coach, and Gale Sayers, the first African-American Division I athletic director.

We also included those icons who did not neatly fit categories, such as Coach Eddie Robinson at Grambling State and renaissance man Paul Robeson. There were three "events" that shaped their times, including the clenched fist, black glove salute of John Carlos and Tommy Smith at the 1968 Mexico City Olympics; the 1975 NBA Finals, when two African-American head coaches first faced each other for any championship; and the 2007 Super Bowl, when two African-American head coaches faced each other for the NFL title for the first time.

100 Pioneers was a mixture of historical research and interviews with those who broke down color barriers on college campuses and in cities around the country. I believed sharing the inspiring life stories of those who paved the way for other people of color in the world of sports can continue to make this world a better place. Such important figures deserve a platform from which to tell their stories and share what their experiences have meant to them. I was part of a team of writers and researchers made up of my graduate assistants at the DeVos Sport Business Management Graduate Program in the College of Business Administration at the University of Central Florida. As with *100 Heroes*, the team was led by Jessica Bartter. The writers included Stacy Martin, Horacio Ruiz, Jennifer Brenden, and Marcus Sedberry. The editor was Catherine Lahey, and research support was offered by Zoie Springer. We were all proud to play a role by publishing these stories that include the adversities each conquered, the decisions each faced, and the accomplishments that each individual achieved.

But we knew there was yet more to do and thus a new team, also led by Jessica Bartter, was formed to write about the women who blazed new trails in sport.

The book is organized into two parts. The first covers the women who were the decision makers and organizational leaders whose courage and conviction helped open so many doors for others. This section includes the women who were presidents of the Association for Intercollegiate Athletics for Women (AIAW), whose very success forced the NCAA to take over their work in putting on women's collegiate championships and infusing women's college sport with deep-seated values not apparent in men's college sport. There are also the stories of the women who were athletic directors of departments with Division I-A football programs. Also included are the stories of Donna Lopiano and the Women's Sports Foundation (WSF), Tina Sloan Green and the Black Women in Sports Foundation, Anita DeFrantz for her work with the Olympics, and Val Ackerman as the first president of the Women's National Basketball Association (WNBA).

It was the lifelong commitment made by this group of women who fought the fight in the courts, in their colleges and universities, at the conference and NCAA levels, and in Olympic and pro sports. In many cases the great athletes, especially those who benefited from Title IX, might not have had the chance to compete. Many of the women discussed in the section on administrators were also great athletes. Yet, some could never show that on a wide stage.

Then there were many athletes in the specific sports sections who also could have been profiled for the leadership they showed in advancing Title IX or in their leadership roles in the WSF, founded by Billie Jean King. Among those who have been president or leading board members of the WSF are Nancy Hogshead-Makar, Julie Foudy, Carol Mann, Donna deVarona, Diana Nyad, and Willye White.

There were many who succeeded the trailblazers in different sports who not only never had to think about fighting the fight for women's rights but could think outside of the box as to what they could do competitively as female athletes. Annika Sorenstam played in spots on the Professional Golfers Association (PGA) tour. So did Michelle Wie. We had women coaching men's Division I men's basketball teams and playing Division I-A football. There have been winning women in motor sports, as jockeys, and in the Iditarod sleddog race. According to the National Federation of State High School Associations, nearly 3,000 girls play high school football. On the level of men's professional sports, women have been owners, team presidents, assistant general managers, referees, team physicians, trainers, and radio and television broadcasters.

We are no longer thinking about exclusivity. In many ways, we owe that sea change of thinking to the administrators featured in *100 Trailblazers*.

The second part is on 11 of the sports in which women have been most successful and focuses on the trailblazers in each rather than the modern-day greats. There are rare exceptions to that, such as in tennis, where Serena and Venus Williams are featured along with Hazel Wightman, Margaret Osborne duPont, Billie Jean King, Maureen Connolly, Althea Gibson, Evonne Goolagong, and Chris Evert. It was, of course, in tennis where Billie Jean King's victory over Bobby Riggs helped change all women's sport for all females. Anything seemed possible after that magical day.

There were women who were great at several sports who were hard to place. One early star was Eleonora Randolph Sears, whose full story is not included in this book. Before Annika Sorenstam was winning major after major on the links; before Venus and Serena Williams were competing for Grand Slam titles; before Danica Patrick was winning Indy Racing League competitions; and even before Amelia Earhart was flying across the Atlantic, Sears was participating in each of these sports, not to mention boating, football, hockey, boxing, skating, swimming, and trap shooting! Not only was she participating, she was competing at a very high level. In fact, a 1910 magazine article proclaimed her "the best all-around athlete in American society."

Of all the sports she competed in, Sears seemed to take tennis and squash racquets most seriously. She captured four U.S. women's doubles tennis championships. She won two titles with Hazel Hotchkiss Wightman in 1911 and 1915, and two more with Molla Bjurstedt Mallory in 1916 and 1917. She also won the mixed doubles championship in 1916 with Willis E. Davis. In addition, she was a two-time finalist for the national singles championship.

Sears became the first woman to ever play squash racquets when, in 1918, she demanded that the local men's-only club allow her to play on its courts. The game, now referred to simply as squash, is an indoor variation of tennis. Sears beat the best local male player the first time she ever played the game, inspiring women to take up tennis. In 1928, she won the first national squash racquets championship for women. The mere fact that there was even a squash racquets championship for women was due almost entirely to Sears's influence. This is just one example of her impact on the growth of women's sports. In her era, Sears was called the trailblazer for women's entrance into sports.

Babe Didrikson Zaharias was in a category by herself and was such a great all-around athlete that she could have been included in several sections of this book, including golf. However, you will find her in the track and field section. Of all the great women golfers, we have selected as our trailblazers Glenna Collett-Vare, Louise Suggs, Patty Berg, Betty Jameson, Mickey Wright, Carol Mann, Kathy Whitworth, JoAnne Carner, Nancy Lopez, and Annika Sorenstam. More recently, women from other countries have dominated the women's tour. In the major 2008 championships, Mexican Lorena Ochoa won the Kraft Nabisco, Chinese golfer Yani Tseng won the Ladies' Professional Golf Association (LPGA) Championship, and South Koreans Inbee Park and Ji-Yai Shin won the U.S. and British Opens, respectively.

In the figure skating section, we featured Sonja Henie, Mabel Fairbanks, Tenley Albright, Peggy Fleming Jenkins, Katarina Witt, and Kristi Yamaguchi. There were so many phenomenal skaters in the second half of the 20th century that many in the 1990s and in the new millennium could not be included. We also featured Bonnie Blair for her domination of speed skating.

The same was true for those whom we selected to feature as swimmers and divers, with Eleanor Holm, Florence Chadwick, Janet Evans, Tracy Caulkins, Debbie Meyer, Mary Meagher Plant, Nancy Hogshead-Makar, Diana Nyad, and Donna de Varona as our swimmers and Micki King and Pat McCormick as our divers. These swimmers and divers set the way for today's greats. At the 2008 Beijing

Olympics, the U.S. women's team totaled 31 medals, including two gold, 18 silver, and 11 bronze. Natalie Coughlin, Rebecca Soni and Dara Torres won the headlines and hearts of the fans.

Like swimming, every four years, gymnastics becomes one of the world's favorite sports and the Beijing Olympics proved to be no exception. The performances of American gold medal winners Nastia Liukin in the women's individual all-around and Shawn Johnson in the women's balance beam dominated the headlines. While there was an age controversy about how old the Chinese girls were, the level of performance of women's team competition gold medalists Fei Cheng, Kexin He, Yuyuan Jiang, Shanshan Li, Yilin Yang, and Linlin Deng cannot be challenged.

Gymnastics has a rich history that has often transcended nationalism. The three women profiled in the gymnastics section became beloved across borders; Olga Korbut, Nadia Comaneci, and Mary Lou Retton were the sport's antifreeze to the Cold War.

Tennis, golf, figure skating, and gymnastics all have a rich history and are sports where it generally was expensive to compete, which therefore made them largely the sports of the economically elite. The emergence of the more recent popularity of track and field, soccer, softball, basketball, and volleyball yield a slightly more modern history and more inclusive list of competitors. Motor sports is in a unique category, as it is both expensive and perhaps the most white-male-dominated sport.

There are more African-American women in our track and field section than any other. We included athletes Babe Didrikson Zaharias, Helen Stephens, Alice Coachman, Mae Faggs Starr, Wilma Rudolph, Madeline Manning Mims, Wyomia Tyus, Florence Griffith-Joyner, Evelyn Ashford, Valerie Brisco-Hooks, Jackie Joyner-Kersee, Joan Benoit, and Willye White and coaches Nell Jackson, Barbara Jacket, and Beverly Kearney.

Women's soccer, propelled by Title IX, is now so popular in the United States that it is easy to forget this popularity is quite new and thus our trailblazers are more contemporary. They are Michelle Akers, Mia Hamm, and Julie Foudy.

The year 1996 is often talked about as the year of women in the Olympics. Women's soccer and basketball were expected to be huge and they were. It was also time for softball to join the stage. Lisa Fernandez, Joan Joyce, Margie Wright, Sharon Backus, and Dr. Dot Richardson are among the historical stars of the game of softball. Donna Lopiano could have been included in this section, but her advocacy efforts for Title IX and leadership at the WSF have her elsewhere in the book. Joyce, Wright, and Backus became legendary coaches. We have included the story of Effa Manley because she played such a unique role in baseball. There are only a few women in 2008 with responsibilities of the magnitude that Manley had 60 years ago with her sport franchise. We also included Toni Stone because she became the first woman to play professional baseball when she broke the gender barrier in a 1953 Negro League baseball game in Omaha.

Choosing those to include in our basketball section was difficult. In the end we picked coaches Pat Summitt, Vivian Stringer, Tara VanDerveer, and Margaret Wade. The players are Nancy Lieberman, Ann Meyers Drysdale, Cheryl Miller, Sheryl Swoopes, and Lisa Leslie. Betty Jaynes is like the thread that runs through the modern story of women's basketball. She was the long-time director and CEO of the Women's Basketball Coaches Association (WBCA).

When I think about women and volleyball, I see two shining stars: Flo Hyman and Misty May-Treanor. While we lost Flo Hyman when she was too young and May-Treanor may have successors in the wings, they both remain as inspirations.

Finally, the motor sports industry historically has seemed to be the most exclusive white male club in sports. Tennis, golf, and swimming, the so-called country club sports, had the same label but slowly—very slowly—barriers began to fall. Then, on April 19, 2008, Danica Patrick won the race at Twin Ring Motegi in Japan and became the first woman ever to win an IndyCar race. It was a whole new world for women in motor sports. But she stood on the shoulders of the other two women in the section on motor sports: Lyn St. James and Janet Guthrie. These three women are featured in *100 Trailblazers*.

The final part is the conclusion, with a look at the future of women in sport that has been created by these amazing historical trailblazers featured in this book.

As I wrote in *100 Heroes*, I recognized that sport reaches all kinds of people for all kinds of reasons. Sport can be played competitively or recreationally or sport can be watched and enjoyed as entertainment. We watch sports we never play and we play sports we never watch. Sport can help build friendships, families, respect, confidence, and character. Sport provides health benefits some medical professionals can only begin to understand.

Most important, sport is unique in the boundaries it crosses with both its participants and its audience. Differences in gender, race, physical and mental abilities, age, religion, and cultures are irrelevant in the huddle, on the field, in the gym, or in the water. Sport smashes these barriers like nothing else can. The athletes in *100 Heroes*, *100 Pioneers*, and *100 Trailblazers* represent that better than anyone because of their own life experiences.

Yet many of today's young women as well as athletes of color do not realize how different their field looked 100, 50, or even 25 years ago. The history of race and gender in the United States may be studied by young Americans but too many cannot relate. But young people do relate to sport. By illustrating the history of America's racial and gender barriers through the vehicle of sport, the picture may become clearer. It can be the role of those who lived it to educate the next generation and there will be no better time to do so than now.

Young athletes who look up to Danica Patrick, Venus and Serena Williams, Natalie Coughlin, Nastia Liukin, Shawn Johnson, Lorena Ochoa, Candace Parker, LeBron James, and Tiger Woods should know of those who came before them to pave the way. For without these pioneers and trailblazers, today's heroes might still just be knocking at the doors.

2

ADMINISTRATORS BREAK DOWN THE WALLS

Introduction by Richard Lapchick

All the great athletes featured in *100 Trailblazers* were remarkable pioneers within their own sports. However, this book would be incomplete if we failed to feature the lifelong commitment made by a group of women who fought the fight in the courts, in their colleges and universities, at the conference and National Collegiate Athletic Association (NCAA) levels, and in Olympic and pro sports. In many cases the great athletes, especially those who benefited from Title IX, might not have had the chance to compete. Many of the women discussed in this chapter were also great athletes. Some could never show that on a wide stage.

Then there were many athletes in the specific sports sections who could have been profiled here for the leadership they showed in advancing Title IX or in their leadership roles in the Women's Sports Foundation (WSF), founded by Billie Jean King. Among those who have been president or leading board members of the WSF are Nancy Hogshead-Makar, Julie Foudy, Carol Mann, Donna deVarona, Diana Nyad, and Willye White.

There were many who succeeded the trailblazers in different sports who not only never had to think about fighting the fight for women's rights but could think out of the box as to what they could do competitively as female athletes. Annika Sorenstam played in spots on the Professional Golfers Association (PGA) tour. So did Michelle Wie. We had women coaching men's Division I men's basketball teams and playing Division I-A football. There have been winning women in motor sports, as jockeys, and in the Iditarod sled-dog race. According to the National Federation of State High School Associations, nearly 3,000 girls play high school football. On the level of men's professional sports, women have been owners, team presidents, assistant general managers, referees, team physicians and trainers, and radio and television broadcasters.

We are no longer thinking about exclusivity. In many ways, we owe that change of thinking to the administrators in this section.

Association for Intercollegiate Athletics for Women

The Association for Intercollegiate Athletics for Women (AIAW) was founded in 1971 to govern collegiate women's athletics and to administer national championships. The AIAW became a center for advocacy for women's sports by defining these sports on their own terms and not as identified by men in sport. When it was founded, men had little interest in women's sports. That all changed as women's sports started to get noticed with their own national championships and also, of course, because Title IX of the Education Amendments was passed in 1972. The new federal law prohibited discrimination based on gender in any activity at an educational institution that received federal funds, forcing institutions of higher education to fund women's athletics and offer women athletic scholarships. Championships gained significance quickly.

The Division of Girls and Women's Sports (DGWS) was an organization of physical educators and was a division of the American Alliance for Health, Physical Education and Recreation (AAHPER). It is now known as the National Association for Girls and Women in Sport (NAGWS). DGWS became the first nationally recognized collegiate organization for women's athletics and was the forerunner of the AIAW. The Commission on Intercollegiate Athletics for Women (CIAW) operated under the auspices of the DGWS and governed from 1966 to 1972, conducting championships in seven sports.

It did not take long to realize that a group of professionals could not run or govern a membership collegiate athletic governance system; they called a convention. The result was the creation of the AIAW.

During the 1972–73 season, its first year of actual operation, the AIAW offered its first seven national championships in badminton, basketball, golf, gymnastics, swimming and diving, track and field, and volleyball. In 1972, Immaculata College won the first of three consecutive AIAW women's national collegiate basketball championships. In 1975, Immaculata and Queens College met in Madison Square Garden before 12,000 fans.

The AIAW had different values than the NCAA, emphasizing participation as much as competition. The student in the "student-athlete" was the top priority. They wanted to avoid the NCAA's drive toward commercialization. None of this was relevant to the women until their basketball championships took off in popularity. In the 1970s and even into the 1980s, the NCAA actively sought to limit the impact of Title IX. Suddenly, the NCAA did get interested, culminating in the NCAA voting in 1981 to establish women's championships in a number of women's sports with basketball being the prize. The AIAW sued to prevent the NCAA from implementing the new championships. The suit was dismissed, so schools had to choose between the NCAA and AIAW. Realistically, the NCAA had all the power. The AIAW match-up between Rutgers and Texas was its last championship. Louisiana Tech defeated Cheyney State, becoming the first NCAA Division I women's basketball champion.

The women who led the AIAW are included in this section.

Judy Sweet became the first female athletic director of a combined intercollegiate athletic program in the nation. Her teams won a remarkable 25 NCAA Championships and were national runners-up 32 times in her 24 years. In 1997–98, UC San Diego won the Division III Sears Director's Cup for program excellence. This marked the first time that an athletic department directed by a woman had been awarded the Cup. Judy was the first female president of the NCAA from 1991 to 1993. She became the first female senior vice president for championships and education services for the NCAA in 2003, in addition to maintaining her role as the senior women's administrator.

Charlotte West had an amazing 42-year career at Southern Illinois as a coach, instructor, professor, and administrator. West coached women's basketball for 16 years, golf for 12 years, badminton for seven years, and volleyball for a year. In 1969, her golf team won the national championship and the basketball team finished fifth in the nation in the National Invitational Tournament (NIT) Women's Basketball Tournament. In 1959, she was named the director of women's athletics. When the men's and women's programs merged in 1986, she was named an associate athletic director, a post she would hold until her retirement in 1998. As women's athletic director, West was able to build a nationally recognized program that included 11 sports and had an operating budget of more than $1 million.

West became heavily involved with Title IX legislation. She served as a consultant for the Health, Education, and Welfare portions of Title IX that related to athletics. West worked with the AIAW and was elected president. She was instrumental in landing television contracts for women's sports, increasing both participatory and financial opportunities for women in sports through federal legislation, and in drawing the guidelines for the AIAW.

Christine Grant was the acting president of the AIAW from 1979 to 1980, when it became clear the association was near the end of its reign. She was president in 1980–81 and helped members of the AIAW try in vain to keep the association alive. Grant knew how important it was to provide women with leadership roles in college sport.

After the presiding judge ruled against the AIAW in its suit against the NCAA, many women left intercollegiate athletics and never returned. Grant says she was blackballed by the NCAA but she still was the athletic director of the women's athletic department at the University of Iowa. Under her leadership, Iowa's athletic department grew to include 12 NCAA championship sports. Iowa teams won a 27 Big Ten Conference titles during her tenure. It was many years before Grant would participate in NCAA activities. In 2007, she became the fourth recipient of the NCAA President's Gerald R. Ford Award, one of its highest awards. She was president of the National Association of Collegiate Women Athletics Administrators (NACWAA) from 1987 to 1989. Grant testified before Congress on numerous occasions regarding gender equity in sports. She also served as a consultant for the Civil Rights Title IX Task Force, becoming a key figure in drafting Title IX implementation.

Merrily Dean Baker became the first woman to be an athletic director in the Big Ten when she went to Michigan State in 1992. She was the women's athletic director for 12 years at Princeton. There she became a leading proponent for women's athletics on the national level by working with the AIAW, where she played a crucial role in lobbying for Title IX legislation. But with the passing of Title IX, the dissolution of the AIAW, and the absorption of women's sports by the NCAA, Baker saw the possibility of more expansive financial resources to fund women's athletics.

Baker went to the University of Minnesota in 1982 as the athletic director of the women's athletic department. Under her leadership the department took women's athletics to a higher level, increasing the amount of scholarship money available to its athletes and also getting the State of Minnesota to finance the operations of the women's athletic departments due to her lobbying efforts. Baker was also able to secure a television contract for the women's athletic department. In 1988, her final year at Minnesota, she was named one of the "100 Most Powerful Women" in the United States by *Ladies' Home Journal*. Baker was convinced by then–executive director of the NCAA Richard Schultz to serve as the assistant executive director of the NCAA between 1988 and 1992.

In 1992, Michigan State called and Baker headed back to the Big Ten as the first woman to be named athletic director at the conference and only the second at a Division I football–playing institution. Baker resigned from Michigan State in 1995, but she had already left her mark.

Carol Gordon accepted her first coaching and teaching job at the University of New Hampshire in 1948. Six years later, she took her career to the University of Utah. In addition to coaching and teaching at Utah, Gordon added to her educational resume. In 1962, Washington State University hired Gordon to chair its department of physical education for women. She also coached the Cougar field hockey and tennis teams while teaching psychology of sport classes. In addition to her teaching, coaching, and administrative roles at Washington State, Gordon found time to serve as the president of the AIAW in 1973–74. After 21 years at Washington State, Carol Gordon retired in 1983.

Peggy Burke was a founding member of the AIAW. Burke began as a representative at the state level in Iowa, helping to defuse the boycott of Iowa Wesleyan University. From the state level, Burke became a member of the AIAW first delegate assembly in 1972 and eventually served as the organization's president from 1976 to 1977.

The issue was a volatile one, particularly for those like Burke who had worked so tirelessly to create an organization for women by women. "I was very opposed to the NCAA's takeover of women's sports governance. It came at a time when we [the AIAW] were gaining television contracts, a step that would have made the AIAW financially feasible into the future. I resented the takeover then and I resent it today."

When asked if she had any advice for the young women of

today, Burke replied by quoting James McNeill Whistler, "Someone once said 'Women should raise more hell and fewer flowers.' I still think that's a good motto for today."

Dr. Lee Morrison came to Virginia's Madison College, now James Madison University (JMU), because the school offered sports for women. She coached field hockey for 17 years. Eventually she became director of women's intercollegiate sports from 1972 to 1989. During her time at Madison, Morrison's prowess and passion as a champion of women's athletics began to gain recognition in the larger world of sport.

Dr. Morrison played a pivotal role in the two things that significantly contributed to increased opportunities for female athletes: the interpretation and promotion of Title IX and the establishment of a collegiate national championship system for women's sports. From 1970 to 1973, she acted as a founding member and the first president of the Virginia Federation for Intercollegiate Sports for College Women, an organization that helped spawn the AIAW. She became a founding member and also a president.

Dr. Morrison and a small number of athletic directors were summoned to Washington by the Honorable Joseph A. Califano, U.S. secretary of health, education and welfare, in order to assist with "properly" interpreting and promoting Title IX.

When she arrived at SUNY at Cortland in an academic post, Dr. Carole Mushier was drawn into athletic administration after she found the university was trying to organize a serious women's athletic department. At first, she coached the field hockey team and then, when she saw stronger leadership was needed to steer the women's program, she accepted an administrative position. From the moment she returned to athletic administration, Mushier was involved in the development and the passing of Title IX into federal law.

In 1979, Dr. Mushier served as the national president of the AIAW. It was the year in which an interpretation policy was passed for Title IX to determine whether schools were in compliance with the law. As AIAW president, Mushier testified before Congress and the U.S. Commission on Civil Rights. She was partly responsible for keeping football in the equation when how to be compliant with Title IX was considered. That became critical when the NCAA took over women's sport.

Dr. Carol Oglesby realized that sport was as much about physical activity and personal health as it was about winning and losing. She spent her career as an academic pioneer in kinesiology and as a strong voice for women and girls in sport.

Dr. Oglesby's pioneering book, *Women and Sport: From Myth to Reality*, smashed the fallacies about women and girls in sport and set a new stage for them to compete on. Dr. Oglesby wants her legacy to be simple. "I hope to live in the memories of my students and mentees as a person who never gave up and never ever stopped fighting." Dr. Oglesby most recently has been the chairperson of the Department of Kinesiology at California State University, Northridge.

After the passage of Title IX in 1972, UCLA was one of the first schools to comply with the new law and establish a separate women's athletic program. Judith Holland, given her background in coaching and administration, was deemed the best choice to head the new women's department. She was given little more than a green RV located outside the women's gym to house her new athletic department. Furthermore, the women were still a part of the AIAW and were essentially treated like club sports—receiving limited funding for uniforms, facilities, and transportation to events.

She gave her first scholarship to Ann Meyers (Drysdale), a four-time All-American who became one of the most decorated players in UCLA history and the only female to sign a National Basketball Association (NBA) contract.

Holland knew that to take this program to the next level, she needed to take drastic steps. Joining the men in the NCAA was the first of these steps—a bold move given Holland was the former president of the AIAW. In 1981, the NCAA created a division for women and UCLA promptly enlisted.

Holland's next move would be met with even more resistance. After attending an NCAA convention, Holland concluded that the men's and women's programs could not coexist and would need to be joined under the same organization in order for true equality to be present. Although a controversial and very unpopular idea, the two programs merged in 1982. Shortly thereafter, many other collegiate athletic departments followed Holland's model and sought equality by joining forces with the men's department.

Holland's impact extended far beyond UCLA, as many women's departments followed her lead. She was a true pioneer, often having to make controversial and unpopular decisions, but never ceasing the fight for gender equality. The successes of women's sports at UCLA have become legendary.

Laurie Mabry helped to elevate Illinois State University women's programs from recreational status to the level of competitive college teams. During Mabry's 20-year tenure with the university from 1960 to 1980 as director of women's intercollegiate athletics, she significantly impacted opportunities for women at Illinois State and beyond.

The beyond included a term as AIAW president from 1975 to 1976. In that position, Mabry had an opportunity to influence women's athletics at the national level.

Although some of the AIAW's top female administrators made the transition to roles within the NCAA structure, Mabry's prediction about decreased professional opportunities for women largely held true for many years.

The handful of women who currently lead Division I-A programs as athletic directors are advancing such opportunities.

Women Leading I-A Programs

In 1991, Sandy Barbour was recruited to join the administration team at Tulane University as an associate athletic director. Upon the departure of athletic director and mentor Kevin White, Barbour took the helm of Green Wave athletics in 1996. She rejoined White at Notre Dame as a senior associate athletic director.

In 2004, Barbour was offered a job that she called "a dream come true, both personally and professionally"—director of athletics at the University of California, Berkeley (Cal). Under Barbour's leadership, Cal has developed into a regular among the top 10 in the annual National Association of Collegiate Directors of Athletics (NACDA) Directors' Cup standings matching its best-ever finish in 2007–08 with a seventh-place standing, made possible by having seven sports ranked among the top five nationally. The Bears were also seventh in 2005–06 and ninth in 2003, 2004, and 2007.

Under her leadership, Cal programs have captured nine national team championships and 25 individual titles. In 2007–08, the Bears repeated as champions in men's rugby and water polo, while Cal athletes won a school-record 11 individual crowns in 2006–07.

In addition, the Cal football team won three consecutive bowl championships—the Las Vegas Bowl in 2005, the Holiday Bowl in 2006, and the Armed Forces Bowl in 2007—and shared the Pac-10 championship for the first time in 21 seasons in 2006. Overall, Cal supports a 27-sport program with more than 800 student-athletes and a budget in excess of $60 million.

On the academic front, nearly half of Cal's student-athletes maintain a cumulative GPA of 3.0 or higher, and 14 of Cal's 27 programs earned their highest cumulative GPAs ever!

Barbara Burke was a talented athlete in both softball and basketball while attending Western Michigan University from 1976 to 1980. She then coached college basketball and softball at numerous institutions. Her administrative career began at West Virginia State from 1992 to 1994, at Marshall from 1994 to 1997, and at the University of Texas at El Paso (UTEP) during the 1997–98 school year.

She became Eastern Illinois's director of athletics in July 2008 after serving 10 years at the University of Wyoming, most recently as deputy director and senior women's administrator.

In her fifth year as athletic director of the University of Nevada, Reno (UNR), the university has enjoyed an era of program-wide success under Cary Groth. All of Nevada's teams have participated in postseason play. They won 13 Western Athletic Conference championships in the past four years. At the end of the 2006–07 season, UNR won the Western Athletic Conference's Commissioner's Cup as the best overall athletic department in the conference for the first time in school history.

Off the playing field, UNR's graduation rate continues to improve, and 145 student-athletes earned their degrees in the last two academic years. In addition, UNR has been listed as one of the top two athletic departments in the nation in providing opportunities for women for three straight years. UNR also was one of only 10 universities in the country to win a Diversity in Athletics Award.

Previously, Groth was the director of athletics at her alma mater, Northern Illinois University.

Debbie Yow is the middle sister of highly acclaimed college basketball coaches Susan and Kay, who have 65 years of coaching combined. But it is Debbie who is in this section because she has been athletic director at the University of Maryland for 15 years. In Yow's first 14 years at Maryland, its teams won a remarkable 16 national championships, including seven in the past three years. She was one of the first women to lead a department that had a Division I-A football program. But she too started as a basketball coach—at the University of Kentucky, Oral Roberts University, and the University of Florida. Her record was an impressive 160-69. Her success propelled her into positions in athletic administration, serving as an athletic fundraiser at Florida before moving on to the University of North Carolina, Greensboro, and finally accepting the role of athletic director at St. Louis University.

At the time of Yow's hiring at Maryland, the department had been running at a budget deficit for over 10 years and was $51 million in debt. In addition to this financial struggle, the Terrapins were ranked last competitively in the Atlantic Coast Conference (ACC) and also ranked last in fundraising. Now they have balanced all 14 of the department's annual budgets with the total budget closing in on $60 million annually. The inherited debt has been reduced to $7.6 million. Maryland's national all-sports ranking is now in the upper 7 percent of all NCAA Division I institutions.

Yow has previously served as president of the NACDA and is currently president of the NCAA Division I-A Athletic Directors Association.

After 10 years at the helm, Kathy Beauregard, the director of athletics at Western Michigan University (WMU), is the second-longest serving athletic director in the Mid-American Conference. Under her lead, facilities have improved, student-athletes have set new standards in the classroom, and many of WMU's teams have won conference championships.

Beauregard began her coaching career in gymnastics at Western Michigan, while earning her master's in athletic administration. Before becoming athletic director in 1998, she was the senior associate athletic director from 1993 to 1997. In that role, she supervised all revenue sports, the university's compliance with NCAA rules, academic services, student-athlete welfare, and athletic marketing and communications.

Lisa Love was named Arizona State University's (ASU) vice president for university athletics on April 23, 2005. She had been at the University of Southern California since 1989 both as head women's volleyball coach (1989–98) and most recently as senior associate athletic director.

She hit the ground as a running success. While in her position for less than two months, she had less than a week to move ASU's scheduled football game with Louisiana State University (LSU) from Baton Rouge, Louisiana, to Tempe after Hurricane Katrina. ASU raised $1 million in ticket sales from the game to assist with the hurricane relief effort.

Arizona State President Michael Crow said, "In a year of challenge, change, and choice, Lisa Love has confirmed our wisdom in selecting her to lead one of the nation's great athletic programs. She is setting the bar high, both for athletic and academic performance. She has demonstrated strategic skill in hiring, retaining, and developing an exceptional athletic staff. Her vision and personal leadership skills are laying a foundation for sustained success."

The marquee programs—football, men's and women's basketball, baseball—are thriving, donations are on the rise, and the Sun Devils ranked eighth in the Director's Cup standings in 2008.

In the past two years, the number of donors has grown by 1,286 to 9,386 and total fundraising has increased from $10.2 million to $15 million. Love has also amassed $26.6 million in pledges to build the indoor football practice facility and the Weatherup Center, a 30,000-square-foot facility that will house the men's and women's basketball teams. Like the other women athletic directors in this section, Lisa Love has silenced those who feared a woman could not lead a Division I-A program.

National Reform Leaders

Donna Lopiano is one of the women in this section who could just as easily been in the softball section, as she was one of the sport's greatest players ever. In 1963, Lopiano was discovered by the Raybestos Brakettes, an amateur softball team for whom she played until 1972. During her 10 seasons, Lopiano earned All-American honors nine times and was named MVP three times. She was a great pitcher and hitter. Lopiano compiled a .910 winning percentage with 183 games won and just 18 games lost. In 817 innings she struck out 1,633 opponents. Lopiano twice led her team in batting average with .316 and .367. One of the most amazing aspects of Lopiano's amateur softball career is the fact that it spanned over her high school, collegiate, and postgraduate educations.

Lopiano's career as a Raybestos Brakette also did not interfere with her success on the field hockey, volleyball, and basketball teams. Including her amateur career, she played in 26 national championships in the four sports. The success she earned as an athlete led her to coaching positions for collegiate men's and women's volleyball, women's basketball, and women's softball programs.

Lopiano was hired by the University of Texas, Austin, as the director of intercollegiate athletics for women when she was 28 years old. She made it clear to her staff that winning, as well as education, was a priority. Lopiano warned coaches that their jobs depended on whether or not their teams were top 10 programs. Lopiano also stressed that their jobs were equally dependent on the success their student-athletes achieved in the classroom. During her 17 years at the University of Texas, the Longhorns graduated 95 percent of their women athletes who completed their athletic eligibility. Lopiano's Longhorns were equally successful athletically. Eighteen National Championships (AIAW and NCAA), 62 Southwest Conference Championships, more than 300 All-Americans, and over a dozen Olympians made Lopiano's women's program a dominant one in collegiate athletics.

At each stage of her career, Lopiano has served women and girls everywhere with her advocacy for Title IX. It was perfect when she moved to the WSF in April 1992 to continue her advocacy for female athletes' rights. In her 15 years as executive director, Lopiano secured funding for girls' and women's sport programs and educated the public and corporations about the importance of women's health and gender equality in sport.

Tina Sloan Green could have been in a section on lacrosse as an athlete and coach. But she has been creating opportunities for women and African-Americans as players and coaches in sports like lacrosse, tennis, golf, and field hockey for more than 40 years, so we listed her in this section.

After she started as a field hockey player at West Chester State University in Pennsylvania, Sloan Green was recruited to the lacrosse team by her field hockey coach, who doubled as the coach for both teams. Sloan Green also added badminton to her varsity repertoire for three years. Sloan Green received All-American field hockey honors in 1965 and 1966 and played on the U.S. National Field Hockey Squad in 1969. She also competed with the U.S. Women's Lacrosse team from 1968 to 1972. In doing so, she became the first African-American woman to be named to the squad. In 1970, she earned her master's in physical education from Temple University.

She became the coach of the field hockey and lacrosse teams at Temple University in 1974.

She stayed on the Temple Owls lacrosse field sidelines for 18 seasons, boasting a record of 207-62-4 (a .758 winning percentage), including an NCAA record 29 straight wins from 1984 to 1985. Between 1973 and 1992, she guided 18 of her players to follow in her prestigious footsteps of earning All-American honors. In 1988, Sloan Green's Temple team earned its first undefeated season with a 15-7 victory over Penn State University in the NCAA Championship. This victory was the team's second national championship under Sloan Green, as they had captured the 1984 lacrosse title as well.

Sloan Greene became the first African-American head coach in the history of women's intercollegiate lacrosse. She was also the first female African-American and only the second African-American head coach ever to win a NCAA Division I title in 1984.

In 1992, she left the coaching sidelines but not Temple University. She turned her focus entirely on her teaching and advancing opportunities for African-American females in sport. As co-founder and head of the Black Women in Sports Foundation, Sloan Green has provided young females the exposure and opportunity to participate in typically white "preppy" sports like tennis and golf.

Olympic Sport

Anita DeFrantz is often described as the most powerful or influential woman in sport in the world!

She rowed in college and was on an academic scholarship. She won an Olympic medal in rowing after only five years in the sport. She was the first African-American to medal in rowing. She led the athletes' protest against President Jimmy Carter's decision to boycott the 1980 Moscow Olympics. She is president of one of America's largest foundations dealing with the power of sport to affect children. She was elected vice president of the International Olympic Committee (IOC). No woman held that position before her. Before the world made such a big issue out of performance-enhancing drugs, DeFrantz took the lead internationally after the 1988 Olympics. She has been a leading advocate for athletes' rights in the IOC. She has fought at the elite level but even more so at the grassroots. DeFrantz has worked tirelessly to provide opportunities for underprivileged youth, ensuring opportunities exist for males and females alike. As president of the LA84 Foundation, she focuses its commitment to Southern California but mainly on Los Angeles. And while no child is turned away, special emphasis is placed on girls, ethnic minorities, the physically challenged and developmentally disabled, and other underserved community members. In its first 20 years of existence, DeFrantz has led the LA84 in its endeavors that have provided nearly $50 million in grants to youth programs and has trained over 50,000 coaches.

Pro Sport

There are not many women to discuss as commissioners of major professional sports leagues. The first big exception was Val Ackerman, who became the president of the Women's National Basketball Association (WNBA) when the WNBA was launched in 1997. She was president from 1996 through 2005.

Ackerman was a four-year starter and graduated as a two-time Academic All-American from the University of Virginia in 1981. Ackerman played professional basketball in France for one season and then earned a law degree from UCLA. After two years at a New York law firm, she joined the NBA as a staff attorney and special assistant to NBA Commissioner David Stern.

She was a driving force behind the creation of the historic USA Basketball Women's Senior National Team program in 1995 that led to a gold medal at the 1996 Atlanta Olympics and an incredible 60-0 record.

She led the WNBA from 1996 until her resignation in February 2005. She is now the first woman to be president of USA Basketball.

So these have been the women we chose to represent—those whose lifelong commitment to fight for the rights of female athletes has changed the gender landscape in sports in America. These women created organizations like the AIAW, fought the fight in the courts, in their colleges and universities, at the conference and NCAA levels, and in Olympic and pro sports. Today's great athletes, women and men alike, all should stand and salute these warriors for change.

Judy Sweet

Trailblazer of the Association for Intercollegiate Athletics for Women (AIAW)

by Stacy Martin-Tenney

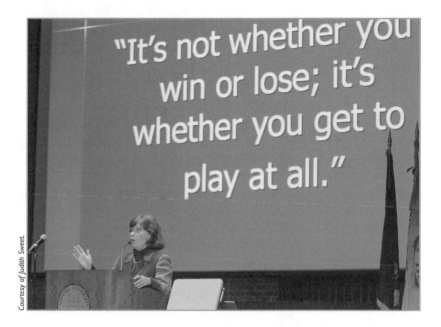

"It's not whether you win or lose; it's whether you get to play at all."

Judy Sweet is no stranger to change. In fact, for most of her life she has been a proponent of change in sports. She pioneered the landscape of college athletics and helped transform it from a barren scene for women to one full of opportunity and promise. The idea of diversity is more commonplace today, but when Judy Sweet was growing up in Milwaukee, Wisconsin, in the 1960s it was radical. Her first groundbreaking move came when she walked onto a sandlot to play a game with her brothers and cousins. She quickly proved herself and enjoyed plenty of opportunities to play sports, as long as she didn't stray outside the confines of the neighborhood. The sandlot was only the first of many changes she would make throughout her life and it was a valuable lesson to push the barriers of what was allowed. Judy Sweet has broken many barriers in her quest to cultivate women's participation onto the sporting landscape.

Sweet's journey has not been without struggle and opposition. Change is hard to accept for most people, and many take a great deal of comfort in doing things the way they have always been done. She left the sandlot and went on to high school and college only to be stifled by the lack of intramural programs that should have been instituted for educational and recreational purposes. Sweet missed the proverbial boat for women's sports when Title IX was passed in 1972, banning the unequal opportunity that Sweet had experienced in her playing career. She had graduated with honors from the University of Wisconsin three years prior to its inception. Sweet had majored in physical education and mathematics, which led her to take a position at Tulane University as a physical education teacher. Her quiet start soon flourished and she moved across the country to Arizona. The Painted Desert's majestic scene surely inspired her to create her own landscape.

Sweet began teaching at the University of Arizona and simultaneously pursued a master's degree in education, eventually graduating with honors. Sweet remained at the university for one more year and began her career in athletic administration. A taste for change persuaded her to move closer to the ocean. She arrived in San Diego and taught at a local high school for one year before she began her long career at the University of California, San Diego, joining the faculty as both a teacher and a coach. Her attachment to student-athletes and her mission to safeguard their welfare began. After only a year she became an associate athletic director. As previously demonstrated, Sweet is a woman who quickly excels at any task she undertakes, so just over a year later she was promoted to the director of athletics at UC San Diego. Sweet had made her first sweeping stroke of change to the inhospitable sporting landscape on a grand scale.

Control of both the men's and women's athletic programs was nonexistent in 1975, until Judy Sweet took a brave step into a constantly changing yet rigidly resistant environment for women. She became the first female athletic director of a combined intercollegiate athletic program in the nation. At the time, athletic directors were typically former male coaches who received a promotion and an increase in responsibilities. In fact, some even served dual roles as a head coach and athletic director. Sweet broke the mold. She faced opposition and hesitation from her peers. Some were hesitant to accept her at all. The coaches whom she had befriended to shape student-athlete talents just two years prior became antagonistic when she cut their budgets so she could create a more equitable athletic environment. Every landscape has its own unique color scheme, and the sports realm is no different. Color was added to Sweet's landscape by "the most colorful" negative language that expressed resentment and biases for her newly acquired position. Sweet soon realized "the hurdles that had to be overcome."[1]

Pioneers have climbed mountains to pursue their dreams, and Sweet learned on the sandlot how to overcome such barriers. During her 24 years of service at UC San Diego, she experienced unrivaled success and started establishing new landmarks in the expanding environment for women's athletics. Her athletic department supported 23 varsity sports and brought 25 National Collegiate Athletic Association (NCAA) Championships home to San Diego. UC San Diego teams were National Runners-up 32 times in her 24 years. In 1997–98, UC San Diego won the Division III Sears Director's Cup for program excellence. This marked the first time that an athletic department directed by a woman had been awarded the Cup. Additionally, it was the first time an athletic department without a football program had won the award. Sweet not only kept her department in the forefront of success, but she continued to foster her education and earned a master's of business administration with distinction from National University in San Diego.

Sweet committed herself to improving student-athlete welfare throughout her career without regard to gender, although she had a distinctive viewpoint to guard opportunities for future female athletes. Her perspective has been sought out by 20 different NCAA committees over the years and her contribution has broadened her impact on college sports. Being "the first" is not a new concept for Sweet, as she served as the first female secretary-treasurer of the NCAA from 1989 to 1991 and then as the first female president of the NCAA from 1991 to 1993. She was the first female president of the Association during a time when the position was voluntary and not contracted. She helped create more opportunity for her female counterparts. Sweet's commitment to student-athletes has never been contingent on contracts of service. She truly cares about providing the best experience possible for student-athletes in any way she can. She has also served on the NCAA Council and Executive

Committee as well as the Review and Planning Committee. For seven years she served as chair of the Special Advisory Committee to Review Recommendations Regarding Distribution of Revenues, a committee formed in response to the $1 billion television contract with CBS.

Exhibiting leadership is second nature to Sweet. She has made ethical choices and implemented policy that benefited student-athletes. More important, she motivates others to join her cause. She has been recognized for her exemplary leadership with a variety of awards throughout her career, including being named Outstanding Young Woman of America in 1984 and receiving the honor as the *Los Angeles Times*'s selection for Top Southern California College Sports Executive of the 1980s. Southern California is an arena historically filled with fierce sports competitors in the administration as well as on the playing fields. The *Times*'s selection speaks volumes about her extraordinary leadership at UC San Diego.

Her commitment to excellence transcended decades and the 1990s were no exception. Just like wines have very good years, 1992 was Judy Sweet's year. She was named the Administrator of the Year by the National Association of Collegiate Athletic Administrators, and the Women's Sports Advocates of Wisconsin, Sweet's native state, inducted her into their Lifetime Achievement Hall of Fame. She has convincingly demonstrated her abilities.

One year later she was named Woman of the Year in District 38 by the California State Senate. She then lent her service and experience to the United States Olympic Committee Task Force on Minorities for two years. Her wealth of knowledge and firsthand experience on the front lines of the gender equity fight was invaluable to the minority task force. In 1998, Judy Sweet was the recipient of The Honda Award for Outstanding Achievement in Women's Collegiate Athletics. Sweet served on the board of directors for the National Association of College Directors of Athletics (NACDA). Sweet stepped down from her longtime position of director of athletics at UC San Diego in 1999 but remained on the faculty.

Sweet's expertise was requested by the NCAA once more in 2001 to serve in the prestigious role of vice president for championships. Sweet would oversee planning and organization for all of the 88 NCAA Championships except Division I men's and women's basketball, football, and baseball. Cedric Dempsey, the NCAA president at that time, said, "Her depth of knowledge of college sports and administrative experience in running a broad range of events will ensure that NCAA Championships continue to be great experiences for student-athletes."[2] Sweet understood how valuable the experience of a championship is for student-athletes and wanted to ensure that the event would also be unforgettable.

Sweet joined the NCAA national office team and quickly took on additional responsibilities as the senior women's administrator. The position was initially established at universities in 1981 as a way to monitor and grow women's roles in athletic departments. This position grew in importance through increased responsibilities by 1990, but lacked reflection in the national office. Sweet was once again the first woman to take the job and has left a lasting impression on sports that will benefit her successors. The position may have originated with the idea of guaranteed female involvement at the top of the NCAA governance, but it has evolved into a position with appropriate responsibility and accountability in all facets of the organization that has the added benefit of a female perspective. Sweet never made the fact that she was a woman an issue but instead used it as a competitive advantage. She has been described as "a quiet, effective fighter for opportunities" by Dale Neuberger, the former president of the Indiana Sports Corp.[3] Her focus on gender equity encompasses suggestions that come from both men and women.

Sweet constantly seeks out new challenges and thus she accepted the promotion to senior vice president for championships and education services in 2003, in addition to maintaining her role as the senior women's administrator. Her last role in education was to implement leadership programs. Leadership is a concept that Sweet knows inside and out. Myles Brand, the current NCAA president, has described Sweet as the "conscience of college sports" and regularly consulted with Sweet for her indispensable knowledge.[4] She was one of the four senior vice presidents who reported directly to Brand, and the only woman. Sweet gained so much status and prestige with the NCAA that she was the only active college sports icon to have a meeting room named after her at the NCAA Headquarters.

Sweet is widely respected for creating an equitable environment that provides a positive experience for both young men and women. Her hope is for them to become the leaders of tomorrow when the sun sets on her majestic landscape. Sweet retired in 2006 from the NCAA but still serves as a consultant. The awards have already accumulated congratulating her on a distinguished career. The National Association of Collegiate Women Athletic Administrators (NACWAA) presented her with their first NACWAA Legacy Award and established the Judith M. Sweet Commitment Award to honor those that follow in her awe-inspiring footsteps. Furthermore, in 2007, the Institute for International Sports proclaimed that she was one of the Top 100 Most Influential Sports Educators in America. Judy Sweet's leadership is impressive and resilient, and she worked every day to instill the same drive and values in student-athletes. There are thousands of student-athletes, coaches, and women applauding her and the difference she has made.

Notes

1. Mark Montieth, "Clearing the Path," *The Indianapolis Star*, October 30, 2005.

2. Wallace I. Renfroe, "Judy Sweet, Long-time Athletics Leader and Administrator, Joins NCAA Staff as Vice-President for Championships," *The NCAA News*, November 1, 2000.

3. Montieth, "Clearing the Path."

4. Ibid.

Charlotte West

Trailblazer of the Association for Intercollegiate Athletics for Women (AIAW)

by Horacio Ruiz

"I pretty much devoted my life to creating opportunities for girls and women in sports,"[1] said Dr. Charlotte West, the former president of the Association for Intercollegiate Athletics for Women (AIAW). There is nothing but truth in that statement, but West says it so humbly. West, whose 42-year career at Southern Illinois University (SIU) as a coach, instructor, professor, and administrator, had built a sphere of influence that indeed created opportunities for others. As head coach of the SIU women's basketball team, she recruited a player who grew up in a neighborhood so dangerous that on a recruiting trip she could not visit the player's home. Instead, the recruit was escorted to West's car, decided to play for West, and is now a successful Division I coach. West helped many women adjust to life on a college campus, which seemed a world away from where many of them grew up. Her influence also extended to men.

"I learned as much or more from her than I have anybody in athletics," said longtime Arizona athletic director Jim Livengood. "Everything that I do, there's a part of me that certainly has a Charlotte West stamp on it."[2]

West arrived at Southern Illinois in 1957 as a coach and instructor in the department of physical education, and then she became so much more. She was the coach of the women's golf team for more than 12 years, badminton for seven years, and volleyball for one year. She also coached women's basketball from 1959 to 1975. In 1969, her golf team won the national championship and the basketball team finished fifth in the nation in the National Invitational Title (NIT) Women's Basketball Tournament. West's role on these teams extended past her coaching duties, as she also raised money through bake sales and car washes, coordinated travel on a limited budget, served as the public relations manager for the team, and also worked as the athletic trainer.

"We had our traditional bake sales and selling some merchandise, and mainly I think we didn't raise a lot of money but we lived on a nickel and a dime," West said. "Traditionally now, people go up the day before an event, spend the night, then they have a practice and are fresh for the contest that day. We never did that. We got up at 5:30 a.m. or 6 then bused up the same day then played and came back the same night. That way we only had to take care of lunch and dinner."[3] By 1959, she was named the director of women's athletics, and in 1986, she was named an associate athletic director when both the men's and women's athletic departments merged, a post she would hold until her retirement in 1998. As director of women's athletics, West was able to develop the program from a "nickel and dime" operation in the beginning of her career, to a nationally recognized program that included 11 sports and an operating budget of more than $1 million.

West had many opportunities to play sports as a child growing up in St. Petersburg, Florida, but upon arriving at Florida State University (FSU) as an undergraduate, she was shocked that there were no opportunities for women to compete outside of the university. "As I reflect back to FSU and not having that opportunity, it motivated me," she said.

After double majoring in physical education and math at FSU, she continued her graduate studies by enrolling at the University of North Carolina at Greensboro, where she received her master's degree in physical education with an emphasis in dance. She fondly remembers being able to teach dance classes to a studio full of excited women eager to learn. West had danced since she was a girl and had a background in folk dance, square dance, tap dance, and ballet. Upon finishing her doctoral work, she moved to the SIU campus in Carbondale, Illinois, partly because of the opportunities for women to play sports, as the women's teams had extramurals and received funding from student government because of their status as recognized club sports.

In the 1970s, West became heavily involved with Title IX legislation. She served as a consultant for the Health, Education, and Welfare portions of Title IX that related to athletics. The Southern Illinois legal counsel consulted with West to make sure they were in compliance with Title IX legislation at the school. West worked with the AIAW and was elected president. She was instrumental in landing television contracts for women's sports, increasing both participatory and financial opportunities for women in sports through federal legislation, and drawing the guidelines for the AIAW.

"The '70s as far as we're concerned was just a glorious time because we were involved with the AIAW," West said. "It was such an exciting time for those of us committed to providing opportunities. Individually we couldn't have accomplished what we did. Collectively, we accomplished more than we could have dreamed. It was a tremendous volunteer organization."

As much as the 1970s were what West calls the golden age, she recalls the 1980s as the decadent decade. In 1981, West was saddened to see the AIAW cease to exist when the National Collegiate Athletic Association (NCAA) took over women's intercollegiate sports. By 1981, the AIAW had grown to include 41 national championships for women in different sports, and West was serving as the AIAW commissioner of national championships. In an attempt to save the AIAW, she proposed an alliance between the NCAA and AIAW in which the NCAA would give its female counterparts five years before taking over women's athletics. She never heard a word back. As saddened as she was to see her organization fold and as much as she considered the NCAA to be "public enemy number one" in the 1980s, West calls the 1990s an age of renaissance in which women became increasingly involved in the NCAA. Her own involvement in policymaking did not diminish either.

West served on the NCAA's Committee on Financial Aid and Amateurism, the Committee on Athletic Certification, and the Gender Equity Task Force. She spent five years on the NCAA Council, a 44-member group that governed collegiate athletics until 1997. Upon restructuring its governance, the NCAA elected West as the Missouri Valley Conference's representative to the NCAA Division I Management Council. She also was the first woman member of the National Association of Collegiate Directors of Athletics (NACDA) and later would be inducted into the NACDA Hall of Fame. West also became the first recipient of the Honda Award, given for outstanding achievement in women's athletics.

In 1998, West retired from Southern Illinois, active as ever with her beloved school and the NCAA. At the time of her retirement she was close to breaking the record for longest-tenured faculty member. "Someone said to me, 'You know, if you had stayed one more year you would have broken the record.' I said, 'No, I don't want to break that record." West added, "I really worked hard, I mean very hard, my last five or 10 years to get full scholarship funding for our men and our women."[4] In 2003, SIU named its new softball stadium after Charlotte West. "Dr. West has been such an important figure for women's athletics, not just at SIU, but all over the country," said SIU softball coach Kerri Blaylock. "She's well known and well respected everywhere. When I go to conventions and recruiting, I always run into someone who mentions her name and asks if I know her or worked for her."[5]

Looking back on her career, she's most proud of developing the women's athletic program at Southern Illinois prior to merging with the men's program, noting the academic performance of its women athletes and the behavior of the athletes and staff. "I couldn't have asked for more," West said. "I've just had a very happy life here."

Notes

1. Unless noted otherwise, all quotes in this article are by Charlotte West, from an interview with the author, June 2, 2008.

2. Ethan Erickson, "Coach Charlotte West Helps Put Southern Illinois on the Map," *Daily Egyptian*, October 23, 2003.

3. Ibid.

4. Ibid.

5. Saluki Athletics. New softball stadium named charlotte west stadium in honor of athletics pioneer, http://siusalukis.cstv.com/sports/w-softbl/spec-rel/021303aaa .html, February 13, 2003.

Christine Grant

Trailblazer of the Association for Intercollegiate Athletics for Women (AIAW)

by Horacio Ruiz

Listening to Dr. Christine Grant over the phone, one can hear, in her gentle Scottish voice, that behind the pride she has for the Association for Intercollegiate Athletics for Women (AIAW), there is a trace of sadness that remains from its ultimate demise. Grant loved the AIAW. Looking back on a career full of accomplishments and hard-fought battles, the former University of Iowa women's athletic director and professor, and one of the nation's leading proponents of Title IX legislation, fondly remembers the Association she believes was coming close to creating the perfect model for intercollegiate athletics. "There was tremendous respect for each person and it was just such an exciting time," she said of the AIAW. "We were starting this organization from scratch."[1] As Grant speaks, it is barely a week after the 25th anniversary of the official dissolution of her beloved organization. She makes it a point to say that policies made during the AIAW's 10 years of existence always kept the student-athlete in mind. "Every decision that we made we would ask ourselves, 'Is this in the best interest of the student-athlete?'"

Grant was the acting president of the AIAW from 1979 to 1980, when it became clear the Association would be shut down. Members of the AIAW tried in vain to keep the Association alive, knowing it provided women with substantial leadership roles in significant administrative positions. As the National Collegiate Athletic Association (NCAA) took over women's athletic departments because of Title IX financial and legal implications, women who previously held the highest posts in their departments were suddenly moved to less influential posts in departments directed by men. The AIAW and the NCAA differed in philosophies relating to athletics, not the least of which included financial aid for student-athletes, the sums of money dedicated to athletics, and the purposes for which the finances were used. The AIAW sued the NCAA in 1983, but the presiding judge ruled against the organization. "To this day, I do not

know how we lost that lawsuit," Grant said. Many women left intercollegiate athletics altogether, never to return because of the differences. Grant says she was blackballed by the NCAA, which was fine
by her because she still was the athletic director of the women's athletic department at the University of Iowa. It would take many years
before Grant would again participate in NCAA committees.

Her fight for equality can be traced back to her native Scotland. Grant grew up surrounded by sports as a child, falling in love
with field hockey because of the freedom she felt while running
around an open field. For her, it was natural to include sports in her
life. After receiving her diploma in physical education in 1956 from
Dunfermline College in Aberdeen, Scotland, Grant was a high
school teacher and coach in Graeme, Scotland, until 1961, when she
moved to Canada. In Canada, she became heavily involved with
field hockey, helping to organize pockets of field hockey clubs into
a national field hockey association. In nine years in Canada, Grant
would be chosen as the National Coach of the Canadian Women's
Field Hockey team, and she also organized national field hockey
tournaments. In 1969, Grant pursued graduate studies in the United
States and enrolled at Iowa. Grant did not want to spend more than
one year at Iowa, but with the creation of a new women's athletic department at the university, and with her international experience
combined with her leadership skills, she was hired as women's athletic director in 1973. Grant would go on to earn a bachelor's degree
in physical education and her master's and doctoral degrees in sports
administration.

"I could not believe the opportunities for men in this country,"
she said. "There was nothing like a football Saturday in Iowa City,
and on the other hand, I could not believe the opportunities for
women because there were none."

With her position independent of the men's athletic department
and with support from the University of Iowa, she was able to become an expert witness on Title IX legislation. Grant said that many
of her colleagues who made the transition into working for a merged
athletic department were afraid to speak on Title IX issues because
they were afraid of the reprisals from the athletic director to whom
they reported. "I was in a position to speak, so I felt an obligation to
do what I could," she said. Grant testified before Congress on numerous occasions regarding gender equity in sports. She also served

as a consultant for the Civil Rights Title IX Task Force, becoming a key figure in drafting Title IX implementation. The University of Iowa has a collection of Christine Grant's papers that she wrote throughout her career, including those she prepared for congressional testimonies, as well as her scholarly publications. During her time as women's athletic director until her retirement in 2000, she grew the department to include 12 NCAA championship titles and 27 Big Ten Championships.

Teaching, Grant said, had always been her true love. Teaching came naturally to her as a former coach. Since 1975, Grant was associate professor of Health and Sport Studies. Even after retiring from her post as athletic director, she remained teaching in the graduate sport administration program at Iowa until 2006. By the late 1980s, Grant returned to work directly with the NCAA when she saw a change in leadership that embraced women's athletics. She credits Dr. Myles Brand of the NCAA as one of the greatest proponents of Title IX. Grant has been instrumental as a consultant and chair in many of the NCAA's most important committees regarding NCAA certification requirements, gender and equity issues, and amateurism reform. "In the '70s I was the biggest opponent of the NCAA," she said. "Now I am one of the NCAA's biggest supporters."

Grant has been inducted into the University of Iowa Athletics Hall of Fame and the Iowa Women's Hall of Fame. In 2006, Grant was the recipient of the NCAA President's Gerald R. Ford Award, which was awarded to her at the NCAA National Convention. The award honors individuals who have provided significant leadership in the areas of higher education and intercollegiate athletics throughout their careers. She was the first woman to receive the honor. That same year, she was named one of the 100 most influential educators in the United States by the Institute of International Sport. "On behalf of the entire University of Iowa family, I'd like to congratulate Dr. Grant on this wonderful honor," said Iowa athletic director Gary Barta when Grant was recognized by the Institute of International Sport. "People around the country are now finding out what we Iowans have known for a long time; Dr. Christine Grant was a wonderful teacher, coach, athletic administrator, and proponent of women's athletics. There's no question the status of women, in today's athletic world, is in large part due to the ideals and efforts championed by Dr. Christine Grant."[2]

Currently, Grant is an associate of the consulting firm Sports Management Resources (SMR) started by former CEO of the Women's Sports Foundation Donna Lopiano. The firm works to consult athletic directors about policies in education and gender equity, and in the implementation and management of those policies. When she speaks about her career in sports and her involvement in creating opportunities for student-athletes, one can't help but notice the passion in her voice. "To have had sports as a career has been delightful," Grant said. "Sports have brought me so much joy and friendships that I wanted other young ladies to have the same opportunities I did." During an interview a little more than one year after her retirement as women's athletic director at Iowa, the interviewer asked, almost as if to extract an inspiring quote, why Grant had bothered to try and change the atmosphere of college athletics. The interviewer got just what he was looking for. "Because we in education have a responsibility to try to help society understand that in educational sport, winning is not the most important thing and losing is never failure," Grant responded. "We can teach society that. I truly believe that, but we've got to believe it ourselves."[3]

Notes

1. Unless noted otherwise, the quotes in this article are by Christine Grant, from an interview with the author, July 8, 2008.

2. University of Iowa News Services. Christine Grant honored as one of 100 most influential sports educators, October 17, 2007, http://www.news-releases.uiowa.edu/2007/october/101707christine_grant_honor.html.

3. Ross Atkin, "A Voice in the Wilderness for Sports as Education," *The Christian Science Monitor*, November 30, 2001.

Merrily Dean Baker

Trailblazer of the Association for Intercollegiate Athletics for Women (AIAW)

by Horacio Ruiz

Merrily Dean Baker tells aspiring students and sport professionals to take three pills at the start of every day: one for courage, a second for commitment, and a third for compassion. It was, she says, these three characteristics that carried her through a career in athletics that saw her build athletic programs from scratch and blaze a trail for women by going where many had never been before. It would take a lot of courage, commitment, and compassion for Baker to work beneath a constant microscope. The challenges of running athletic departments were very real, but for Baker, sometimes the challenges went beyond the job description.

"Virtually every job I had I was the first woman there or starting a new program," she said. "I had to assure people that it was okay that I was there and that I was able to do it. Everywhere I went people were not used to having a woman as a boss."[1]

Initially drawn to a career in teaching and coaching, Baker received her undergraduate degree in physical education from East Stroudsburg University, where she was a six-sport athlete. From an early age, Baker was involved in athletics, as her father taught her how to swim when she was three years old and she started competitive field hockey by the fifth grade. She would continue a coaching career in gymnastics and field hockey through the university and high school ranks before finishing her master's degree in fine arts and dance in 1968 from Temple University. Baker took her first administrative position in 1969 at Franklin & Marshall College in Lancaster, Pennsylvania, as the university's first director of the women's athletic department. In 1970, Princeton University asked her to be a consultant for its new women's athletic department. After three days of consulting at Princeton, the university offered her their position as the women's director of athletics.

"I felt like that was raising another child," said Baker of Princeton. "I started the Princeton athletic department from scratch. We started with nothing; they handed me a five-year plan that was a slow progression." Initially, Princeton had intended for Baker to plan and implement a women's athletic department in five years, but after consulting with the women on campus, the five-year plan was scrapped in three weeks. Women wanted to participate in sports a lot sooner and Baker eagerly undertook the challenge of building an athletic department for them. She implemented some of the first sports women would play at Princeton, including basketball, field hockey, tennis, swimming, and lacrosse. "Princeton women's athletics did extremely well," Baker said. "Everybody loves winners and the Princeton teams, from day one, won championships. It set the tone for acceptance of women in a very major way." The 1970s was a decade of great professional and personal growth for Baker. She would spend 12 years at Princeton as the women's athletic director, and she would also marry and become a mother. Baker also became a leading proponent for women's athletics on the national level by

Courtesy of Merrily Dean Baker.

working with the Association for Intercollegiate Athletics for Women (AIAW). Under the AIAW, Baker played a crucial role in lobbying for Title IX legislation, which would give women in universities more opportunities to play sports at the collegiate level. But with the passing of Title IX came the dissolution of the AIAW. What was then strictly a male-only National Collegiate Athletic Association (NCAA) absorbed the AIAW with its far more expansive financial resources to fund women's athletics.

Baker was the last president of the AIAW, where she was tasked with holding together an organization that would soon disappear. Baker and her colleagues made one more attempt to preserve the organization with a lawsuit against the NCAA, but they lost.

"Donna Lopiano and I spent hours and hours in D.C. getting ready to file that suit," Baker said. "We all had to testify in federal district court. They found the NCAA not in violation of antitrust laws. We could not compete with their financial resources. I was talking to women who were professional friends for years. It was a very difficult time emotionally and all I could do was traverse the country and calm people down. All of us grew up in the AIAW. Before the AIAW I knew nothing about politics. I was thrust into leadership positions with people telling me I was their mentor before I had found a mentor for myself. We were thrust into positions where somebody had to do something and so you did what had to be done. We all experienced tremendous personal and professional growth. I certainly didn't expect that my presidential experience would be to shut out the lights and close the door. But it was a decade-long experience that gave birth to women's intercollegiate athletics today. Women's sports survived and it got better. The AIAW wasn't a failure. The AIAW was a huge success. It set the stage for what is happening today. Do not ever look at the AIAW as a failed experiment—it was a very successful experiment. So successful that someone took it over. I feel privileged to have been part of the leadership. I will be forever grateful to that opportunity and to the people that made it happen. It has shaped all of us."

In 1982, Baker was wooed to the University of Minnesota as the athletic director of the women's athletic department. Under her leadership the department took women's athletics to a higher level, increasing the amount of scholarship money available to its athletes and also getting the State of Minnesota to finance the operations of the women's athletic departments due to her lobbying efforts. Baker was also able to secure a television contract for the women's athletic department. In 1988, her final year at Minnesota, she was named one of the "100 Most Powerful Women" in the United States by the *Ladies' Home Journal*. She also coauthored an $85 million athletics facilities plan that was part of the university's effort to build an Aquatics Center that opened in 1990. For all her efforts in her tenure at Minnesota, she was inducted into the M Club Hall of Fame in 2005.

Baker can laugh with colleague Christine Grant about their first Big Ten athletic director meeting. At the time, Baker and Grant were both directors of the only separate women's athletic departments in the Big Ten, and they were the only women at the meeting. Baker and Grant were asked by another athletic director if they would mind stepping out of a picture at the resort where the meetings were being held. They did not step out of the picture. But they would later find out that there was another picture taken in the back of the resort of all the athletic directors—excluding them.

"They were products of their upbringing but it didn't make it any more palpable to deal with," Baker said. "Every single man was fine with us one on one, but in a group it was different. The worst of them I could have dinner with or have a drink with and we would be

Courtesy of Merrily Dean Baker.

fine. But then they would get with their buddies and their attitude would be completely different. I tried to change it instead of being angry about it."

After serving in the Big Ten with Minnesota, Baker calls her career between 1988 and 1992 at the NCAA her corporate piece because it was the only time she was not working on a college campus. Baker was convinced by then–executive director of the NCAA Richard Schultz to serve as the assistant executive director of the NCAA. Schultz convinced Baker to join the NCAA by telling her that what she could do for 100 schools she was doing for one. It took Baker nine months to make a decision, but she ultimately accepted. She became the first woman appointed to the NCAA Executive Committee. Some of her colleagues could not understand why Baker would work for the NCAA after it absorbed the AIAW, but she saw the NCAA as a continuation of her and her colleagues' hard work in the 1970s. "I suddenly was now on the Executive Committee of the enemy," she said. "We spent 10 years building something that we really believe in and this is the organization that is going to continue this and I want to make sure it's done right."

At the NCAA, Baker created scholarship and internship opportunities for women and ethnic minorities. She wanted to create more professional opportunities and to enhance their education. She administered two national youth programs that served more than 67,000 youth each year through sport and education enrichment programs. She also initiated the NCAA Student-Athlete Advisory Committee (SAAC), which gave student-athletes a voice in matters concerning them.

In 1992, Michigan State University (MSU) called and Baker headed back to the Big Ten as the first woman to be named athletic director at the conference and only the second at a Division I football-playing institution. Only four years after returning to the Big Ten, Baker could sense a different level of respect from her peers, because, as she puts it, a new generation of administrators had taken up the athletic director posts and "a lot of the old-timers had retired by then." Baker's arrival at Michigan State was not without its share of turmoil. On her first day on the job, the president that hired her called Baker at her office. Thinking she was receiving a phone call wishing her good luck on her first day, she soon realized that the president had instead called to inform her that he was resigning.

Baker would serve under three presidents her first two years at Michigan State. During her time at Michigan State, she was able to fundraise at higher levels than her predecessors while increasing student-athlete graduation rates and concentrating on enrichment programs for student-athletes, including community outreach and mentor programs. But she was also stifled by what she says was the most political institution she had ever been involved with. At one point she had a trustee of the university telling her to cheat.

"It was a cauldron of controversy at Michigan State," Baker said. "I never shied away from challenges before so I said let's get on it. I met wonderful people. It's a wonderful institution, it just happened at a time when they subjugated their values for politics. There are parts of me that had the energy to stay longer and accomplish some things. To me, MSU was an institution that lost its moral compass. I had to look in the mirror and I said I can't do it. It was probably the most challenging of all the experiences I had. I feel very good about the things we accomplished and the things we got done."

Baker resigned from Michigan State in 1995, but even amid detractors who said she could not deal with managing football, men's basketball, and men's hockey, one of her greatest legacies was hiring basketball coach Tom Izzo. At the time of his hiring, Baker was criticized for elevating Izzo from the assistant coach position to the head coach position in 1995. "I felt Tom was the hire to make," she said. "A lot of the old boys gave me a lot of grief that he's too young, he's too that."

But in 1999, when the Michigan State basketball team made the Final Four for the first time in Izzo's tenure, he called Baker to tell her that he never forgot who hired him and that she was welcome to as many tickets to the Final Four as she wanted. She accepted the invitation. The next season, she again accepted Izzo's invitation to the Final Four when the Spartans won their second basketball national championship in school history. Baker partied along with all the other people that had criticized her years before for hiring Izzo.

In 1998, she was asked to be a part-time consultant for Florida Gulf Coast University, which was starting an athletic department from the ground up. What was supposed to be a six-month job to write a 10-year strategic plan and to help fundraise, turned into two and a half years during which she was appointed as the interim athletic director. She hired the first four coaches at the university for the men's and women's and golf and tennis teams. "It was another start from scratch," Baker said. "It was an incredible experience. Someone handed me a blank slate and they said to me, 'Fill it.'"

Looking back on her career, Baker says one of the most difficult parts was balancing her work with her family life, but she found ways to make it work. She also encouraged her coaches to bring their kids to sporting events, and she let them know it was okay to incorporate their family into their careers. It wasn't accepted by all people, but Baker knew her responsibilities lay in being both a mother and a professional. At Michigan State, Baker made it a point to leave every Thursday at 4:00 p.m., with no exceptions, because her daughter needed to be at her Girl Scout troop meeting. "I did it with three children in tow," Baker said. "I did it when it wasn't supposed to be done. I really didn't have any role models or mentors that fit what my life was like. I wanted other women to know they could have this career and still have a family. You have to find ways to make it work, but you can make it work without question."

Baker said someone once told her it takes three generations to have changes truly take place. Two generations have passed since she became a leading voice for the passage of Title IX through the AIAW, so she thinks it should be soon when she will see the fruition of her labors and women will be on a level playing field.

"I was so blessed to have all these opportunities and experiences," Baker said. "It was not all a bed of roses. But rewarding? Absolutely. We all met people who helped us along the unknown path. A lot of trial and error, a lot of mistakes were made, but you have to be strongly committed to stand up for what's right. The overall joy is it stretched over 38 years and I had a lot of opportunities to go where a lot of women did not have opportunities to go. I'd do it all again in a minute."

Note

1. All of the quotes in this article are by Merrily Dean Baker, from an interview with the author on July 11, 2008.

Carol Gordon

Trailblazer of the Association for Intercollegiate Athletics for Women (AIAW)

by Sara Jane Baker

When Carol Gordon joined Washington State University's (WSU) faculty in 1962, no one could have predicted her widespread influence and impact. Gordon was originally hired as a teacher; however, she quickly expanded her role to one of a mentor, coach, and administrator. At a time when opportunities for women and sport were disparate, Carol Gordon advanced women's athletics and fought for many of the opportunities that are apparent today.

Despite the societal stereotypes that sports were "unladylike" and the limited opportunities for women in the 1930s, Gordon competed in numerous sports during her youth. A native of Goffstown, New Hampshire, she played basketball at Goffstown High while also serving as a "curtain raiser" for the men's basketball team. Gordon then took her athletic talents to Oberlin College in Ohio. Although opportunities for women and sport were still limited at Oberlin, Gordon amazingly lettered in four sports: field hockey, tennis, basketball, and volleyball.

Gordon's involvement in sport as an athlete influenced her decision to make coaching and teaching her life's work. "I always was convinced of the importance of activity—both athletics and dance—and that it should be an important part of life."[1] Gordon accepted her first coaching and teaching job at the University of New Hampshire in 1948. Six years later, she took her career to the University of Utah. In addition to coaching and teaching at Utah, Gordon added to her educational resume. She received her master's degree in psychology, as well as her doctorate in educational psychology. Gordon was twice honored with Utah's Faculty Woman of the Year honors.

Psychology of sport became Gordon's specialty, which eventually led her to WSU. In 1962, WSU hired Gordon to chair its department of physical education for women. She also coached the Cougar field hockey and tennis teams while teaching psychology of sport classes. Gordon's impact at WSU was extensive. At a time when there was a large disparity between men's and women's sports, Gordon campaigned for women's athletics at the state and national levels.

In addition to her teaching, coaching, and administrative roles at Washington State, Gordon found time to serve as the president of the Association for Intercollegiate Athletics for Women (AIAW) in 1973–74. The AIAW, founded in 1971, was the most important organization in the progression of women's sports. The AIAW governed collegiate women's athletics and administered national championships until 1982, when the National Collegiate Athletic Association (NCAA) finally adopted women's sports. Gordon was also a member of the AIAW/NCAA Joint Committee and the NCAA Long Range Planning Committee.

After 21 years at Washington State, Carol Gordon retired in 1983. She continues to live in Pullman, Washington, while in retirement. Fortunately, her accomplishments as a pioneer for women's athletics have been widely recognized. In 1988, she received a Lifetime Achievement Award from the National Association of Collegiate Women Athletic Administrators. Although this proved her widespread influence, Carol Gordon, perhaps, made the biggest impact at WSU. In fact, recently in 2004, Gordon was inducted into Washington State University's Athletic Hall of Fame. Joining an elite group of former coaches, administrators, and athletes, her induction has ensured that her contributions to women's athletics will never be forgotten.[2]

Notes

1. Pat Caraher, "WSU Hall of Fame Adds 5 Who Excelled," *Washington State Magazine*, 2004.

2. WSU Hall of Fame, "WSU Athletic Hall of Fame Induction Feb. 21," Washington State University Athletics, http://wsucougars.cstv.com/genrel/012104aab.html (accessed June 20, 2008).

Dr. Peggy Burke

Trailblazer of the Association for Intercollegiate Athletics for Women (AIAW)

by Catherine Lahey

When asked what the climate of women's sports was like when she first became interested in athletics, Dr. Peggy Burke laughs a little. "Really, there was no climate, because there were little to no formal opportunities for women. At least, that was the case where I grew up."[1] Though women's teams didn't exist in her area (in fact, there wasn't even physical education in her high school), Burke had the fortune of being introduced to sports through playing with her brothers. Despite the absence of athletic opportunities during her own formative years, Burke would soon become one of the most influential voices in garnering increased opportunities in sport for women.

The community of women's athletics narrowly missed losing Burke's influence entirely. Upon entering college Burke declared a business major, completely unaware of the opportunity to study physical education. When she realized that the physical education major was open to women, she quickly made a switch, incurring a date with her own destiny. When asked why she elected to change majors, Burke says "It was purely my own desire—no one pushed me toward athletics." From that point forward, Burke was fully dedicated to her field, becoming actively involved in women's athletics administration at a number of levels.

Since 1977, Burke has been an active promoter of athletic opportunities for women. Much of her career was spent as an associate professor of sport, health, leisure, and physical studies at the University of Iowa. While there, she mentored numerous women while establishing collegiate athletic opportunities for women. One of the ways she did this was by participating as a founding member of the Association for Intercollegiate Athletics for Women (AIAW). Burke began as a representative at the state level in Iowa, helping to defuse the boycott of Iowa Wesleyan University. From the state level, Burke became a member of the AIAW's first delegate assembly in 1972 and eventually served as the organization's president from 1976 to 1977.

During her presidential tenure, Burke tackled numerous issues in women's athletics, including Title IX interpretation, six-player girls' basketball in Iowa, AIAW policy and structure, and the National Collegiate Athletic Association's (NCAA) increasing interest in overseeing women's championship play. "I'm very proud of the fact that we implemented a system of student-athlete representatives—that was something that took place during my presidency," says Burke. An unselfish leader, Burke shortened her own tenure as president by implementing streamlined election practices, so that presidents were chosen at the delegation rather than by mail-in vote. Burke also took great pride in the work that AIAW did in promoting Title IX and addressing its correct interpretation.

The issue that Burke and many others within the organization felt most strongly about was the NCAA's increasing encroachment on the governance of women's intercollegiate athletics. Though the NCAA initially snubbed women's sports, functionally prompting the formation of the AIAW, its apathy didn't last long. As the AIAW built a strong base for women's athletics and Title IX began to truly take effect, the NCAA began to develop an interest in uniting men's and women's sports governance under one organizational umbrella. Soon the NCAA began to actively pursue gaining oversight of women's athletics from the AIAW. The issue was a volatile one, particularly for those like Burke who had worked so tirelessly to create an organization for women by women. "I was very opposed to the NCAA's takeover of women's sports governance. It came at a time when we [the AIAW] were gaining television contracts, a step that would have made the AIAW financially feasible into the future. I resented the takeover then and I resent it today." These strong feelings were shared by many women who had dedicated their time and talent to providing opportunities to females—in student-athlete, coaching, officiating, and administrative roles—through the AIAW. In 1982, governance of women's athletics was officially transferred to the NCAA and the AIAW, a truly innovative and empowering organization, closed its doors.

Regardless of the organization's ultimate end, the AIAW and its leaders accomplished an incredible amount in creating opportunities for women through athletics and beyond. For her work with the organization and for women, Burke has been honored numerous times. A copy of one of her speeches was published in the 1979 edition of *Vital Speeches of the Day*, and she authored many journal articles and book chapters. Burke has been honored with the University of Iowa Distinguished Achievement Award and the Women's Sports Foundation's Pioneer in Women's Sports Award. The National Association for Girls and Women in Sport (NAGWS) had lauded Burke twice, first with the Honor Fellow Award and then with the 1999 Pathfinder Award.[2] Her passionate work with the AIAW set the foundation for increased opportunities for females through sports.

Today there is a place for women's sports in American society, largely due to the work of Burke and her colleagues in the AIAW. When asked if she had any advice for the young women of today, Burke replied, "Someone once said, 'Women should raise more hell and fewer flowers.' I still think that's a good motto for today." The quote, by James McNeill Whistler, is an excellent summation of the vigor with which Burke plowed through the obstacles that stood in the way of equality for women through sport. Burke is also quick to remind women that the fight is not over. The greatest honor that today's female athletes can give her is to remember the past and work for a brighter future.

Notes

1. Unless noted otherwise, the quotes in this article are by Dr. N. Peggy Burke, from a telephone interview with Catherine Lahey, May 28, 2008.

2. Mary Geraghty, "Burke Wins Pathfinder Award for Promotion of Women in Sports," The University of Iowa News Services, May 24, 1999.

Dr. Lonnie Leotus "Lee" Morrison

Trailblazer of the Association for Intercollegiate Athletics for Women (AIAW)

by Catherine Lahey

Venus Williams. Pat Summitt. Jennie Finch. Lisa Leslie. Michelle Wie. Danica Patrick. All of these women have achieved unprecedented success in their respective disciplines, becoming idols to aspiring young athletes and household names to even the most casual American sports fans. What these phenomenal female athletes may not know is that they likely owe their athletic opportunities to a true trailblazer whose name most sports enthusiasts would not recognize: Dr. Lee Morrison.

Born in Savannah, Georgia, in 1926, Lonnie Leotus "Lee" Morrison was a self-proclaimed "tomboy" from the start, although organized sports opportunities for girls were relatively nonexistent.[1] In the absence of organized sports, Morrison spent her youth becoming an accomplished equestrian and trying every activity that even remotely involved athletics, including roller skating, bike riding, and thoroughly unorganized neighborhood baseball. Finally in high school, Morrison had the opportunity to try more traditional sports like swimming, tennis, and softball. She was hooked.[2]

Morrison began her career in athletics administration early, being elected president of the Women's Athletic Association at Ward Belmont Junior College during her time as a student there. A strong proponent for the necessity of education, Morrison quickly earned her bachelor's of science degree in education from Georgia State College for Women, her master's degree from George Peabody College, and her doctoral degree in physical education from Indiana University. Armed with this impressive academic background, she set out to coach and teach, determined to help others, particularly women, achieve their dreams through education and exercise.

After spending time teaching in South Carolina, Morrison came to Virginia's Madison College, now James Madison University (JMU), enticed by the fact that the school offered sports for women. Slowly but surely, she became involved in the Madison intercollegiate athletics program, coaching field hockey for 17 years, dabbling in the coaching of a number of other sports and eventually acting as director of women's intercollegiate sports from 1972 to 1989. During her time at Madison, Morrison's prowess and passion as a champion of women's athletics began to gain recognition in the larger world of sport. Soon, major organizations beyond Madison began seeking Morrison's talent and expertise.

Dr. Morrison played a pivotal role in the two events that significantly contributed to increased opportunities for female athletes: the interpretation and promotion of Title IX and the establishment of a collegiate national championship system for women's sports. From 1970 to 1973, she acted as a founding member and the first president of the Virginia Federation for Intercollegiate Sports for College Women, an organization that spawned the Association for Intercollegiate Athletics for Women (AIAW), of which she was also a president and founding member. The AIAW, a passionate and pioneering organization, supported and sponsored collegiate athletics for women so successfully that the National Collegiate Athletic Association (NCAA), historically opposed to overseeing women's national collegiate championships, began to accept their merit and eventually sponsor them. Following this groundbreaking work, Dr. Morrison and a small number of athletic directors were summoned to Washington by the Honorable Joseph A. Califano, U.S. secretary of health, education and welfare, in order to assist with "properly" interpreting and promoting Title IX. Dr. Morrison's outstanding and inspired work with this group paved the way for the modern era of equity and equality through athletic activities.[3] Millions of women, young and old alike, have found their lives touched by the opportunities that Dr. Morrison's work has afforded them.

As if these accomplishments weren't stellar enough, Dr. Morrison has also been feted with numerous honors and Hall of Fame inductions. She has served in a number of roles on the United States Olympic Committee, acted as the president of the National Association for Girls and Women in Sport (NAGWS), and has been a speaker at the First International Congress on Women and Sport in the Americas. She has traveled to Germany, Venezuela, France, and Greece as an ambassador for the benefits of sporting opportunities for women.[4]

Though Dr. Morrison traveled the globe promoting the importance of athletic opportunities for women, JMU has always held a special place in her heart. In 2004, JMU honored her contributions to the university and the women of Virginia with the opening of The Morrison-Bruce Center for the Promotion of Physical Activity for Girls and Women, a community and research center that fully embodies all of the philosophies that Dr. Morrison has made her life's work. Upon the Center's opening, Dr. Morrison was asked what advice she might offer to today's girls and young women. She offered these thoughts: "Include some physical activity in your lifestyle as young as you can and find groups (co-ed and female) for participation. And if you don't know a sport or skill, don't be bashful. More than likely the others are also. Be brave."[5]

Dr. Lee Morrison has certainly been brave over the course of her 50-plus-year career in athletics administration. Never looking for a fight, but also never backing down from her convictions, Dr. Morrison and her colleagues have truly paved the way for the hundreds of thousands of young, female athletes who have benefited from Title IX and the newly available funding and support for women's athletics. Female athletes, from those little girls busting a move on their first skateboard to the women on the Olympic podium singing the national anthem, owe a debt of gratitude to Dr. Morrison. The greatest honor they afford her is to instill courage, passion, and drive into the next generation of women in sports.

Notes

1. Sean Coughlin, "Morrison a Pioneer for Female Sports," *Savannah Morning News*, May 2, 2008.

2. "Lonnie Leotus 'Lee' Morrison—A Women's Sports Rights Trailblazer," Greater Savannah Athletic Hall of Fame Biography, emailed to author, April 7, 2008.

3. Betty Jaynes, Nomination Letter—Greater Savannah Athletic Hall of Fame, emailed to author, April 7, 2008.

4. Sports Accomplishments, Nomination Form—Greater Savannah Athletic Hall of Fame, emailed to author, April 7, 2008.

5. "Dr. Lee Morrison," Notable Women, JMU: The Morrison-Bruce Center for the Promotion of Physical Activity for Girls & Women, http://www.jmu.edu/kinesiology/cppagw/leemorrison.html.

Dr. Carole Mushier

Trailblazer of the Association for Intercollegiate Athletics for Women (AIAW)

by Horacio Ruiz

Before Dr. Carole Mushier became an activist and a leading voice of Title IX legislation, the former athlcte, coach, administrator, and academic remembers playing on as many as five varsity teams in one year during high school. Growing up on the north shore of Long Island, New York, she knew that most girls did not have the same opportunities in their communities and schools to play varsity sports as she did. But when it came to playing sports in college, the opportunities were not there, and those experiences laid the foundation for her life's work.

"The one thing I remember when I was graduating from high school and I was going to college is when my father said to me, 'These boys are getting scholarships to play sports. You were voted best athlete for your class. Why can't you get a scholarship?'" Mushier said, "That would be a scholarship to a nonexistent program."[1]

When she enrolled at Boston University (BU) in the mid-1950s, there were no varsity teams on which Mushier could compete. She remembers cutthroat intramural competition, but nothing resembling intercampus competition. She would satisfy her competitive spirit by playing lacrosse, field hockey, and basketball on adult association teams. The nationwide associations in field hockey and lacrosse were highly competitive and, in many instances, were the grounds for picking the best players to represent the United States in international competition. After graduating with a degree in physical education from Sargent College at BU, Mushier was a high school teacher for three years while coaching the girls' lacrosse, field hockey, track and field, and basketball teams.

Mushier attended Columbia University for her master's degree from 1961 to 1962. During that time, she was the director of women's physical activities at St. John's University and she continued her own participation in sports, adding golf to her repertoire.

In 1962, she moved to East Stroudsburg State College as an assistant professor. She coached both the women's basketball and lacrosse teams and from 1965 to 1967 she served as the director of women's athletics. In 1964, still active as a player, Mushier represented the U.S. lacrosse team during a nine-week tour of Great Britain and Ireland.

From 1967 to 1969, Mushier enrolled at the University of Southern California to work on her doctoral degree. At USC, she became heavily involved with research in sport psychology and sociology. Mushier's dissertation, titled "Personality and Selected Women Athletes," was published in 1972 in the *International Journal of Sport Psychology*. Mushier's study found that "the similarities between the athletes regardless of age or experience level suggests that self-selection into sports competition on the basis of existing personality factors may be the prime reason for the personality structure of competitors and not the effect of the experience of sports competition." Even after her dissertation was published, Mushier hoped to continue her research and expand on the findings. In 1970, she accepted a position at SUNY College at Cortland as an associate professor, ready to leave the world of athletics and to continue her research.

"I felt my career had taken a different turn and after getting my PhD, I was an academic," she said. "Once you get a PhD, you should do regular research. The research I did for my dissertation is still considered a classic in the field."

When she arrived at SUNY at Cortland, Mushier couldn't help but be pulled back into athletic administration. She found the university was trying to organize a serious women's athletic department. At first, she coached the field hockey team and then, when she saw stronger leadership was needed to steer the women's program, she accepted an administrative position. "I got thrust back and I'm not sorry," Mushier said. "It was a wild ride, but a great ride."

Beginning in 1972, Mushier became involved with the Association for Intercollegiate Athletics for Women (AIAW). She first became involved at the state level when she was elected president of the New York State AIAW and she served in that capacity from 1974 to 1976. From the moment she returned to athletic administration, Mushier was involved in the development and the passing of Title IX into federal law.

In 1976, Mushier served as the president of the Eastern Region of the AIAW, continuing to form the policies that directly affected the AIAW and women's athletics in the United States. In 1979, she served as the national president of the AIAW, the year in which an interpretation policy was passed for Title IX to determine whether schools were in compliance with the law. As AIAW president, Mushier testified before Congress and the U.S. Commission on Civil Rights. She is proud of her colleagues for staying the course during the passing of Title IX.

"In the fall of 1979 the 'final guidelines' came out for Title IX and that was during my term," Mushier said. "We were successful in them not excluding football from the equation. The NCAA [National Collegiate Athletics Association] spent millions against us to exempt football from Title IX."

With the passing of Title IX, Mushier was keenly aware of the consequences the AIAW would face. The AIAW had formed a model for women's athletics that differed from the NCAA. In December 1979, Mushier made this statement: "We're going to win the law of the land, but we're going to lose our organization."

"With the passing of Title IX and with football included, women's athletics was going to become very important," Mushier said. "It was going to be such a ripe plum on the tree that somebody had to come and pluck it."

In 1982, armed with more money and influence, the NCAA took over as the governing body of women's intercollegiate athletics and the AIAW ceased to exist. Mushier wanted more time to develop the model the AIAW had created for women athletes, hoping that the NCAA would incorporate more of that outline. "I hoped that they would give us a little more time," Mushier said. "We had a model for women's intercollegiate athletics. It was not a business model. We wanted to keep it more academic—no less competitive, however."

Mushier is also proud of signing million-dollar contracts with NBC and then-fledgling ESPN. She said the two networks were primarily focused on airing women's basketball, but under her presidency, the AIAW negotiated the inclusion of other women's championships. Mushier also helped negotiate the broadcasting of women's sports at the Division II and III levels. She looks at Title IX as a revolutionary step in women's athletics, but she also knows that more than 35 years after Title IX was passed into law, not all women are receiving equal opportunities to play. "There's no doubt that Title IX changed the face of sport—men's and women's—not that it's been without its problems," she said. "I know there are still people that ask, 'Why does a girls' softball team have to have a decent practice field?' It's certainly better than it was. Is it perfect? No. Is there a perfect world? I doubt it."

Today, Mushier is retired and living in Fort Pierce, Florida, continuing her work as an activist by becoming a leading voice for her community. In 2007, she was elected president of the Fort Pierce South Beach Association, an 800-member organization that represents more than 3,000 residents of the barrier island. She also remains active with the Women's Sports Foundation as a volunteer, where she served on the Foundation's executive board in 1979. At the 2008 Women's Basketball Final Four, Mushier attended a "Women of Experience" luncheon and met with many of her colleagues from the AIAW and others, whom she affectionately re ferred to as the "oldie goldies." Mushier credits her opportunities to coach as an influence in building a philosophy for her career and in leaving a legacy for women in sport.

"If you look back, most of the presidents of the AIAW were coaches," Mushier said. "I think it gives you a perspective of what's going on out [in the playing fields]. I had an educational model for my kids. It was not win at all costs—it can't be in my mind."

Note

1. All of the quotes in this article are by Carole Mushier, from an interview with the author on May 30, 2008.

Dr. Carole Oglesby

Trailblazer of the Association for Intercollegiate Athletics for Women (AIAW)

by Sara Jane Baker

Growing up in the 1940s, most women were discouraged from participating in sports, but not Carole Oglesby. Luckily, she had influential parents and mentors who encouraged her to pursue her dreams. Most of these dreams surrounded sport, and this passion provided the motivation for her life's work. Oglesby has dedicated the majority of her life to encouraging physical activity and sport participation among women while attempting to close the gender equity gap in athletics.

Oglesby grew up in a very athletic family. Her father was a semiprofessional baseball player and avid golfer, and her mother had always been athletic as well. Sports naturally became an outlet for Oglesby's competitive and intense nature. She was addicted to everything about sport: the challenge, the goal setting, and the idea of mastery. After playing on a softball team, Oglesby found another group of women who shared this same love, a rarity for that era.

Oglesby was eager to share this love for sport with other women as she pursued her physical education degree at UCLA. However, she quickly discovered that not all women shared her passion. She described her first student teaching experience as miserable. "The girls were not about to even change into gym clothes and complained about sweating."[1] Thankfully, Oglesby did not let this attitude stall her teaching career. In fact, it actually provoked her to learn why her students were behaving that way. This should have been no surprise to Oglesby, given societal ideals for women at this time. "I was raised in a time when aspects of traditional feminism were perceived as laughable and expressiveness was looked at as a flaw."[2] Oglesby never felt that women should fit into one mold, so instead, she searched for the flexibility of the whole of human nature and not just half of it.

One of the turning points in her professional development came after a 1972 trip to Finland. At the time, Oglesby was a new professor at the University of Massachusetts. She was amazed by how important personal fitness was to the Fins. All over the country there were signs detailing the kilometers one had traveled, so the Fins always knew how far they were walking or running. Because she had always been surrounded by the competitive-natured Americans, Oglesby realized that sport was as much about physical activity and personal health as it was about winning and losing.

Early on, Oglesby got involved with the women's political movement even though sport was not on the agenda at that time. She addressed women's sport issues as a positive and encouraged physical activity among people of all ages. After meeting Katherine Switzer, who would later become the first woman to run in the all-male Boston marathon, Oglesby began doing advocacy work for women's marathons. She organized rallies, publications, and seminars providing evidence and facts supporting physical activity among women. For decades, there was a gross misconception about women in sport, sometimes even claiming it was bad for their health. Oglesby hoped to clear up many of these fallacies in her book, *Women and Sport: From Myth to Reality*. Betty Spears, a contributor to this book, writes:

> Sport for women has been more a myth than a reality because the western world has both accepted and rejected women in sport. Society has always been enthralled by the athletic skill and prowess of a few women, for these women, sport is real. But for most women society has created a role which excludes them from sport and, for these women, sport has been a myth. While accepting the idea of sport for a few women, society has created many myths and folk tales which reinforce the reject of sport for most women.[3]

Oglesby eventually extended her work to include not just women, but everyone. After all, everyone should have an equal opportunity to participate in sports and stay physically active. Oglesby focused on Olympism, an idea dating back to ancient Greece. The goal of Olympism is "to place sport at the service of the harmonious development of man [humankind], with a view to promoting a peaceful society concerned with the preservation of human dignity."[4] Oglesby strove to change perceptions about participation along with winning and losing, specifically among the United States Olympic Committee (USOC). "The Olympic Committee, especially in the 1970s, 1980s and early 1990s, was only paying attention to the gold medalist. Only one winner was recognized and only one person was thought to win."[5] In Oglesby's eyes, to focus only upon the Olympic Games was not an effective use of money or resources. Instead, all governing bodies should place high importance on their grassroots programs bringing high-level sport to everyone—including women. Furthermore, there should be equitable funds for men's and women's sports. Not surprising for the time, Oglesby's views were met with incredible resistance.

Ignoring her critics, Oglesby pressed on. She continued teaching while becoming more involved in sport psychology. One of Oglesby's few regrets in life is that she was never seriously viewed as an athlete, even though she was a really good athlete. However, looking back on her experience in athletics, Oglesby realized the psychology aspect did not come easy to her. "I struggled with performing at my best due to the pressure that I put on myself."[6] After gaining expertise in the field of sport psychology, Oglesby realized she never had access to this information growing up. In fact, there still is a large imbalance between the hundreds of thousands of U.S. athletes and the only 300+ certified sport psychology consultants. Oglesby has made it her mission to provide athletes with what she had never been given. One of her current athletes, Renee Hykel, recently competed in the Beijing Olympics. Hykel rowed in the lightweight women's doubles placing in the top 10 and was less than one second away from competing in the Olympic Finals.

Currently, Dr. Oglesby serves as the chairperson of the department of kinesiology at California State University, Northridge (CSUN). Although she plans on retiring from CSUN soon, she is looking forward to getting involved with, and continuing, other initiatives. In 2007, Oglesby worked with the United Nations Division of Advancement for Women (DAW) in releasing a publication titled, "Women, Gender Equality, and Sport." This publication was translated worldwide and should help in advocacy especially in developing countries. She plans to continue her work with this publication as well as her work with Women Sport International (WSI), an organization over which she once presided.

Fortunately, Dr. Oglesby's work has not gone unnoticed. In fact, she has a distinguished list of awards and honors. The Women's Sports Foundation's Billie Jean King Contribution Award, the National Association of Girls and Women in Sport Honor Fellow, and the Association of Intercollegiate Athletics for Women Award of Merit are just a few of her many awards.

Despite these honors, Carole Oglesby wants her legacy to be simple. "I hope to live in the memories of my students and mentees as a person who never gave up and never ever stopped fighting."[7] This is a humble request for such an amazing woman. Women—and sports participants everywhere—should be indebted to Carole Oglesby for her countless contributions to society and sport. After all, she is a big reason for the opportunities in sport we see today.

Notes

1. Carole Oglesby, phone interview, May 16, 2008.

2. Ibid.

3. Carole Oglesby, *Women and Sport: From Myth to Reality* (Philadelphia: Lea & Febiger Publishers, 1978), 3.

4. Ibid.

5. Ibid.

6. Ibid.

7. Ibid.

Judith Holland

Trailblazer of the Association for Intercollegiate Athletics for Women (AIAW)

by Sara Jane Baker

In 1968, only 16,000 females participated in college sport. Today, this number has grown to over 180,000.[1] With this increased participation for women in sport, some may take these additional opportunities for granted. Not Judith Holland. She is one of the many women who fought for gender equality in sport. When she was hired as UCLA's first athletic director for the women's program, Holland knew she had a tough road ahead of her.

After the passage of Title IX in 1972, UCLA was one of the first schools to comply with the new law and establish a separate women's athletic program. Holland, given her background in coaching and administration, was deemed the best choice to head the new women's department. She was given little more than a green RV located outside the women's gym to house her new athletic department. Furthermore, the women were still a part of the Association for Intercollegiate Athletics for Women (AIAW) and were essentially treated like club sports—receiving limited funding for uniforms, facilities, and transportation to events.

The men's program, in contrast, had established themselves as one of the most successful programs in the country. Holland wasted no time in attempting to close the gap between these two programs. To get the coaches and athletic staff on board with the department's new goals, Holland, always a visionary, organized a handbook detailing how she planned to run the new department. "I wanted to have a program that would equal the success of UCLA's men's athletics. That's what my vision was so I had to build it day-by-day."[2]

Holland was given a measly budget of $263,000—an unrealistic amount given the program needed money for uniforms, facilities, transportation, and coaches' salaries. "We spend more than that now on shoelaces,"[3] Holland later joked. Not letting this financial challenge deter her, Holland found ways to cut costs and stretch out the budget. Rather than hiring full-time coaches, she hired part-time coaches who also taught to earn extra money. Holland would also participate in fundraisers each year, lobbying student registration fees for additional money for the women's teams. Michele Kort, a former UCLA basketball player, remembers these tumultuous times. "Road games? That was a four-hour drive to Fresno in clunky university station wagons, followed by an immediate return trip. Forget any overnights at a hotel."[4]

Although UCLA had to monitor its spending, Holland refused to be frugal with scholarships, knowing that in order to attract the best players, she would have to entice them with scholarships. However, due to the lack of money, Holland could not afford to be reckless with her decisions—and she was anything but careless. In fact, her choices were flawless. She gave her first scholarship to Ann Meyers, a four-time All-American who became one of the most decorated players in UCLA history and the only female to sign a National Basketball Association (NBA) contract.

The lack of scholarships for women was not the only place Holland saw a disparity between the two programs. Despite the passage of Title IX in 1972, which sought to eliminate gender discrimination, women were still lacking equality. Women, for example, were not eligible for academic tutoring like the men. Holland knew that to take this program to the next level, she needed to take drastic steps. Joining the men in the National Collegiate Athletic Association (NCAA) was the first of these steps—a bold move given Holland was the former president of the AIAW. "I thought it was right for UCLA," Holland said. "Only the NCAA could take women's sports to the next level of better recruitment, greater funding, and, ultimately, more recognition."[5] In 1981, the NCAA created a division for women and UCLA promptly enlisted. Although the AIAW would go out of business shortly thereafter, joining the NCAA would make a huge impact on women's teams across the country.

Holland's next move would be met with even more resistance. After attending an NCAA convention, Holland concluded that the men's and women's programs could not coexist and would need to be joined under the same organization in order for true equality to exist. Although a controversial and very unpopular idea, the two programs merged in 1982. Shortly after, many other collegiate athletic departments followed Holland's model and sought equality by joining forces with the men's department.

Holland retired in 1996, but not before leaving behind a legacy. Under her reign, the Lady Bruins won 24 collegiate team titles and earned the National No. 1 Overall Athletic Program title on 10 different occasions. As incredible as these statistics are, her greatest contribution to UCLA was more intangible. "She helped me a lot just in terms of always striving for the best and never settling for anything else. You didn't have an excuse. She wanted the best out of you. And she would let you know that that performance was good but you could do better,"[6] a former athlete remembers.

Today, thanks in large part to Holland's work, the UCLA women's department has seen tremendous success. UCLA is currently home to 12 women's teams that have gone on to win over 30 national championships. Her impact on UCLA has not gone unrecognized. In 1988, she was the recipient of UCLA's Alumni Association's University Service Award, as well as the Women's Basketball Coaches Association (WBCA) Administrator of the Year award.

Judith Holland transformed an athletic department housed in an RV with a budget of $263,000 into one of the most distinguished programs in the nation. Her impact extended far beyond UCLA, as many women's departments followed her lead. She was a true pioneer, often having to make controversial decisions, but never ceasing the fight for gender equality. For women's progress in sport over the past four decades, Judith Holland deserves much of the credit. UCLA's former sports information director would give Judith Holland *all* of the credit: "Women athletes today owe everything to Judith Holland. Without her, UCLA wouldn't be recognized as it is. She was so ahead of her time that it gave UCLA an edge."[7]

Notes

1. AP. "Despite Record Female Participation in Athletics, Percentage of Women Coaches Declines," Diverse: Issues in Higher Education, http://www.diverseeducation.com/artman/publish/article_11232.shtml.

2. Chen, Alice I. "Athletics for Women," UCLA, http://www.english.ucla.edu/ ucla 1960s/7274/chen.htm (accessed May 23, 2008).

3. Kort, Michelle, "The Journey toward Excellence," UCLA TODAY, http://www .today.ucla.edu/1999/990222the.html (accessed May 23, 2008).

4. Chen, "Athletics for Women."

5. Chris Umpierre, "After 28 Years, UCLA Women's Athletics on Even Ground." University Wire, http://www.highbeam.com/doc/1P1-25811539.html (accessed May 22, 2008).

6. Ibid.

7. Bruin Athletics, "In a league of their own," UCLA, http://uclabruins.cstv.com/ genrel/040999aaa.html (accessed May 23, 2008).

Dr. Laurie Mabry

Trailblazer of the Association for Intercollegiate Athletics for Women (AIAW)

by Catherine Lahey

Sometimes you have to fight for what you know is right—regardless of what the authorities tell you. Dr. Laurie Mabry knows this sentiment well. During Mabry's time with the Association for Intercollegiate Athletics for Women (AIAW), she was scheduled to speak before a congressional committee regarding Title IX implementation and interpretation. Upon picking up the prepared remarks from her attorney, Mabry noticed something that seemed odd. Part of the speech discussed the fact that men's football and basketball would be exempt from consideration in Title IX issues. Mabry balked. The attorney and others expressed concern that there was a possibility of losing all benefits associated with Title IX if concessions weren't made for popular established sports like football and basketball. Mabry stood her ground, refusing to give the remarks unless the policies of Title IX were applied to all sports. Her stubborn persistence paid off—not just for her or the AIAW, but for all future generations of American women.

The best outcome of Title IX says Mabry is that "it's okay to be a girl and be athletic."[1] This was not the case when Mabry was growing up, although she did participate in softball, basketball, and golf. Formal sports opportunities were few and far between, but Mabry's father encouraged her by helping to manage a summer softball team. Later in life, these early experiences with sport would help shape Mabry's path. Mabry, like her AIAW colleague Dr. Peggy Burke, didn't go to college with intentions of studying physical education. After entering Northwestern University, Mabry discovered that physical education was her calling and quickly changed her major. A profound and powerful career was born.

After graduation, Mabry found a home with Illinois State University athletics, helping to elevate its women's programs from recreational status to the level of competitive college teams. During Mabry's 20 year tenure with the university (1960–80) as director of women's intercollegiate athletics, she significantly impacted opportunities for women at Illinois State and beyond. Part of her professional duties included being involved with the AIAW at the state level. Mabry eventually served the organization as commissioner before being elected AIAW president for the 1975–76 term. In that position, Mabry had an opportunity to influence women's athletics at a national level.

Like many others within the AIAW, Mabry felt that the greatest challenge facing the organization was the impending fight with the National Collegiate Athletic Association (NCAA) over governance of women's sports. This was also her greatest point of pride. Slowly but surely, the NCAA's interest in undertaking the oversight of women's intercollegiate championship competitions increased. During her presidency, Mabry fought off their encroachment while actively promoting the need for women's equality within sports. Though Mabry didn't like it, she had the foresight to see that all intercollegiate athletic governance would eventually have to fall under a single organization. In anticipation of this inevitable conclusion, Mabry championed an "equal voice" structure for national athletic governance in order to preserve opportunities for women in coaching, officiating, and athletic administration.

Unfortunately, this "equal voice" model was not to be. In 1982, governance of women's athletics officially switched to the NCAA and the AIAW was forced to close its doors. Although some of the AIAW's top female administrators made the transition to roles within the NCAA, Mabry's prediction about decreased professional opportunities for women largely held true. In looking back, Mabry comments that although the AIAW "lost, we accomplished a lot." Her observation is certainly true, considering the organization's absolute focus on achieving equal opportunities for women through sport.

In addition to her involvement in the AIAW, Mabry also had plenty of responsibilities at her own university. Outside of her role in overseeing women's athletics at Illinois State, Mabry also taught in the physical education department. As director of women's athletics, Mabry organized and hosted the first women's national basketball tournament held in 1972 at Illinois State. Her service to the university and to the community of directors of athletics earned her the honor of being inducted into the National Association of Collegiate Athletic Directors' Hall of Fame. Mabry is particularly proud of her work with the university in hosting those early women's basketball tournaments and in her professional achievements with the AIAW. Like a pebble thrown into a pond, the ripples of Mabry's influence continue to affect female athletes today.

With all of these experiences behind her, Mabry has a wealth of knowledge to share with young women. Her advice is simple and powerful. "You have to stand up for what you believe is right and fair and equal. Things aren't quite equal yet across the board. Fight for it." During her career as an athletic administrator, Mabry was unafraid to practice what she preaches now. Laurie Mabry's ability to stand up for what she felt was right and equal has positively impacted generations of women, within sports and far beyond.

Notes

1. Unless noted otherwise, the quotes in this article are by Dr. Laurie Mabry, from a telephone interview with author, May 28, 2008.

2. Laurie Mabry, biography, Illinois State Athletics website.

Anne "Sandy" Barbour

Leader at the NCAA Division I-A Level

by Catherine Lahey

Life in a military family is typically characterized by discipline, structure, and constant relocation. The Barbour family, headed by Henry, a Navy pilot who was shot down twice over Korea, was no exception. The Barbours spent time both on U.S. soil and abroad during their children's formative years. Sandy, the youngest of three girls, later recalled that life as a Barbour was militaristically " 'Yes, Sir,' 'No, Sir,' or 'I'll find out, Sir.' " She once complained about being kicked out of basketball practice for mouthing off to the coach, and her father stood her up in front of the hall mirror and pointed out, in no uncertain terms, that such behavior was unacceptable.[1] Needless to say, expectations were high in the Barbour household.

Although strict, Henry had a deep love of sports that he instilled in his youngest daughter. In her youth, Sandy was banned from playing Little League baseball based on her gender, even though her skills were on par with those of her male counterparts. A consummate champion for his children, Henry fought for her inclusion, but ultimately was unsuccessful. Despite the disappointment, Sandy's love for sports grew as she and her father attended innumerable Navy and Baltimore Colts football games. For Sandy Barbour, a childhood passion quickly turned into a successful professional career.

Barbour attended Wake Forest University, where her superior athletic skills garnered her four varsity letters as captain of the field hockey team and two more as a varsity basketball player. After graduating with a degree in physical education, Barbour continued her education at the University of Massachusetts, earning a master's degree in sports management while working as an assistant coach for both the field hockey and lacrosse teams. She then moved into athletic administration at Northwestern University, eventually holding the position of assistant athletic director for intercollegiate programs for six years, as well as earning an MBA from Northwestern's Kellogg School of Management. Post-graduation, Barbour spent a short time working in programming and production for FOX Sports Net in Chicago before returning to college athletics.

In 1991, Barbour was recruited to join the administration team at Tulane University as an associate athletic director. Upon the departure of athletic director and mentor Kevin White, Barbour took the helm of Green Wave athletics. Over her three year tenure as athletic director, she led Tulane to an unprecedented 12 conference championships, including an undefeated season and a national ranking in football with Coach Tommy Bowden. After leaving Tulane, White had been appointed athletic director at Notre Dame and Barbour eventually joined him there as an associate athletic director before being promoted to the role of senior athletic administrator.[2] Remembering the commitment to excellence that her father had instilled in her, Barbour raised the bar in each of these positions, drawing attention from the collegiate athletic community.

Her hard work paid dividends in 2004, when Barbour was offered a job that she called "a dream come true, both personally and professionally" director of athletics at the University of California, Berkeley (Cal).[3] Although some likened the difficulty of her task to "being sent straight to the mound in the bottom of the ninth," Barbour accepted the honor and the challenge with open arms.[4] On the academic front, nearly half of Cal's student-athletes maintain a cumulative GPA of 3.0 or higher, and 14 of Cal's 27 programs earned cumulative GPAs higher than their historical average. Barbour has also worked diligently to upgrade facilities, improve relationships with Cal supporters, and champion community involvement for student-athletes.

Though Barbour often seems like superwoman, delicately balancing a mind-boggling number of critical tasks, she can sum up her plan for Cal athletics in three short words—"athletics done right." For Barbour, this mantra entails focusing on four specific areas (athletics, academics, community, and fiscal responsibility) in order to build a healthy, model collegiate athletics program.[5] She gives careful attention to each area, setting benchmarks and goals in order to help define achievement. Each day may present new challenges, but Barbour's map to success is clearly focused on the big picture.

Even so many years later, it is still the lessons of her father Henry that make Barbour a perfect fit at Cal. His commitment to integrity and education are at the heart of the University of California, Berkeley, and Sandy Barbour alike. In a 2007 statement regarding Title IX compliance, Barbour stressed that even in greatness "we can always strive to be better."[6] It is this acute ability to always endeavor for more that sets Sandy Barbour apart from the crowd and makes her truly excellent.

Notes

1. Jake Curtis, "The Time Is Now," Profile: Sandy Barbour, *San Francisco Chronicle*, November 1, 2004.

2. "Sandy Barbour," Athletic Director, CAL Athletics, http://calbears.cstv.com/genrel/barbour_sandy00.html.

3. "UC Berkley Announces New Athletic Director, Notre Dame's Sandy Barbour," Press Release, *UC Berkeley News*, http://berkeley.edu/news/media/releases/2004/09/15_Barbour.shtml.

4. Curtis, "The Time Is Now."

5. Sandy Barbour, interview by Chris Avery, The Bear Insider. August 22, 2007.

6. Sandy Barbour. "Athletic Director Sandy Barbour's statement on women's athletics at Cal," UC Berkeley Web Feature, August 24, 2007, http://berkeley.edu/news/media/releases/2007/08/24_title9-barbour.shtml.

Barbara Burke

Leader at the NCAA Division I-A Level

by Stacy Martin-Tenney

Courtesy of the University of Wyoming Athletics.

There have been nine full-time directors of athletics at Eastern Illinois University. Recently, Barbara Burke became the first woman to hold the position. Her accomplished and lengthy career in athletics has prepared her for every facet of her new job. She began her athletic career as a student-athlete, grew into coaching, and finally administered athletics in several capacities. The spectrum of opportunity that she experienced will provide a unique perspective whether she is looking for qualities when hiring a coach, relating to student-athlete needs, or representing the university in conference, national, or corporate decisions. Burke's leadership will guide Eastern Illinois into the next century of its athletic and academic endeavors in championship style.

She is no stranger to the daily dedication and commitment that is required for student-athletes to reach championships. Burke was a talented athlete in both softball and basketball while attending Western Michigan University from 1976 to 1980. Hard work became second nature because there was no off-season for her. The native of Kalamazoo, Michigan, reaped the benefits from Title IX, while leading the Western Michigan Broncos to the Women's College World Series in 1980 before graduating with a bachelor's of science degree. Her commitment to athletics did not cease upon graduation, as she immediately began her coaching career.

Burke broke into the coaching profession at Kalamazoo Central High School, but was soon up for another challenge, as she began her collegiate coaching career at Tennessee Temple University in 1980. Again, Burke did not understand the meaning of over-commitment. She was hired as the head softball coach and the assistant basketball coach for the university. Four years later, she found the time to earn her master's of education from the University of Tennessee at Chattanooga to further her understanding of collegiate athletics and ultimately her career. Her coaching career took her south, back north, to the Midwest, and to the East, with stops at Clearwater Christian College (Florida), Cornerstone College (Michigan), Indiana University Southeast, and West Virginia State College. At each one of these stops, her commitment to softball and basketball continued, and so did her success. She was named district coach of the year three different times during her journey. Only eight years removed from her alma mater, the Broncos enshrined her into their hall of fame in 1988 for her post-collegiate achievements in athletics.

Soon after Burke's induction, she took yet another step into athletics and pursued a career in administration. Her experience began with West Virginia State University from 1992 to 1994. She went on to hold administrative roles at Marshall University from 1994 to 1997 and the University of Texas at El Paso (UTEP) during the 1997–98 school year. Burke learned the game and its rules adeptly and honed her talents quickly. When UTEP faced a chasm between their past and future directors of athletics, they instilled their confidence in Barbara Burke to guide them through the transition. Her experience and professionalism made her an excellent choice for the University of Wyoming as they faced a new conference alignment. Burke began her career at Wyoming by serving as one of the original members of the Mountain West Conference Joint Council. The conference took shape and so did her 10-year career at Wyoming. She served on several conference- and national-level committees committed to educational merit and veracity for student-athletes. The most notable of these appointments was the National Collegiate Athletic Association (NCAA) Division I Women's Basketball Committee. Since she had experienced the sport as both an athlete and a coach, it was her opportunity to shape and guide the sport on a national level.

She actively participated in the National Association of Collegiate Directors of America (NACDA) and the National Association of Collegiate Women Athletic Administrators (NACWAA). She still managed to direct the day-to-day operations of the athletic department of Wyoming and determined and implemented a strategic plan for the university and its athletic program. The variety of roles available to her at Wyoming prepared her to become deputy director of athletics and senior women's administrator during the last two years of her tenure at Wyoming. She also served as interim athletic director for Wyoming during a similar transition period, which included the management of all 17 sports and their $19 million budget.

Burke accelerated her career to encapsulate a lifetime of experiences, and so her name certainly circulated as some director of athletics positions began to open during 2008. Programs were looking for someone with professionalism and a rich fabric of experiences, and Barbara Burke's name was promptly put on the short list. Burke credits Dr. Tom Buchanan, president of the University of Wyoming, and Mr. Tom Burman, director of athletics for the University of Wyoming, with her development through the experiences that they created for her under their leadership.[1] Dr. William Perry and Dr. Daniel Nadler saw an opportunity for their university, Eastern Illinois, to hurriedly acquire Burke's experience, brilliance, and passion. She immediately stood out from the other short-list candidates according to President Perry when he announced her as the new director of athletics for Eastern Illinois University. "Barbara stood out as the top candidate in an extremely strong pool of candidates for the position. Her career experience, planning skills, and organizational abilities are first rate. Her commitment to our objectives in the integration of the athletic department into the life of the university, to the development of our student-athletes, and to the progress of our athletic programs is first rate."[2]

Burke echoed the sentiments of Perry and described her decision to accept the position as simply the right thing to do. "When the offer came (from Eastern), I had a very good feel for Dr. Perry and Dr. Nadler," she said. "It just felt right. I can't explain it. For those of you who have done job searches before, you just know. North Dakota was a wonderful opportunity, but Eastern Illinois was ahead of Dakota and I had made a commitment to Eastern and that was the right thing to do. I have no regrets, not one."[3]

Burke's impact at Eastern Illinois will be felt almost immediately, as she will begin to shape her new athletic department by striving to find those qualities she admires in a new swimming coach.

She also plans on implementing various program development strategies to elevate Eastern as a prominent athletic power. Given Burke's background as a student-athlete and coach, she will enthusiastically greet Eastern's athletes and coaches and together they will partner to develop a better future for all of the programs. Burke assumes responsibility for 21 sports, 108 years of athletic tradition, and the relationship with the school's primary conference, the Ohio Valley Conference, which hosts 17 of Eastern's 21 sports in conference play throughout the year. The Mountain West Conference recently bestowed her with the prestigious Dr. Albert C. Yates Award, to recognize her as an individual that successfully supported the University of Wyoming, one of its member institutions, and promoted the ideals of athletic and academic excellence. Burke begins her new journey with a tremendous vote of confidence from her peers and a lifetime of enthusiasm for athletics. More awards and tremendous contributions to athletics are sure to follow her footsteps.

Notes

1. Eastern Illinois University Athletics, "Barbara Burke Hired As EIU Athletic Director," Eastern Illinois University Athletics, http://www.eiupanthers.com/News/gen/2008/3/21/08barbaraburkeadhire.asp.

2. Ibid.

3. Matt Daniels, "It Just Felt Right," *The Daily Eastern News*, March 21, 2008, News Section.

Cary Sue Groth

Leader at the NCAA Division I-A Level

by Catherine Lahey

The last time Cary Groth was referred to as a "girl" she wasn't in junior high school, she was in the process of being hired as director of athletics at National Collegiate Athletic Association (NCAA) Division I Northern Illinois University (NIU). Before her hiring, some athletic department employees complained that the university couldn't possibly "hire 'this girl' to run the athletic program."[1] Much to their dismay, the university proudly turned over control of Huskie Athletics to Groth, an alumna who had been with the department for 10 years. The "girl" promptly began to flex her administrative muscle, dedicating herself to the improvement of the NIU athletic department for the good of the student-athletes and the university at-large.

Groth came to NIU as a student-athlete and, after spending three years teaching at a high school, returned as an assistant tennis coach. Over the next 10 years she climbed the ranks in the Huskie athletic department, eventually being selected to fill the role of athletic director in 1994. Gender aside, Groth was facing a number of major challenges, including looming facility upgrades, questionable leadership in the football program, and funding issues. Groth never blinked.

Despite any doubts that her detractors may have had about a woman's ability to make the difficult decisions required of a Division I athletic director, Groth stood strong in her defense of the best interests of Huskie athletics. After a disappointing 1995 football season, Groth made a major coaching change and hired a new head coach in hopes of introducing "stability and direction" to the struggling NIU football program.[2] She had officially been on the job for over a year, but this decisive coaching change effectively announced Groth's arrival as a force to be reckoned with in collegiate athletic administration. Although the next two years of Huskie football proved to be rough, the new coach turned the program around, allowing Groth to focus on other pressing issues within the department.

Groth's next big task was removing NIU from the Big West Conference, an awkward fit for a Midwestern school, and realigning the university with the Mid-American Conference to the benefit of all Huskie sports programs. With this accomplished, Groth tackled major fundraising and facilities projects, including the building of the 10,000-seat Convocation Center and the revival of the Huskie booster club. Even with major projects like these successfully completed, Groth considered her proudest accomplishment to be the "improvements in graduation rates and the growing recognition on campus of what a successful athletic program can bring to an institution."[3] In keeping with these points of pride, Groth took great pains to establish the AIM Program to address discrepancies in African-American student-athlete graduation rates and the Academic Excellence Program to recognize student-athletes with high or improving GPAs. To Groth, all of these tasks contributed to the establishment of a strong and well-rounded athletic department.

After over 20 years of service to NIU, Groth made a major decision in 2004. She elected to accept the position of athletic director at the University of Nevada, Reno, having previously been a finalist for the same position at Northwestern University. Although she found it difficult to leave the university that had been her home for so many years, Groth was clearly excited about the possibility offered by the University of Nevada Wolfpack. Upon her hiring, she commented on Nevada's commitment to "building things the right way, from the ground up."[3] This concept of the "right way" forms the core of Groth's philosophy for athletic administration. She has committed herself to making each decision with the big picture in mind, taking into account the needs of the student-athletes, the athletic department, the university, and the community. Each day brings new challenges, but Groth's values and goals remain consistent.

Under Groth's guidance, the Wolfpack achieved a new level of athletic achievement with numerous teams winning Western Athletic Conference Championships and Tournament Titles. In 2007, Nevada won the Western Athletic Conference Commissioner's Cup, recognizing the Conference's best athletic department, for the first time in school history. The department has also won awards for its commitment to diversity and equality, including the Diversity in Athletics Award from the Laboratory for Diversity in Sport. In addition, Groth has helped facilitate a number of capital improvements and fundraising opportunities and continues to helm the Wolfpack as they strive to attain new milestones.

Personally, Groth has garnered awards and honors throughout her career for her abilities as a leader and commitment to athletic excellence. Street & Smith's *Sports Business Journal* in 1998 named her one of the "Super 50: Women's Sports Executives," and she has since been lauded by the National Association of Collegiate Women's Athletic Administrators (NACWAA). In 2002, while still at NIU, Groth was appointed to the Title IX "Commission on Opportunities in Athletics," a role that allowed her to take part in innovative policy interpretation.

Even with all of these accolades, Groth takes pride in the fact that the main responsibility of her job is service to student-athletes. When asked to look back on her involvement in athletics, Groth comments, "I have been extremely blessed to have been a part of intercollegiate athletics for the past 30 plus years as an athlete, coach, and administrator. The life I have been fortunate to live has been one of great experiences and joy due to the many students and colleagues that I have worked with throughout the years. I can't think of a better profession to be involved with."[4] Groth, through her dedication, perseverance, and commitment to the "right way," has passed these blessings along to her student-athletes and colleagues.

Notes

1. "Q&A with Cary Groth," Athletic Management, 14.6, October/November 2002.

2. Ibid.

3. Melanie Magara, "NIU AD Cary Groth Accepts Top Job at University of Nevada," Northern Today, March 9, 2004, http://www.niu.edu/northerntoday/2004/mar9/carygroth.shtml.

4. Magara, "NIU AD Cary Groth Accepts."

Deborah A. Yow

Leader at the NCAA Division I-A Level

by Catherine Lahey

To look at the Yow sisters today is to see one of the most storied families in the history of women's athletics. The youngest, Susan, has been a professional and collegiate Division I basketball coach for nearly 30 years. The oldest, Kay, is a living legend in her 33rd year as head women's basketball coach at North Carolina State, having coached both of her sisters through their collegiate careers. In women's basketball, the Yow name is synonymous with faith, hard work, and excellence. But there is one more Yow sister—the middle one, Debbie. The one who dropped out of college to "find herself" and experimented with recreational drugs. The one who is "wired for 220 volts in a 110 volt world."[1] The one who found her faith reborn. The one who is in her 14th year as the athletic director at the University of Maryland, making her one of only a handful of women running collegiate athletic departments.

Throughout her life, Debbie Yow has always been full of surprises. When her family thought she was interested in being a majorette, Debbie instead announced she would be trying out for basketball, following in the footsteps of her mother and older sister. After high school, Yow attended East Carolina as a freshman before briefly getting caught up in the turbulence of the 1960s and striking out on her own. Having spent a year working menial fast food jobs, Yow returned to the world of academia, graduating with honors from Elon College, where she played basketball for her sister Kay.[2] From that point forward, Debbie Yow was unstoppable.

From fast food to fast breaks, Yow went on to coach women's basketball at the University of Kentucky, Oral Roberts University, and the University of Florida, amassing an impressive 160-69 win-loss record. Her success propelled her into positions in athletic administration, serving as an athletics fundraiser at Florida before moving on to the University of North Carolina, Greensboro, and finally accepting the role of athletic director at St. Louis University. When the University of Maryland began the search for a new director of athletics in 1994, Yow's background and accomplishments sparked interest. On August 15, 1994, Deborah A. Yow was hired to take the helm of the Terrapin athletic department, making her the first female athletic director in the Atlantic Coast Conference (ACC) and only the fourth among all National Collegiate Athletic Association (NCAA) Division I-A schools.[3]

Mothers always seem to know their children best. Yow's mother, Lib, herself an excellent basketball player and star at Gibsonville High School in North Carolina, was no exception. "Debbie," she once said, "really loves a challenge."[4] Yow's strong willed, adventuresome spirit was never more evident than the day she accepted the position of athletic director at Maryland. Although many people focused on the challenges Yow faced as a woman in a traditionally male-dominated field, Yow instead focused on the many challenges of leading Terrapin athletics. At the time of Yow's hiring, the department had been running at a budget deficit for over 10 years and was quickly accumulating debt. In addition to this financial struggle, the Terrapins were ranked last competitively in the ACC and also ranked last in fundraising. Yow's challenge began the moment she arrived on campus.

Over the next 14 years, Yow made great strides in her quest to elevate Terrapin athletics to the position of a nationally ranked and universally respected athletic program. Immediately upon her arrival, Yow began balancing all 14 departmental budgets and establishing an influx of dollars through marketing and fundraising. Her efforts have paid off monumentally, as private gifts to athletics and corporate sponsorships have increased over 300 percent. Over her tenure, athletic facilities at Maryland have been upgraded dramatically, student-athlete graduation rates have improved significantly,

Courtesy of University of Maryland Athletics.

and Maryland programs have garnered seven national champion-ships over the past three seasons. As a capstone, Terrapin athletics was named one of the top 20 programs in the nation by *U.S. News and World Report* and *Sports Illustrated*.

All of these milestones and achievements have caused the col-legiate athletic community to look beyond Yow's gender and to rec-ognize her skill as a leader. She has previously served as president of the National Association of Collegiate Directors of Athletics (NACDA) and is currently president of the NCAA Division I-A Ath-letic Directors Association. Numerous organizations have honored her for her leadership and vision and she has been recognized as one of the most influential people in collegiate athletics. She is a highly sought after speaker and has written many articles on athletics man-agement. Even with all of these additional responsibilities, Yow's true passion is still leading the Terrapins to greatness. On a daily basis, she asks her colleagues, student-athletes, and herself to "raise our sights and sharpen our tools . . . to work hard and work smart . . . to recognize that our only limitations are those that we place upon ourselves."[5]

Although Yow's path to the helm of Terrapin athletics may have been unconventional, her success is undeniable. Excellence is in the Yow blood, passed down through Lib and husband Hilton to their highly acclaimed, hard-working children. Yow has worked tire-lessly to pass that sense of success and dedication on to the Univer-sity of Maryland community and, as she tells everyone who will lis-ten, "It's a great time to be a Terp."[6] What is left unspoken is that this sense of hope, optimism, and greatness in Terrapin territory is due in large part to the efforts of barrier breaker and Director of Athletics Debbie Yow.

Notes

1. Staci D. Kramer, "One to Watch," *The Sporting News*, September 5, 1994.

2. Bill Brubaker, "Maryland's Debbie Yow," *ACC Area Sports Journal*, September 17, 1999.

3. David Nakamura and Mark Asher, "U-Md. Names Yow Athletic Director; First Woman to Hold Post in ACC History," *The Washington Post*, August 16, 1994.

4. Kramer, "One to Watch."

5. "Deborah A. Yow," Director of Athletics, University of Maryland Athletics, http://umterps.cstv.com/school-bio/md-athdir.html.

6. "Deborah A. Yow."

Kathy Beauregard

Leader at the NCAA Division I-A Level

by Stacy Martin-Tenney

Kathy Beauregard has become the cornerstone of Western Michigan University (WMU). She became involved in athletics at an early age and was even inducted into the Loy Norrix High School Athletic Hall of Fame for her preparatory accomplishments. After growing up in Kalamazoo, Michigan, and graduating from Hope College in 1979, she began her coaching career in gymnastics at Western Michigan, while earning her master's in athletic administration. Throughout her nine-year coaching career, she led her team to two championship titles and was named Coach of the Year for the Mid-American Conference (MAC) twice. The experience she gained while coaching her gymnasts provided her with firsthand knowledge of the athletic department, which would prepare her for her future in athletic administration.

She left the coaching ranks in 1988 for a role at the university as an associate athletic director. During this time, she learned the ins and outs of the National Collegiate Athletic Association (NCAA) compliance rules and she was naturally suited for student-athlete academic support after her coaching experience. After only a few years of administrative experience, she was named senior associate athletic director in 1993. Women have grown in numbers in the ranks of athletic departments, but it has not been an easy path to the top. When women garner these positions in the upper echelon of the athletic department, they are rarely given supervision over the typically male revenue generating sports. However, Beauregard was different. She supervised all of the revenue sports at Western and continued to manage the NCAA compliance process, student-athlete academic support, athletic marketing and communications, and her natural role of looking out for the welfare of the student-athletes. She invested herself in her profession by serving on the MAC Gender Equity Committee and as a chairperson of the MAC Marketing Committee. Beauregard also served on the NCAA National Compliance Coordinator Committee. Her investment paid dividends in 1998 when she was appointed director of athletics for WMU.

WMU President Diether Haenicke expressed his delight in the decision to place Beauregard at the helm of his school's athletic department. She replaced James Weaver, who had held the position since 1995. "As an athlete and former coach, she is ideally suited to provide the kind of leadership we need for our athletic program. Kathy has a broad range of administrative experience, ranging from NCAA rules compliance to student-athlete academic support. This, combined with her leadership, enthusiasm and loyalty to WMU and the community, make her the ideal choice to take the Broncos to the next level."[1] She became the first woman to hold the director of athletics position at WMU, and only the third to hold the position in the MAC. More staggering still, she is one of only a few women serving as a director of athletics in the nation.

Beauregard accepted the job with enthusiasm and approached it with vigor and tenacity, stating, "Speaking on behalf of my coaches and our athletic staff, we are determined to give the university and the people of West Michigan programs they can be proud of."[2] Truer words could not have been spoken. Beauregard strategically managed all of the university's intercollegiate sports, brokered profitable relationships with corporate sponsors, and preserved the rapport between the student-athletes and coaches. The immediate impact of her leadership and support resulted in the men's teams winning the Reese Cup, the all-sports trophy for the MAC. The university previously finished 10th in the standings, and this was the first Reese Cup in the past 17 years for Western Michigan. Her guidance in her third year led the Western Michigan Broncos to a Western Division football title and MAC Championship game appearance. From 2002 to 2004, Western brought home six conference titles, three for the men and three for the women. Also during that time, the athletic teams of Western Michigan University earned the eighth highest graduation rate in the nation, with 83 percent of its student-athletes graduating with a cumulative 3.0 GPA. Beauregard's women's teams won the

Jacoby Cup for the 2005–06 athletic seasons, the all-sports trophy for women's sports in the MAC. Beauregard is proof that women can run athletic departments and deliver results as well as support.

After equipping the student-athletes and coaches on the playing fields, she quickly improved the university's athletic facilities. Beauregard recognizes the power and the revenue associated with a top-notch football program, and she strives to capitalize on that power to elevate the facilities, the programs, and the performance of all of her institution's intercollegiate sports. She started from the ground up by replacing the grounds of Waldon Stadium with field turf and then she moved on to larger capital projects. The Bill Brown Football Alumni Center, an $8 million capital project, was completed under her watch, as well as a $21 million capital expansion to the Seelye Athletic Indoor Center. The improvements made to Seelye will directly benefit a number of people by providing the best training grounds for Bronco student-athletes. Her determination and passion to improve the facilities continue at Western Michigan with the Hyames Field Renovation Project and other state-of-the-art facility plans. She has changed the face of the campus and therefore is uplifting the athletic department to a more prominent status. The fans rallied around Beauregard's Broncos and quickly set single game and season attendance records. Athletic directors are harshly judged on the numbers—attendance, GPAs, graduation rates, revenue, and win-loss records—and Beauregard has responded to these challenges with poise and excellence.

She committed herself to improving not only the athletic environment at Western Michigan, but also the environment of the NCAA and Olympic Sports. From 2001 to 2003 she served as the chairperson of the NCAA Olympic Sports Liaison Committee, which also included a seat on the board of directors for the United States Olympic Committee. Beauregard and the committee set out to protect the integrity of the Olympic Sports at the collegiate level while ensuring the future of the country's Olympians. Beauregard also served on the NCAA Football Bowl Certification Committee and represented WMU on the NCAA Championships Cabinet. Her commitment to gender equity, diversity, and the inclusion of individuals previously underrepresented in collegiate athletics made her a perfect fit for the NCAA Diversity and Inclusion Committee.

Beauregard has demonstrated the attributes of a leader and a champion throughout her career. She has not only competed in an industry dominated by men, but she excelled to the top. In 1999, less than two years after her director of athletics appointment, Kalamazoo Network bestowed the "Glass Ceiling" award to Beauregard, though she had already crashed through the proverbial ceiling. That same year, *Business Direct Weekly* named her as one of the 26 most influential women in Western Michigan. Her undergraduate alma mater awarded her with the Hope College Distinguished Alumni Award in 2000. She was recognized by the YWCA with the Woman of Achievement Award and also by the Kalamazoo Chamber of Commerce with the Athena Award in 2002. While Beauregard is well known around the athletic fields of Western Michigan, she is better known around her hometown of Kalamazoo, Michigan.

Her 27-year commitment to the university and the town has created a welcoming home for her and her family. Her husband, Rick, taught in the public school system for 32 years before retiring to start his own home security business. Together, they raised their son, Brad. Kathy has made feverish commitments to community causes as well as her beloved Western. Despite the devotion to her family and the steadfast support of 17 intercollegiate sports, she finds time to volunteer for the American Cancer Society and the American Heart Association. Her active involvement in the Kalamazoo Rotary continues to thread her into the fabric of the community. Kathy Beauregard is living proof that women can do it all.

Notes

1. "Beauregard named athletic director," *WMU News*, September 24, 1997, http://www.wmich.edu/wmu/news. (accessed May 20, 2008).
2. "Beauregard named athletic director."

Lisa Love

Leader at the NCAA Division I-A Level

by Catherine Lahey

Few people who have encountered Lisa Love as an opposing player, opposing coach, interviewee, or employee would ever guess that she doesn't even consider herself the most competitive member of her immediate family. The youngest of three daughters born to a talented football and tennis player and a life master duplicate bridge player, competition was king, or perhaps more appropriately queen, in Lisa Love's household. "In my family of five, I'm probably the fourth most competitive. It didn't matter if we were playing table games like Scrabble or cards or charades or backyard badminton or anything. We grew up playing, competing, and enjoying it."[1] Described by her colleagues as a "competitor" and a "dynamo," Love rose through the ranks of collegiate coaching and administration to embrace the role of vice president for university athletics at Arizona State University (ASU), making her one of only six female athletic directors at the 120 Football Bowl Subdivision institutions. Since her 2005 hiring, Love's leadership, vision, and tireless commitment to excellence have pushed Arizona State into a new era of athletic accomplishment and recognition.

Love's passion for athletics was born from the competitive environment of her family. Father Tom Love quickly turned his three little girls into competent, confident wide receivers for backyard football contests. "Sports were a part of our fabric growing up. I loved it. And I always wanted a career in it."[2] Love, trained to be tough through constant battles with her older sisters, grew into an excellent volleyball player, eventually starring at Texas Tech. After spending four years as a starter and earning all-region accolades, Love turned her attention to teaching the game she loved as head coach at Bowie High School in Arlington, Texas.

After five successful years at Bowie, Love was tapped to take the helm of the volleyball team at the University of Texas at Arlington, where she turned the program into a nationally recognized powerhouse after only seven seasons. Following her final season at Texas Arlington, one in which her team achieved a 30-4 record, she garnered National Coach of the Year honors. Love's intensity, skill, and coaching prowess were soon recognized by larger, more prominent athletic departments. In 1989, Love left Texas Arlington to become head volleyball coach at USC, a position that she would hold for 10 seasons. During her tenure, Love led the Trojans to eight finishes in the national top 15 and nine National Collegiate Athletic Association (NCAA) tournament berths while simultaneously adopting an increasing level of administrative responsibility within the USC athletic department. By 1991, Love had left coaching in order to pursue athletic administration full-time with the Trojans, eventually rising to the role of senior associate athletic director. Love was a rising star, known for her foresight, wisdom, and ability to mesh and manage the sometimes disparate needs of a large athletic department.

In 2005, Arizona State president Michael Crow was tasked with hiring a new athletic director, a hugely important task for a university that was striving for excellence on a national stage. Crow interviewed a number of advocates, but fell in love with Love. "She was far and away the best candidate in terms of energy, coaching drive, and just raw talent than anyone I interviewed. She had the perfect combination of drive, skills, and coaching instincts."[3] Some skepticism followed Love's hiring, particularly among the Sun Devil boosters, but Love's confidence and commitment to the best interests of ASU athletics were unshakable. Within the first two years of her tenure, Love fired the two most prominent coaches on campus, the leaders of the underperforming football and men's basketball teams. She replaced them with highly motivated, experienced, and capable coaches who shared her vision for a future of elite-level Sun Devil athletics. Just as President Crow had done, the boosters couldn't help but love Love.

Love's time as athletic director has been characterized by an ever-rising level of unprecedented success for Arizona State. The football and men's basketball teams have consistently increased in strength on a national level. During 2007, the women's track team won an indoor title, the women's golf team achieved a number one ranking in national polls, and the women's basketball team reached the Elite Eight. The softball team, headed by another of Love's early coaching hires, won the 2008 Women's College World Series in dramatic fashion. All of these individual triumphs have added up to increased recognition of ASU as an athletic program to be respected.

In 2008, the Sun Devils were ranked fourth in the prestigious Director's Cup standings and were named the best program in the nation by *Sports Illustrated*. Donations have begun to flow into athletics and strategically planned capital improvement projects are in the process of being completed. But is Love comfortably satisfied? "I have a very strong belief of what this school is capable of. We're not anywhere near where I think we can be."[4]

Lisa Love, an inductee into multiple volleyball Halls of Fame, has grown from a talented young athlete into a high-profile athletic administrator committed to positively impacting the lives of today's talented young athletes. In an era where few women have been called upon to captain the athletic departments of major universities, Love has served as a brilliant example for all young women considering careers in athletic management. Her story is one of strategic intelligence and pure grit, exactly what one could expect of the child of a master bridge player and football star. Although she may not be the most competitive member of her immediate family, many regard her as not only the leader, but also the most competitive member of the Arizona State Sun Devil family.

Notes

1. Alex Espinoza, "The Lisa Love Effect," ASU Web Devil, July 21, 2008.

2. George J. Tanber, "Love guiding light at ASU," NCAA, ESPN.com, March 30, 2007.

3. Tanber, "Love guiding light at ASU."

4. Scott Bordow, "ASU Athletics Experiencing More Than Just Wins," *East Valley Tribune*, April 8, 2008.

Dr. Donna Lopiano

National Reform Leader

by Jessica Bartter

The payback for young girls who participate in sports includes several health and social benefits. Yet for years, marketers have pushed a girly, subordinate demeanor of women, discouraging young girls from being strong, active, and independent. Donna Lopiano ignored such pressures as a child. While many young girls growing up in the 1950s and 1960s viewed sports as a man's game and preferred to watch, Lopiano could always be found playing with the boys. In fact, she did not even notice the difference between her and her neighborhood playmates until her gender denied her a spot on a Little League team that had actually recruited her at age 11. For the previous six years, she had spent hours after school perfecting her baseball pitches against the side of her family's house. She idolized Mickey Mantle, Whitey Ford, and Don Drysdale, and dreamt of pitching for the New York Yankees.[1] When she was lined up at the field to get her uniform, another Little Leaguer's father pulled out the rule book and demanded Lopiano be taken off the team because the rules stated that no girls were allowed. That very team went on to win the Little League World Series without her.

Lopiano was hurt by the exclusion and the subsequent pain drove her to work even harder toward success. She did not appreciate being told she could not pursue her dream and has worked tirelessly over the past four decades to prevent the same from happening to more young, impressionable girls. Until she was old enough to stand up for the injustices in women's sports, Lopiano was forced to conform to the standard that males play baseball and females play softball. Lopiano learned to execute her powerful pitches with an underhand release and quickly excelled on the softball mound. In 1963, Lopiano was discovered by the Raybestos Brakettes, an amateur softball team for whom she played until 1972. During her 10 seasons, Lopiano earned All-American honors nine times and was named MVP three times. Her force from the mound led to a .910 winning percentage with 183 games won and just 18 games lost. In 817 innings pitched she struck out 1,633 opponents at the plate. A force at the plate herself, Lopiano twice led her team in batting average with .316 and .367. In addition to sharpening her softball skills, her career with the Brakettes provided her with the opportunity to travel and explore other parts of the world. By the time she was 18, she had already toured France, Hong Kong, India, and Australia playing the game she loved.[2]

One of the most amazing aspects of Lopiano's amateur softball career is the fact that it spanned over her high school, collegiate, and postgraduate educations. In between long practices, intense training, international travel, and national championships, Lopiano managed to graduate from Stamford High School, Southern Connecticut State University with a bachelor's degree in physical education, and the University of Southern California, where she earned her master's and doctoral degrees. Lopiano's career as a Raybestos Brakette also did not interfere with her success on the field hockey, volleyball, and basketball teams. Including her amateur career, she played in 26 national championships in the four sports. The success she earned as an athlete led her to coaching positions for collegiate men's and women's volleyball, women's basketball, and women's softball programs.

At just 28 years old, Lopiano was hired by the University of Texas, Austin, as the director of intercollegiate athletics for women. Her energetic attitude and high standards appealed to the selection committee. Lopiano put pressure on the coaches both on and off the field. In her first 10 years, she went through 16 coaches in eight different sports. She made it clear to her staff that winning, as well as education, was a priority. Lopiano warned coaches that their jobs depended on whether or not their teams were top 10 programs. Lopiano also stressed that their jobs were equally dependent on the success their student-athletes achieved in the classroom. Just one year after she began holding her coaches accountable for academic performances, the athletic department's mean SAT score increased by 100 points. During her 17 years at the University of Texas, the Longhorns graduated 95 percent of its women athletes who completed their athletic eligibility. Athletically, Lopiano's Longhorns were equally successful. Eighteen National Championships (Association for Intercollegiate Athletics for Women [AIAW] and National Collegiate Athletic Association [NCAA]), 62 Southwest Conference Championships, more than 300 All-Americans, and over a dozen Olympians made Lopiano's women's program a dominant one in collegiate athletics. Her program's success was a direct result of her philosophy that money and coaches were the two key ingredients for a collegiate program. Lopiano believed that if she adequately funded the program then she could attract the best coaches who would accept her demands, athletically and academically.[3] By attracting the best coaches, Lopiano predicted the best athletes would follow. Lopiano developed her department's budget from $57,000 in 1975 to almost $3 million in 1987.[4]

While the short-term numbers prove Lopiano's success, she made great strides for women's sports in the long run as well. A pioneer for her time, Lopiano has served females everywhere with her advocacy for Title IX of the Education Amendments of 1972, a federal law that prohibits discrimination on the basis of sex in all education programs and activities receiving federal funds. Title IX is commonly referred to for its impact on sports, but it also pertains to drama, band, and other extracurricular student activities. Title IX is credited with increasing female involvement in sport more than tenfold. In 1970, only one in every 27 high school girls played varsity sports compared to one in every 2.5 girls 30 years later. Title IX has led to increased funding and support for women's sports, bringing the ratio of girls playing much closer to the ratio of boys in sports, which is equal to one in every two. Lopiano was instrumental in implementing Title IX at the University of Texas, pushing equal rights for women, something she was denied in her youth.[5]

Lopiano moved to the Women's Sports Foundation (WSF) in April of 1992 to continue her advocacy for female athletes' rights. The WSF is a 501(c)(3) nonprofit organization that was founded in 1974 by tennis legend Billie Jean King to advance the lives of girls and women through sports and physical activity. The Foundation's programs, services, and initiatives are dedicated to participation, education, advocacy, research, and leadership for women's sports. In her 15 years as executive director, Lopiano secured funding for girls' and women's sport programs and educated the public and corporations about the importance of women's health and gender equality in sport. Lopiano believes the 1996 Summer Olympics was a celebration of Title IX, showing the first generation of success stories in gymnast Kerri Strug, sprinter Gail Devers, softball player Dot Richardson, swimmer Amy Van Dyken, and basketball player Lisa Leslie who all took home gold medals. Young girls everywhere suddenly had female role models in the sports world despite the lack of professional athletic opportunities for females in the United States. Individuals and parents under the age of 40 are also of the Title IX generation and have been a major influence on children, according to Lopiano, by encouraging both sons and daughters to participate in sports.

The Sporting News named Lopiano one of "The 100 Most Influential People in Sports"; *College Sports* magazine ranked her among "The 50 Most Influential People in College Sports"; *Ladies Home Journal* named her one of "America's 100 Most Important Women"; and she was named as one of the century's greatest sportswomen by *Sports Illustrated Women*. She is an inductee of the National Sports Hall of Fame, the National Softball Hall of Fame, and the Texas Women's Hall of Fame. In honor of her many contributions to women in athletics at the University of Texas, the crew team christened the Varsity Eight shell "Donna A. Lopiano" in April 2005. Lopiano sat on the United States Olympic Committee's executive board for many years and was awarded the 2005 International Olympic Committee (IOC) Women and Sport Trophy. Since 2000, the IOC Women and Sport Trophy has been awarded annually to a person or organization in recognition of their outstanding contributions to developing, encouraging, and strengthening the participation of women and girls in physical and sports activities, in coaching, and in administrative, journalism, and media positions.

In August 2007, Lopiano announced her retirement from the Women's Sports Foundation. In 2008, she founded Sports Management Resources (SMR), a consulting firm specializing in educational sport. As president of SMR, Lopiano is helping sports organizations solve integrity, growth, and development challenges. A champion athlete in her own right, Donna Lopiano is similarly considered a champion of equal opportunity for women in sports. Her educational advocacy of ethical conduct garnering gender equality in sports made Lopiano a pioneer whose bravado, intelligence, and determination have left an everlasting—and feminine—effect on American sports.

Notes

1. Alexander Wolff, "Prima Donna: Women's Athletic Director Donna Lopiano Has Taken the Bull by the Horns at Texas," *Sports Illustrated*, December 17, 1990.

2. Ibid.

3. Ibid.

4. Texas Woman's University, "Texas Women's Hall of Fame: Donna Lopiano," http://www.twu.edu/twhf/tw-lopiano.htm, August 18, 2004 (accessed July 27, 2005).

5. Women's Sports Foundation, "Title IX and Race in Intercollegiate Sport," http://www.womenssportsfoundation.org/cgi-bin/iowa/issues/disc/article.html?record=955, June 23, 2003 (accessed April 2, 2008).

Tina Sloan Green

National Reform Leader and American Star of the Women's International Sports Hall of Fame

by Jessica Bartter

The National Collegiate Athletic Association (NCAA) basketball tournament is so greatly followed that the term "March Madness" has been coined to refer to the month-long, über-popular championship series. Yet, contrary to popular belief, it is the Men's Lacrosse Championship that is the most highly attended NCAA national championship. The 2008 NCAA finals included a record 48,970 fans in attendance. If you haven't been there in person, it may be hard to imagine the magnitude of the lacrosse finals.

It may be even harder to imagine a tradition born to breed warriors using hundreds, even thousands of men to compete across a territory that spread miles and days long and resulted in serious injuries and even death has evolved into the game we now know as lacrosse. But this history would not surprise those who have stepped on the field to battle their opponents while whipping hard sticks, or "crosses," to send a little, hard ball traveling over 100 miles per hour while wearing minimal protection. Lacrosse, the original sport of the North American continent, actually predates the United States by hundreds of years. First invented by Native Americans, it was intended to settle inter- and intra-tribal disputes, or to prepare warriors for battle and was sometimes played for religious purposes. The game of lacrosse, "born of the North American Indian, christened by the French, and adapted and raised by the Canadians" is still known as "The Creator's Game" to Native Americans.[1]

A creator in her own right, Tina Sloan Green has been creating opportunities for women and African-Americans as players and coaches in sports like lacrosse, tennis, golf, and field hockey for more than 40 years. After receiving the rare opportunity for a young girl in the 1950s and 1960s to get a chance to play organized sports, Sloan Green credits team sports with her taking more of an interest in her teachers, friends, and grades.[2] She has since dedicated her life to ensure that other young girls are afforded the same opportunities and life lessons sport has provided her.

After she started as a field hockey player at West Chester State University in Pennsylvania, Sloan Green was recruited to the lacrosse team by her field hockey coach who doubled as the coach for both teams. Sloan Green's field hockey passion was matched by her discovery of lacrosse and she learned to juggle both, a choice certainly supported by her coach, who discovered she could utilize Sloan Green's talent on both fields. Sloan Green also added badminton to her varsity repertoire for three years. While earning her bachelor's degree in health and physical education, Sloan Green received All-American field hockey honors in 1965 and 1966 and played on the U.S. National Field Hockey squad in 1969. She also competed with the U.S. Women's Lacrosse team from 1968 to 1972. In doing so, she became the first African-American woman to be named to the squad. In 1970, she earned her master's in physical education from Temple University.

Upon completion of her graduate degree and while continuing her international touring with the national lacrosse team, Sloan Green served as the lacrosse coach, basketball coach, cheerleader advisor, and physical education instructor at Lincoln University. She stayed at Lincoln for four years.

In 1974, Sloan Green returned to her first passion of field hockey, this time on the sidelines with the Temple University women's team as its head coach. She led the field hockey team for five years, earning a 44-33-10 record and three Association for Intercollegiate Athletics for Women (AIAW) National Championships.

Also in 1974, Sloan Green added the Owls lacrosse team to her coaching responsibilities and was the coach of both teams until 1980, when she left her field hockey coaching position. She stayed on the Temple Owls lacrosse field sidelines for 18 seasons, boasting a record of 207-62-4 (a .758 winning percentage), including an NCAA record 29 straight wins from 1984 to 1985. Between 1973 and 1992, she guided 18 of her players to follow in her prestigious footsteps of earning All-American honors. In 1988, Sloan Green's Temple team earned its first undefeated season with a 15-7 victory over Penn

State University in the NCAA Championship. This victory was the team's second national championship under Sloan Green, as they had captured the 1984 lacrosse title as well.

Though she had a late start in lacrosse, she has left her impression on the sport nonetheless. When she accepted Temple's head coaching position in 1975, she became the first African-American head coach in the history of women's intercollegiate lacrosse.[3] She was also the first female African-American and only the second African-American head coach ever to win a NCAA Division I title in 1984.

All the while, Sloan Green was a professor of sport and culture at Temple University. In 1992, Sloan Green left the coaching sidelines, but not Temple University. She turned her focus entirely on her teaching and advancing opportunities for African-American females in sport. As co-founder and head of the Black Women in Sports Foundation, Sloan Green has provided young females the exposure and opportunity to participate in typically white "preppy" sports like tennis and golf. She also founded the Inner City Field Hockey and Lacrosse Program in Philadelphia. Also while a professor at Temple, Sloan Green was co-principal investigator of Sisters in Sports Science, a National Science Foundation-funded program, and directed the university's National Youth Sports Program. She also authored two books, *Black Women in Sport* and *Modern Women's Lacrosse*, before becoming professor emeritus in the College of Education in 2006 after 32 years of teaching.

In her retirement, Sloan Green gets her greatest satisfaction from watching the prospering career of her daughter, Traci Green. While it was no secret where her passion lay, Sloan Green did not push lacrosse on Traci. Regardless, Traci inherited her mother's passion for sports, both playing and teaching. But Traci's skill was undeniably in tennis. Fortunate enough to have Arthur Ashe as a mentor and her mother as a constant supporter, Traci was destined for greatness. After a championship collegiate career, Traci filled the tremendous shoes of her mother and became Harvard University's first African-American female head coach in the Ivy League school's history of intercollegiate sports in 2007. Prior to Harvard, Traci coached Temple's tennis team to its first ever nationally ranked season.

To African-American women like her daughter, Sloan Green offers the following advice, "Education is power." She suggests,

"Get a terminal degree if possible—a law or doctorate degree in your chosen field. Learn your craft. Learn and understand the corporate model of sports, but appreciate and understand the grassroots model as well."[4]

Sloan Green's advice on diversity is equally important. "It is not enough to tolerate diversity," she says. "To be an effective leader in this day and age, you must embrace diversity. You must treat everyone with dignity and respect." Coming from someone who has walked the walk more often than talking the talk, it can be as simple as "Be real. Be yourself."[5]

Upon her induction into the Black Lacrosse Hall of Fame in 2007, Sloan Green described lacrosse as "the best sport on two feet." She said, "You can run and gun all the way down the field, you can be physical if you need to be, it's graceful, especially the women's game, it's powerful, and you have to be smart. It requires teamwork, and a level of timing and athleticism and skill that is unparalleled."[6] Most would use such words as physical, graceful, powerful, smart, team player, athletic, and unparalleled skill to describe Tina Sloan Green in all aspects of her career, not just on the field. It is no wonder why she has mastered the art—or rather sport—of lacrosse.

Notes

1. The National Governing Body of Lacrosse, http://www.lacrosse.org/the_sport/index.phtml (accessed March 31, 2008).

2. Ben Hammer, "Reconstructing the status of Title IX; critics say the mandate shortchanges some men's teams, while proponent argue women's sports remain under funded," *Black Issues in Higher Education*, April 10, 2003.

3. www.cstv.com Temple: Sloan Green to be honored at 1st annual black lacrosse hall of fame induction ceremony, November 17, 2006.

4. Email from Tina Sloan Green to author, June 24, 2008.

5. Ibid.

6. Carla Peay, "Black Lacrosse Pioneers Honored at Hall of Fame Ceremony," BlackAthlete Sports Network, February 10, 2007, www.blackathlete.net/artman/publish/printer_2877.shtml (accessed March 4, 2008).

Anita DeFrantz

National Reform Leader—Olympic Sport

by Jessica Bartter

Anita DeFrantz has lived a life defying the odds. She did not play sports as a child despite the fact that she grew up in Hoosier basketball territory in Indiana. She rowed in college despite the fact that she was on an academic scholarship. She won an Olympic medal in rowing despite the fact that she had been introduced to the sport just five years prior. She defied President Jimmy Carter's 1980 Moscow Olympic boycott despite the fact that the United States Olympic Committee (USOC) had not previously contradicted any president's orders and sent Olympians into competition. She was elected vice president of the International Olympic Committee despite the fact that no female before her held that position. And that was just during the first 50 years of her life.

DeFrantz was born in Philadelphia but grew up in Indianapolis, where she learned a great deal of compassion and strength from her parents. Both her mother, who was a teacher, and her father, who ran an organization called Community Action Against Poverty, displayed commitments to youth, community, and education, and encouraged their daughter to do the same. In 1970, DeFrantz enrolled at Connecticut College on an academic scholarship with no athletic intentions, but, as a sophomore, discovered the sport of rowing. While walking on campus one day, DeFrantz stopped to ask a man about the long, thin object he was carrying. The man, Bart Gulong, turned out to be the rowing coach and the object he was carrying was a rowing shell. DeFrantz's interest and 5-foot-11-inch build caused him to encourage her to participate in the new sport at Connecticut College.

Though DeFrantz had never tried the sport before, she knew most of the girls who went out for the team would also be beginners; so she gave it a shot. Gulong had been right in predicting DeFrantz's athleticism and shortly thereafter, he suggested she consider training for the Olympics. At the time, DeFrantz was not even aware that rowing was an Olympic sport for women because it had just been chosen to make its debut in the next Olympics.

DeFrantz graduated with honors in 1974 with a bachelor's degree in political philosophy after competing at the collegiate level for three years. Her excellence in the rowing shell earned her a spot on the national team every year from 1975 until 1980. Coach Gulong's suggestion came to fruition as DeFrantz traveled to Montreal for the 1976 Olympic Games. Just five years after learning the sport, DeFrantz, and the rest of the American team, came in third place behind the East Germans and Soviet Union in the Olympic debut of women's rowing. In the midst of Olympic training, DeFrantz applied to and enrolled in law school at the University of Pennsylvania. After graduating in 1977 and passing the bar exam, DeFrantz began practicing law representing children.

In October 1977, DeFrantz participated in her first of many changes involving the Olympic Committee. She and three other Olympians were summoned to testify regarding the rights of athletes. Their testimony helped produce the Amateur Sports Act of 1978, which restructured the way Olympic sports are governed in the United States.

While a bronze medal in the Olympics is nothing short of an amazing accomplishment, DeFrantz hoped to return to the 1980 Olympics and capture the gold. Her participation with the national team kept her in tiptop shape while she was simultaneously fulfilling her professional career as a lawyer. DeFrantz worked for a public interest law firm in Philadelphia that protected children before taking a year off in 1979 to focus on what would be her last Olympic opportunity. To DeFrantz's dismay, then-President Jimmy Carter announced in January 1980 that the United States planned to boycott the 1980 Olympics in Moscow because of the Soviet invasion of Afghanistan.

As a lawyer, DeFrantz immediately knew she and her teammates had rights as athletes. She did not want to stand by and watch President Carter strip away the athletes' Olympic dreams. DeFrantz believed the Olympics were pure of political confrontations between countries and that a boycott represented the exact opposite of the Olympic ideology. DeFrantz had been a member of the USOC's Athletes Advisory Council since her Olympic debut in 1976. She and other members pleaded with the USOC to defy President Carter's order and eventually filed suit to allow them the opportunity to compete. DeFrantz knew the USOC could enter a team regardless of President Carter's suggestions. Despite this, the Carter administration's threat to ruin the USOC's funding was taken seriously enough that DeFrantz, her teammates, and every other 1980 Olympic hopeful would have to wait another four more years.

Until the boycott decision was official in April 1980, DeFrantz continued to train, hoping for the best. She had become the face and name connected with the opposition to Carter's position and the associated unpatriotic accusations left her very unpopular, making her the recipient of disturbing hate mail. Though the suit was lost, DeFrantz's fight for athletes' rights was just beginning.

While the opposition DeFrantz presented made her disliked by many, she certainly attracted notice, not all of which was negative. In 1981, Peter Ueberroth hired her on the management team of the 1984 Summer Olympic Games scheduled to take place in Los Angeles. Ueberroth asked her to serve the Los Angeles Olympic Organizing Committee as liaison with the African nations and as chief administrator of the Olympic Village. DeFrantz is credited with helping to save the 1984 Summer Games by preventing African nations from boycotting because South African runner Zola Budd was allowed to run for Great Britain. She had the credibility because she

Courtesy of Anita DeFrantz.

1976 Montreal Olympics.

had actively opposed apartheid and had worked with Richard Lapchick and the American Coordinating Committee for Equality in Sport and Society (ACCESS) to keep South Africa out of international sports contests. Lapchick, who became a lifelong friend, calls Anita "one of sport's greatest leaders and heroes. She always stands up for justice." She has had many opportunities to do so.

DeFrantz was named vice president for the newly created Amateur Athletic Foundation (AAF) of Los Angeles, which was established from $93 million of the $230 million profit the Games produced. In 1987, she became president of the AAF, which has since changed its name to The LA84 Foundation. During the previous year, the International Olympic Committee (IOC) was looking to fulfill a lifetime position and found 34-year-old DeFrantz. Her appointment makes her a voting member of the IOC until the age of 80, when the position will become honorary in 2032. DeFrantz is one of two Americans to represent the United States and was the first woman and the first African-American to do so. DeFrantz finally gained the platform necessary to make her case for athletes' rights.

In 1988, DeFrantz spoke out against the injustice she witnessed at the Olympic Games. Canadian Ben Johnson tested positive for performance-enhancing drugs after running the 100-meter dash in 9.79 seconds. DeFrantz refused to shy away from the controversy and spoke out publicly to fight for pure, drug-free Olympic competitions. Eight years and two Olympic Games later, DeFrantz continued to fight for clean sports by preventing the Atlanta Committee for the Olympic Games from using less expensive and not as concise drug testing methods for the 1996 Atlanta Games.

As a member of the IOC, DeFrantz made an impact fighting for athletes' rights and the purity of the Games. Yet, her commitment and intelligence made her worthy of a position with the IOC that exhibits more power. From 1992 until 2001, DeFrantz sat on the executive board and in 1997 she accomplished a feat no female had successfully done in the past. DeFrantz was named one of the four vice presidents of the IOC, serving a four-year term. In the history of the IOC, which dates back to 1894, a woman had never held such a prestigious position.

DeFrantz, whose high school did not offer team sports for girls, has worked tirelessly to provide opportunities for underprivileged youth, ensuring opportunities exist for males and females alike. The

LA84 Foundation is committed to the eight counties of Southern California but focuses mainly on Los Angeles. And while no child is turned away, special emphasis is placed on girls, ethnic minorities, the physically challenged and developmentally disabled, and other underserved community members. DeFrantz knows sports can change one's life and bring so much opportunity to a child, socially and physically. Nonetheless, she is realistic with the children, informing them of their slim chances in becoming professional athletes and encouraging them to focus on their education as well. DeFrantz believes this message should also be carried by the coaches and has committed the LA84 to a special coaching education program since 1985. In its first 20 years of existence, DeFrantz has led the LA84 in its endeavors that have provided nearly $50 million in grants to youth programs and has trained over 50,000 coaches.

DeFrantz is active in several youth, sport, and legal organizations, including Kids in Sports, the NCAA Leadership Advisory Board, the Juvenile Law Center, The Knight Foundation Commission on Intercollegiate Athletics, the Institute for International Sport, and FISA (the International Rowing Federation). DeFrantz also sits on several different Olympic committees, utilizing her historic position to the fullest.

In 2004, the First Lady of California, Maria Shriver, created The Minerva Awards in an effort to honor women for their humanity and commitment to service. Shriver chose four special women whose stories she believed would inspire others in the community, state, and nation. Fittingly, DeFrantz was a 2005 recipient of The Minerva Awards. Shriver named the Awards after the Roman goddess portrayed on the California State Seal who represents both a warrior and a peacemaker.

The great great-granddaughter of a Louisiana plantation owner and one of his slaves, Anita DeFrantz has proven herself to be a true leader. She has achieved many firsts, both for her family and for our nation. This internationally known figure has put so many before her selflessly and persistently. She truly is a warrior and a peacemaker.

Val Ackerman

National Reform Leader—Pro Sport

by Horacio Ruiz

Val Ackerman was appointed president of the Women's National Basketball Association (WNBA) in August 1996, when the women's league was just a concept in development. Tip-off for the inaugural season was set for June 1997, leaving Ackerman with less than one year to find coaches, players, and cities to host franchises. In her first year, Ackerman was making decisions on everything from the size and color of the basketball and the way the uniforms would look, to setting the salaries for her players. There had already been 15 documented attempts at establishing a women's basketball league, all of which failed for one reason or another. Ackerman's job was to make sure that what had happened 15 times before did not happen to the WNBA.

Ackerman had an early recollection of her first failure. The granddaughter and daughter of collegiate and high school athletic directors, Ackerman grew up playing sports with the boys on her block. In the seventh grade, she tried out for the only organized team that her middle school provided for girls—the cheerleading squad. She practiced every day and at night she tried to perfect the routines in front of her bedroom mirror. When it was time to find out if she had made the squad, Ackerman did not see her name on a list posted outside the locker room. She was so embarrassed that she did not want to go back to school for a week. But Ackerman's father reminded her that in high school she would be able to play any sport that she wanted. Once in high school, she earned 10 varsity letters in field hockey, track, and basketball. She earned a scholarship to play basketball at the University of Virginia, where she was a four-year starter, three-year captain, and two-time Academic All-American. Ackerman would go on to play professionally for one year in France, then earn her law degree from the University of California, Los Angeles, in 1985.

By 2004, Ackerman's last year as president of the WNBA, she had grown a business that included 17 highly recognizable corporate sponsors and television contracts that broadcast games on ABC,

ESPN, and ESPN2. Sure, the WNBA had received a tremendous amount of support from its brother association, the National Basketball Association (NBA), but women's basketball had been woven into the social fabric of major professional sports leagues. The WNBA had become the leading women's basketball league in the world, with broadcasts across more than 125 countries and with a number of the best international players playing in the league. Despite encountering some tough labor issues, changes in team ownership, team relocations, and the dissolution of some franchises, Ackerman was the first woman to successfully launch a women's team-oriented sports league and she guided the league for its first eight seasons, averaging more than 9,300 fans over the course of her tenure. She had done the exact opposite of fail; she had been a grand success as the founding president and more than anything, she shined a light on women's basketball players like never before.

Through the marketing, sales, and financial plans, Ackerman was working to achieve something deeper than making sure her league succeeded financially. In May of 2000, she told a reporter a story about a girl that asked for her autograph. Standing to the side was the girl's father. "You must be the dad, you must be proud," Ackerman said to him.[1] A few days later, Ackerman received a note from the father, thanking her for giving him an opportunity to bond with his daughter and noting that the girl had higher self-esteem for being a fan of women players. Ackerman had created an institution different from the surroundings she grew up in. As a teenager, she hung up posters of her sports heroes, John Havlicek and Jerry West—both men. She also cited that nearly 75 percent of WNBA attendees were women and girls, giving them, to some sense, a league of their own.

"We were able with the WNBA to get women's basketball to its rightful place in our country, meaning a place where we can have not only young girls playing at the youth level and the high school and collegiate levels, but also a viable pro outlet for the very best players," Ackerman said. "There had been many attempts to start leagues prior to the launch of the WNBA. None of them made it and I think the fact that the WNBA has been here 12 seasons is a testament to how strong the women's game has gotten, how popular it is as a spectator sport, and how much potential it continues to have. With each passing year, the quality of play only escalates and the number of people who accept as a fact of life that women's pro basketball is here to stay, that number of people solidifies."[2]

Just as the man had thanked Ackerman for allowing him to bond with his daughter, Ackerman realized she needed to do the same with her two daughters. In 2004, Ackerman resigned from her post as president of the WNBA to spend more time with her daughters. "This was entirely my decision, and it's a very difficult one because in many ways I think of the WNBA as a third child," Ackerman said at the time. "But it's required a great deal of time and it's required a great deal of energy. I felt very strongly that this was, and is, the right decision for my two daughters. I would hope this isn't taken in any way as an indictment on working motherhood because it can absolutely be done. We have many women in the league who are parents and have been able to form balanced situations. I didn't feel that in this job that was possible."[3]

Ackerman stayed as a consultant with the WNBA and in 2005, she was the first woman elected as president of USA Basketball to lead the organization through the 2008 Beijing Olympics. Under her leadership, both the men's and women's basketball teams won gold medals at Beijing. Her previous Olympic experience extended from 1995 to 1996, when Ackerman was the main force in directing the Women's Senior National Team that finished with a 60-0 record and a gold medal at the 1996 Atlanta Olympics.

Just after arriving in the United States following the successes at Beijing, the Naismith Memorial Basketball Hall of Fame honored Ackerman with its highest distinction outside of enshrinement, awarding her with the John W. Bunn Lifetime Achievement Award. In addition to recognizing her pioneering work with the WNBA and USA Basketball, the Hall of Fame took into consideration her work with the New York law firm of Simpson Thacher & Bartlett for two years, her post at the NBA League Office as a staff attorney where she worked closely with Commissioner David Stern, and her positions as NBA director and, later, vice president of Business Affairs, before being chosen to lead the WNBA.

"This is a tremendous and very unexpected honor, and I'm deeply grateful to the Hall of Fame for the recognition," said Ackerman after learning of the award. "It has been a privilege for me to work in basketball and to witness many of the exciting developments in our game over the past 20 years, especially in women's basketball, which I know will only continue to grow in popularity in the years to come."[4]

Ackerman currently serves on the Executive Committee of the Naismith Memorial Basketball Hall of Fame, the National Board of Trustees for the March of Dimes, the National Board of Girls Incorporated, and the Knight Commission on Intercollegiate Athletics. In her role as president of USA Basketball, she restructured the board of directors to include youth basketball organizations and is looking to partner with the National Collegiate Athletic Association (NCAA) to spearhead youth basketball initiatives.

Notes

1. Jan Hoffman, "A League President in the Dreams Business," *New York Times*, May 26, 2000.

2. John Hareas, Q & A with Val Ackerman. http://www.nba.com/news/ackerman_080904.html (accessed September 22, 2008).

3. Patricia B. McGraw, "Family Needs Come First for Ackerman," *Daily Herald*, October 23, 2004.

4. Naismith Memorial Basketball Hall of Fame, Val Ackerman recipient of 2008 hall of fame John W. Bunn lifetime achievement award, http://hoophall.com/genrel/082008aac.html (accessed September 22, 2008).

3

WOMEN COURT EQUALITY AND RESPECT IN TENNIS

Introduction by Richard Lapchick

When we watch the incredible play of today's women tennis stars, it is hard to imagine a more delicate breed of tennis players as they were in the early days of the game. A year after lawn tennis was first played—many believe in Bermuda in 1873—the game was introduced in the United States by Mary Ewing Outerbridge on the grounds of the Staten Island Cricket and Baseball Club.

Three years later, the name Wimbledon was introduced to the world of tennis when the first "world amateur championships" for men were held there at the All-England Lawn Tennis and Croquet Club. The championships for women started in 1884.

The game was spread throughout the British colonies by the end of the 19th century.

In the United States, local rules and standards for the game varied widely until 1881, when the United States Lawn Tennis Association (USLTA—now the USTA) was organized to make rules and equipment uniform. The USLTA started singles championships for men in 1881 in Newport, Rhode Island, where they were played until 1915, when they were moved to Forest Hills, New York, to the West Side Tennis Club.

Philadelphia was the home of the national women's singles matches between 1887 and 1921. The matches were played at the Philadelphia Cricket Club. Women joined the men at Forest Hills, where they were both played until 1978, when they were moved nearby to the National Tennis Center in Flushing Meadows-Corona Park in New York City. The events took the name of the U.S. Open in 1968.

Wimbledon and the U.S. championships were the ultimate prizes in tennis well into the 20th century. Among the women Dorothea Douglass Lambert Chambers of England won the women's title at Wimbledon seven times in 11 years starting in 1903. Americans Elisabeth Moore and Hazel Wightman, who became known as the "Queen Mother of Tennis," both won several U.S. women's championships in the early 1900s. But they were dominated by Norwegian-born Molla Mallory, who won eight titles between1915 and 1926. Wightman's story is profiled in *100 Trailblazers*.

In the 1920s, American Helen Wills Moody and Suzanne Lenglen of France were the leading female players. In the 1930s, Moody continued to dominate. In all, she won eight Wimbledon titles, seven U.S. championship titles, and four French championship titles. Her top opponents were Americans Alice Marble and Helen Jacobs, and Dorothy Round of England. Tennis was very segregated in this era. In 1929, Ora Washington, an African-American woman, won her first American Tennis Association's (ATA) singles title, a title she held for seven years. She won an eighth ATA title in 1937. Her record stood until Althea Gibson broke it with nine titles. The ATA was all African-American.

During the war years and into the 1950s, there were two dominant female players who began their careers at this time. Pauline Betz won four U.S. championships between 1942 and 1946 and Louise Brough captured four Wimbledon titles between 1948 and 1955.

Maureen Connolly was a top female player of the early 1950s. Connolly won the grand slam in 1953. Althea Gibson won both the Wimbledon and the U.S. championships in 1957 and 1958, becoming the first African-American player to win those tournaments. The stories of both Connolly and Gibson are included in this section of the book.

During the 1960s and 1970s, leading female players included Maria Bueno of Brazil, Margaret Smith Court of Australia, Virginia Wade of England, and Billie Jean King, who won an amazing six Wimbledon titles between 1966 and 1975 and became tennis's bigger than life figure.

In the 1970s, Court, Wade, and King were joined by Australian Evonne Goolagong. It was during this decade that Czech-born Martina Navratilova came onto the tennis scene like a lightning bolt. Navratilova won 167 singles titles, including nine Wimbledon titles, between 1978 and 1990. Her biggest rival was American Chris Evert, who won seven French and six U.S. Opens in the 1970s and 1980s.

In 1988, Steffi Graf captured the grand slam and Olympic gold in Seoul. Other female stars of the 1980s included American Tracy Austin and Hana Mandilikova of Czechoslovakia.

Graf and Monica Seles became great rivals. Seles won the U.S., French, and Australian opens in 1991 and 1992. Navratilova remained one of the highest-ranking players until her retirement from singles competition in 1995. Arantxa Sánchez Vicario of Spain, Jennifer Capriati of the United States, and Gabriela Sabatini of Argentina were also consistent winners on the tour.

The women we profiled in *100 Trailblazers* are Hazel Wightman, Billie Jean King, Maureen Connolly Brinker, Althea Gibson, Evonne Goolagong, Margaret Osborne duPont, Chris Evert, Martina Navratilova, and Venus and Serena Williams. All of the great women mentioned above could have been highlighted.

"Queen Mother of Tennis" is one of the many nicknames Hazel Wightman has donned. It was one of many, not because people changed their minds about her during her 45-year-long career, but because she had a hand in almost every aspect of the game of tennis. In 1919, at the age of 32, she won her fourth singles title, at the U.S. Championships. She went on to win the women's doubles title at the same tournament and continued prolonged success in doubles tournaments until 1954, when she won her 45th and final title at age 68.

Also known for her longevity, Margaret Osborne duPont won her first of 37 Grand Slam titles in 1941 at the U.S. Championships in women's doubles. She went on to win a total of 21 women's doubles, 10 mixed doubles, and six singles titles at the U.S Championships, Wimbledon, and French Open, spanning from 1941 to 1962. Osborne duPont's title-tally still ranks her fourth on the all-time list despite never competing in the fourth Grand Slam event, the Australian Open.

Althea Gibson won both Wimbledon and the U.S. Championships in 1957 and 1958. In 1957 she earned the No. 1 ranking in the world and was named the AP Female Athlete of the Year in 1957 and 1958. She was the first African-American female to win the AP award.

She suddenly retired from amateur tennis in 1958 in her prime at age 31. There was no prize money and were no endorsement deals for women in that era. Male tennis players had to give up their amateur status but there was no pro tour for women so Gibson could only earn money in exhibition matches.

Growing up in an impoverished Harlem, Gibson changed tennis. She became the first African-American tennis star to be hailed internationally and seemed to be opening the door during an era when sexism and racism were abundant. The door was slow to open wider for others. The successes of Serena and Venus Williams, while so important, have been but faint knocks on the door at the elite level of tennis.

Her tennis career lasted just three and a half years but in that time Maureen Connolly won all nine Grand Slam tournaments she entered and lost only five matches. She was the first woman to achieve a Grand Slam by winning each of the four major national championships (United States, Great Britain, France, and Australia) in a single year. Connolly repeated her victories at the French and Wimbledon championships in 1954, but little did she know they would be the last of her career. She was thrown from a horse and had to retire at 20 years old. The tragedy continued when she died of cancer in 1969 at the age of 34.

Although she has so many great victories, including six Wimbledon singles championships and four U.S. Opens, Billie Jean King may be best remembered for a single match played against a 55-year-old man when she was at the top of her game. Bobby Riggs was a cocky, arrogant Wimbledon champion himself, circa 1939. He was somebody who loudly bragged about the dominance of men over women to raise the ire of women's organizations and possibly, to get more attention for himself. It worked. In 1973, he defeated the great but fading star, Margaret Smith Court.

This propelled Billie Jean King to accept a match against Bobby Riggs. Among the firsts that Billie Jean King achieved were that she was the first woman commissioner in professional sports history (World Team Tennis [WTT], 1984); the first woman to coach a co-ed team in professional sports (Philadelphia Freedoms, WTT, 1974); the first female athlete in any sport to earn more than $100,000 in a single season ($117,000, 1971); and the first woman to have a major sports venue named in her honor (USTA Billie Jean King National Tennis Center—2006).

The 19-year-old 1971 Wimbledon and French Open champion, Evonne Goolagong, did not realize the significance of her success.

Goolagong's success in the tennis circuit drew attention as she was the first Aboriginal to reach such a pinnacle in Australia. She was able to overcome the discrimination against Aboriginals. She helped educate her country and the world about Aboriginals while smashing stereotypes.

Chris Evert stunned the tennis world when, as a 15-year-old, she upset the World's No. 1 player, Margaret Smith Court, in 1970. She later won 125 consecutive matches (24 tournaments) on clay between 1973 and 1979. This stretch still stands as the longest winning streak of any player on any single surface. One loss broke the streak, but she followed it by winning the next 72 matches on clay. Evert retired in 1989 with a total of 1,309 match victories in a sport where no one had won 1,000 matches before her. She won the big ones: three Wimbledons, seven French, two Australian, and six U.S. Opens. Evert's Grand Slam total remains the third best in professional tennis history.

Venus and Serena Williams helped bring tennis out of the country clubs and into the inner cities with the great talent they developed in Compton, California, known for its gang violence and poor neighborhoods. Both turned pro at age 14: Venus in 1994 and Serena in 1995. In 1999, Serena was the seventh seed at the U.S. Open when she upset No. 4 Monica Seles, No. 2 Lindsay Davenport, and No. 1 Martina Hingis to take the U.S. Open title. Thus she became the second African-American woman to ever win a Grand Slam event four decades after Althea Gibson was the first African-American Grand Slam Champion when she won the French Open in 1956.

By the time of this writing, Venus had won five Wimbledon titles, two U.S., one French, and one Australian Open. She has won seven grand slam doubles. Her sister Serena had won two Wimbledon titles, three U.S., one French, and three Australian Opens. She has also won seven grand slam doubles. And they are still going strong.

As the Williams sisters reached the 2008 Wimbledon finals, many noted the great athletic accomplishments of the sisters while fewer noted it as another racial milestone in sports. Venus's fifth singles title was surely remarkable but it paled in comparison to the trailblazing efforts of Althea Gibson at Wimbledon in 1957, 51 years earlier. Women's tennis has come a long way, with some great pioneers having helped blaze the trail.

Hazel Wightman

American Star of the Women's International Sports Hall of Fame

by Jessica Bartter

"Queen Mother of Tennis" is one of the many nicknames Hazel Wightman has donned. It was one of many, not because people changed their minds about her during her 45-year-long career, but because she had a hand in almost every aspect of the game of tennis. Wightman was a talented player, a well-respected teacher, a mentor to many aspiring players, an advocate for a women's playing platform, and, obviously, a motherly-figure to other female tennis players. Through it all, Wightman was an amateur, never receiving a dime for the 45 tennis titles she earned during her lengthy playing career.

Born as Hazel Hotchkiss on December 20, 1886, in Healdsburg, California, Wightman was not introduced to tennis until she was 16 years old. Her interest was sparked after watching fellow Californian May Sutton battle one of her sisters. The five Sutton sisters dominated Southern California's tennis territory, winning every singles title in the region's championships between 1899 and 1915. Wightman's interest went from a spark to a full-fledged flame after watching the more rapid pace of a men's doubles game packed with power and volleying.

Volleying would become a key ingredient of Wightman's game. She practiced tennis around and against her house with her four older brothers, but because of the dirt and gravel ground, they were forced to hit the ball before it bounced or simply volley back and forth. Wightman honed her game on the only court near her home in Berkeley, California. The lone court at the University of California, Berkeley, restricted female players from using the court after 8:00 a.m. Therefore, Wightman showed up at 6:00 a.m. every day.

It did not take long before Wightman was known as the best tennis player in Northern California. And therefore, it was inevitable that she would face her Southern California counterpart and inspiration, May Sutton. In 1909, the 22-year-old traveled to the Philadelphia Cricket Club for the U.S. Championships. Despite learning on clay and never having played on grass before, Wightman won the grass tournament with her net-attacking style and dominant volley. With a single tournament, Wightman introduced a new style of play to women's tennis. Wightman also won the women's doubles and mixed doubles titles in 1909. She defended all three titles in 1910 and 1911. As could have been predicted, Wightman faced May Sutton in the 1911 finals, where she went on to win the close match 8-10, 6-4, 9-7.

In 1912, Hazel Hotchkiss married George Wightman of Boston, Massachusetts, and took a retreat from tennis to start a family. The true competitor inside her jumped back into tennis after a simply-stated challenge from her father. Mr. Hotchkiss pointed out that no American women had ever won a singles title after giving birth to a child. Though easier said than done, Wightman was up for the challenge. In 1919, at the age of 32, she won her fourth (and last) singles title, again at the U.S. Championships. She went on to win the women's doubles title at the same tournament and continued prolonged success in doubles tournaments until 1954, when she won her 45th and final title at age 68.

While juggling motherhood with her tennis career, proving to be up to her father's challenge, Wightman also focused on equality for women's tennis. In 1919, she urged tennis officials to offer an international team tournament for women similar to the men's Davis Cup. The Davis Cup began in 1900 as a competition between the United States and Great Britain, but has now expanded to 127 entering countries. Wightman wanted the women's version to "include Great Britain, the United States, France, and all other nations with prominent women players." Wightman went so far as to spend $300 of her own money on a trophy that she presented to United States Lawn Tennis Association (USLTA) with her idea. The tall, slender, silver cup sat on their shelves for four years before Wightman's dream was realized. In 1923, the West Side Tennis Club in Forest Hills, New York, opened a new tennis stadium and decided the "Ladies International Lawn Tennis Challenge" would be the perfect event to celebrate its opening. The tournament continued until 1989, but was always known by its unofficial name, the Wightman Cup.[1]

The Wightman Cup was alternately played in the United States and Great Britain each year. In England, it was generally played before Wimbledon and "helped generate tremendous interest in the women's game."[2]

Wightman remembered 1924 as the prime of her tennis career. She traveled to England with Helen Wills to win the women's doubles title at Wimbledon, which she described as nothing less than "a big thrill."[3] She then traveled to Paris, France, for the 1924 Olympic Games, where she won two gold medals, one each in the women's doubles and mixed doubles.

In 1940, the mother of five divorced George Wightman, but remained living in Massachusetts. She moved to Chestnut Hill near the Longwood Cricket Club, where she instructed tennis clinics and coordinated many tournaments. The now single woman opened up her three-story home to young aspiring female tennis players from every stretch of the globe. She was known for motherly yet rigid hospitality:

> Guests slept everywhere, from the basement to the solarium, coexisting peacefully with Mrs. Wightie's cats, which came and went as they pleased through the open windows.
>
> Mrs. Wightie rose at dawn. She would whip up batches of brownies and chocolate-chip cookies for her guests and to satisfy her own sweet tooth. Then she headed for the washing machine. "She did all the laundry for us," recalled Doris Hart, a Wimbledon and United States champion in the 1950s. "She didn't want us to mess with her machine. It wasn't like the machines today. It had one of those ringers. It was always going."
>
> Shirley Fry, another champion, recalled that Mrs. Wightman washed the dishes herself, too, "because during the war she had learned to save soap, and no one else could do it right." She shook out just the necessary amount of flakes from a little basket.
>
> Following an evening meal at a large table, Hazel played bridge or poker with her guests. Women who went out for the evening signed out and in on a blackboard. There was no curfew, but Hazel watched over her girls with the eye of a hawk, or perhaps the eye of a mother hen. "Shirley!" she would say, narrowing in on a too-casual teenager, "Stand up straight!"[4]

Wightman's career lasted long enough for her to compete in doubles tournaments with her pupils. She taught many of the best, including

Helen Wills (with whom she won Wimbledon and the Olympics) and Sarah Palfrey. She was ranked in the U.S.'s top 10 in 1915, 1918, and 1919, when she was the nation's top-ranked player. In 1973, the California native was named an honorary Commander of the British Empire by Queen Elizabeth II. In 1999, the Boston Globe named her 85th on its list of the Top 100 New England sports figures of the 20th century. Wightman's sports figure fame extended far beyond her win-loss record or long-standing doubles reign. Wightman's volley-changing style of play, outspokenness for female tennis players, end-less teaching, and maternal care for the game of tennis made her stature far from short, despite being a meager five feet tall. Billie Jean King once wrote that "Hazel Wightman's name is woven into the tapestry of women's tennis like a shining golden thread that stretched from the 1900s through the 1920s, 1930s, 1940s, 1950s, and 1960s. Champion, patron, coach . . . she devoted her life to teaching, encouraging, sheltering, and enlightening aspiring young tennis stars. In a statistic not recognized by the record books, 'Mrs. Wightie' will be remembered as the most beloved tennis figure of all time."[5]

Notes

1. Billie Jean King, *We Have Come a Long Way* (New York: McGraw-Hill Book Company, 1988), 20–22.

2. King, *We Have Come a Long Way*, 21.

3. Barbara Matson, "She Was Queen of Court: Wightman Had Regal Reign in Women's Tennis," *The Boston Globe*, October 8, 1999.

4. King, *We Have Come a Long Way*, 21–22.

5. Ibid.

Margaret Osborne duPont

American Star of the Women's International Sports Hall of Fame

by Jessica Bartter

As the epitome of a trailblazer, Margaret Osborne duPont made her own path as she became an American tennis star whose career spanned across four decades from the late 1930s to the early 1960s. Born on a farm in 1918 in the small community of Joseph, Oregon, she cannot recall having any heroes to aspire after. Instead, she blazed her own trail.

Osborne duPont has since retired to El Paso, Texas, but the time in between has been a journey. The Osborne family left the Oregon farm due to the health of Margaret's father. After two years in Spokane, Washington, they moved to San Francisco, where he found work as a car mechanic in a garage that was much more conducive to his medical condition in comparison to the hard labor of a farm.

One summer in Spokane, when Osborne duPont was 10 years old, her mother bought her and her older brother tennis racquets. Yet, rather than signing them up for tennis lessons, she sent the children to music classes. On her way to her music lesson, Osborne duPont made sure to pass the tennis courts, where she would stop to watch or shag balls. Then upon moving to San Francisco, Margaret and her brother, already familiar with the game, discovered the public courts at Golden Gate Park. She says they "played on every public court in San Francisco."[1]

The lack of heroes or heroines did not make Osborne duPont exempt from being impressionable at a young age. She does recall a junior high graduation speaker who spoke about sports. He explained to the adolescents that "there is no such thing as a bad sport or a good sport. You are either a sport or not a sport. And from that day forward, sportsmanship was very high in [her] book."[2]

Upon her High School of Commerce graduation in January 1936, Osborne duPont focused her attention on a career in tennis since her family could not afford to send her to college. Tennis brought her great opportunities to travel the world and she started with a trip to the Junior Nationals, where she won both the singles and doubles titles at 18 years old. She accepted side jobs writing for *The American Lawn Tennis Magazine* and working for the Northern California Tennis Association as the secretary treasurer to help sustain her while she focused most of her time on the practice court.

Despite her early victories at the Junior Nationals, Osborne duPont was not happy with her tennis game. She said she "couldn't do what I wanted to do with the game I had,"[3] so she took a year off solely to train with legendary coach Tom Stow. Day in and day out, she hit the court with him for a full year without getting burned out, because, as she told me, she had "too much ambition."[4]

Osborne duPont won her first of 37 Grand Slam titles in 1941 at the U.S. Championships in women's doubles. She went on to win a total of 21 women's doubles, 10 mixed doubles, and six singles titles at the U.S Championships, Wimbledon, and French Open spanning from 1941 to 1962. Osborne duPont's title-tally still ranks her fourth on the all-time list despite never competing in the fourth Grand Slam event, the Australian Open.

When reading Osborne duPont's tennis bio, it is the numerous records she set and still holds that immediately jump out. Even more impressive is the length of time her records have stood, considering most were set over 50 years ago. Yet longevity is a theme of Margaret Osborne duPont's career. Very few can claim the length of dominance Osborne duPont earned on the international tennis circuit. Writer and tennis enthusiast Stan Hart declared in his book *Once a Champion* that, in fact, no one can be compared with Osborne duPont's longevity. Hart wrote, "for longevity, there is no one that I can think of who equals Margaret Osborne duPont."[5]

While her career was lengthy, Osborne duPont is also known for a couple of particularly lengthy matches. The 1948 U.S. Championships final lasted the longest of any women's singles final of that tournament. Osborne duPont battled Louise Brough point for point before edging her out 3-6, 6-4, and 15-13 at Forest Hills, New York. Margaret and Louise then joined the same side of the net to win the women's doubles final, one of nine consecutive championships they earned together from 1941 through 1950. The Osborne duPont and Brough duo actually won a record of 20 Grand Slam women's doubles titles, a number that has since been matched (but not exceeded) by partners Martina Navratilova and Pam Shriver.

In what she remembers as the toughest doubles match she ever played in, Osborne duPont and partner Billy Talbert played a 71-game, two-day spanning match against Gussy Moran and Bob Falkenburg, also in 1948, during the mixed doubles' semifinal. She recalls, "We had to end it on the first day at 22-all and then continued the next day. The wind was so strong that day at the grandstand court at Forest Hills that you couldn't possibly win a game on one side of the court and you couldn't possibly lose a game on the other. We just never could finish the set."[6] Finally, on their second day of competition, they did finish a set and were victorious 27-25, 5-7, 6-1. The 71-game record stood for 43 years until the 1991 Wimbledon final went 77 games.

Margaret Osborne duPont went on to win titles up until 1962. Between 1938 and 1958, she was ranked among the top 10 in the world 14 times. Fifty years later, in 2008, when asked what advice she could offer today's stars, Osborne duPont doesn't think she has much to offer. She points out the drastic difference in tennis from the World War II era to the new millennium by saying, "We played with wooden racquets, and the balls are much harder now. Our game was more about finesse, not so much power as today." She adds that the stars of her day "did not receive any money," so they truly played for the love of the game.[7] The humble Margaret Osborne duPont did not realize that that is the best advice she could give: "play for the love of the game."

Notes

1 Stan Hart, *Once a Champion: Legendary Tennis Stars Revisited* (New York: Dodd, Mead & Company, Inc., 1985), 397.

2 Ibid..

3 Interview with author, August 14, 2008.

4 Ibid.

5 Hart, *Once a Champion*, 391–92.

6 Ibid., 394.

7 Interview with author, August 14, 2008.

Billie Jean King

American Star of the Women's International Sports Hall of Fame

by Richard Lapchick

Billie Jean King was an early teacher for me on the issue of Women's Rights. She used the world of sport to help educate many young girls and women, boys and men, about the inequitable and sexist world in which she competed. I have been lucky to know Billie Jean King since the mid-1980s. I have been around her as a fan, as a fellow committee member for various organizations, as an advocate for the Women's Sports Foundation (WSF), which she founded, and in organizations dedicated to improving the situation of people of color in America. She is beyond any question an iconic hero in my lifetime. When I mention her name to other people, I know that it is hardly unique, as she stands tall for so many others.

Although she has so many great victories, including six Wimbledon singles championships and four U.S. Opens, she may be best remembered for a single match played against a 55-year-old man when she was at the top of her game. Bobby Riggs was a cocky, arrogant Wimbledon champion himself, circa 1939. He was somebody who used his braggadocio about the dominance of men over women to raise the ire of women's organizations, and possibly, to get more attention for himself. It worked. In 1973, he defeated the great but fading star, Margaret Court.

This propelled Billie Jean King to accept a match against Bobby Riggs. She knew she had to win because on her shoulders were riding the hopes of so many young girls and women. The match became known as the "Battle of the Sexes." On September 20, 1973, in the Houston Astro Dome, Billie Jean King dismantled Riggs, 6-4, 6-3, 6-3. The New York Times Neil Amdur wrote, "Most important, perhaps, for women everywhere, she convinced skeptics that a female can survive pressure-felt situations and that men are as susceptible to nerves as women." Fifty million people watched that tennis match, which has been hailed ever since as the greatest step forward for women's equality in sports. Billie Jean King showed every woman that it was okay to be an athlete at a time when many men were trying to persuade young girls and women not to compete in sports because it was "not feminine." When *LIFE Magazine* named its 100 most important Americans of the 21st century, there were only four sports figures on the list and only one female athlete—Babe Ruth, Jackie Robinson, Muhammad Ali, and Billie Jean King.

Born into a family that produced two professional athletes (her brother was the Major League Baseball player Randy Moffitt), King started her journey when she was born on November 22, 1943. She grew up in Long Beach, California. Her father, Bill, worked for the Long Beach Fire Department and her mother, Betty, was a homemaker. She had told her mom at age five that "I am going to do something great with my life."

She knew after her first tennis lesson that she was going to be a tennis player. At age 11, Billie told her mom, "I am going to be No. 1 in the world."

By the time she was 17, she had won the doubles championship at Wimbledon with Karen Hantze. She would eventually win a total of 20 titles at Wimbledon, including ten doubles and four mixed, along with six singles championships. She gained the No. 1 ranking in 1966 after her first Wimbledon Singles Championship. The next year she won again at Wimbledon and also captured her first U.S. Championship.

She started when there were no women's tennis professionals and by the end of her playing career had won close to $2 million in prize money. She became a strong advocate for women to gain equal pay with men for tournaments that they competed in. Billie Jean King helped launch the Virginia Slims Tour, which broke away from the regular tour. She signed a $1 contract to play in the Virginia Slims tennis tournament, which became the first professional tour for women, in 1970. She helped launch the first women's players union, the Women's Tennis Association. She told the U.S. Open officials in 1972 that if men's and women's champions did not receive the same prize that she and other women would not compete. In 1973, the U.S. Open became the first major tournament to offer equal prize money. Wimbledon didn't comply until 2007!

She was off and running. Within a year, she had founded the WSF and *Women's Sports Magazine* and then World Team Tennis

(WTT). The WSF became the leading advocacy group for girls and women in sport and has remained so for more than three decades.

King's personal life became a lightning rod of controversy when her sexual orientation became public after a palimony suit by her assistant. Although King won the suit, she felt that she lost, perhaps, hundreds of thousands of dollars in endorsements because of the controversy caused by her becoming known as a bisexual player. She and her husband were divorced shortly after.

But she was hardly stopped. She became a leader in the fight for equality and recognition in the Gay, Lesbian, Bisexual and Transgender (GLBT) community, and has been honored by many of the leading GLBT organizations.

Among the firsts that King achieved was the first woman commissioner in professional sports history (World Team Tennis, 1984); the first woman to coach a co-ed team in professional sports (Philadelphia Freedoms, WTT, 1974); the first female athlete in any sport to earn more than $100,000 in a single season ($117,000, 1971); and the first woman to have a major sports venue named in her honor (USTA Billie Jean King National Tennis Center—2006).

In 2008, the Sports Museum of America opened in New York, where the Billie Jean King International Women's Sports Center will be the nation's first permanent women's sports hall of fame and exhibit.

In a 2008 interview with Cokie Roberts of *USA Today Weekend*, King was asked, "Over time, have you seen a tangible difference for women in sports?" Her response was direct, "Oh, we're shockingly off. Just for example, we get 8 percent of the sports page. We have about $1 billion in sponsorship worldwide—men have more than $25 billion. And that's just the beginning. We have so far to go in the sports world. And yet, sports are a microcosm of society. If you know where we are in sports, you kind of know where the world is."

On the importance of female role models for girls, she told Roberts, "You have to see it to be it. If a girl sees a woman succeed at something new, the sky truly is the limit." King has been that role model and "shero" for generations and there is no sign of her slowing down.

Elton John wrote his song, "Philadelphia Freedom," for Billie Jean. Like her, it became No. 1. She has been a freedom fighter.

Still active after all these years and in great demand, Billie Jean King, at age 65 as of this writing, remains young at heart and in the hearts of women and girls around the country. She has also helped men, like me, gain a greater appreciation of how important sports are to women and girls.

Maureen Connolly Brinker

American Star of the Women's International Sports Hall of Fame

by Jessica Bartter

Despite a tennis career that lasted just three and a half years, Maureen Connolly Brinker was so well respected for her talent that the International Tennis Hall of Fame inducted her in 1969 and the Women's International Sports Hall of Fame inducted her in 1987. Perhaps it was her 100 percent victory rate in each of the nine Grand Slam tournaments she entered, or the fact that in three and a half years, she won all but five matches. Better yet, maybe it was the fact that she was the first woman to achieve a Grand Slam by winning each of the four major national championships (United States, Great Britain, France, and Australia) in a single year. There are certainly many arguments that rightfully place Maureen Connolly Brinker in several halls of fame.

Born in San Diego, California, on September 17, 1934, Connolly Brinker initially fell in love with horses. Her parents divorced when she was three and she was raised by her mother and aunt. Her single mother could not afford horseback riding lessons, but luckily, Connolly Brinker's passion for tennis blossomed, and later, provided her the opportunities with horses that she had always dreamt about.

At nine years old, Connolly Brinker discovered tennis while watching two men competitively rally on the University Heights' courts just down the street from her home. Though her mother could not afford tennis lessons, Connolly Brinker made herself a useful presence on the courts by shagging balls for the tennis pro Wilbur Folsom, who had a prosthetic leg. In return, Folsom gave Connolly Brinker lessons and her first racquet. His first order of business was to change the natural left-hander into a righty. Through practicing three hours a day, five days a week, Connolly Brinker mastered the transition, though some attributed her weak serve to the fact that she was not a natural right-handed player.

Connolly Brinker increased her practice hours and intensity when, at 12 years old, she came under the tutelage of Eleanor "Teach" Tennant. "Teach improved Maureen's game technically and molded her into an unyielding competitor by sheltering her and refusing to let her socialize or even practice with the other women players."[1] Teach also embedded a deep hatred into Connolly Brinker, forcing her to believe she had to loathe each of her opponents to be victorious.

Victories were not a problem for Maureen Connolly Brinker, with or without the hatred she embodied for her competitors. By 14, Connolly Brinker had won 56 consecutive matches and was "beating the very best in the Los Angeles area."[2] In 1949, at age 14 she became the youngest player to ever win the National Girls 18 and under Championship. She defended her title at age 15. The young Connolly Brinker had been nicknamed "Little Mo" by a *San Diego Tribune* sportswriter after the battleship USS Missouri, which was known as "Big Mo." The nickname "Little Mo" might conjure the image of a sweet, dainty, girlish individual, but she was nothing but a fierce, explosive competitor on the court, just like "Big Mo" was at sea.

Part of Connolly Brinker's fierceness came from her preference to play the baseline. As a child, Connolly Brinker was hit in the face while playing the net and, as a result, she feared volleying. Conse-

Compliments of the Maureen Connolly Brinker Tennis Foundation.

Maureen "Little Mo" Connolly winning the Grand Slam in 1953.

quently, she developed a fierce drive from the baseline, and she routinely hit the ball within inches of her competitor's baseline with tremendous force.

In 1951, Connolly Brinker won the U.S. Championships, just weeks shy of her 17th birthday. This victory made Connolly Brinker the second youngest American champion since May Sutton, who had won at age 16 in 1904. The following year, Connolly Brinker defended her U.S. title and became the second youngest winner of Wimbledon when she defeated Louise Brough:

Small and compact, she hit with a tremendous power which she developed through more intensive practice than any woman who has yet played at Wimbledon . . . Her concentration was enormous and in order to unwind she would normally go straight from a tournament win to a practice court where she could gradually relax through hitting the ball smoothly and easily, rather than with the power and determination of match play. Even when she won the Wimbledon final she followed this routine, her perfectionist approach completely overcoming the natural glee of a seventeen-year-old girl winning what is virtually the championship of the world.[3]

During 1953, Connolly Brinker had a new coach, Australian Harry Hopman, who convinced her for the first time to enter all four Grand Slam tournaments. Together they set their sights on Connolly Brinker becoming the first female player to win all four championships in a single season. She hoped to be the next Don Budge, who had successfully won his Grand Slam in 1938, "a year after he conceived of the idea."[4] Connolly Brinker first won the Australian title, then the French Open, where she lost the only set of the entire Grand Slam. She continued winning in England without dropping a set and played against Doris Hart in what many regarded as one of the greatest women's finals ever played at Wimbledon. With a final score of 8-6 and 7-5, both sets were so close even Hart left the court feeling victorious, despite being defeated. At three-quarters of the way to her Grand Slam, Connolly Brinker traveled to New York to compete in the U.S. Championships. The stellar play of this 18-year-old was unstoppable and though she again met Doris Hart in the finals, Connolly Brinker handled Hart much easier this time in just 43 minutes with a score of 6-2, 6-4.

Despite Connolly Brinker's period of great success in the tennis world, she went largely unrecognized by the major media outlets. At the pinnacle of her career, only devout tennis fans would have noticed Connolly's feat of winning all four title tournaments. Despite the fact that Connolly Brinker was the first woman to accomplish such a feat, the *New York Times* had the men's U.S. Open champion on the front page while mention of Maureen Connolly Brinker's Grand Slam sweep could only be found buried within the sports section, no doubt indicative of the era's attitude toward women.

Connolly Brinker repeated her victories at the French and Wimbledon championships in 1954, but little did she know they would be the last of her career. Connolly Brinker returned home to San Diego and was horseback riding with friends "on a narrow side road when a noisy cement truck passed between them. [The horse] whirled. The truck's rear mudguard caught Maureen's right leg, throwing her to the ground. The impact tore the muscles below her knee and broke and exposed the bone."[5] The accident occurred just weeks after Connolly Brinker's third Wimbledon title. A few months later, Connolly Brinker was forced to announce her retirement. She was only 20 years old and though she had accomplished many great challenges in the tennis world, it was almost certain she had not yet reached her prime.

Notwithstanding this calamity, Connolly Brinker did not steer clear of horses. In 1955, she married Norman Brinker, who was a member of the 1952 United States Olympic equestrian team. Together they had two children.

It was common knowledge, and Connolly Brinker agreed, that her tennis stroke was never affected by the accident. She continued to hit with immense power and pinpoint accuracy until the day she died, the only difference being her undeniable lack of movement to the ball. Maureen Connolly Brinker suffered another undeserved blow to her health in 1966, when she was diagnosed with cancer. While on vacation in Europe, Connolly Brinker experienced terrible back pains for which she sought treatment upon her return to the United States. The doctors informed her that she had cancer. Like her tennis career, Connolly Brinker fought for three years, but unlike her success on the court, she lost her battle with cancer on June 21, 1969, at the age of 34. Billie Jean King sums up Maureen Connolly Brinker well: "Her life, like her career, was fulfilling but too short."[6]

Notes

1. Billie Jean King, *We Have Come A Long Way* (New York: McGraw-Hill Book Company, 1988), 84.

2. Ibid.

3. James Medlycott, *100 Years of the Wimbledon Tennis Champions* (New York: Crescent Books, 1977), 61.

4. King, *We Have Come a Long Way*, 87.

5. Ibid., 88.

6. Ibid., 89.

Althea Gibson

American Star of the Women's International Sports Hall of Fame

by Richard Lapchick

As the Williams sisters reached the 2008 Wimbledon finals, many noted the great athletic accomplishments for the sisters while fewer noted it as another racial milestone in sports. Venus's sixth Grand Slam singles title was surely remarkable, but it paled in comparison to the trailblazing efforts of Althea Gibson at Wimbledon in 1957, 51 years earlier.

We honored Arthur Ashe when I was director of Northeastern University's Center for the Study of Sport in Society. After tennis luminary Bud Collins rightly extolled all of Ashe's accomplishments and virtues, the first thing Ashe said in his acceptance speech was that "I would not have had the chance to do what I have been able to do if Althea Gibson had not blazed the way for me."

This daughter of a sharecropper titled her autobiography, *I Always Wanted to Be Somebody*. By the time the book was released in 1958, she definitely was somebody. It came out two years after she had won her first Grand Slam event with victories in both the singles and doubles in the French Open. Her doubles partner was Angela Buxton, who was Jewish. Buxton and Gibson had confronted anti-Semitism and racism, respectively. They repeated their doubles victory at Wimbledon. Buxton was the first Jewish champion at Wimbledon and Gibson was the first African-American champion. An English newspaper reported their victory at Wimbledon under the headline "Minorities Win."

Gibson was to win a great deal more, including Wimbledon in 1957 and 1958 and the U.S. Championships in 1957 and 1958. In 1957, she earned the No. 1 ranking in the world and was named the AP Female Athlete of the Year in 1957 and 1958. She was the first African-American female to win the AP award.

She suddenly retired from amateur tennis in 1958 in her prime at age 31. There was no prize money and were no endorsement deals for women in that era. Male tennis players had to give up their amateur status, but there was no pro tour for women so Gibson could earn money only in exhibition matches.

Gibson was driven to succeed and became a historical figure in and out of sport. Growing up in an impoverished Harlem, Althea Gibson would change tennis. She became the first African-American tennis star to be hailed internationally and seemed to be opening the door during an era when sexism and racism were abundant. The door was slow to open wider for others. The successes of Serena and Venus Williams, while so important, have been but faint knocks on the door at the elite level of tennis.

Although hopes were high when Gibson won at Wimbledon, it took 42 years for a repeat by an African-American woman. Other women of color to win that coveted crown were Australian Evonne Goolagong Cawley (1971 and 1980), Maria Bueno (1959, 1960, and 1964), and Conchita Martinez (1994).

Born in 1927 in Silver, South Carolina, in 1930 Gibson moved with her family to Harlem in New York City, where they lived on welfare for most of her youth. Gibson often skipped school and ran away from home.

Developing her early skills from table tennis in public recreation parks, she actually won Police Athletic Leagues and Parks Department sponsored tournaments. Musician Buddy Walker gave her the first opportunity to play tennis and helped her to become a member of the Harlem Cosmopolitan Tennis Club, a group of all African-American athletes. In 1942, Gibson played and won her first tournament, which was sponsored by the American Tennis Association (ATA). Later, Gibson was introduced to a physician from Lynchburg, Virginia, Dr. Walter Johnson. He mentored her and gave her the opportunity to play more and better tennis. Dr. Johnson would later be an influential person in the life of Arthur Ashe. In 1946, Gibson decided to further pursue her tennis career and moved to Wilmington, North Carolina, to work under Dr. Hubert A. Eaton while attending high school in North Carolina. Honing her great skills through steady practice, Gibson won her first of 10 straight ATA National Championships in 1947.

Her tennis career continued to rise fast while she was a student at Florida A&M University in Tallahassee, where she graduated in 1953.

Tennis was virtually a 100 percent segregated sport. In 1949,

Gibson competed against white tennis players for the first time. Alice Marble wrote an editorial for the July 1950 edition of *American Lawn Tennis Magazine*. Marble said, "Miss Gibson is over a very cunningly wrought barrel, and I can only hope to loosen a few of its staves with one lone opinion. If tennis is a game for ladies and gentlemen, it's also time we acted a little more like gentlepeople and less like sanctimonious hypocrites . . . If Althea Gibson represents a challenge to the present crop of women players, it's only fair that they should meet that challenge on the courts." Marble said that if Gibson were not given the opportunity to compete, "then there is an uneradicable mark against a game to which I have devoted most of my life, and I would be bitterly ashamed." Gibson played in the U.S. Championships in 1950 for the first time.

In 1953, Gibson competed on a U.S. State Department to Southeast Asia goodwill tennis tour. When she returned from the tour, the big victories piled up and she won the 1956 French Open.

Gibson won 56 singles and doubles titles during her amateur career in the 1950s and won 10 major titles after the 1956 French Open. Gibson was inducted into the International Tennis Hall of Fame, the International Women's Sports Hall of Fame, the International Scholar-Athletes Hall of Fame, and many others.

After her retirement from amateur tennis, she released a record album, *Althea Gibson Sings*, and later appeared in the film, *The Horse Soldiers*. Her "pro" tennis career included when she toured with the Harlem Globetrotters playing exhibition tennis, for which she reportedly made $100,000 in these matches before the Globetrotters games. In 1964, Gibson began playing professional golf on the Ladies Professional Golf Association (LPGA) tour.

She married Will Durben. In 1971, Gibson again tried to play professional tennis but was far past her prime at the age of 44 and could not compete with many of the younger players.

She became a tennis professional and taught instead. In 1975, Gibson was named the manager of the East Orange, New Jersey Department of Recreation and held the position for 10 years. She was also the New Jersey state commissioner of athletics from 1975 to 1985. Gibson then served on the State's Athletics Control Board until 1988 and the Governor's Council on Physical Fitness until 1992, when she retired.

Gibson began experiencing health problems in the 1990s and

suffered from a stroke in 1992. She also had two cerebral aneurysms. These health problems caused a significant financial burden on her and she became a recluse, rarely seeing people or being seen in public. Again living on welfare, Gibson was unable to pay for her medical or living costs. Eventually, Gibson called her old doubles partner, Angela Buxton, and told her she contemplated suicide. Without informing Gibson, Buxton arranged for a letter requesting support to appear in a tennis magazine. Nearly $1 million poured in from around the world.

I attended the funerals of both Arthur Ashe and Althea Gibson. Arthur, who hailed her as his champion and role model, drew thousands from across the globe to his funeral in Richmond. Hundreds came to Gibson's service, but did not quite fill the Trinity St. Phillip Cathedral in Newark, New Jersey.

Alan Schwartz, president of the United States Tennis Association, told those gathered that, "She simply changed the landscape of tennis . . . Gibson was no less a trailblazer than baseball great Jackie Robinson or tennis champion Arthur Ashe, although she received less recognition for her accomplishments. Arthur Ashe's job was not easy, but if he had to climb a hill, Althea Gibson had to climb a mountain. She was the original breakthrough person."

Zina Garrison was the next African-American woman after Gibson to reach the finals of Wimbledon 33 years later when she played Martina Navratilova in 1990. Garrison eulogized that Gibson was her inspiration: "Althea used to say she wanted me to be the one who broke her barrier, to take the burden off of her (as the only black woman to have won Wimbledon). She showed me the stall where she dressed and where she popped the champagne when she won. She knew she opened the door for all of us, and she was so excited about all the women who followed her."

Venus Williams released a statement after Gibson passed away saying she had been a role model for her tennis career. "I am grateful to Althea Gibson for having the strength and courage to break through the racial barriers in tennis. Althea Gibson was the first African-American woman to rank number one and win Wimbledon, and I am honored to have followed in such great footsteps." I surmised that Althea was there in spirit in June 2008 when Venus took her fourth Wimbledon title.

Her legacy is being carried on by the Althea Gibson Foundation, which was founded "for the primary purpose of identifying, encouraging, and providing financial support for urban youth who wish to develop their skills and talents in the sports of tennis or golf, and have decided to pursue a career as a student-athlete at the post-secondary level. The Foundation will continue her work to encourage young people to utilize sports to help improve upon the social condition of urban America and to promote global unity."

Gibson once said, "I hope that I have accomplished just one thing: that I have been a credit to tennis and my country." She was a credit to all of humanity.

Evonne Goolagong

International Star of the Women's International Sports Hall of Fame

by Jessica Bartter

Evonne Goolagong's talent stood out right away. Mrs. Martin, one of Evonne's first instructors, said, "The first thing we noticed was the way Evonne moved. She was a natural athlete." But it was more than her talent that drew eyes on the tennis court. She also stood out for her appearance, recalled Mrs. Martin, because she was "darker than the rest of the kids."[1] The Goolagong family are Australian Aboriginals, something Evonne equated to "aliens" in her memoir, *Evonne! On the Move.* "Now we are aliens in our own country. Another civilization has taken over, and we are second-class citizens. Aborigines. We left our mark across the continent, and I've left mine across the world, but I grew up as a bushie—a country girl—in Barellan, Narrandera Shire, New South Wales, Australia."[2] Australian Aborigines were the first inhabitants of the continent. They were tribal people who hunted on foot using spears, traps, and boomerangs. They moved often, following the abundance of food and good weather. A "bushie" by birth, Evonne left the countryside, not for superior weather or plentiful crops, but to globetrot from court to court, trampling many international competitors along the way.

Evonne Goolagong was playing with tennis balls before she was walking or talking. When she was just 12 months, her parents discovered how much tennis balls and chewing gum could entertain their daughter. It was almost like a free babysitter and an important form of entertainment since Evonne was the third of eight Goolagong children. Eventually, at two years old, when she did learn to walk, she could often be seen carrying her tennis ball around the neighborhood. But before Goolagong learned what to do with that tennis ball, she was outside playing rugby, cricket, and soccer with her brothers and other neighborhood boys. These games taught her to run and forced her to do so quickly. Her tennis game later became known for the way she moved, as is suggested from the title of her memoir. Goolagong said, "Speed has been a prime factor in my tennis . . . Running makes me feel good and free; it's the best part of any sport."[3]

Though her mother was worried about her walking late, she quickly caught up and by the age of nine, her running on the court attracted the attention of Australian teaching pro Vic Edwards. Goolagong was fortunate that while growing up in Barellan, she was welcomed on the War Memorial Tennis Club courts next to her home. By age 13, she had moved to Sydney to train and live with the Edwards family. Sydney was about 400 miles northeast of Barellan and strikingly different in population. Barellan was a wheat-farming town with just 900 inhabitants (down to 359 in 2001). It was in the fast-paced, densely-populated Sydney that Goolagong was first made to feel different for being an Aboriginal.

Goolagong quickly made headlines by surprising competitors and winning tournaments, but the headlines often read "colored this or Aboriginal that."[4] Goolagong's success in Australia's tennis circuit drew attention as she was the first Aboriginal to reach such a pinnacle, not necessarily because she was the best, but because unlike those before her, Goolagong was able to overcome the discrimination Australians reserved for Aboriginals. Goolagong's success helped educate her country and the world about Aboriginals. She dismissed many of the stereotypes, including the assumption that she was practically professional at the Aboriginal custom of throwing a boomerang, something she had actually never even tried.

By the time Goolagong was 16, she'd won all of the Australian national junior titles. In 1970, at age 18, she made her international debut. Her first match at Wimbledon quickly made her a fan favorite. She always "walked onto the court with a smile on her face," says Billie Jean King, "and it was apparent to all that, win or lose, tennis was a sheer joy for her."[5] By January 1971, Goolagong made it to the finals of the Australian Open, where she nearly beat fellow countrywoman Margaret Court. Court and Goolagong teamed up to win the women's doubles of the 1971 Australian Open. Goolagong soon revenged her singles loss by beating Court in the 1971 Wimbledon despite being seeded third. Goolagong completed her triumphant year with the French Open title as well.

The 19-year-old Wimbledon and French Open champion did not realize the significance of her success. In fact, Goolagong shied away from the attention because she never thought tennis was, nor wanted tennis to be, her life. Rather, Goolagong found joy in what her victories provided her with the ability to do: "The best present I ever bought anybody, a huge refrigerator, Mum's first . . . You should have seen her the afternoon the men from the appliance store in Griffith knocked on the door and began carrying in this fridge. I'm sure she enjoyed that more than my winning Wimbledon. And so did I."[6]

Goolagong took her game seriously but never allowed it to control her life or emotions. Even in the middle of a match, she often let anything but tennis roam her thoughts. She suffered a long mental lapse in one match while trying to remember the words to a song. Once they came to her, the "Goolagong fog" lifted and she seemed to flip a switch before going on to win the match easily after a loss appeared imminent. She joked in her memoir that she cried more over sappy movies than the loss of any championship game and was often distracted in a match if her opponents didn't push her to run after each ball. After her 1974 loss to Billie Jean King at the U.S. Open, Goolagong said, "It will probably take me until tomorrow to forget it,"[7] as if that was an unusually long time to dwell on a huge tournament loss.

Perhaps Goolagong wasn't gravely fazed by her losses because they were so greatly outnumbered by wins (704-165 career). Goolagong won the Australian Open in 1974 and 1975 before marrying British tennis player Roger Cawley. At 25 and pregnant, she gladly put tennis aside to welcome her new role of motherhood. She continued to compete until she was four months along and then continued playing recreationally until she was seven months pregnant. Her eldest daughter, Kelly, was born in 1977 and Goolagong had no trouble returning to professional tennis several months later. In 1980, she was the Wimbledon Champion again and was the first mother to achieve such a feat since Dorothea Lambert Chambers did the same in 1914. Goolagong had her son Morgan in 1981 but did not officially retire until 1983.

Goolagong's career ended with 43 singles titles and nine doubles titles, including 14 Grand Slam titles (seven in singles, six in women's doubles, and one in mixed doubles). The calmness of Evonne's play coincidently matched the translation of her surname

Goolagong which "is an Aboriginal word meaning tall trees by still water."[8] Though "still" is not a word often used to describe her, her calm and serene approach to tennis is perhaps what made her the successful player she is known as today.

Notes

1. Evonne Goolagong, *Evonne! On the Move* (New York: E. P. Dutton & Co., Inc., 1975), 48–49.

2. Ibid., 29.

3. Ibid., 38.

4. Ibid., 67.

5. Billie Jean King, *We Have Come a Long Way* (New York: McGraw-Hill, 1988), 131.

6. Goolagong, *Evonne!* 146.

7. Ibid., 25.

8. Ibid., 64.

Chris Evert

American Star of the Women's International Sports Hall of Fame

by Jessica Bartter

The line between sports stardom and Hollywood celebrity has been blurred in the past few decades, leading sports fans to revel in the drama behind the scenes as much as the score on the field. Sports fans love winners, but even more so, they love the story leading up to the competition, they love the rivalry, they love watching the underdog succeed, and, perhaps most of all, they love the juicy details of the athletes' personal lives. While the vast majority of us cannot relate to the perfection we see on the field or court, it is more likely that we were once the underdog or that a long-standing rivalry once brought out the best of us as competitors. In addition, it is the controversy in the locker room that is most relatable, bringing today's celebrity-athlete out of the untouchable realm and down to earth with the rest of us, despite their seven-figure salaries. "Years before Anna Kournikova or Serena Williams arrived, [Chris] Evert was women's sports first crossover star. *People* magazine covered her romances. Andy Warhol asked her to sit for a portrait. *Saturday Night Live* invited her to be the first female athlete to host the show."[1] Evert won stardom both on and off the tennis court, but the controversy surrounding the tennis-celeb Chris Evert's career was that there was no controversy.

Chris Evert first entered the stage as a cute, naïve, humble 15-year-old just along for the ride when she upset the world's No. 1 player, Margaret Court, in 1970. The high school sophomore was so unknown, the scoreboard mistakenly listed the amateur as "Everet," but it wasn't long before the tennis world learned her true name and bona fide talent. She quickly became a fan favorite, as there weren't many teenage stars on the tennis circuit. At the time, the rules prohibited an individual from turning professional before turning 18 years old. Evert's big upsets, subtle charm, and sweet demeanor won the hearts of tennis fans and sportswriters alike. She was nicknamed "Cinderella in Sneakers" by the *New York Times* and "Little Miss Sunshine" by New York's *Daily News*. But her name was not always synonymous with good press. As she stoically progressed, and made a habit of consistently winning, the fan favorite lost her appeal by playing with an almost unprecedented level head. The British sportswriters re-nicknamed her "Ice Princess" in 1972 because of her outwardly cold appearance during matches. Some fans felt betrayed to see so much seemingly easy success come to an American woman who appeared emotionless and unimpressed by her own victories. But the fans' assumptions could not have been further from the truth. Evert was filled with emotion on the inside, but externally portrayed the mental concentration that she had mastered, and that every competitor envied. Opponent Billie Jean King wrote, "Winning meant everything to Chris, the most competitive person I have known and one of the toughest competitors ever . . . unsmiling on the court . . . Chris had the ability to concentrate at all times. Her unwavering focus, combined with her great, natural coordination and her father's marvelous training, made Chris Evert one of the giants of the game."[2] While sportswriters everywhere praised Evert's talent but bashed her emotionless façade, it is surely words like these from a respected peer that meant the most.

As King mentioned, Evert stuck to the poised play she learned from her greatest coach, her father, Jimmy Evert. You could say it flowed through the veins of his five children, the bloodline of a tennis-playing family, but more important than passing on his talent was the ability of Jimmy to spend time with his children while juggling his life as a tennis pro. What better way to succeed as a professional and a father than to be able to share the joys of both? Especially when Jimmy often spent 12 hours a day, seven days a week on the tennis courts. To mixed answers depending on who you ask (Chris or Jimmy), it seems Jimmy Evert dragged his five-and-a-half-year-old daughter away from the swimming pool with friends and the weekend slumber parties to his tennis courts at the Holiday Park municipal facility, where he could pass along his honed racquet skills. Jimmy Evert had competed at Forest Hills (now known as the U.S. Open) five times and was ranked as high as 11th in the country in 1943. His stellar amateur circuit earned him a tennis scholarship to the University of Notre Dame and a Canadian National Championship. While the dream of a college scholarship for each of his children would have been nice, Jimmy was just happy to have them on the court. He could never have expected each of his five children would go on to reach at least the final round of a national championship as junior players.

Perhaps even further from Jimmy's mind was the two-handed backhand craze he and Chris would eventually start. As a young girl, Chris was not strong enough to handle the racket single-handedly on her backswing so her father and coach let her use two hands, hoping that as she grew in strength and size, she would outgrow this technique. To his initial displeasure, Chris managed to master the two-handed backhand and utilized it during her entire career. The success she had with her backhand led to tennis youth everywhere emulating her movements. Today, the two-handed backhand is a common weapon on the pro-tour, something almost nonexistent on the tour in the late 1960s and early 1970s.

After Evert's initial show-stopping victory over Margaret Court just weeks after Court had won the 1970 Wimbledon, Evert really made a name for herself as she landed in the living rooms of tennis fans nationwide during the 1971 U.S. Open, where the un-renowned teen made it to the semifinals before she fell to Billie Jean King, who would eventually become that year's champion. At the time, Evert was the youngest player ever to reach that stage at just 16 years, eight months, and 20 days old. Evert played in about five tournaments a year until she was 18 and could turn professional. Until then, her sparing tournament play allowed her to focus on graduating from high school and practicing tennis without burning out.

December 21, 1972 marked Chris Evert's 18th birthday and the day she declared her professional status. She might as well have declared her unstoppable status as well. Evert's skill first learned on the clay courts of Fort Lauderdale, Florida, led her to win 125 consecutive matches (24 tournaments) on clay between 1973 and 1979. This stretch still stands as the longest winning streak of any player on any single surface. After the single loss that broke the streak, Evert went on to win the next 72 matches on clay. Evert's records would be hard to list, but another great streak includes the 55 straight matches that she won in 1974 on all surfaces. That record stood for more than 10 years. It is not surprising that Evert was the first player to win 1,000 singles matches; she retired in 1989 with a total of 1,309 match victories (out of 1,454) in her career. It was obvious that Evert did not expect anything less than a victory from herself. She reached the finals or the semifinals in 52 of her 56 Grand Slams, 18 of which she took home the title (three Wimbledons, seven French Opens, two Australian Opens, and six U.S. Opens). Evert's Grand Slam total remains the third best in professional tennis history.

There is a widely-believed premise that good news never makes the news. Because sports fans gravitate toward the controversy, sportswriters are forced to seek the drama off the court, or in some cases, invent the controversy on their own. Chris Evert experienced this firsthand as she repeatedly faced Martina Navratilova. Sportswriters were desperate to paint the picture of an evil rivalry but the truth was far from ill will of either competitor. In fact, Evert and Navratilova could often be found in the locker room after a finals match where the winner would be consoling the crying loser with an arm around her shoulders. It was not a coach or a mother doing the consoling, but it was the very person who had just beat them, hardly a sign of hatred between the two women. The only debate was around who would be victorious as the winner and the loser seemed endlessly interchangeable. Their early meetings went favorably to Evert, who was 20-5 in their first 25 meetings. But with Evert in mind, Navratilova changed her training regiment and began to gain more W's against her. With Navratilova's 1984 Wimbledon win over Evert, their draw was a clean 30-30.[3] The latter 20 match-ups went 13-7 to the defected-Czechoslovakian. Their final tally from 1973 to 1988 was 43-37, with Navratilova slightly edging out Evert. Most important, though, was the friendship they groomed along the way. Both competitors credit each other for their lengthy careers, agreeing it was the other who gave them the strength and motivation to keep training and competing. Navratilova and Evert even shared the same side of the net at times to compete together as a doubles team. The duo produced doubles championships in 1975 and 1976 at the French Open and Wimbledon, respectively. The friendship/rivalry produced such extensive hype and intrigue that a book was published specifically about the two women 16 years after Evert's retirement. In it, author Johnette Howard best describes their relationship:

> They were two people who fervently wanted the same thing, found the other blocking the way, and ultimately forgave each other for it. They were bound by their athletic superiority. They were operating so far above everyone else on tour, needing to fear only each other, and they realized that

they were the only two people who really, truly understood what the other was going through.[4]

Despite exchanging the No. 1 ranking 17 times, there was no one on tour who the other would rather cede it to.

Before her 1989 retirement, Evert spent seven years of her two-decade-spanning career ranked No. 1 and remains there in the hearts and memories of many fans. Tennis prodigies seek Chris Evert's advice at the Evert Academy in Boca Raton, Florida, where she instructs. She offers tips about their forehand, one- or two-handed backswing, drop shot and lob, but most important offers the secret of her success; "the mental side was my strength . . . I was a really good athlete, but I wasn't a great athlete."[5] While each of her competitors would almost certainly agree with her undeniable mental prowess, we would be hard pressed to find anyone who would agree that she wasn't a great athlete, especially seeing as how she practically beat them all!

Note

1. Johnette Howard, *The Rivals* (New York: Broadway Books, 2005), 4.

2. Billie Jean King, *We Have Come A Long Way* (New York: McGraw-Hill, 1988), 135.

3. Howard, *The Rivals*, 6.

4. Ibid., 9.

5. *The Oprah Winfrey Show*, April 8, 2008.

Martina Navratilova

International Star of the Women's International Sports Hall of Fame

by Horacio Ruiz

I was an intern at the 2006 NASDAQ-100 Open in Key Biscayne, Florida, where I was taking a short cut to the concession stands for lunch. As I walked by the player drop-off and pick-up, I passed right by Martina Navratilova for the first and only time in my life, where she was waiting to be picked up. She was sitting on a bench talking to a group of guys standing around her. She looked relaxed and young even as she was only a few months away from turning fifty. A big part of me wanted to stop and introduce myself to just say hello because there were a number of players I saw that week, all of them much younger, but not one of them was as striking or as fit as Navratilova.

When I was as young as nine years old, my father told me about Navratilova and the other great tennis players he grew up watching and reading about. To me, those players were just images of the past on the television—characters in a different dimension. Every week, I was allowed to check out two books from my elementary school library. One time I decided to read about Navratilova and to see her in the pictures in the book. To see her at the NASDAQ was a validation of my childhood sports fandom. The legend was only a few feet away from me, and in that moment, the legend had become real.

Many believe Navratilova is the greatest women's tennis player ever. Billie Jean King, one of the greatest, said of Navratilova, "She's the greatest singles, doubles and mixed doubles player who's ever lived."[1] Navratilova made her first mark as a singles player in 1978 when she captured the Wimbledon title, the first of a record nine Wimbledon singles titles. All told, Navratilova won eighteen Grand Slam singles titles, an all-time record thirty-one Grand Slam women's doubles titles, and 10 Grand Slam mixed doubles titles.

In a 1973 match in Akron, Ohio, Navratilova caught the attention of Chris Evert, another tennis great with whom she would begin a tremendous rivalry. "She was overweight, but eager and gifted," Evert remembered. "It was a close match. Even though I'd never heard of her, and couldn't pronounce or spell her name, I could tell she'd be trouble. Especially if she got in shape."[2]

Navratilova defected from the former communist Czechoslovakia shortly before her 19th birthday in 1975. At the time, it was strictly a tennis decision. Navratilova felt as if the government in Czechoslovakia was trying to stifle her tennis career. The year before she defected, the government demanded that she return home from a tennis tournament in Amelia Island off the coast of Florida. Shortly after that incident, she defected at the 1975 U.S. Open.

While setting up residency in the United States, the 5-foot-7 $1/2$-inch Navratilova struggled with her weight, getting up to 167 pounds. But beginning in the 1980s Navratilova concentrated on her fitness, and as Evert had predicted she was trouble for the rest of the field, becoming the most dominant tennis player of the decade. With her dominance, Navratilova ushered in a new era in tennis. With her weight down to 145 pounds, her tightly wound physique, cut and muscular, was in sharp contrast to that of the women tennis players of her day, many of whom kept the curves and round shapes of their bodies associated with femininity.

"I'm not saying she's the first to do it," said Mary Carillo, a former player who is now a television commentator. "Margaret Court did it and Billie Jean King did it. But when Martina did it, everybody followed her lead. Martina soared so far beyond everybody else the only thing to do was to follow her lead. She did more than dominate the early 1980s. She set a whole new standard. She changed her diet and her fitness status. She made it scientific. She made it specific."[3]

The year 1983 would be a banner one for Navratilova. After dropping a match in the fourth round of the French Open, Navratilova went on to claim the other three Grand Slam titles that year, bringing her record to 86-1, a year-long winning percentage that has never been matched. She was named the Associated Press Female Athlete of the Year in 1983. Navratilova was named WTA Player of the Year seven times, including five times in the 1980s. She was named the Female Athlete of the Decade of the 1980s by the national Sports Review, Associated Press, and United Press International.

Navratilova's star shined brightest at Wimbledon, where she used the grass surface and her aggressive, quick-paced game to her advantage. She reached the Wimbledon singles final 12 times, including nine consecutive years from 1982 through 1990. Navratilova is tied with King for the all-time record in Wimbledon titles with 20. Her Wimbledon triumph in 1990 was her last Grand Slam singles title, but she made two more Grand Slam finals appearances, including her final appearance in 1994 at Wimbledon, when she made headlines by losing a hard-fought three-set match to Conchita Martinez, who was more than 15 years younger. Shortly after her bout with Martinez, Navratilova retired from full-time competition in singles play. At that point in her career, she was receiving standing ovations from adoring fans, both before and after her matches. The fans were cheering for her to stay, they were cheering for her to win, and they were cheering to thank her for all the masterful tennis.

The International Tennis Hall of Fame inducted Navratilova into its halls in 2000, the same year she came out of retirement to play doubles events and, on occasion, singles matches. In 2003, she won the mixed doubles events at the Australian Open and Wimbledon, making her the oldest Grand Slam champion ever at 46 years and eight months of age. She capped off her illustrious career with a win after capturing the mixed doubles event at the 2006 U.S. Open. Navratilova said her retirement in 2006 was absolutely final.

She finished as one of just three women to have accomplished a career Grand Slam by winning the singles, women's doubles, and mixed doubles at all four Grand Slam events. She holds the open era records for most singles titles with 167, and doubles titles with 177. She also recorded the longest winning streak in tennis history at 74 consecutive matches. Navratilova, Margaret Court, and Maureen Connolly Brinker share the record for the most consecutive Grand Slam singles titles with six. Navratilova reached 11 consecutive Grand Slam singles finals, second all-time to Steffi Graf's 13. In women's doubles, Navratilova and Pam Shriver won 109 consecutive matches and won all four Grand Slam titles in 1984. They also tied Louise Brough Clapp's and Margaret Osborne duPont's record of 20 Grand Slam women's doubles titles as a team.

Since her final retirement in 2006, Navratilova has been an ambassador not just for tennis but for a number of different communities to which she has emotional connections. Never one to shy away from her sexuality for fear of the public's criticism, Navratilova has been at the forefront of promoting the Rainbow Endowment and the National Center for Lesbian Rights. In 1999, she was ranked #19 on ESPN's Sports Century Top 50 Athletes. Navratilova remains in tennis as a commentator for both the Wimbledon and French Open tournaments, and she has also worked in the art world through her Art Grand Slam project with fellow tennis player Juraj Kralik. In 2007, Navratilova accepted the role of AARP's Health and Fitness Ambassador. In April 2008, she was able to get her Czech citizenship back and gained dual citizenship with the United States. Thinking back to when I saw Navratilova, I wish I could have stopped and said "hi" to her to at least make myself, and only in my mind, a part of her growing legend.

Notes

1. DeSimone, Bonnie. 2006. Act II of Navratilova's career ends with a win. ESPN.com. http://sports.espn.go.com/sports/tennis/usopen06/news/story?id=2578105 (accessed December 2, 2008).

2. International Tennis Hall of Fame, "Martina Navratilova," http://www.tennis fame.com/famer.aspx?pgID=867&hof_id=219 (accessed December 2, 2008).

3. Answers.com, "Who 2 Biography: Martina Navratilova, tennis player," http://www.answers.com/topic/martina-navratilova (accessed December 3, 2008).

Venus and Serena Williams

Future Hall of Famers

by Jessica Bartter

In 1973, seven and eight years before Venus or Serena Williams were born, Bobby Riggs, the 1939 Wimbledon champion, claimed that the women's tennis game was so inferior to that of the men's that he, at 55 years old, could beat any of the current top female players. I imagine Venus and Serena would have gladly accepted Riggs's challenge, but it was before their time, so another tennis-great, Billie Jean King, accepted his offer. In front of more than 30,000 spectators in the Houston Astrodome on September 20, 1973, King made Riggs eat his words as she diligently laid to rest his sexist claim with three-straight set victories, 6-4, 6-3, and 6-3. Perhaps Riggs cannot bear all the blame for his chauvinistic attitude, as it seemed to be the product of the times. In 1972, the Association of Tennis Professionals (ATP) was established. Though the name doesn't suggest any exclusion, its purpose was to protect the best interests of male professional tennis players. Perhaps as an afterthought or perhaps thanks to Billie Jean King's "Battle of the Sexes" victory, the Women's Tennis Association (WTA) was born a year later in 1973. Women in general have faced such inequalities and underestimations, as well as this afterthought mentality for centuries.

Nonetheless, the year 2000 marked a new millennium and this new century would suggest the tables have turned, at least in tennis. Even John McEnroe, who was known for his criticism of the women's game, among other things, acknowledged in 2000 that "you can't deny it . . . right now the women have the better product." A *USA Today* poll supported McEnroe's claim when it published the fact that 75 percent of tennis fans preferred the women's game to that of the men's.[1] Thanks in part to the powerful, dominant strength and style of the Williams sisters, tennis fans have not only expanded in quantity, but have also expanded in age, race, creed, and economic status.

Venus and Serena Williams helped bring tennis out of the country clubs and into the inner cities with the great talent they developed that was first learned on the old, rundown courts of Compton, a city in Los Angeles known for its gang violence and poor neighbor-hoods. One day while practicing around the potholes and raggedy nets of the Compton municipal courts, Venus and Serena found them-selves in between two rival gangs and narrowly escaped the ex-changed gunfire.[2] Gunfire was not uncommon at night either, but luckily the sisters shared a room and therefore a safety in each other's presence. Jon Wertheim, author of *Venus Envy*, shared their typical conversation after having "listened nightly to an urban symphony of car horns, screams, sirens and the occasional rat-a-tat of gunfire":

> Venus, Serena would whisper.
> What is it, Serena?
> Don't go to sleep before me.
> I'm tired, Serena.
> Well, I'm scared.
> Venus would sigh, but she would force herself to stay awake until Serena had drifted off. "Same thing every night," Venus recalls, shaking her head. "That was Serena, getting her way." ("My responsibility in life is to be the annoying little sister and I've always taken that responsibility seriously," re-sponds Serena with a laugh.)[3]

Their candor is well established and long evolved. Their mother, Oracene Williams, once said, "They love each other so much they're almost like a husband and a wife."[4] Oracene had long ago pulled them aside and taught them that while matches with any other oppo-nents could be treated as war, it was just a game when played among sisters.[5] This lesson remains with them.

Compton's dangerous gunfire and sleepless nights pushed their father, Richard Williams, to coach them to success and off the streets of Los Angeles. Richard had first recognized the lucrative business that tennis was, even for women, after he witnessed Virginia Ruzici win tens of thousands of dollars after a fourth-round defeat in the late 1970s. Thus, Richard put each of his two youngest daughters on the court when they were just four or five years old. Though not fa-miliar with the game himself, Richard bought a book about tennis and shouted instructions from the sidelines to his daughters who played with used balls they had found since they could not afford new ones.[6] At times he even made them return balls with a slim base-ball bat rather than the large face of a racket.[7]

After their skill showed true potential, the Williams family relocated to Florida, where Venus and Serena accepted scholarships to the Rick Macci Tennis Academy, though father/coach Richard never stepped too far from the court. When Venus was nine and Serena was eight, they entered their first tournament, where they met each other in the finals. Age presided in this tournament and Venus was victorious in their first of what would become many head-to-head match-ups. They continued to enter junior tournaments and continued to be victorious. However, it was only a couple of years before Richard pulled them off the junior circuit to refocus his daughters' attention on their educations. Both straight-A students, they excelled in the classroom enough for Richard to believe they could return their attention to tennis a few years later.

At age 14, Venus turned pro, playing in tournaments sparingly, but really made a name for herself in 1997, when she joined the tour more regularly at age 17 and reached the finals of the U.S. Open.

In 1995, a year after Venus, also at the age of 14, Serena joined the pro-circuit tour. She entered the 1999 U.S. Open seeded seventh. She went on to upset the World No. 4 Monica Seles, the World No. 2 Lindsay Davenport, and the World No. 1 Martina Hingis to take the U.S. Open title. She became the first Williams sister and the second African-American woman to ever win a Grand Slam event (French Open, Australian Open, U.S. Open, and Wimbledon). Althea Gibson was the first African-American Grand Slam Champion when she won the French Open in 1956.

After early rumors of her retirement and despite battling tendonitis in her wrists that sidelined her for four months, 2000 turned out to be a great year for Venus, as she defeated World No. 1 Hingis in the quarterfinals, Serena in the semifinals, and defending champion Lindsay Davenport in the finals to win her first Grand Slam title at Wimbledon. The Williams duo joined forces to win the Wimbledon doubles title that year as well, after already notching doubles victories together at the French and U.S. Opens in 1999. Venus faced and conquered the still-World No. 1 Hingis in the semifinals and the World No. 2 Davenport in the 2000 U.S. Open to win her second Grand Slam singles title. At the 2000 Olympics, the pair teamed to represent the United States and earned gold medals in the doubles at Sydney. Venus also took home the coveted gold medal in the singles. To cap it off, 2000 marked Venus's $40 million endorsement deal with Reebok that was the largest ever awarded to a female athlete (until Serena signed a $60 million deal with Nike in 2003). Dad/ Coach Richard had tremendous foresight in identifying tennis as a lucrative means to succeed financially and rise above the struggles of living in a rough neighborhood.

Venus successfully defended her Wimbledon and U.S. Open titles in 2001. She won three more Wimbledon championships in 2005, 2007, and 2008. While it appears Wimbledon has been good to her, Venus has criticized tournament officials and those of the French Open for paying its female competitors less than their male counterparts. After unsuccessfully pleading with the tournament officials in 2005, she went public with an essay in *The Times* on June 26, 2006, in which she stated, "Wimbledon has sent me a message: I'm only a second-class champion: The time has come for it to do the right thing: pay men and women equal prize money," a struggle that still exists more than 30 years after Billie Jean King's victory over Bobby Riggs.[8]

Serena's Grand Slam title total currently matches her big sister's seven titles. Though she ran dry for a couple of years after her 1999 U.S. Open win, 2002 brought Serena three Grand Slam titles,

Venus Williams celebrating her 2008 Wimbledon Championship.

winning the French Open (after defeating her sister in the finals), Wimbledon, and the U.S. Open again. In 2003, she defended her Wimbledon title and beat her sister Venus in the finals of the Australian Open. Serena earned Australian Open titles in 2005 and 2007 as well. In September 2008, Serena beat Venus in the quarterfinals and went on to win the U.S. Open, which helped her regain a world ranking of No. 1 as of this writing.

The WTA pro tour consists of more than 50 tournaments year round, including the four Grand Slam events. As of September 2008, Venus had 37 WTA titles and her career singles record was 503-119 (106-20 in doubles play) and she was ranked eighth in the world. Similarly, Serena had 32 WTA wins and her career singles record was 398-83 (110-17 in doubles play) with a world ranking of No. 1. Despite two early upsets in single play at the 2008 Beijing Olympics, the Williams sisters brought home the doubles' gold medal. Afterward, in response to questions about their poor singles play, Serena said, "I'd much rather win with Venus than without her."[9] Though their professional tennis dominance is undeniable with no signs of slowing down, both Venus and Serena recognize that tennis will not dominate the rest of their lives.

Venus has already pursued her interests in fashion, designing a line of clothing available at any budget called EleVen. At its launch in November 2007, it was the largest line of clothing launched by a female athlete. Venus named the line EleVen so that every woman can feel like an 11 on a scale of 1 to 10. Venus serves as a global ambassador for the United Nations Educational, Scientific, and Cultural Organization (UNESCO). She donates all of the proceeds from a specially designed t-shirt in her EleVen collection to UNESCO. Venus also designs a line of women's leather apparel for Wilson's Leather. Venus's creativity extends beyond fashion with her interior design company called V Starr Interiors. In addition to her fashion and interior design interests, after tennis she would like to further pursue choreography and music production.

In June 2004, Serena launched her own line of clothing, Aneres. Aneres is designed for "the independent woman who works, enjoys life, and is at the prime of her life . . . She chooses to wear Aneres because Aneres is in style yet follows its own trend. Aneres reflects Serena's style at its best; complex simplicity."[10] In addition to fashion, Serena is interested in acting.

Among the popular fan favorites, Venus and Serena Williams have often experienced the peaks and valleys of support and criticism drawn from their occasional lackluster appearances, seemingly timely injuries, and their contentiously outspoken father and coach who appears to appreciate the spotlight more than either of his daughters desire. But, as many athletes would argue, the wins column is the most important and the only aspect worthy of criticism, leaving naysayers with little argument. Talent is not something anyone can attack when it comes to the Williams sisters, who have traded world rankings of No. 1 and No. 2, most often remaining in the top 10 for the past 10 years. Known for their strong returns and serves as well as their strong attitudes and opinions, there is no doubt both Venus and Serena will continue to make names for themselves, both in and out of tennis. The story of Venus and Serena Williams may just be beginning. The first act has been quite enjoyable to watch and may certainly be hard to follow. But I'd bet there are many more acts to come and many more fans eager at the sidelines to see what they can achieve next.

Notes

1. John Wertheim, *Venus Envy* (New York: HarperCollins, 2001), 4.

2. "Venus and Serena Williams: Such Devoted Sisters," *The Scotsman*, July 6, 2002.

3. Wertheim, *Venus Envy*, 173–74.

4. Ibid., 175.

5. "Venus and Serena Williams: Such Devoted Sisters."

6. "Venus and Serena Williams: Queens of Women's Tennis," *Westside Gazette*, February 17, 2005.

7. "Venus and Serena Williams: Such Devoted Sisters."

8. Venus Williams, "Wimbledon has sent me a message: I'm only a second-class champion," *The Times*, June 26, 2006.

9. Serena Williams, *Access Hollywood* on NBC, August 18, 2008.

10. Aneres, "Mission," http://www.aneresdesigns.com/aneres.html (accessed April 3, 2008).

4

GOING THE DISTANCE IN GOLF: WOMEN DRIVE THE FAIRWAYS

Introduction by Richard Lapchick

When most people think of women as athletes, golf would be one of the first sports that come to mind. Few know the role of a woman in the sport going back five centuries. Mary Queen of Scots reportedly commissioned the building of St. Andrews Golf Course in 1552 and is thought to be the first woman to play golf, thus becoming the sport's first trailblazer. Ironically, women were not allowed to play at St. Andrews for nearly 400 years after it was built, as golf continued to be an exclusive sport for white men.

In 1893, the British Ladies Golf Union sponsored the first of a long line of British Ladies' Championships. In 1895, the Australian Women's National Golf Championship was launched.

The United States Golf Association held the first national women's amateur championship tournament in 1895. The Rhode Island Women's Golf Association was formed in 1914. Elizabeth Gordan won the first four titles starting in 1916, but women golfers were not getting much attention until Babe Didrikson Zaharias put a spotlight on the sport in the 1930s.

The first Curtis Cup Match was staged in May 1932 at England's Wentworth Golf Club and drew 15,000 spectators. The U.S. team narrowly beat the British team. The Curtis Cup match was then held every two years, alternating between the United States and England. The 2008 Curtis Cup was won by the team from the United States for the sixth consecutive win for the Americans.

The women played the Cup on the Old Course at St. Andrews, where they had been banned for so many centuries. The modern-day series is between a team from the United States and one representing England, Scotland, Northern Ireland, Ireland, and Wales. The last Great Britain & Ireland (GB&I) win came in 1996.

However, except for Didrikson Zaharias and the Curtis Cup every other year, female golfers were virtually unnoticed by the mainstream public or media. That began to change after World War II.

Patty Berg won the first U.S. Women's Open in 1946. The Ladies Professional Golf Association (LPGA) was formed in 1950 with stars like Berg, Didrikson Zaharias, and Louise Suggs.

Kathy Whitworth still holds the all-time tour mark with 88 career wins, and she won eight Player of the Year awards between 1966 and 1973.

Nancy Lopez burst onto the scene in 1978 when she won both the Rookie of the Year and Player of the Year honors. Her personal popularity further popularized the game itself.

More recently, women from other countries have dominated the women's tour. Australian Karrie Webb, Sweden's Annika Sorenstam, Se Ri Pak and dozens of Asian golfers, and Mexican Lorena Ochoa have become the stars of the professional ranks. In the major 2008 championships, Ochoa won the Kraft Nabisco, Chinese golfer Yani Tseng won the LPGA Championship, and South Koreans Inbee Park and Ji-Yai Shin won the U.S. and British Opens, respectively. Since 2000, Americans Julie Inkster, Cristie Kerr, Morgan Pressel, Meg Mallon, Hilary Lunke, and Sherri Steinhauer have won a total of only six of the 36 majors played. Between 1990 and 1995, Americans won 21 of the 24 majors played.

Of all these great women golfers, we have selected as our trailblazers Glenna Collett-Vare, Louise Suggs, Patty Berg, Betty Jameson, Mickey Wright, Carol Mann, Kathy Whitworth, JoAnne Carner, Nancy Lopez, and Annika Sorenstam.

Glenna Collett Vare was called the female Bobby Jones and was considered the greatest female golfer of her time. She played when there was no LPGA. Vare won a record six U.S. Women's Amateur Championships, two Canadian Women's Amateurs, and a French Women's Amateur. In 1924, Collett won 59 out of 60 matches. She was driving 300 yards off the tee in the 1920s. Glenna Collett Vare was a member of the American team that won the first Curtis Cup played at the Wentworth Golf Club in England in 1932 and was the team captain and player in 1934, 1936, 1938, and 1948. She ended her competitive golf career at the age of 56 with a victory at the 1959 Rhode Island Women's Golf Association tournament after winning 49 championships. As stated elsewhere, the Vare Trophy was named after her for the woman with best scoring average on the tour.

Not only was Louise Suggs the lowest-scoring professional in the LPGA's very first event, she was the tour money leader that year, with a lower scoring average than Berg and less than half a percentage point higher scoring average than Didrikson Zaharias. She won the U.S. Women's Amateur and the British Women's Amateur in 1947 and 1948, respectively. She then capped off her amateur career by playing on the 1948 U.S. Curtis Cup team. Upon turning professional in 1948, she won 11 more major championships including an LPGA Championship in 1957, two U.S. Women's Opens (1949 and 1952), four Western Opens (1946, 1947, 1949, and 1953), and four Titleholders Championships (1946, 1954, 1956, and 1959). Today, the LPGA awards the tour's newest star with the "Louise Suggs Rolex Rookie of the Year Award."

Patty Berg was a founding member, the first president, and a leading player on the LPGA Tour during the 1940s, 1950s, and 1960s. She turned pro in 1940 after winning 29 amateur titles. Her 15 major title wins remains the all-time record for most major wins by a female golfer. Berg won the U.S. Women's Open in 1946; the Western Open in 1941, 1943, 1948, 1951, 1955, 1957, and 1958; and the Titleholders in 1937, 1938, 1939, 1948, 1953, 1955, and 1957.

She was voted the AP Woman Athlete of the Year in 1938, 1942, and 1955. She won 60 LPGA events. Since 1979, the LPGA has given the Patty Berg Award to an individual who "exemplifies diplomacy, sportsmanship, goodwill, and contributions to the game of golf."

While Betty Jameson's 13 tour victories do not compare with many of the win totals of her fellow golfers in this book, she was one of the most influential women in golf history. Her major championships include back-to-back titles in the U.S. Women's Amateur in 1939 and 1940. As a professional, she went on to win two Western Opens (1942 and 1954), as well as the 1947 U.S. Women's Open, making her one of only six women to ever win both the U.S. Women's Open and U.S. Women's Amateur championships. Jameson was the first woman golfer to score under the 300-stroke mark in a

72-hole event when she set the women's scoring bar at 295 during the event in the 1947 U.S. Open. Jameson was one of the 13 women who co-founded the LPGA in 1950. Her contributions to the organization include coming up with the idea to annually award the woman golfer with the lowest scoring average on tour with the Vare Trophy, named in honor of Jameson's idol, Glenna Collett Vare.

Mickey Wright won at least one tournament on the LPGA tour each of the first 14 years she competed from 1956 to 1969. That 14-year winning streak is second to only Kathy Whitworth in LPGA history. Wright was also second to Whitworth with 82 victories. And she retired young at the age of 35. She also won 13 major championships, including a record four U.S. Women's Opens (1958, 1959, 1961, and 1964), four LPGA Championships (1958, 1960, 1961, and 1964), three Western Opens (1962, 1963, and 1966), and two Titleholders Championships (1961 and 1962).

During her 22-year-long career, Carol Mann amassed 38 tournament wins, including the U.S. Women's Open championship in 1965. Mann was also the lowest average scorer taking home the Vare Trophy in 1968, as well as being the LPGA Tour money leader in 1969. Other highlights from her career include winning multiple tournaments in eight of her 22 years on Tour. She won 10 tournaments in 1968.

While Mann's achievements in the game are certainly admirable, her true legacy is as a powerful president of the LPGA and as an outspoken advocate for women in sports. The period of Mann's LPGA presidency was perhaps that of the most growth in the organization's history and brought in the "modern era" to the LPGA. She took strong stands on many women's issues in sport as well as taking on racial issues in golf over the Shoal Creek controversy and the exclusivity of golf courses.

What Kathy Whitworth lacked in major championships she made up for in statistics, earnings, and honors. She is a seven-time winner of the Vare Trophy (1965–67, 1969–72). She also had two different four-year streaks, 1965–68 and 1970–73, where she was the LPGA Tour money leader. She won seven LPGA Player of the Year honors, earning that distinction each year from 1966 to 1969 and 1971 to 1973. Her 85th tournament win made Whitworth the winningest golfer, male or female, of all time. She finished her career with 88 total victories.

JoAnne Carner became an absolute dominant force during her 14 years in the amateur ranks starting in 1956. Carner won a total of five U.S. Amateur Championships (1958, 1960, 1962, 1966, and 1968), trailing only the lifelong amateur Glenna Collett-Vare, who won six. Then in 1969, a year before turning professional, Carner won the Burdine's Invitational, and is still the last amateur to win an LPGA event.

As a pro, Carner claimed 43 victories, including the 1971 and 1976 U.S. Women's Opens. She also is a five-time winner of the Vare Trophy for being the tour's lowest average scorer. Her other achievements include being named the LPGA Tour Player of the Year in 1974, 1981, and 1982, and being the tour's money leader in 1974, 1982, and 1983. She was a four-time member of the U.S. Curtis Cup team and captained the 1994 U.S. Solheim Cup team. At age 64 in 2004, she became the oldest woman to make the cut at the Chick-fil-A Charity Championship.

Nancy Lopez burst into the professional spotlight in 1978 by placing second in the Women's Open and winning nine titles. That same year, Lopez became the first woman to be named Rookie of the Year and Player of the Year, and to win the Vare Trophy all in the same season. She experienced her career year in her first full season on the LPGA tour. She won two more Vare trophies in 1979 and 1985 and three more Player of the Year awards in 1979, 1985, and 1989.

Annika Sorenstam took the world of golf in her hands in her rookie year with three Top 10 finishes, including a tie for second at the 1994 Women's British Open. In her prime, she was as dominant on the women's tour as Tiger Woods was on the men's. Here are just some of her accomplishments over the next 14 years: 72 LPGA career victories, including 10 majors, eight Rolex Player of the Year awards, and six Vare Trophies. She is the only woman to have shot a 59 in competition and holds various all-time scoring records, including the lowest season scoring average: 68.7 in 2004. Sorenstam was the first player in LPGA history to cross the $20 million mark. In 2003, she was an obvious choice as the winner of the Patty Berg Award for her contributions to women's golf.

Whether American women will regain the top of the game is open to question as the tour is dominated by international players. What is obvious is that the game is getting better and better and is now a major global sports enterprise.

Glenna Collett-Vare

American Star of the Women's International Sports Hall of Fame

by Ryan Sleeper

You will not find the name Glenna Collett-Vare in the Ladies Professional Golf Association (LPGA) Hall of Fame, nor in the pages of books paying homage to the LPGA's greats. After all, she didn't win a single competition on tour. However, by all accounts, Collett-Vare was one of the greatest female golfers of all time. She certainly dominated women's golf during her time, prior to a professional tour for women. Her accomplishments and notoriety likely went a long way in opening the door for women to make money playing golf, but Collett-Vare certainly did not set out for this glory. She was simply playing for her love of the game.

It should be of no surprise then that she was often referred to as the "female Bobby Jones." Jones, whose career started slightly before, but mostly overlapped with Collett-Vare's, exemplified sportsmanship before he chose to retire from competition when he was just 28 years old. The magnitude of his sportsmanship can be summed up in one short story. At the 1925 U.S. Open at the Worcester Country Club, Jones called a two-stroke penalty on himself for accidentally moving his ball even though nobody else saw it happen. He ended up losing the prestigious tournament by just one stroke. When the press praised Jones after the match for his honesty, he replied, "You may as well praise a man for not robbing a bank."[1] The United States Golf Association's (USGA) sportsmanship award is named after him, and Collett-Vare fittingly won this award in 1965. Bobby Jones personally mentioned that "aside from her skill with her clubs, Miss Collett typified all that the word 'sportsmanship' stands for."[2]

Another moniker Collett-Vare earned was "Queen of American Golf." Although she surely must have preferred a less royal nickname, her accomplishments in golf undoubtedly garnered such an honorable handle. She won six U.S. Women's Amateur titles in 1922, 1925, 1928, 1929, 1930, and 1935. She also participated in several

U.S. Curtis Cup teams. The Curtis Cup is an international competition held biennially that pits teams from the United States, England, Ireland, Northern Ireland, Scotland, and Wales. Collett-Vare actually played a hand in starting the famous event. In 1930, she took a team of American golfers with her to compete against British teams in unofficial matches. The following year, the British Ladies Golf Union and the USGA agreed to make these regular match-ups. She was a member of the first Curtis Cup team in 1932 as well as the 1938 squad, a player-captain in the 1934 and 1936 contests, and a captain of the 1948 and 1950 players. She also earned a place in the World Golf Hall of Fame.

Beyond the achievements and honors and in case any doubt remains, Collett-Vare simply dominated golf around the world in her day. "The women amateurs felt that they had a chance to win a tournament only when Collett-Vare did not play."[3] In addition to her U.S. titles, she also won two Canadian Women's Amateurs and one French Women's Amateur. Her most dominant year came in 1924, when she won a remarkable 59 of 60 matches in which she competed. Perhaps the only thing more extraordinary than that accomplishment is the fact that the only event she lost was the 1924 U.S. Women's Amateur and how she lost it. Despite setting a record in the qualifying round, Collett-Vare lost the tournament when Mary K. Browne's ball caromed off Collett-Vare's and fell into the cup on the 19th hole! The only real gap on Collett-Vare's golfing resume was a victory in the British Women's Amateur, where she was twice the runner-up to her rival Joyce Wethered in 1929 and 1930. Despite this one disappointment, Collett-Vare's dominance in golf is undeniable and her mark on golf has been honored since 1953, when the LPGA began awarding the Vare Trophy to the golfer with the lowest scoring average in tournament play each year.

Glenna Collett was born in New Haven, Connecticut, on June 20, 1903. However, when she was six years old, she and her family moved to Providence, Rhode Island, where they remained during her transformation into a golfing legend. While there was no golfing tradition in her family, like many star players, there is typically some form of athletics in their blood, and Collett-Vare was no exception. Her father was a great bowler and a famous bicyclist, having won the national amateur championship in 1899. Collett-Vare possessed an interest in sports from a very young age, swimming and diving when she was nine and driving automobiles when she was 10. However, she was most fond of the game of baseball, which she played with her brother Ned and his team on a local field until she was 14, when her mother suggested she pick up a more feminine game. So she tried her hand at tennis and said she would have played indefinitely had she not accompanied her father out to the Metacomet Golf Club one afternoon.[4] "As I came off the course after the first game, my destiny was settled. I would become a golfer."[5] She would later comment about her fate: "There was little or no choice in the matter, like many others who are intensely interested in the sport, the love of competition and the outdoors was in my blood. My temperament, natural ability, environment, and inclination pointed to such a hobby and all I had to do was 'follow through.' "[6] By the time Collett-Vare was 18 years old, at 5 feet, 6 inches and 128 pounds, her drive had been measured at 307 yards. This distance was 36 yards longer than Babe Ruth's longest drive and the farthest ever recorded for a woman golfer. She would win her first U.S. Women's Amateur a year later at the age of 19 and the rest is women's golf history.

An intensely focused golfer and intelligent woman, Glenna Collett-Vare was well aware of not just the sports history, but the world history she was a part of, writing in one of two books she published in the 1920s, *Ladies in the Rough* (1928):

> It was my happy fortune to come on the athletic scene at a most significant time—a period when women were breaking through the barriers in all fields of endeavor, from politics to swimming the English Channel, or flying across the Atlantic. American women in the first quarter of the twentieth century have won two rights: the right of exercising the suffrage and the right of participating in sport. The second of these seems to be as important as the first for the happiness and welfare of women themselves and of the world at large.[7]

No, you will not find Glenna Collett-Vare's name in the LPGA Hall of Fame, but you will still see her impact on sports and society nearly a century after she began playing.

Notes

1. John Boyette, August.com, "Winning by the Book," posted April 6, 2008, http://www.augusta.com/stories/040608/mas_193309.shtml (accessed May 25, 2008).

2. Brent Kelley, About.com: Golf, "Biography of Golfer Glenna Collett Vare," http://golf.about.com/od/golferswomen/p/glennacollett.htm (accessed May 23, 2008).

3. Terri Leonard, In the Women's Clubhouse: *The Greatest Women Golfers in Their Own Words* (Chicago: Contemporary Books, 2000). 71.

4. Ibid., 72.

5. Ibid,. 73.

6. Ibid., 72.

7. Ibid., 75.

Louise Suggs

American Star of the Women's International Sports Hall of Fame

by Ryan Sleeper

Louise Suggs won a total of $3,000 in prize money during her rookie season in 1950. A year before turning professional she predicted, "I believe I may have arrived 20 years too soon, but the day is dawning for women golfers."[1] Twenty years later, Rookie of the Year, JoAnne Carner collected nearly $15,000 in prize money—five times that of her legendary predecessor. Beyond the ever-increasing growth of tournament purses from which she could have benefited, Suggs brought a business-like personality to the links well ahead of her time. When she originally co-founded the Ladies Professional Golf Association (LPGA) nearly 60 years ago, Louise Suggs could not have prophesied the level of corporate partnership the game has today or that the 2007 money leader would collect $4,364,994.

This prediction probably would have been even harder for Suggs to imagine while she was competing against Babe Zaharias, a colleague with an opposite personality from herself, in what has been described as a flamboyant, sometimes sideshow atmosphere during the tour's early years.[2] The two had a fierce rivalry, and were often matched with Patty Berg, who brought her own, more comedic, personality to the game. Suggs described those matches "like watching three cats fighting over a plate of fish."[3] Zaharias, who by many accounts is the greatest athlete of all time, male or female, attracted great media attention and figured out this interest could reap financial rewards. Suggs felt that Zaharias's boisterous personality unfairly overshadowed the accomplishments of herself and other golfers on tour. After all, Suggs frequently defeated the much more well-known Berg and Zaharias. For evidence of Suggs's belonging in the "Big Three," you need not look any further than the inaugural year of the LPGA. Not only was Suggs the lowest-scoring professional in the LPGA's very first event, she was the tour money leader that year, with a lower scoring average than Berg and less than half a percentage point higher scoring average than Zaharias.[4]

In her true stoic fashion, Suggs never commented publicly on her feelings toward Zaharias and the environment on the tour in their day, but it is evident that she struggled to find a place for her personality in the early days of the LPGA. For taking the high road throughout her career, Suggs was awarded the Bob Jones Award in 2007, which recognizes distinguished sportsmanship in the game of golf.

Due to their shared character, Suggs was often referred to as the "Ben Hogan" of women's golf. Ben Hogan, another of the greatest golfers in history, was known internationally as the "ice man" for his emotionless demeanor on the course. Suggs and Hogan also shared an uncanny ball-striking ability. This talent prompted comedian Bob Hope, himself a very competent golfer, to give her the nickname "Miss Sluggs."[5]

Mae Louise Suggs was born September 7, 1923, in Lithia Springs, Georgia, just outside of Atlanta. Like many star athletes who are often born with competition in their blood, Suggs was no exception. Her father, Johnny Suggs, was a star pitcher for the Atlanta Crackers. The Crackers, a Class AA Southern Association minor league affiliate, won more games than any other team in the history of the association, and were Atlanta's home team until the Braves moved in from Milwaukee in 1966. Johnny gave up his spot on the team and joined the front office after meeting and marrying the owner's daughter. Plans for the young couple changed drastically when Johnny lost his job after a fire destroyed the all-wood stadium and offices on September 7, 1923, the same day Suggs was born.

After moving on from baseball, the family owned and operated a golf course where Suggs began learning the game. "At age ten, during the height of the Depression, the young Suggs found that golf was one of the few forms of entertainment easily available to her."[6] She would grow into one of the most accomplished golfers, male or female, the world has ever seen, and despite her quiet demeanor, her opinions about women playing golf are as strong as her golf game. In an excerpt from her 1953 book, *Golf for Women*, Suggs writes:

> Golf has been a part of my life for twenty-six years, so it's not easy for me to be objective about it. By and large, it's been a good life, too, so the prejudices show up more than they might with someone else. But when it comes to this fascinating and frustrating game, there are a few convictions I hold that are based on observation and are not to be classified as prejudices.

One of these convictions has to do with women and golf. There's been far too much of this nonsense, so far as I'm concerned, about women being inferior on the golf course, the people who make this claim usually basing their argument on the female's physical structure. To them I say, "If a woman can walk, she can play golf!"[7]

Not only did Suggs play golf, she dominated the game. As an amateur, she won both the U.S. Women's Amateur and the British Women's Amateur in 1947 and 1948, respectively. She capped off her amateur career by playing on the 1948 U.S. Curtis Cup team. The Curtis Cup is an international competition held biennially that pitted teams from the United States, England, Ireland, Northern Ireland, Scotland, and Wales. Upon turning professional in 1948, she won 11 more major championships, including an LPGA Championship in 1957, two U.S. Women's Opens (1949 and 1952), four Western Opens (1946, 1947, 1949, and 1953), and four Titleholders Championships (1946, 1954, 1956, and 1959).

Her honors also include two years as the tour's money leader (1953 and 1960) and a Vare trophy in 1953 for being the tour's scoring leader, culminating in spots in the Georgia Athletic, LPGA Teaching and Club Professional, and the World Golf Halls of Fame. To truly bring her victories, awards, and honors full circle, each year the LPGA awards the tour's newest young star with the "Louise Suggs Rolex Rookie of the Year Award." Suggs must surely be proud that the organization she co-founded warrants such corporate sponsorship. Women's golf has come a tremendously long way since Louise Suggs so accurately predicted the day was dawning for women in professional golf in 1949.

Notes

1. Jackie Williams, *Playing from the Rough: The Women of the LPGA Hall of Fame* (Las Vegas: Women of Diversity Productions, 2000), 59.

2. Ibid., 60.

3. Terri Leonard, *In the Women's Clubhouse: The Greatest Women Golfers in Their Own Words* (Chicago: Contemporary Books, 2000), 145.

4. Williams, *Playing from the Rough*, 63.

5. Brent Kelley, About.com: Golf, "Biography of Golfer Louise Suggs," http://golf.about.com/od/golferswomen/p/louise_suggs.htm (accessed May 23, 2008).

6. Williams, *Playing from the Rough*, 61.

7. Leonard, *In the Women's Clubhouse*, 146.

Patricia "Patty" Berg

American Star of the Women's International Sports Hall of Fame

by Ryan Sleeper

"I'm very happy I gave up football, or I wouldn't be here tonight," said Patty "Dynamite" Berg upon her inception into the Ladies Professional Golf Association (LPGA) Hall of Fame in 1951.[1] Indeed, thousands of women's golf fans around the world should be happy she gave up football, and perhaps owe some gratitude to her father, who insisted she stop playing contact sports with growing boys when she became a teenager. After all, some have said that Berg introduced golf to more women than any other player. In recognition of this sentiment, the LPGA's Patty Berg Award was established in 1978, and continues to be awarded annually to "the lady golfer who has made the greatest contribution to women's golf during the year." This award has been given to the likes of Kathy Whitworth, Louise Suggs, and, most recently, Annika Sorenstam. All recipients of the Patty Berg Award have done an honorable job of carrying on her legacy of not only growing women's golf, but doing so in a classy way. Berg often encouraged people to "shake a hand, and make a friend."[2]

Patty Berg was born February 13, 1918, in Minneapolis, Minnesota, where she would later attend the University of Minnesota before becoming a golf legend. She grew up a tomboy with an interest in sports and was a very talented track and field athlete as well as a speed skater; in fact, she was the runner-up in speed skating in the 1933 national girls' championships. Another sport she enjoyed playing was football. As a youngster, she played quarterback for a local all-boys team, the 50th Street Tigers, where she shared snaps with the eventual, legendary coach of the Oklahoma Sooners, Bud Wilkinson. Also, as a guard and quarterback just years after his time with the Tigers, Wilkinson would lead Berg's alma mater, the Minnesota Golden Gophers, to three consecutive national football titles from 1934 to 1936. Holding her own with such talent was not uncommon for Berg, but her parents became concerned about her participation with males in aggressive, contact sports such as football. To promote her transition to, as they called it, a more "lady-like" game such as golf, her father purchased a used set of clubs for her as well as a country club membership. Berg's love of her new game was evident from the start, as she was so enamored with her new gift that she would bring her clubs with her to sleep every night and stack them against her bedroom wall. Her passion for golf and her dedication to improving her skills would result in her winning the Minneapolis City Championship and reaching the semifinals of the United States Women's Amateur tournament just three years after picking up the game. Berg once said, "There is nothing in this game of golf that can't be improved upon if you practice."[3]

While it has been said that "Patty Berg's achievements in golf are not measured by tournaments won or checks received," she certainly did more than her fair share of both during her career.[4] After winning her first amateur title in 1934, Berg would go on to win more than 28 amateur titles. Along the way, she gained national notoriety by playing in the finals of the 1935 U.S. Women's Amateur, where she lost to Glenna Collett-Vare in what was Collett-Vare's final amateur victory. Upon turning professional in 1940, at the age of 22, Berg had won every single amateur championship title the United States had to offer. Among her most notable amateur achievements are three Minnesota Women's State Amateur titles in 1935, 1936, and 1938, as well as the U.S. Women's Amateur title in 1938. She was also a two-time member of the U.S. Curtis Cup team in 1936 and 1938. The Curtis Cup is an international competition held biennially that pits teams against each other from the United States, England, Ireland, Northern Ireland, Scotland, and Wales. Berg was recognized as the AP Female Athlete of the Year, for the first of three times, as an amateur in 1938.

There was no organized professional golf tour for women in 1940, but that did not stop Berg from turning professional that year. Riding the fame she had gained through her countless amateur achievements, she was able to travel the country and charge for clinics and exhibitions. It was estimated that she traveled 60,000 miles per year to make her living, and by her own account, she taught over 16,000 clinics and introduced the game to over 500,000 new players in her lifetime. Patty also signed a lucrative endorsement deal with Wilson Sporting Goods, who produced a set of Patty Berg Golf Clubs.

Unfortunately, Berg's first stint at making money while playing the game she loved was curtailed by injuries she sustained in a serious automobile accident in 1941. These injuries would set her back 18 months in the prime of her career. Most professional athletes would be eager to return to work after a serious injury so as to maximize their short window of opportunity to compete at the highest possible level. Instead, upon recovery, Berg enlisted in the Marine Corps and served four years as a lieutenant during World War II. She passed on the opportunity to make thousands of dollars from 1942 to 1945 so that she could serve her country. Berg's sense of community and patriotism are truly admirable. Actions like these make it even clearer why people that knew Berg would tell you her accomplishments should not be measured by the amount of tournaments she won or how much money she made.

After the war, Berg rededicated herself to golf full-time. Without even missing a beat after being away from the game for five years, she won her first U.S. Women's Open Championship in 1946. During this time, the Women's Professional Golf Association (WPGA), the first professional tour for women, was developing. Despite Berg's undeniable dominance, the tour struggled. Then in 1950, Berg, along with other notable female golfers of the time Mildred Didrikson Zaharias, Betty Jameson, and Louise Suggs, formed the LPGA. For their contribution to the game, these four women were the first four inducted into the LPGA's new Hall of Fame in 1951. While this is perhaps Berg's biggest and most lasting contribution to not only golf, but to the world of sports, her resume is loaded with titles, awards, and honors. As a professional, she earned 60 tour victories, including 15 major championships. She also garnered two additional AP Female Athlete of the Year awards. She was the LPGA Tour money leader in 1954, 1955, and 1956, as well as the tour's scoring leader in 1953, 1955, and 1956. She would preach "the will to win, not the wish to win."[5]

Perhaps more important, she was also honored with the 1963 Bob Jones Award, recognizing sportsmanship and respect for the game, and the 1976 Humanitarian Sports Award by the United Cerebral Palsy Foundation. Furthermore, for her dedication to community service, she was recognized by the Professional Golfers Association (PGA) in 1995 as their Distinguished Service Award winner, as well as by the Minnesota Golf Association a year later as their Distinguished Service Award winner. Finally, in 1997, Patty Berg was awarded the Spirit Lifetime Achievement Award after 66 years in the game of golf.

Sadly, Berg had to endure cancer and hip and back surgeries from 1971 to 1989, but she never gave up playing golf, and even recorded a hole-in-one in 1991 at the age of 73. Patty Berg passed away September 10, 2006, in Fort Meyers, Florida, from complications that arose from her Alzheimer's disease. To hear her speak late in her life, she was as electrifying as ever. In an interview with The Golf Channel, she said, "Our key thing was to get women's professional golf off the ground."[6] When Berg started playing, spectators were charged $2.20 and Berg's official professional tour winnings totaled $190,760. Last year, the LPGA's total prize money amounted to $54,285,000. Congratulations, Patty Berg—women's professional golf is off the ground.

Notes

1. Judy Hasday, *Extraordinary Women Athletes* (Danbury, Conn.: Children's Press, 2000), 40.

2. Brent Kelley, About.com: Golf, "Biography of Golfer Patty Berg," http://golf.about.com/od/golferswomen/p/patty_berg.htm (accessed March 23, 2008).

3. Kelley, About.com: Golf, "Biography of Golfer Patty Berg."

4. Elinor Nickerson, *Golf: A Women's History* (Jefferson, N.C.: McFarland & Company, Inc., 1987), 49.

5. Greg Hardwig, Naplesnews.com, "Berg Keeps Giving Back to the Game She Loves," http://www.naplesnews.com/news/2006/sep/13/berg_keeps_giving_back_game_she_loves/?printer=1/ (accessed March 23, 2008).

6. LPGA.com, "Patty Berg," http://www.LPGA.com/content_1.aspx?pid=8002& mid=2 (accessed March 12, 2008).

Betty Jameson

American Star of the Women's International Sports Hall of Fame

by Ryan Sleeper

During the peak of her golfing career, Betty Jameson worked as a truck driver at an Army depot in San Antonio, Texas. This is one of the last jobs anybody would have imagined golf's first "glamour girl" working in the early 1940s during the meteoric rise of women's golf. Jameson simply had no choice. Starting in 1942, most major golf events throughout the United States were suspended due to World War II. Still having to make a living, Jameson turned to writing and took a job in her hometown at the *Dallas Times Herald*. She enjoyed writing, but was a slow typist and struggled to meet deadlines. That's when she decided to move south and assist the war effort by transporting generals. It was the war that actually caused Jameson to turn professional when the Spalding Company talked her into leaving the base to tour the country teaching golf clinics. While this certainly seemed like the more appropriate occupation at the time, little did Jameson know how much she would miss the amateur ranks. She later recollected:

> At least I would be making money. I could not afford the amateur game. I did not dream that without match play the whole essence and drama of golf would disappear. I did not realize how humdrum it is, playing hole-after-hole and not daring to take chances. I love match play. The fact that you knew you could make six on one hole and not be out of the match made you a little more daring—you were never protective. For me, it was just a little more exciting.[1]

Being that Betty Jameson was born May 9, 1919, just as World War I was drawing to a close, this is certainly not the first time world history would shape her life. After all, Betty began playing golf at 10 years old when her parents got her a set of golf clubs for Christmas in 1929, just two months after the catastrophic stock market crash and during the first year of the Great Depression. The clubs were the only thing Betty had asked for after taking an interest in golf after seeing a particularly meaningful newsreel at the movies. "I saw a newsreel one afternoon about Betty Hicks beating Collett Vare in the national amateur championship," Jameson recalls. "Betty was only 19 and she had beaten the best player in the world. I really did not know anything about golf, but the story of Hicks' win impressed me. That this young girl could dethrone the national champion caught my attention."[2]

You could definitely say Jameson's life in golf had humble beginnings. The clubs were a family friend's well-used-hand-me-downs, which Jameson's parents cut down for her so she could use, but she could not have been happier with her one and only gift that bleak Christmas morning. She began playing as many as 50 holes per day on the cheapest local course around. "It was a little course with sand greens—my father called it 'Cow Pasture Country Club,'" Betty fondly jokes.[3]

While Jameson's 13 tour victories do not contend with many of the win totals of her fellow golfers in this book, she was one of the most influential women in golf history. Her major championships include back-to-back titles in the U.S. Women's Amateur in 1939 and 1940. As a professional, she went on to win two Western Opens (1942 and 1954), as well as the 1947 U.S. Women's Open, making her one of only six women to ever win both the U.S. Women's Open and U.S. Women's Amateur championships. Her Open win in 1947 would add Jameson's name to the record books in more ways than one, as she also earned the distinction of being the first woman golfer to score under the 300-stroke mark in a 72-hole event when she set the women's scoring bar at 295 during the event. Jameson's best year came in 1955, when she won four events on tour. These wins would be the last of her career, as she would not win another event before her retirement in 1970. Most important to her legacy in golf, Jameson was one of the 13 women who co-founded the Ladies Professional Golf Association (LPGA) in 1950. Her contributions to the organization include coming up with the idea to annually award the woman golfer with the lowest scoring average on tour. In 1952, she donated the original trophy for the award, which was soon named the Vare Trophy in honor of Jameson's idol, Glenna Collett Vare.[4] Jameson was one of 11 charter members in the LPGA Hall of Fame, and her achievements also earned her a spot in the World Golf Hall of Fame.

Due to Betty's blue eyes and blonde hair, as well as the fact that she was a tall, stylish woman, she is known as the first "glamour girl" of golf. While she did not resent this title, her thoughts on women in sport as well as in society are much deeper. "She is almost a solitary voice among women athletes of her generation to speak about both the 'place of women' and her personal beliefs on 'a woman's place,'" says Jackie Williams, women's golf historian and author.[5] Jameson credits the women in her life for shaping her feminist views:

> My mother and grandmother were great figures in my life. My mother knew I could be a world beater—that was the old fashioned term—and my grandmother, on the other hand would say, "Are you still playing golf?" As a woman I always thought I was swimming with the tide. I thought women could do anything and I still do. Women's place in the world meant something to me.[6]

From starting her golf life by playing on a course of "sand greens" with used clubs tailor-cut to her height, to taking an unwelcome sabbatical from the game to be a truck driver, to eventually turning into golf's "glamour girl," Betty Jameson experienced several places in this world, proving along the way that women truly can do anything.

Notes

1. Jackie Williams, *Playing from the Rough: The Women of the LPGA Hall of Fame* (Las Vegas: Women of Diversity Productions, 2000), 43.
2. Ibid., 40.
3. Ibid., 41.
4. Wgv.com: Hall of Fame, "Biography of World Golf Hall of Famer Betty Jameson," http://www.wgv.com/hof/member.php?member=1068 (accessed May 23, 2008).
5. Williams, *Playing From the Rough*, 42.
6. Ibid.

Mary Kathryn "Mickey" Wright

American Star of the Women's International Sports Hall of Fame

by Ryan Sleeper

Valentine's Day, 1935, Arthur Wright, an expectant father, was certain his wife Dorothy would give birth to a son he would call Michael. When the couple had a daughter, they ended up naming her Mary Kathryn Wright. Arthur had to improvise by nicknaming his girl, "Mickey."

Since birth, Mickey has been challenging conventional gender roles and expectations.

Unlike her famous predecessors such as Babe Zaharias, who although an amazing athlete in her own right, packaged her abilities with extracurricular, attention-grabbing activities, Wright made no qualms about simply being a great golfer for a man or a woman, whether anybody liked it or not. While perhaps no other female player shattered barriers and stereotypes quite like Wright, she never purposely set out to do so. Her natural ability was enough to make people step back and think about everything women are capable of.

In an excerpt from *Playing From the Rough: The Women of the LPGA Hall of Fame*, author and golf insider Jackie Williams talks about Wright's place in the golf world:

> Wright had no "private agenda" to challenge accepted gender roles. Wright's talent and hard work, and possibly fate had put her in a position that made her a threat—albeit, an unknown one—to conventional thought. Wright's ability to play golf at a phenomenal level forced others in the golf world to deal with the issue as best they could.
>
> Mickey Wright did not seek this role. Once placed in the situation, Wright demonstrated that she had the intelligence and courage to play it out with grace and honesty. In doing so, she unintentionally played a key role in unlocking a door which future women golfers would more easily open.[1]

"I wanted to be the best at something," Wright said in a 1997 interview.[2] Many certainly argue that she was the best women's golfer of all time due to her awe-inspiring accomplishments. Wright won at least one tournament on the Ladies Professional Golf Association (LPGA) tour each of the first 14 years she competed from 1956 to 1969. That 14-year winning streak is second in LPGA history only to the great Kathy Whitworth, who also stands alone in front of Wright for most career tournament wins of all-time with 88; Wright's career mark stands at 82 victories. These marks are even more impressive when you consider Wright retired at the age of 35. This means she potentially left many playing years on the table by retiring at a much younger age than most golfers. She also won 13 major championships, including a record four U.S. Women's Opens (1958, 1959, 1961, and 1964), four LPGA Championships (1958, 1960, 1961, and 1964), three Western Opens (1962, 1963, and 1966), and two Titleholders Championships (1961 and 1962). Her amateur highlights include a U.S. Girls Junior Championship in 1952, a World Amateur Championship in 1954, and the U.S. Open low amateur score in 1954.

You could call Wright the prodigy of the group of women golfers among the pages of this book, having technically been introduced to the game by her father when she was just seven years old. That's when her father bought her a complete set of toy golf clubs from a dime shop in San Diego. Wright swung the clubs so hard that she broke every one of them.[3] A bit of grace was added to that powerful swing over the years and eventually her swing was transformed into what fellow hard-hitting legend Ben Hogan would describe as "the finest I ever saw, man or woman."[4] This is quite a statement, considering Ben Hogan is renowned as the utmost authority on the mechanics of the golf swing, having revolutionized golf swing theory.

Wright likely inherited some of her athletic prowess from her father, who played football at the University of Michigan. Her athletic ability was present at a very young age when she started walking at nine months old and she has been very coordinated ever since. She attributes her great "ball sense," which many female golfers consider so important, to the fact that her father began playing baseball with her when she was just four years old. However, when Wright began pestering her father to allow her to accompany him to the golf course when she was 11, he was reluctant.

"Take some lessons first and then I'll play golf with you," he promised.[5] So Wright immediately began taking lessons with Johnny Bellante at the La Jolla Country Club. Bellante was also the first teacher of another great golfer, Gene Littler. In 1961, Bellante's two star pupils, Gene Littler and Mickey Wright, captured both the Men's and Women's U.S. Opens!

Bellante was so impressed with Wright during their three years together that he asked the *San Diego Union* newspaper to send out a photographer to witness his future golf legend. *The Union* not only printed Wright's picture in its paper, they captioned the photo, "The Next Babe?"[6]

This question was a sign of things to come, as just a few years later at the age of 19, Wright would have the torch symbolically passed to her by Babe Zaharias. It happened in 1954 at Wright's very first U.S. Women's Open when, on the last day of the tournament, Wright was paired with Zaharias. Although Zaharias ended up winning, Wright broke 80 in each round and she hung tough with arguably the greatest athlete of all time the entire day. Wright ended up finishing fourth overall, but was the lowest scoring amateur, and a star was born.

Despite this success, her father was still hesitant to give his daughter his blessing to pursue a career in golf. "I was ready to play professionally. My father was not that enthusiastic. He believed that women should have something that would offer security if they were unmarried. To him security meant a teaching certificate."[7]

In order to pursue her dream, Wright made a deal with her father. Her father agreed to give her $1,000 to give the tour a shot. She promised that if she ran out of money, she would go back to school. Eighty-two victories and hundreds of thousands of dollars later, Wright has never looked back. This is quite a far cry from the $2,000 a year she would have earned teaching had she accepted the safer, gender-accepted role.

Notes

1. Jackie Williams, *Playing from the Rough: The Women of the LPGA Hall of Fame* (Las Vegas: Women of Diversity Productions, 2000), 84–85.

2. Ibid., 83.

3. Terri Leonard, *In the Women's Clubhouse: The Greatest Women Golfers in Their Own Words* (Chicago: Contemporary Books, 2000), 165–166.

4. Ibid., 178.

5. Ibid., 168.

6. Ibid., 169.

7. Williams, *Playing from the Rough*, 88.

zation's positive exposure, but they also dramatically improved the size of the purses in tournaments because of the increase in corporate partnership.

In addition to Mann navigating the LPGA through its most tumultuous time, she joined the Women's Sports Foundation (WSF) as a trustee during a controversial time in women's sports. In 1981, the affair between tennis-star Billie Jean King and Marilyn Barnett was a very hot topic in the media. "The press presented the situation as a scandal that could adversely affect the future of all women's sports."[4] Mann took a stand in *Women's Sports* magazine:

> I'm especially concerned with the public reaction to King's admission. In recent years it's been gratifying to see how much more acceptable it is for girls and young women to pursue sports as amateurs and professionals. It would be a terrible injustice if parents didn't continue to encourage such active lifestyles.
>
> Participating in sports is probably the most valuable experience girls can have while growing up. What they discover on the field, court and course spills over into the rest of their personal lives. They learn how to win, how to lose, how to rely totally on themselves and how to work together with a team. They come to understand defeat without being devastated by it, and how to channel their energy and anger.
>
> I've done a lot of thinking lately about the value of being an athlete and about the golf tour's success story. I wouldn't trade my experiences for anything in the world.[5]

Toward the end of her term with the Women's Sports Foundation, Mann once again found herself speaking out against discrimination. After nearly a decade since her article in *Women's Sports* magazine, she was outspoken in 1990, when the PGA Championship was moved from Shoal Creek Country Club in Birmingham, Alabama, because they did not admit African-American golfers. Mann had this to say about the incident:

> Playing a game professionally is a very narrow existence. These players have little breadth of experience or knowledge of the real world. They live inside the ropes. Frankly, you almost have to have a narrow outlook to succeed at this.

They don't see it, but golf and society have changed this week. Who you hire and who you promote, who you accept and where you socialize, are all eventually going to be different. Through humanizing straight talk, we're about to learn we have things in common. The ripple is going to be long and wide.[6]

Carol Mann came a long way from a shy, 19-year-old who questioned her belonging in the LPGA, to arguably the most influential and outspoken woman golfer the tour has ever seen. The ripples of her impact are still being felt throughout golf and society today.

Notes

1. *Time Magazine*, "How About That Mann?" May 17, 1968, http://www.time .com/time/printout/0,8816,838366,00.html# (accessed May 23, 2008).

2. Jackie Williams, *Playing from the Rough: The Women of the LPGA Hall of Fame* (Las Vegas: Women of Diversity Productions, 2000), 132.

3. Brent Kelley, About.com: Golf, "Biography of Golfer Carol Mann," http://golf .about.com/od/golferswomen/p/carol_mann.htm (accessed May 23, 2008.)

4. Williams, *Playing From the Rough*, 137.

5. Ibid., 138.

6. Ibid., 139.

Kathy Whitworth

American Star of the Women's International Sports Hall of Fame

by Ryan Sleeper

Kathy Whitworth once said, "Nobody ever conquers golf."[1] While that may be true, she sure did come close. During her career, which spanned more than four decades, she compiled one of the most impressive resumes the history of golf has to offer. She did not earn her first Ladies Professional Golf Association (LPGA) win until the 1962 Kelly Girl Open during her fourth year on tour. However, once she captured her first title, she would never look back. In fact, that first victory marked the beginning of an astounding streak where she would win at least one title for 17 years in a row. Those titles would include six major championships starting with back-to-back Title-holders Championships in 1965 and 1966. The next year she won the Western Open and her first LPGA Championship. She would go on to win two additional LPGA Championships in 1971 and 1975. It should be noted that there were only two major championships played on the LPGA tour from 1968 to 1971 and from 1973 to 78, spans that overlapped the prime of her career. Most golfers who played before and after Whitworth generally competed in at least three, usually four, major championships per year.

What Whitworth lacked in major championships, she made up for in statistics, earnings, and honors. She is a seven-time winner of the Vare Trophy (1965–67, 1969–72), which is the award given to the LPGA player with the lowest scoring average each season. She also had two different four-year streaks, 1965–68 and 1970–73, where she was the LPGA Tour money leader. This enabled her to become the first woman golfer to reach the $1 million in earnings milestone.[2] This feat is even more amazing when you consider the purses were much smaller in those days. For example, during a four-year span in the 1960s, she won an astonishing 35 tournaments, yet only earned $143,491 during that period.[3] Today, LPGA golfers easily clear that amount with just one tour victory. As a consolation for Whitworth, money does not buy LPGA Player of the Year honors, and she earned more than her fair share of those. She won seven in total, earning that distinction each year from 1966 to 1969 and from 1971 to 1973. She also garnered AP Athlete of the Year honors in 1965 and 1967. In addition to these awards, she also captained the 1990 and 1992 Solheim Cup teams. The culmination of these accomplishments is a spot in both the LPGA and World Golf Halls of Fame.

Her tournament wins total, for which Whitworth is most famous, surely did not hurt her bid to become immortalized in multiple golf and women's sports halls of fame. She became the winningest women's golfer in history when she won the Lady Michelob Classic at the Brookfield West Country Club in Atlanta, Georgia, in 1982. The victory marked her 83rd, passing fellow golf legend, Mickey Wright, who finished her career with 82 wins. Whitworth was not done there because she knew that Sam Snead's record of 84 career victories on the men's side was just one win away. She tied Snead's mark in dramatic fashion the very next year by sinking a 40-foot putt on the 18th green to win the Women's Kemper Open. Then, on July 22, 1984, she passed Snead by winning the Rochester International. Her 85th win made Whitworth the winningest golfer, male or female, of all time.[4] She would go on to win three more tournaments to finish her career with 88 total victories.

Kathryn Ann Whitworth was born September 27, 1939, in Monahans, Texas, but she mostly grew up in Jal, New Mexico. She did not pick up a golf club until she was 15 years old. One day a reporter was talking to Whitworth about then 14-year-old phenom Michelle Wie and asked her, "How good were you at that age?" Whitworth laughingly responded, "I hadn't even started."[5] Whitworth got her start in golf when, by chance, she tagged along with her tennis team for a nine-hole outing. She had a tough game, which was a rare occurrence for such a natural athlete, but she was so enamored during her first encounter with the sport of golf that she never played tennis again.[6] Whitworth turned professional just four years later. Her humility and drive to succeed would be themes throughout her career. She played with two central beliefs: never give up and never get too full of yourself.[7] This mentality was developed in part because of Betsy Rawls's approach to "work harder to shoot 80 than 70." Whitworth idolized Betsy Rawls for her "great mind" when it came to the game of golf. Whitworth credits much of her success with not getting down on herself during poor tournaments and focusing on the positives. Once she adopted this theory, she started placing in the money.

The first time she placed, she earned \$33.[8] She went on to win \$5,000 during her second year on tour, but obviously the winnings would begin to pick up for Whitworth, even if she was not very concerned about them. "You know, money was never a motivation,"[9] Whitworth has said. However, she does acknowledge primarily going on the professional tour to get experience playing when her family could not afford to have her compete locally in New Mexico. She even left a scholarship at Odessa Junior College in Texas after just one year to pursue a professional career.

The bigger concern for Whitworth, though, was playing the game she loved and helping women's golf grow. She would eventually serve as president of the LPGA four times. Whitworth was known as a very good sport who rarely showed any negative emotion on the links. Fellow golfers took notice of Whitworth's modesty and drive to help women's golf. Rival golfer JoAnne "Big Mama" Carner noted, "Everyone likes her, because she always treated people with such respect and worked so hard to improve the LPGA."[10]

Arguably the best women's golfer of all time, Kathy Whitworth played in an era after the original trailblazers such as Mildred Babe Didrikson Zaharias and Patty Berg, yet did not receive the benefits of big attention and even larger purses that players like Annika Sorenstam and Michelle Wie have received in the era that followed Whitworth's playing days. Today's players owe a debt of gratitude to Whitworth for bridging this gap, and almost anonymously exerting the tireless efforts required to continue the growth of women's golf. Despite not receiving the wealth and attention that she would have garnered had she played just a few years later, Whitworth has always had a positive outlook. Her philosophy on golf is simple. When asked about her lifetime commitment to the game, she said, "Why not continue to do what you love to do, if you're successful at it and get some enjoyment out of it? Even if you're not as successful as some people think you should be, who cares?"[11] But few have had more success in any sport than Kathy Whitworth.

Notes

1. Brent Kelley, About.com: Golf, "Biography of Golfer Kathy Whitworth," http:// golf.about.com/od/golferswomen/p/kathy_whitworth.htm (accessed April 5, 2008).

2. Judy Hasday, *Extraordinary Women Athletes* (Danbury, Conn.: Children's Press, 2000), 67.

3. Jenni Carlson, "Whitworth Arrived Ahead of Schedule," *Daily Oklahoman*, May 25, 2006.

4. Hasday, *Extraordinary Women Athletes*, 69.

5. Carlson, "Whitworth Arrived Ahead of Schedule."

6. Jaime Aron, "Whitworth Doesn't Expect to Add to Record for Pro Golf Titles," *AP Worldstream*, August 5, 2002.

7. Ibid.

8. Ibid.

9. Ibid.

10. Hasday, *Extraordinary Women Athletes*, 68.

11. Ibid., 66.

JoAnne Carner

American Star of the Women's International Sports Hall of Fame

by Ryan Sleeper

JoAnne Carner was born April 4, 1939, in Kirkland, Washington. She was the youngest of five Gunderson (her maiden name) children. She had three sisters, but it was her brother Bill, the second youngest, born just 13 months before JoAnne, who would help shape her life by introducing her to the game of golf. Bill worked at a nine-hole public course and JoAnne tagged along whenever possible. "We played after the customers went home, with old taped up clubs, wearing gloves 'til they fell apart," JoAnne said.[1] She also attributes these after-hour practices with developing her "feel" for the game, which so many Ladies Professional Golf Association (LPGA) players talk about as being so vital to their success. JoAnne reminisces, "We played in the moonlight, which is why I'm such a feel player."[2]

This experience paid off and JoAnne Carner became a local celebrity after notching her first couple of victories as an amateur. After winning the Junior National title in 1956, the 17-year-old was rewarded with a ticker tape parade from Seattle to her hometown of Kirkland 12 miles away. "The Great Gundy," as she would come to be known, became an absolute dominant force during her 14 years in the amateur ranks. In addition to her U.S. Girls Junior Championship in 1956, Carner won a total of five U.S. Amateur Championships (1958, 1960, 1962, 1966, and 1968), trailing only the lifelong amateur Glenna Collett-Vare, who won six. Carner also was a runner-up in the prestigious event two times to boot. She made four appearances in the Curtis Cup (1958, 1960, 1962, and 1964), an international competition held biennially that pits teams from the United States, England, Ireland, Northern Ireland, Scotland, and Wales. Then in 1969, a year before turning professional, Carner won the Burdine's Invitational, and is still the last amateur to win an LPGA event.

Carner had become the best amateur golfer in the world. What is even more amazing about her accomplishments is that unlike most golfers who make a career in the game, Carner focused on more than just golf during her time as an amateur. She completed a four-year degree at Arizona State University in physical education, where her skills on the greens earned her one of the first athletic scholarships in golf for a woman. Upon graduating, Carner spent time at several jobs, including at an insurance company and an electronics store. Before turning professional, she also owned and operated a nine-hole golf course with her husband.

She thrived in the match play scenarios that the amateur competitions present. This style of play suited Carner because she worked hard to scout the competition on how they would handle certain circumstances and used her intimidation to propel her to victory after victory. Eventually, she turned professional because she had simply outgrown the challenge of competing as an amateur. "I had no desire to be a pro," Carner recalls. "I loved amateur golf. Then I ran out of goals. My USGA record was something like 910 victories out of 1,000 matches."[3]

So, in 1970, armed with a new nickname because "The Great Gundy" no longer suited her after she adopted the last name of her husband, Don Carner, JoAnne "Big Momma" Carner joined the LPGA Tour. "When I first came on tour, some of the lady pros didn't care for me too much, probably because of my amateur success," Carner remembers. "They tried some mental games on me. I thought it was poor sportsmanship." This inhospitable welcome did not shake Carner's confidence one bit, but success on the pro tour would come slower than she was accustomed. "I expected to take over the tour immediately," Carner said. "Sandra Haynie told me it would take four years, and I said baloney, but it did. I was used to match play and winning, not staying there and grinding it out for $500."[4] To help her get back to her winning ways, Carner began playing her own mind games with opponents. She would practice vigorously away from the tournament so that nobody ever saw her practice, then show up early the day of the competition to relax, smoke, and drink coffee in front of everybody. "It drove some of them crazy,"[5] Carner smugly recalls.

Something must have worked for Carner, as she amassed 43 victories on the professional tour, including two major championships: the 1971 and 1976 U.S. Women's Opens. She also is a five-time winner of the Vare Trophy for being the tour's lowest average scorer. Her other achievements include being named the LPGA Tour

Player of the Year in 1974, 1981, and 1982, and being the tour's money leader in 1974, 1982, and 1983. She was a four-time member of the U.S. Curtis Cup team and captained the 1994 U.S. Solheim Cup team. Carner was inducted into the World Golf Hall of Fame in 1985.

Carner's legacy in golf will be for bringing a big game and an even bigger personality to the links. She once said she would never retire and in 2004 at the Chick-fil-A Charity Championship, when she became the oldest woman to make the cut, doing so at the age of 64 years 26 days, people believed maybe she would never have to. However, if there is one thing Carner loves more than golf, it is her husband Don. Amazingly, despite JoAnne's rigorous tour schedule, during the first 20 years of their marriage, the couple was only apart for a total of 19 days! To accomplish this, the Carners traveled in a trailer during JoAnne's early career. But when Don was diagnosed with Parkinson's disease, JoAnne immediately cut her tour schedule and eventually decided to call it quits for good in 2005. JoAnne Carner is a prime example of how people can be successful while being themselves and she shows us that happiness in life comes from knowing our priorities and pursuing them accordingly.

Notes

1. Jackie Williams, *Playing from the Rough: The Women of the LPGA Hall of Fame* (Las Vegas: Women of Diversity Productions, 2000), 145.

2. Ibid.

3. Ibid.

4. Ibid.

5. Ibid.

Nancy Lopez

Future Hall of Famer

by Ryan Sleeper

It is the most coveted championship in women's professional golf. The only tournament that has been recognized as a major event by the Ladies Professional Golf Association (LPGA) since its founding in 1950. The U.S. Open has been won by many of the greatest golfers in history, several of whom can be found in the pages of this book, including Patty Berg, Betty Jameson, Louise Suggs, Mickey Wright, Carol Mann, JoAnne Carner, and Annika Sorenstam. However, the victors list is missing one woman, Nancy Lopez, who has been credited with touching women's golf like none other before or since.[1] Lopez is different from the aforementioned legends in that she transcended the game of golf and impacted so many, not solely by her talents on the course, but with her endearing personality and down-to-earth approach to the game and its fans.

Lopez did come very close to capturing the championship that eluded her during her illustrious golf career, placing second on four occasions. Never was she closer than in 1997, when she became the first woman to post all four of her U.S. Open scores in the 60s (69-68-69-69), but still lost to Alison Nicholas by just one stroke.[2] As she tearfully watched the trophy presentation, many others in the crowd were also moved to tears. Wearing her emotions on her sleeve and allowing the public to see her true feelings was just one way Lopez connected with fans all over the world. She had a more lighthearted runner-up finish in 1977, and still jokes today about why she fell short. Believe it or not, that year she got a hole in one. Unfortunately, it wasn't on the course. Instead, it was in a pair of her pants.

In another, not-so-close run at the Open, Nancy marched down her final fairway of the tournament waving a putter with a white towel wrapped around it in surrender before missing the cut by shooting a 71 and an 83 in the first two rounds of the competition. She has said, "Do your best, one shot at a time and then move on. Remember that golf is just a game."[3] These stories illustrate why she is such a fan favorite on the tour. She is a fierce competitor who is not afraid to let her emotions be known, yet humble, with a sense of humor. Quite simply, Nancy Lopez is herself whether she is at home with her husband and three daughters, or playing on television in front of millions of spectators. It should be of no surprise, then, that she has been compared to Arnold Palmer, perhaps the most loved player in the history of men's golf. Like Palmer, who had a large fan base nicknamed "Arnie's Army," Lopez's following is similarly called "Nancy's Navy." What appeals to fans is her humility and willingness to talk to everyone and anyone while paying them the same individual attention she would bestow a best friend. She fondly explains her fan encounters, saying, "I feel like I'm wearing a shirt these days that says 'Talk to me.' So many people come up to me and feel they know me, like we have been friends. It's nice, because you meet a lot of nice people that way."[4] Despite winning only three major championships during her career, and never winning the Open, there is one category Lopez never placed second in: gallery size. Lopez had the ability to fill the stands with fans who would enjoy watching her even miss a cut (a rare occurrence) more than seeing any of the other golfers on the tour win the tournament.[5]

While Nancy Lopez was best known during her career for the way she played the game and not whether she won or lost, make no mistake about it, she had her moments of greatness on the greens. She started her winning ways at the age of 12, when she won the New Mexico Women's Amateur. She also won the U.S. Junior Girls Amateur in 1972 and 1974. A year later at the age of 17, she would place second for the first of four times in the U.S. Women's Open. She continued her amateur career by attending Tulsa University for two years, where she was named an All-American in 1976 before turning pro after her sophomore year in 1977. She burst into the professional spotlight in 1978 by again placing second in the Women's Open. That year she also won nine titles, including a streak of five in a row, and became a superstar when she graced the cover of *Sports Illustrated*. That same year, Lopez became the first woman to be named Rookie of the Year and Player of the Year, and to win the Vare trophy all in the same season. The Vare trophy is awarded annually to the woman golfer with the lowest scoring average over the season. She experienced her career year in her first full season on the LPGA tour.

Lopez's style was marked by extremely aggressive play. "I think when I came out on tour, I wanted to beat the JoAnne Carners and Judy Rankins and I didn't have any pressure on me," Lopez said. "I wanted to beat them really bad. I felt like they had a lot to lose if I beat them, but I didn't have anything to lose if I shot 80. I was just somebody starting on the tour. So I played very aggressively and I loved it. The tour was comfortable to me and golf was fun. Still is." She stuck with what worked for her and went on to win two more Vare trophies (1979 and 1985) and three more Player of the Year awards (1979, 1985, and 1989). She was also a member of the 1976 Curtis Cup, a member of the 1990 Solheim Cup, and the captain of the U.S. team in the 2005 Solheim Cup. These achievements earned her spots in the LPGA Hall of Fame and the World Golf Hall of Fame.

Lopez said her inspiration came from her first and only golf teacher, her father. Domingo Lopez, who introduced her to the game when she was just eight years old, and did not have to train his daughter that much considering she was such a natural that she could out-drive both her mother and father the first day she ever picked up a golf club. "My dad was such a great inspiration to me," Lopez said. "He always told me to enjoy what I was doing. And always smile."[6] Lopez would benefit greatly from learning to play the game in such a supportive environment, with people who encouraged her to be herself with everything from her personality to her unconventional style of play. She actually attributes having never changed her unorthodox swing to the discriminatory practices of a local country club where she grew up in Roswell, New Mexico. Lopez and her family are Mexican-Americans, and they were unwelcome guests at the nicest course in her neighborhood. She believes that if an instructor from the club latched onto her and influenced her golf development, she may have never became the Hall of Fame golfer she is today. She learned to be comfortable with her swing, especially after seeking guidance from fellow Mexican-American golfer, Lee Trevino. She asked, "Mr. Trevino, what should I do about my golf swing? I have a bad golf swing and yet I play very well." Without even seeing her swing, he responded, "You can't argue with success. If you swing badly but still score well and win, don't change a thing."[7]

Nancy Lopez, while humbly never dwelling on the fact, became a role model for athletes all over the world. She is living proof that people can be successful without sacrificing who they really are. As she walked up her final U.S. Open fairway in 2002, she cried, and thousands cried with her. "Well, I knew eighteen would be tough,"[8] she said through the tears. She befriended so many by being genuine and approachable with fans, showing she was just like them. She returned every letter and offered encouragement to every young boy and girl. She never put up a wall like so many high-profile athletes and entertainers do today. "If I can make somebody feel good by smiling at them or saying 'hi' to them then I'm doing my job," she said during her touching sendoff, "at least for my dad."[9]

Notes

1. Joe Posnanski, "Nancy Lopez Touched Many and Many Touched Her," *The Kansas City Star*, July 6, 2002.

2. Brian Wicker, "Queen of the LPGA," *Minneapolis Star Tribune*, August 16, 1998.

3. Brent Kelley, About.com: Golf, "Biography of Golfer Nancy Lopez," http://golf.about.com/od/golferswomen/p/nancy_lopez.htm (accessed March 30, 2008).

4. Wicker, "Queen of the LPGA."

5. Ibid.

6. Posnanski, "Nancy Lopez."

7. Nancy Lopez, *The Education of a Woman Golfer* (New York: Simon and Schuster, 1979), 24.

8. Posnanski, "Nancy Lopez."

9. Ibid.

Annika Sorenstam

Future Hall of Famer

by Ryan Sleeper

Courtesy of Arizona Athletics Media Relations.

Annika Sorenstam is such an extraordinary golf talent, it should be no surprise that she actually spent time on a golf course before she was even born! Like so many of the storied athletes found in this book, Annika came from very athletic genes. Her mother and father both enjoyed golf, and her mother happened to do so when she was pregnant with Annika.

Born October 9, 1970, in Stockholm, Sweden, Annika grew up playing badminton, soccer, and ping-pong. She also skied the famous slopes of Sweden and even dreamt of growing up to become a fighter pilot. Although Annika's parents exposed her early in life to the game she would eventually take over by storm, her first love was tennis. At the age of 12, she was one of Sweden's best junior tennis players, and only picked up golf because it was an activity she could do alone. "In tennis you need someone to play with," Annika said, "but in golf I could go and hit balls when I wanted."[1] In fact, she initially found golf quite boring. It did not take long, however, for Annika to find enjoyment in the game, and she joined a youth golf program. Her dedication was evident from the start. Her 12 teammates were impressively dedicated for young teenagers, practicing an extra hour after each round, but Annika's commitment to the game was even more apparent, as she always practiced three hours after each round. The extra work paid off and by the age of 16, Annika gave up tennis to pursue her shot at a career in golf.

Sorenstam was quickly ascending the ranks of Sweden's junior golfers, but her extreme shyness was literally costing her victories.

In an excerpt from her book, *Golf Annika's Way*, Sorenstam recalls how bad this problem was:

> I can't count the number of times I three-putted on the final hole of a tournament—on purpose—so that I wouldn't have to give a victory speech. I thought the real reason for my three-putts, pure shyness, was my little secret. But some of the coaches were watching me and noticing my not-so-coincidental misses. So they announced that, at the next tournament, both the winner and the runner-up would have to give a speech. I figured, what's the point of finishing second if I had to face the crowd anyway. I won that tournament and never looked back.[2]

In 1987, Sorenstam joined Sweden's national junior golf team, and soon was winning tournaments all over Europe. At one tournament, Sorenstam caught the eye of Coach Kim Haddow from the University of Arizona, who offered her a golf scholarship. Sorenstam says it took her about three seconds to decide if she should accept the offer, and in 1990, she made the 5,500-mile trip from Sweden to Tucson, Arizona, to begin her collegiate career.

Nearly as quickly as she made her decision to come to America, Sorenstam made her impact on the collegiate golf scene. In 1991, in her very first year in college, she captured the National Collegiate Athletic Association (NCAA) Championship. After another successful year during her sophomore season, Sorenstam had already won a total of seven tournaments. Also in 1992, she captured the World Amateur Championship. Having clearly established her dominance on the amateur scene, Sorenstam turned pro in 1993, going back home to join the European Tour. There she captured Rookie of the Year honors and decided she was ready to join the world's best golfers on the Ladies Professional Golf Association (LPGA) Tour. So in 1994, Sorenstam returned to the United States to begin her illustrious LPGA career.

It did not take long for Sorenstam to begin writing her long list of accomplishments. She started by winning her second Rookie of the Year award in as many years, this time in the United States, thus beginning another chapter in golf history. Sorenstam would not win her first tournament on the LPGA Tour until her second year in

1995, but when she did, the triumph would be a big one. In fact, her first victory would be her first of three U.S. Women Open titles (1995, 1996, and 2006), a title many consider to be the most important in women's golf. She would eventually win seven additional major titles over the course of her career, including three Kraft Nabisco Championships (2001, 2002, and 2005), three LPGA Championships (2003, 2004, and 2005), and the Women's British Open (2003). Sorenstam's other remarkable achievements include being a six-time recipient of the Vare trophy for having the lowest average score on tour (1995, 1996, 1998, 2001, 2002, and 2005), leading the tour in prize money winnings eight times (1995, 1997, 1998, 2001, 2002, 2003, 2004, and 2005), and being named the LPGA Player of the Year eight times (1995, 1997, 1998, 2001, 2002, 2003, 2004, and 2005). In 2001, she broke the LPGA's single round scoring record when she shot a 59 at the Standard Register Ping. A year later, she broke the women's average scoring record with a 68.70. All of these achievements and more culminated with a 2003 induction into the LPGA Hall of Fame.

It is easy to see why most people call Annika Sorenstam the greatest woman golfer of all time. It is not as easy to pick which one of her feats is the greatest, but many would make an argument for her appearance in the 2003 Colonial Professional Golfers Association (PGA) Tour tournament. It was there that Sorenstam made history when she became the first woman golfer to play with the men since Babe Didrikson Zaharias did so in 1945. Amid immense pressure and the media circus that surrounded her, Sorenstam shot a respectable 71–75. Although she missed the cut, she placed better than eleven men, and showed she could compete at golf's highest level. She had accomplished her goal of playing in the tournament and considered her effort a success. Sorenstam was never out for attention or to prove she was better than the men; she simply wanted to drive herself to become a better player for herself. "This is a way to push myself to another level," she explained.[3] This attitude says a great deal about her humility despite her undeniable greatness.

Surely this grace played into Sorenstam's May 2008 retirement announcement. At the young age of 37, with 72 victories, and a more-than-good chance of breaking Kathy Whitworth's record of 88 wins, Sorenstam announced she would be leaving the tour at the end of the season. However, she was very reluctant to say she was retiring, and never even used what she called "the r-word." She simply wanted to move on to pursue "greater priorities in life," including running her golf academy for children, designing golf courses, and getting married. "While I'm stepping away from competition, I will be very engaged and very involved in the game of golf, but in a very different way," Sorenstam said after her announcement. "I want to make sure that I can get back to the game that's been great to me, by helping and inspiring young kids to develop and reach their dreams."[4] Annika Sorenstam may be retiring from the game whose record books she completely rewrote, but she will never retire from so gracefully helping society through sport.

Notes

1. Jeff Savage, *Annika Sorenstam* (Minneapolis: Lerner Publishing Group, 2005), 10.
2. Annika Sorenstam, *Golf Annika's Way* (New York: Penguin Group Inc, 2004), 8.
3. Savage, *Annika Sorenstam*, 25.
4. Jason Sobel, ESPN.com: Golf, "Annika gracefully entering last phase of her career," http://sports.espn.go.com/golf/columns/story?id=3394148 (accessed September 14, 2008).

5

FIGURE SKATING AND SPEED SKATING: GRACE AND POWER ON ICE

Introduction by Richard Lapchick

Just as gymnastics, swimming, and track and field seem to dominate television coverage and the interest of Olympic sports fans during the Summer Games, figure skating steals the show in the Winter Games.

In fact, figure skating has become so popular that a survey indicated that only the National Football League (NFL) was more popular in the United States. Like gymnastics, it draws in adults and children, especially young girls, who can visualize themselves on the ice making those moves in elegant costumes. Speed skating's popularity has also increased dramatically after the ascension and dominance of Bonnie Blair. Speed skating for men was added to the Winter Olympics in 1924. Speed skating for women was demonstrated at the Winter Olympics in Lake Placid but women had to wait more than three decades until 1960, when it became an official event.

The history of women's world championship figure skating goes back to the London World Championship of 1902, when a woman slipped into the field and nearly won when competing against men. Madge Syers of Great Britain finished second behind Ulrich Salchow, a Swedish male skater. Women were subsequently banned and a separate women's event was created in 1905.

Madge Syers won the first two annual championships in that competition. Syers then won the first Olympic gold medal for women's figure skating (1908).

Beatrix Loughran is the only American to have won three medals in figure skating. She won silver in 1924 and the bronze in 1928 in the women's singles and then a silver in the 1932 games in pairs. She also was the U.S. women's champion in 1925, 1926, and 1927 and won the U.S. pairs title from 1930 until 1932 with Sherwin

Badger as her partner. She won the 1932 pairs silver medal with Badger.

Norwegian Sonja Henie dominated figure skating like no one before or since. She won three consecutive Olympic gold medals in 1928, 1932, and 1936. She had participated in the 1924 Games as an 11-year-old. She brought a ballerina-like approach to skating. She was the icon for aspiring young skaters and really popularized the sport. Her fame as a Hollywood actress added to her luster. However, it was her skating that won her the stage on which to act. She had won nearly 1,500 medals and trophies by the time she retired in 1936. At the age of 14 in 1927, Henie won the first of her astonishing 10 World Figure Skating Championships. Her life was filled with controversy as she had an association with members of the Nazi regime, including Hitler himself. But this somehow did not stop her career as a skater or as an actress.

Mabel Fairbanks was the first African-American to be inducted into the U.S. Figure Skating Hall of Fame. Fairbanks was sent to New York City to live with an older brother as a very young girl. Her skating was hindered at first because the skating rinks were segregated and she was often turned away. But famed skater and coach Maribel Vinson saw her skill and helped Fairbanks earn great public recognition. However, in the segregated world of 1930s and 1940s, Fairbanks's race made her talent, skill, and grace largely irrelevant at the competitive level. But it did not stop her from opening the doors for the next generations.

Over the next 50 years, Fairbanks dedicated herself to coaching, teaching, and promoting the sport of figure skating, particularly to young people of color. Her students included Atoy Wilson, the first African-American winner of a national title; Richard Ewell III and Michelle McCladdie, the first African-Americans to win a national title in pairs; Tai Babalonia and Randy Gardner, who she paired together and who later won a world pairs championship and five national titles; and Kristi Yamaguchi, an Olympic legend.

Tenley Albright loved to skate, but when she was 11, she was diagnosed with polio in an era when little was known about the disease itself or how to treat or cure it. Her parents were told that Tenley might never walk again and she endured several painful procedures and was restricted from moving her back, neck, and legs during her treatment.

Miraculously, only five years later, Albright won a silver medal at the 1952 Winter Olympic Games in Oslo, Norway. She then started a string of five consecutive national titles in the same year.

She trained hard for the 1956 Winter Olympics in Cortina, Italy, suspending her studies at Radcliffe to focus on her Olympic performance. Two weeks before the Games, Albright fell while practicing and sustained a serious cut to her right ankle. Immediately, her father, who was a prominent doctor, flew to Italy in order to repair the damage to both vein and bone. She became the first American woman to win the gold medal in figure skating.

Albright became one of only five women accepted to a class of 135 total students at the Harvard Medical School. Again, she persisted against the odds, eventually becoming a successful surgeon and a leader in blood plasma research. She also maintained her ties to skating by becoming the first woman to serve as an officer on the U.S. Olympic Committee. She helped make the future of American skating look bright indeed.

Carol Heiss finished second to Albright in the 1956 Olympics in Cortina d'Ampezzo and then won the gold in 1960 at Squaw Valley. She had finished fourth in the 1953 World Championships when she was only 13. In 1955 she was runner-up to Albright in the World Championship, but from 1956 until 1960, she was World Champion. Heiss never lost again after the silver in Cortina d'Ampezzo. She retired after Squaw Valley.

Things changed so dramatically after a tragic plane crash in 1961 took the lives of all 18 members of the U.S. Figure Skating Team and numerous coaches, officials, friends, and family members. The early 1960s marked a dark period in U.S. figure skating. At a time when the national anthem should have been booming over podiums full of American skaters, there was only an eerie silence. The victims of this crash, on their way to an undoubtedly brilliant showing at the World Championships in Prague, comprised the heart of the American figure skating community. Among the deceased were Maribel Vinson Owen, an extremely talented skater and one-time coach to Tenley Albright and Mabel Fairbanks; her 16-year-old daughter Laurence, the 1961 U.S. Ladies Champion; and 20-year-old daughter Maribel, the 1961 U.S. Pairs Champion. It was devastating and demoralizing.

Peggy Fleming's rise brought back hope to U.S. figure skating. She surprised many by winning her first World Championship in 1966. Although many female skaters forced themselves into a powerfully athletic approach, Fleming sought to be "ballet-like" and the judges loved her for it. She was often compared to Tenley Albright, who was known for her beauty, grace, and competitive creativity. Fleming soon won over the figure skating world and won two more World Championships in 1967 and 1968.

Though already a World Champion, Fleming's greatest triumph came during the 1968 Grenoble Winter Olympics, where she took the gold medal with a nearly flawless performance. It was only seven years after the loss of the best American skaters and coaches. Peggy Fleming brought the United States back to the top of the skating world. In 1999, *Sports Illustrated* named Fleming one of seven "Athletes Who Changed the Game," an honor whose elite company included Billie Jean King and Jackie Robinson.

The year 1984 marked a breakout year for Katarina Witt as she captured a World Championship and competed in her first Olympic Games, where she won the gold although she was not the favorite to win the Sarajevo Games. Witt awed the judges and the audience with her performance.

Instantly, Witt's beauty and playful charm catapulted her to international superstardom both on and off the ice. Witt's hard work paid off as she again won the title of World Champion in 1985, 1987, and 1988. She became a national hero in East Germany. Entering the 1988 Winter Olympic Games, Witt was absolutely determined to go out on top.

In what has been referred to as the "Dueling Carmens," Witt and American Debi Thomas faced off in Olympic competition, both skating their long programs to music from the opera Carmen. Sonja Henie was the last figure skater to defend her Olympic title 52 years before. Witt proved to be the better Carmen, again earning Olympic gold.

Thomas was a pre-med student at Stanford University during this time, and she became the first and only African-American to hold U.S. National titles in ladies' singles figure skating. Her bronze medal at the 1988 Winter Games made her the first black athlete from any nation to achieve this accomplishment. Tai Babilonia, who is of black and Filipino decent, was previously a U.S. and World champion in pair skating. Debi Thomas became an orthopedic surgeon.

American figure skater Kristi Yamaguchi won the gold for the United States in the 1992 Games in Albertville after she won two World Championships in 1991 and 1992 and a U.S. Championship in 1992. Yamaguchi's mother was a second-generation Japanese-American whose grandparents were sent to an internment camp during World War II. Yamaguchi's mother was born in the camp.

The drama around Nancy Kerrigan's life was not something she sought. She received the bronze medal behind Kristi Yamaguchi and Tonya Harding at the 1991 World Figure Skating Championships, where the U.S. team scored a medal sweep. Kerrigan then won the bronze in the 1992 Winter Olympics. She won the silver medal at the 1992 World Championships and became the U.S. Champion. Kerrigan seemed on target to win gold at the World Championships in Prague when her long program collapsed and she finished fifth. Oksana Baiul finished first.

In January 1994, she was clubbed in the knee by an assailant hired by Tonya Harding's ex-husband Jeff Gillooly. Although Kerrigan was not able to take part in the Olympic trials due to the assault, the United States Olympics Committee (USOC) placed her on the team. Only one month after the assault, Kerrigan managed to win the silver medal in the 1994 Winter Olympics. Oksana Baiul again finished first.

The expectations for Michelle Kwan were high, and she has won everything but the Olympic gold. In 1996 she won the U.S. and World Championships and was favored at the 1998 Winter Olympics in Nagano. Her poor performance in the free skate gave the gold medal to teammate Tara Lipinski while Kwan won a silver medal. Kwan roared back later in the year to win the World Championships. She was still at the top of the skating world and favored to win in the 2002 Salt Lake City Winter Games. The free skate event killed her again and Kwan took the bronze with her teammate, Sarah Hughes, winning the gold medal. Even without a gold medal in the Olympics, Kwan has been U.S. champion nine times and World Champion five times.

Sasha Cohen led the 2006 Torino Winter Olympics after the short program, but like Kwan in 1998 and 2002, the free skate set her back. She lost points on her first two jumps and although she completed the rest of her routine, Cohen slipped to win silver instead of gold. The Olympic gold went to Shizuka Arakawa of Japan.

In pairs figure skating, the USSR's Irina Rodnina was the most successful pair skater in history with three Olympic gold medals in 1972 with Aleksey Ulanov and in 1976 and 1980 with Aleksandr Zaytsev. She dominated the World Championships for 10 successive years (1969–78), the first four with Ulanov and the next six with Zaytsev.

Bonnie Blair's accomplishments as an athlete are incredible. Blair, a speed skater, is the most decorated American woman in winter Olympic history. Her performance in the 500-meter event earned her gold medals in three consecutive Olympic Winter Games (1988, 1992, and 1994). In those same games she garnered a bronze and two gold medals in the 1,000-meter distance. In 1992, Blair was named the winner of the James E. Sullivan Award, an honor reserved for America's top amateur athlete. She was only the second American to win Norway's Oscar, an award recognizing the world's best speed skater. ESPN counts her as the 69th greatest athlete of the 20th century.

As always, it was hard to narrow down the field to pick who to highlight in this chapter. There were so many phenomenal skaters in the second half of the 20th century that many in the 1990s and in the new millennium could not be included. But make no mistake that they will write their own history in the years ahead. As they do, hopefully they will look back on the trailblazers in skating highlighted in this section.

Sonja Henie

International Star of the Women's
International Sports Hall of Fame

by Jessica Bartter

The sport of figure skating that we view today as majestic and grace-ful was not known for such qualities until figure skater Sonja Henie took the ice in the 1920s. Grace and dignity followed Henie off the ice as well, as the wealthy heir of Norwegian furriers lived a lavish lifestyle of fur coats, fancy clothes, extravagant jewelry and art collections, and extensive international travel.

Born in Oslo, Norway, in 1912, Henie was encouraged by her parents to take up any and all sports. She first excelled at skiing and even became a nationally ranked tennis player and a skilled swimmer and equestrienne. But Henie found her niche on skates. She began competing at age six and won her first major competition, the Norwegian National Championship, at age nine, at which time her formal schooling was cut off by her parents. Her father simply hired the best tutors so that the majority of Henie's efforts could be spent on building her celebrity stardom.

While her father paid the best experts in the world to make Henie an exquisite figure skater, and eventually, a popular Hollywood actress, it was her own heart and passion for life that allowed her to excel at each. Sonja's father was born into money from his parents' fur and paint equipment trades. Sonja's mother also came from a wealthy family who made millions in transportation and timber exploration. Their privileged daughter fit right into what many consider a sport of the privileged. They used their wealth to shop all over Europe for the best coaches who would develop Sonja's career on the ice. They even hired Russian ballerina Tamara Karsavina to train Sonja. Ballet elements had never before been used on the ice but the Henies could afford to look for any extra edge as a means to success.

Just two years after her national title, Henie made her Olympic debut at the 1924 Olympics in Chamonix, France. Her scores were high enough to put her in third place after the freestyle skate, but her scores in the compulsory events set her back to eighth place. Her naivety and inexperience were evident as she skated to the side of the rink several times during her program to ask her coach questions. Although Henie finished eighth out of the eight competitors at the 1924 Games, her presence alone was golden enough given that she was just 11 years old.

The Olympic experience warranted great returns as she would not compete in another Olympic Games without bringing home the gold medal—a feat she accomplished first at the 1928 St. Moritz, Switzerland Olympic Games, then at the 1932 Lake Placid Olympics, and finally at the 1936 Olympic Games in Germany. Henie was the first figure skater to win three gold medals back-to-back-to-back. One week after her fourth Olympics, Henie won her 10th consecutive World Championship, a record that remains unbroken. Also in 1936, she won her sixth consecutive European Championship.

Young girls wanted to skate like her, competitors wanted to beat her, and companies couldn't wait for her to endorse their products. She was an international sensation and one of the few female athletes of her time to receive sponsorship deals. Police officers often had to be called to control the crowds at her events. Henie revolutionized figure skating with her short skirts and dancing elements. At first, she got away with wearing a knee-length skirt rather than the traditional calf-length because of her young age, but as she grew, her skirt length did not. She could afford to spend more on her costumes than most competitors and always did, hoping to shock and surprise her audience. While it may perplex today's figure skating fans, prior to Henie's influence on the sport, spins and jumps were not standard on the ice. It is Henie who is credited with introducing today's staple elements to figure skating; "Henie's triumphs changed figure skating as rivals deserted the conventional, boring routines that had characterized the sport."[1]

With Henie's success came criticism and controversy. While skating at an exhibition in Berlin, Germany, Henie raised her right arm and cried, "Heil Hitler!" toward the chancellor's box. The Norwegian press had a field day and there was a public outcry from her countrymen who had already heard rumblings of the Nazi-committed atrocities. Yet, Henie didn't end her public showings of support and friendliness. Rumored to be family friends, Henie often visited Hitler at his German mountain retreat. It was no secret that he was fond of her image, which epitomized his vision of a pure, blonde

Aryan race. It was also reported that at the 1936 Olympic Games in Garmisch-Partenkirchen, Germany, the Norwegian skater shook hands with Chancellor Adolf Hitler after winning her third consecutive gold medal and accepted his invitation to lunch. After more public criticism from her home country, Henie was forced to call a press conference where she turned down rumors of an affair with Hitler and defended their relationship by saying, "Nazi-shmatzy! Hitler is the German leader, and I was honoring Germany, not the Nazis. I don't even know what a Nazi is."[2] It would not be long before Henie would find out, as the Nazis invaded her native Norway in 1940. It is believed that the autographed photo of Hitler that was prominently displayed in the Henie family home is what kept them all safe.

Following her three international titles in 1936, Henie decided to turn professional. She moved to the United States to pursue her lifelong dream of Hollywood stardom. Her father paid for and arranged an ice show in Hollywood to display his daughter's showmanship and get her foot—or skate—in the film industry's door. Darryl F. Zanuck of 20th Century Fox signed her to a contract for a series of films. Not known for her acting abilities, movie executives hired big stars for her to share the screen with and used her "natural effervescence and enchanting smile—together with her physical and athletic attributes" to cover up her "thespic deficiencies."[3] She even won 1944's Sour Apple Award given to the industry's "least cooperative actress." Nonetheless, each of her 11 feature films was a box-office hit. And each film included skating numbers choreographed and starred in by Henie herself. Within a year of starting her new career, Henie earned her first quarter-of-a-million dollars despite the fact that it was during the Great Depression. By 1939, she only trailed Clark Gable and Shirley Temple in box-office appeal, and by 1940, she was earning more than $2 million a year.

A portion of Henie's revenue also came from touring ice shows, which she turned to as television starting cutting into the movie industry's profits. She did two tours in the States in the late-1940s and early 1950s before doing the European Holiday On Ice Tour in 1953. Henie's taste for the extravagance and lavish things never wavered. During a show in Chicago, she asked a trusted friend to take the train in from New York just to sharpen her skates. He spent just minutes fixing her skates before boarding the train back to New York for what was an overnight trip each way. Henie officially retired from skating in 1960.

After two failed marriages to Americans, Henie married her childhood sweetheart and fellow Norwegian, shipping magnate Neils Onstad. In the mid-1960s, Henie was diagnosed with leukemia. She spent the remainder of her life fighting the disease. Her body succumbed to the cancer on October 12, 1969, while she was on a plane en route from Paris to Oslo. She was 57 years old. At the time of her death, she was among the world's 10 wealthiest women worth an estimated $47 million, with her art and jewelry collections alone equaling a combined $10 million.

Sonja Henie didn't glamorize the sport of figure skating by simply looking the part; she did so with style and grace, but more important, with victories. During her very publicized and often criticized career, Henie won an estimated 1,473 trophies, cups, and medals. Sonja Henie, the original ice queen, is still considered a member of figure skating's royal family.

Notes

1. Dick Heller, "Among Figure Skaters, Henie Remains Golden," *The Washington Times*, February 20, 2006.

2. Ibid.

3. Ibid.

Mabel Fairbanks

American Star of the Women's International Sports Hall of Fame

by Catherine Lahey

The story of American figure skating great Mabel Fairbanks is one part mystery, one part fairytale, three parts determination and all legendary. Years before athletes like Jackie Robinson and Nat "Sweetwater" Clifton broke racial barriers across the American professional sports leagues, a young Mabel Fairbanks was gliding her way to underground fame on the public ice rinks of New York City. After her athletic career was over, Fairbanks dedicated her life to the advancement of other athletes, particularly those of color, within the sport of figure skating. This is her story.

Though known for her candor with reporters as it regarded figure skating, Fairbanks seldom spoke about the early years of her life, making some aspects of her youth, including her birth date, a mystery. Fairbanks is believed to have been born in 1916 in the Florida Everglades (prompting a manager to later nickname her the "Swanee Snow Bird") to parents of African-American and Seminole descent. As a very young girl, Fairbanks was sent to New York City to live with an older brother. The reasoning for this move is much speculated about, with explanations ranging from poverty and abuse to abandonment and being orphaned.[1] With all of the mystery surrounding her early years, one thing is certain. It is this move to New York City that permanently changed the course of Mabel Fairbanks's life.

In Harlem, Fairbanks's fairytale unfolds. After watching skaters in Central Park, a young Fairbanks purchased a one-dollar pair of skates at a pawn shop and began to teach herself the graceful movements of figure skating. Although often turned away from rinks because of her race, her raw talent soon attracted the attention of famed skater and coach Maribel Vinson. Impressed by Fairbanks's skills, grace, and determination, Vinson began to give free lessons to the gifted, self-taught skater. Gliding on a pair of pawn shop blades, a poor young woman from Harlem quickly became one of America's best amateur figure skaters.

Fairbanks enjoyed a meteoric rise to public recognition, but her fairytale was short-lived. In the elite world of 1930s and 1940s figure skating, Fairbanks's race made her talent, skill, and grace largely irrelevant at the competitive level. A 1943 article in *Time Magazine* states that "experts rate her superior to most amateur whites and unquestionably the best skater of her race," but also points out that "producers who may be impressed draw the color line."[2] Since skating clubs were unwilling to admit a member of color, Fairbanks was never able to compete at the national or international level. Instead, she spent her career displaying her skills on a portable rink in New York nightclubs and touring California, Mexico, and South America with the Rhythm on Ice show.[3] By the 1950s, Fairbanks had hung up her skates.

Although it was her beauty, skill, and novelty that first drew the public's attention, it was her willpower, fortitude, and love of the sport that made her a legend. Over the next 50 years, Fairbanks dedicated herself to coaching, teaching, and promoting the sport of figure skating, particularly to young people of color. Working from Southern California, her early years as a coach were spent teaching the art of the ice to the children of major Hollywood stars. Still facing racism, including a "colored trade not solicited" sign at a Los Angeles area ice rink, Fairbanks inspired her students to rise beyond their surroundings and reach for their dreams. Her students included Atoy Wilson, the first African-American winner of a national title; Richard Ewell III and Michelle McCladdie, the first African-Americans to win a national title in pairs; Tai Babalonia and Randy Gardner, who she paired together and who later won a world pairs championship and five national titles; and Kristi Yamaguchi, an Olympic legend.[4] Already having changed the face of the sport, Fairbanks committed herself to changing the future.

Finally, in the 1990s, Fairbanks began to receive public recognition for her contributions to the figure skating community. In 1997, Fairbanks was inducted into the U.S. Figure Skating Hall of Fame, the first African-American to receive that honor. Fairbanks was posthumously inducted into the Women's Sports Foundation Hall of Fame in 2001, just days after succumbing to myasthenia gravis, a degenerative muscular disease. Upon her 1997 induction, Fairbanks stated, "I was denied opportunities, but [decided] I would do anything I could to make sure other black skaters were not denied a chance to participate at the very highest levels of competition . . . I honestly believe God put me here to help open up skating for all people, regardless of race and color."[5] Fairbanks's dedication and determination certainly paid off.

Jackie Robinson once stated that "a life is not important except in the impact it has on others' lives." His contemporary, Mabel Fairbanks, lived out this statement every day as both an athlete and a coach. Her grace and beauty, perseverance and grit acted as an inspiration to generations of athletes, regardless of race, color, or creed. Mabel Fairbanks reshaped the face and future of American figure skating; her life was important.

Notes

1. Ronald A. Scheurer, "Breaking the Ice: The Mabel Fairbanks Story," American Visions, December 1, 1997.

2. "Swanee Snow Bird," *Time Magazine*, November 29, 1943.

3. Nancy Gavilanes, "A Pioneer at the Rink is Proud of Her Legacy," *New York Times*, January 14, 2001, Figure Skating, Sports section.

4. Women's Sports Foundation, "Mabel Fairbanks: Breaking Down Barriers," Athletes, http://www.womenssportsfoundation.org/cgi-bin/iowa/athletes/article.html?record=71.

5. Ronald A. Scheurer, "Breaking the Ice."

Dr. Tenley E. Albright

American Star of the Women's International Sports Hall of Fame

by Catherine Lahey

Supremely graceful and breathtakingly beautiful, Tenley Albright was the toast of the American figure skating scene in the 1950s. Watching Albright joyfully dance across the ice was like watching an artist turn a blank canvas into a masterpiece. Known for her innovative jumps and spins, Albright was also a master of the compulsory components of her routines. She approached her craft with both style and precision.

Albright excelled at competitive figure skating at a time when the sport was prized for its delicacy, grace, and feminine beauty. Though Albright appeared to fit the traditional image of the privileged, ultra-feminine figure skating icon, this public façade masked a complex array of talents, interests, and conquered challenges. The daughter of a prominent Massachusetts surgeon, Albright was diagnosed with polio at age 11, in an era when little was known about the disease's process, treatment, or cure. The Albright family was warned that young Tenley might never walk again, much less pursue her interest in figure skating. During her treatment, Albright endured several painful procedures and was restricted from moving her back, neck, and legs.[1]

Finally, after months of hospitalization, Albright's doctors slowly challenged her to take a few steps at a time. She met each test with determination and her condition began to steadily improve. Upon her release from the hospital in 1946, her doctors recommended that she return to skating, as the familiar and fun activity might help her reacclimate to "normal" life.

Her first time back to the rink, Albright clung to the barriers— unsteady and unsure on the ice. Just as she had done in the hospital, Albright began to challenge her body to surpass its physical barriers. As an adult, Albright wondered if this recovery process may have sparked her lasting interest in figure skating. "When I found that my muscles could do some things, it made me appreciate them more. I've often wondered if maybe the reason [figure skating] appealed to me so much was that I had a chance to appreciate my muscles, knowing what it was like when I couldn't use them."[2]

Buoyed by the excitement of using her muscles freely, Albright won the Eastern Juvenile Skating Championships only four months after being released from the hospital. This win marked the beginning of a long string of successes in Albright's figure skating career. At the age of 16, Albright stepped into the international spotlight by winning a silver medal at the 1952 Winter Olympic Games in Oslo, Norway. Back at home that same year she continued her winning ways, earning the first of five consecutive national titles.

In 1953, Albright reached a number of milestones. Athletically, she became the first American woman to win a world figure skating championship. To this achievement, she added the titles of North American and U.S. Champion, making her the first winner of figure skating's elusive "triple crown." Personally, Albright enrolled in Radcliffe College, declaring a pre-med major. While other students enjoyed a leisurely collegiate experience, Albright practiced skating from 4:00 a.m. to 6:00 a.m. before tackling her daily studies.

This dedication to her craft paid off as she won the 1955 World Championships and qualified to skate in the 1956 Winter Olympics in Cortina, Italy. An accomplished student, Albright left Radcliffe to focus on her Olympic performance. Two weeks before the competition, Albright fell while practicing and sustained a serious cut to her right ankle. Immediately, her father flew to Italy in order to repair the damage to both vein and bone. Just as she had done while recovering from polio, Albright persevered through the pain. Her brilliant Olympic performance earned her the gold medal, making her the first American woman to achieve such a feat in figure skating.[3]

Upon her return to the United States, Albright shifted her focus back to the world of academia. Though she had not officially graduated from Radcliffe, she applied to Harvard Medical School. After seven interviews, she became one of only five women accepted to a class of 135 total students. Again, she persisted against the odds, eventually becoming a successful surgeon and a leader in blood plasma research. She also maintained her ties to skating by becoming the first woman to serve as an officer on the U.S. Olympic Committee and as an inductee into the World Figure Skating and Olympic Halls of Fame.

Highly successful as both a figure skater and a doctor, Albright lives her life according to some advice she received from her grand-mother while still in high school. A teacher questioned Albright about why she continued to do something "as frivolous as" figure skating when she had aspirations of undertaking the very difficult and serious task of becoming a surgeon. Albright realized that she didn't have an answer. She mentioned the conversation to her grand-mother, who gave her some advice she would never forget. "You have an obligation to do the best you can with whatever you've got. And if you like to do a sport, and you can do it well, that's a way of expressing what God gave you."[4] Her grandmother would be proud of Albright's adherence to these principles. Dr. Tenley Albright, a fig-ure skating champion, prominent surgeon, and groundbreaking medical researcher, has certainly done the best with what she has been given.

Notes

1. "Dr. Tenley E. Albright," Biography, Changing the Face of Medicine, http://www.nlm.nih.gov/changingthefaceofmedicine/physicians/biography_3.html.

2. Tenley Albright, interview, *Academy of Achievement*, June 21, 1991.

3. "Albright, Tenley," Figure Skating Legends, United States Olympic Committee, http://www.usoc.org/26_13369.htm.

4. Tenley Albright, interview, *Academy of Achievement*, June 21, 1991.

Peggy Fleming Jenkins

American Star of the Women's International Sports Hall of Fame

by Catherine Lahey

The early 1960s marked a dark period in the illustrious history of U.S. figure skating. At a time when the National Anthem should have been booming over podiums full of American skaters, there was only an eerie silence. In 1961, a tragic plane crash took the lives of all 18 members of the U.S. Figure Skating Team and numerous coaches, officials, friends, and family members. The victims of this crash, on their way to an undoubtedly brilliant showing at the World Championships in Prague, comprised the heart of the American figure skating community. Among the deceased were Maribel Vinson Owen, an extremely talented skater and one-time coach to Tenley Albright and Mabel Fairbanks; her 16-year-old daughter Laurence, the 1961 U.S. Ladies Champion; and 20-year-old daughter Maribel, the 1961 U.S. Pairs Champion.[1] In a single instant, the best and brightest American skaters and coaches were gone, a devastating and demoralizing loss. Shining out of this darkness came the delicate but steady light of Peggy Fleming.

Just 12 years old at the time of the crash, Peggy Fleming was an exceptional skater already being coached by William Kipp, one of the elite-level instructors killed in the tragedy. Even without a coach, the loss of America's best threw the slight, elegant young lady into the national spotlight almost immediately. In 1964, at the tender age of 15, Fleming competed in her first Olympic Games, finishing an impressive sixth in ladies singles. The same year, she captured her first of five consecutive U.S. National Championships. From the smoldering wreckage of the U.S. National Figure Skating Program, Peggy Fleming was rising like the mythical phoenix, restoring hope and life to American figure skating.

In 1966, Fleming took the world by surprise by winning her first World Championship. While reporters focused on her beauty and diminutive size, Fleming concentrated on approaching her physically demanding routines with precision, skill, and grace. Although many female skaters forced themselves into a powerfully athletic approach, Fleming sought to be "ballet-like" and the judges loved her for it.[2] She was often compared to former U.S. figure skater Tenley Albright, an athlete known for her beauty, grace, and competitive creativity. Fleming soon became the darling of figure skating, drawing compliments from coaches and competitors alike. She would go on to win two more World Championships in 1967 and 1968.

Though already a U.S. and World champion, Fleming enjoyed her greatest triumph during the 1968 Winter Olympics in Grenoble, France. Fleming skated nearly flawlessly, awing the crowd and handily surpassing the talents of her competition. Just seven years after the loss of the best American skaters and coaches, Peggy Fleming won an Olympic gold medal, returning figure skating glory to the United States. She garnered the only gold medal for the United States at those Olympic Games.

Soon after, Fleming embarked on a professional career, starring in highly popular ice shows and televised skating specials. She later accepted roles on popular television shows, did commercial endorsements, and served as an analyst of figure skating coverage for ABC Sports. Fleming has skated at the White House and at the unveiling of the restored Statue of Liberty. Her talents have won her numerous awards and honors, including 1967 ABC Athlete of the Year, 1968 AP Female Athlete of the Year, and the 2003 Vince Lombardi Award of Excellence. In 1999, *Sports Illustrated* named her one of seven "Athletes Who Changed the Game," an honor whose elite company includes Billie Jean King and Jackie Robinson.[3]

While all of these awards are impressive, one of the most telling stories about Fleming took place at a time when her amazing athletic career was just beginning to bloom. After the 18-year-old sensation won her second world title, a reporter asked her how someone of her small stature and delicate nature could possibly perform such physically taxing routines. In response, Fleming smiled and spoke only two words: "Inner guts."[4]

It was these "inner guts" that Fleming called upon in 1998, when she was diagnosed with breast cancer on the 30th anniversary of her gold medal win. With the help of the physical and mental strength she gained over her time as an elite athlete, Fleming was able to approach her cancer as she would an opponent on the rink.

"This is another kind of competition, but I'm being coached by an excellent team and I've got a real strong competitive spirit."[5] Fleming defeated her diagnosis and became an outspoken advocate for breast cancer awareness.

Today, Fleming owns and operates a winery with her husband Dr. Greg Jenkins. Although she has taken many roles and supported many causes, Fleming may be best remembered for being a beautiful, steady light in a dark time in American athletics. Her poise and performance touched a nation and in return, she garnered the courage to face the darkest time in her own life with hope and strength.

Notes

1. "History of the Memorial Fund," U.S. Figure Skating, http://www.usfigure skating.org/About.asp?id=206.

2. Bob Ottum, "Crystal and Steel on the Ice," *Sports Illustrated*, March 13, 1967.

3. "Peggy Fleming," Winter Athlete Bios, United States Olympic Committee, http://www.usoc.org/26_13370.htm.

4. Bob Ottum, "Crystal and Steel on the Ice."

5. "Peggy Fleming," Winter Athlete Bios, United States Olympic Committee, http://www.usoc.org/26_13370.htm.

Katarina Witt

International Star of the Women's International Sports Hall of Fame

by Catherine Lahey

Katarina Witt, a decorated German figure skater, has never been overly concerned by the rules of the game. While she trained relentlessly, followed her diet strictly and strove for athletic greatness, she also drove fast, danced with abandon, and flirted mischievously with all of her adorers. Even as a product of the notoriously rigid East German athletic system, Witt never failed to charmingly assert her individuality. In an East German television interview early in her career, the interviewer attempted to coerce Witt into linking figure skating with physics and scientific development. Witt never budged, refusing to confirm that either aspect was a central part of the sport she loved. While the reporter fumed, Witt glided away on her skates, smiling innocently.[1] For Witt, the most decorated figure skater of all time, figure skating was never about the technicality and the hard science. In keeping with this philosophy, Witt is best known for breathtaking beauty, interpretive and complex routines, and her ability to engage and awe the crowd. For these incredible qualities, Katarina Witt is remembered as one of the most talented and most admired female athletes of all time.

Witt began skating as a five-year-old in her hometown of Karl-Marx-Stadt (now Chemnitz), East Germany. By the age of seven, the young prodigy was winning competitions and at age 10 she became a student of Jutta Müeller, the most successful and demanding coach in the East German system.[2] Under Frau Müeller's watchful eye, the talented and spirited Witt developed into an incredible skater with powerful spins and impeccable style. As a coach, Müeller stressed the importance of presentation, storytelling, and style, focusing on the aesthetic elements of skating as much as the technical ones. Witt, often self-described as a person who "likes to flirt," turned out to be the ideal student for Müeller's skating philosophy.[3]

Soon, Witt exploded to prominence and popularity on a grand level. As a teenager in 1981, Witt won her first of eight consecutive National Championships. Two years later, she won the prestigious

European Championship, the first of six during her career. After these accomplishments, her stardom was beginning to shine on an international level and 1984 marked a breakout year as she captured a World Championship and competed in her first Olympic Games. Although not the favorite to win the Sarajevo Games, Witt awed the judges and the audience with her raw and engaging performance, capturing the gold medal.

Instantly, Witt's beauty and playful charm catapulted her to international superstardom both on and off the ice. Love letters from all over the world began to pile up at her door, eventually filling her bathtub when all other storage spaces were exhausted. Her love of life flowed joyfully through her skating and the world was captivated. Witt soaked up the attention and applied that energy to her skating.

Though many in the skating world expected that Witt would retire from skating soon after the 1984 Olympics, she continued to train behind the iron curtain, ignoring offers of citizenship from other nations. Witt's hard work paid off as she again won the title of World Champion in 1985, 1987 and 1988. Her continued success secured the admiration and respect of her countrymen, elevating her to the status of a national hero. Entering the 1988 Winter Olympic Games, Witt made no secret of the fact that she was ready to retire from amateur skating and that she was absolutely determined to go out on top.

In what has been referred to as the "Dueling Carmens," East Germany's Witt and the United States's Debi Thomas faced off in Olympic competition, both skating their long programs to music from the opera Carmen. As the defending Olympic gold medalist, many saw Witt at a disadvantage because Sonja Henie, in 1936, was the last figure skater to defend her Olympic title. Additionally, the talk of the Games was Witt's performance attire, as competitors sniped that her garments were far too revealing and detracted from the honor and beauty of the sport. Though Witt and Müeller strongly disagreed, they did slightly modify her short program outfit and Witt internalized the criticism to her advantage. Motivated by the controversy and her desire to close her amateur career as a champion, Witt proved to be the better Carmen, again earning Olympic gold.[4]

Shortly after the Olympics, Witt turned professional and began touring with famed U.S. skater Brian Boitano. She also spent four years as a performer in Stars on Ice and has created skating shows entitled "Divas on Ice" and "Enjoy the Stars." In 1990, Witt won an Emmy for her performance in the television special "Carmen on Ice" and has appeared in or produced numerous films and television programs. Also a businesswoman, Witt is a founding partner of the production company With Witt and also has been a spokeswoman for a number of major corporations. Even with all of these roles and achievements, Witt has maintained that "the role I like best is [the role] of the champion."[5]

Remembered as the consummate performer, Witt also gives of herself in order to help others. Due to an unprecedented ruling by the International Skating Union (ISU), Witt and other recently declared professionals were able to participate in the 1994 Winter Olympics in Norway. Witt, remembering Sarajevo, the city of her first gold medal victory, dedicated her performance to those suffering in the Bosnian conflict. Though she did not win, the crowd responded emotionally to her impassioned performance, grasping its gravity.[6] Today, Witt uses her fame to promote the Katarina Witt Foundation, an organization that seeks to return mobility to children who have physical disabilities. Though Witt's external beauty made her memorable, it is her internal beauty that has made a lasting impression. Katarina Witt's talent and commitment to giving back make her the vision of a true champion.

Notes

1. Rick Reilly, "Behold the Shining Star of the G.d.r.," *Sports Illustrated*, January 20, 1986.

2. "Competitive Skating," Biography, Katarina Witt, http://www.katarina.de/index.php?article_id=1&clang=1.

3. Reilly, "Behold the Shining Star of the G.d.r."

4. E. M. Swift, "To Witt, The Victory," *Sports Illustrated*, March 7, 1988.

5. Ibid.

6. Ian Thomsen, "Katarina Witt," *Sports Illustrated*, January 31, 1994.

Kristi Yamaguchi

American Star of the Women's International Sports Hall of Fame

by Jessica Bartter

Through the controversy and scandal on ice that occurred between Nancy Kerrigan and Tonya Harding came a shining star and savior of American figure skating: Kristi Yamaguchi. At first, Yamaguchi struggled with the idea of being an ambassador for figure skating but her undeniable appeal and talent thrust her into the limelight. Despite her resistance, she "always viewed serving as a role model an honor. It's not something one should have to try and be, but simply being yourself and being responsible is what will serve as a positive example."[1] Yamaguchi learned this lesson first from her skating hero and inspiration, Dorothy Hamill, the 1976 Olympic champion.

Born in Hayward, California, on July 12, 1971, Yamaguchi began skating at six years old as a form of therapy for her club feet. The lessons begot great results by improving her ability to walk and also developing her into an international sensation on ice. As a teenager in 1986, Yamaguchi and partner Rudy Galindo won the pairs U.S. Junior Championships. She followed that performance with a World Junior Championship singles title. Yamaguchi and Galindo were unique in that both were successful individual skaters before being paired with one another. Their individual abilities bettered their team appearance while performing difficult elements that today's pairs teams are still unable to coordinate.

Galindo and Yamaguchi enjoyed several years of success as a team with a World Juniors Championship title during the 1987–88 season and two more U.S. Championships during the 1988–89 and 1989–90 seasons. But juggling both an individual career with the pairs competition became taxing on Yamaguchi's overall performance and she was faced with the decision to pick one or the other. In 1990, Yamaguchi was entered in both the ladies singles and the pairs categories for the World Championships and recalls being "exhausted from skating both categories back-to-back" to the point that she "didn't skate well in either event."[2] Even the International Skating Union officials started putting pressure on the 18-year-old to pick between the two events she loved.

In the end, Yamaguchi chose to focus on her individual career. Almost immediately she enjoyed the fruits of her labor with three event victories during the 1990–91 season: the World Championships, Skate America, and the Nations Cup.

In 1991, Yamaguchi took her focus to the next level by moving to Edmonton, Alberta, to train with legendary coach Christy Ness. That year, Yamaguchi earned her third consecutive silver medal at the U.S. Championships, losing to Tonya Harding. Harding, Yamaguchi, and Nancy Kerrigan traveled to Munich, Germany, a month later for the World Championships. Yamaguchi's focus on her individual routines was finally breeding success as she earned her first perfect score while on one of the grandest stages of competition, the World Championship! The American team became the first and only ladies team to sweep the medals as Yamaguchi placed first, Harding second, and Kerrigan third.

The streak of second place finishes at the U.S. Championships was finally broken in 1992, when Yamaguchi again beat out Kerrigan and Harding for the title, her first U.S. title. All three earned the honor to travel to Albertville, France, to represent the United States in the 1992 Winter Olympics. Yamaguchi followed in the skates of her role model, Dorothy Hamill, and became the first American woman to skate to Olympic gold since Hamill had done so in 1976.

Kristi Yamaguchi did not take representing her country lightly, as the third-generation Japanese-American recognizes the significance of the American flag. During World War II, her grandparents were forced into American internment camps, where her mother was actually born. Yamaguchi heard firsthand stories from her grandparents that helped build great pride in her heritage and herself as an Asian-American. Some believe Yamaguchi's Asian heritage has affected her bottom line when it comes to big name endorsements. While marketers may think she lacks the "wholesome All-American" girl image, they can't argue with a recent 2008 Harris Poll that found Yamaguchi in the top 10 of the United States' favorite female athletes. Sixteen years after her Olympic stardom, Yamaguchi's appeal is still undeniable.

Much of Yamaguchi's lasting-appeal can be directly linked to her huge success with Stars on Ice. After the 1992 season, Yamaguchi turned professional and avoided the mistake many athletes make by refusing to go out on top. After winning Olympic gold, Yamaguchi had reached the epitome of her career and though she kept her competitive spirit, she fulfilled her remaining passion for figure skating with the traveling skating show of Stars on Ice until 2002.

While winning the Olympic gold medal in 1992 was the crowning glory of her professional career, Yamaguchi came home from Albertville with an important gift to her personal life as well. While in France she met her future husband and fellow Olympian, Bret Hedican, a member of the American ice hockey team. The ice-loving pair wed in 2000 and now have two daughters, Keara and Emma.

Most recently, Yamaguchi again won over the hearts of Americans through her participation and domination of ABC's Dancing with the Stars. Yamaguchi broke many records with her scores during the show's sixth season. Although she was not new to choreographed routines, dancing on hardwood presented a very different challenge than she was accustomed to on the ice. As always, Yamaguchi practiced hard and performed perfectly to become just the second female star to win Dancing with the Stars.

In 2008, Yamaguchi received the Inspiration Award at the Asian Excellence Awards. Also in 2008, she received the Sonja Henie Award from the Professional Skaters Association. Yamaguchi was also honored with the Women's Sports Foundation Flo Hyman Award. Both Henie and Hyman are trailblazers included in this book. Yamaguchi joins good company.

Equally important, but lesser known than Yamaguchi's Olympic triumphs, is her founding of an organization that "helps children fulfill their dreams." It is rightfully named after her favorite motto: Always Dream. Kristi Yamaguchi's career is one of a young girl who dared to dream big. From hitting the rink at 5:00 a.m. as a six-year-old to standing atop many triumphant podiums along the way, Yamaguchi has given countless young "all-American" girls, particularly Asian-Americans, the opportunity to always dream.

Notes

1. Ethen Lieser, "Golden Girl: Ten Years after Winning the Medal, Kristi Yamaguchi Is Still Celebrating," *AsianWeek*, January 20, 2002.

2. "Magic on Ice: Figure Skater Kristi Yamaguchi," *Today's Woman*, March 31, 2002.

Bonnie Blair

American Star of the Women's International Sports Hall of Fame

by Catherine Lahey

Bonnie Blair's accomplishments as an athlete are incredible. Blair, a speed skater, is the most decorated American woman in winter Olympic history. Her performance in the 500-meter event earned her gold medals in three consecutive Olympic Winter Games (1988, 1992, and 1994). In those same games she garnered a bronze and two gold medals in the 1,000-meter distance. Blair was the first woman to break the 39 second barrier in the 500 meter, speed skating's version of the four minute mile. On her 31st birthday, Blair blazed an American record and a personal best in the 1,000 meters.[1] She retired a champion, still at the peak of her game.

Her accomplishments have led to some of the greatest honors in sports. In 1992, Blair was named the winner of the James E. Sullivan Award, an honor reserved for America's top amateur athlete. She was only the second American to win Norway's Oscar, an award recognizing the world's best speed skater. ESPN counts her as the 69th greatest athlete of the 20th century. She's been named athlete or sportswoman of the year by *Sports Illustrated*, the AP, ABC Sports, CBS, the Women's Sports Foundation, and the United States Olympic Committee. In 2002, she was inducted into the United States Olympic Hall of Fame as America's most decorated winter Olympian. Bonnie Blair's status as a legend is unquestionable.

Although Blair's athletic achievements make her appear superhuman, it is her humanity—her normalcy—that makes her truly inspiring. Blair is the kind of athlete that young people of every race, region, and athletic ability can attempt to emulate. Undersized by traditional speed skating standards, Blair crafted her technique to maximize every ounce of effort. Former U.S. Olympic coach Peter Mueller once called her "the best technician in the world over the sprint distance, man or woman."[2] On the ice, in the heat of competition, Blair was all power, grace, and fluidity—consummately prepared and simply stunning. Beyond the spotlight, she toiled alone in freezing rinks across the globe, missing innumerable family holidays and pushing herself for the love of the sport and the thrill of competition.

Much of her passion and drive seems to be drawn from the Blair family itself. As the youngest of six children, Blair grew up in a house virtually obsessed with the pursuit of speed on ice. In fact, her father and all five siblings were participating in a speed skating meet when Eleanor Blair gave birth to Bonnie. The family was informed of the birth over the rink's loudspeaker, marking the first of many public address announcements about Bonnie Blair. By age two, Blair was gliding across the ice, her feet so small that she wore a pair of shoes inside the smallest pair of hand-me-down skates the Blair family owned.

As the years passed, the Blair children, most of them champions at the national level of competitive speed skating, slowly began to move beyond the sport, leaving Bonnie to make a choice. And so she chose, said her sister Mary, "She dedicated her life to it." Blair spent her high school years training and competing on the speed skating circuit, determined to turn her talent into success. With the financial backing of the Champaign (Illinois) Policemen's Benevolent Association, she moved to Europe to train full-time and learn the intimate nuances of the sport. At 19, only a few short years after making the pivotal decision to fully dedicate herself to speed skating, Blair competed in her first Olympic Games, finishing eighth in the 500 meters.[3]

Through Bonnie, the Blair family recommitted themselves to speed skating. Together with family friends, they formed the Blair Bunch, a group dedicated to supporting Bonnie at all of her major events. They became to Blair what the Cameron Crazies are to Duke basketball. The Blair Bunch strengthened and inspired her, fueling her pursuit of greatness. Perhaps best of all, they shared fully in her joys—after all, no family understands the pure exhilaration of speed on ice better than the Blairs.

While Bonnie drew inspiration from her supporters, one of them, her brother Rob, drew strength and motivation from her. Stricken with an inoperable brain tumor, Rob frequently experienced seizures that left him continually learning how to reuse the right side of his body. When others might despair, the Blairs turn to each other.

"I watch what Bonnie does and that just feeds into me," said Rob in a 1991 *Sports Illustrated* interview. "She has said that I've inspired her and that's nice of her to say. But I've gotten a lot more from her example than the other way around."[4] This attitude is the epitome of the connection the Blair clan shares. Their familial inspiration is not a straight line; it's a circle.

Now, in her retirement, Blair has more time to dedicate to her family, which includes husband and fellow Olympic speed skater David Cruikshank. Though she is one of the winningest female athletes in American history, Blair has never let the shine of a gold medal blind her to the truly important things in life. "Winning doesn't always mean being first," says Blair. "Winning means you're doing better than you've ever done before."[5]

Notes

1. Larry Schwartz, "Blair is special . . . but she doesn't know it," ESPN.com, March 18, 2005. http://sports.espn.go.com/espn/classic/bio/news/story?page=Blair _Bonnie.

2. Schwartz, "Blair is special."

3. Steve Rushin, "Child of Innocence," *Sports Illustrated*, December 19, 1994.

4. Ibid.

5. Bonnie Blair, "Personal Growth," A Gift of Inspiration, http://www.agiftofin spiration.com.au/quotes/personalgrowth.shtml.

6

FEMALE SWIMMERS AND DIVERS: LAPPING EXPECTATIONS IN THE POOL

Introduction by Richard Lapchick

The excitement around swimming at the Beijing Olympics highlighted how popular the sport is in America and around the world. While so much of the attention focused on Michael Phelps's extraordinary achievements, women also caught the attention of the media and fans. It did not hurt that the U.S. team had 41-year-old Dara Torres swimming. She broke the mold of the youthful champions.

There is no record of swimming as a sport until early in the 19th century, when the National Swimming Society of Great Britain, established in 1837, began to conduct competitions in the six pools in London. As the sport grew in popularity more pools were built. By the time the Amateur Swimming Association of Great Britain was organized as a governing body in 1880, there were more than 300 member clubs.

Swimming has been held at every Olympic Games. Women were excluded from swimming in the first several Olympic Games. The man credited with founding the modern Olympics, Baron Pierre de Coubertin, believed that women were too frail to be in competitive sports.

In the early days, prudery slowed the progress of women as swimmers. What the "proper" swimsuit was and what it covered were the issues of the day. Annette Kellerman, one of the 20th century's early great swimmers, was also an activist and became known as an advocate for the right of women to wear a one-piece bathing suit instead of the cumbersome swimsuits of the day, which consisted of a dress and "pantaloons." Kellerman was arrested in 1907 for "indecency" in Boston for wearing the one-piece suit.

On August 24, 1905, Kellerman became the first woman to attempt to swim the English Channel. She was unsuccessful in three attempts.

Women's swimming was first held at the 1912 Stockholm Olympics and has been conducted at all the Olympics since then. Today, men and women compete in an almost identical program with the same number of events. The difference is that the freestyle distance for men is 1,500 meters and 800 meters for women.

Aileen Riggin, who became one of America's first female sportswriters, was the first athlete, male or female, to medal in both the Olympic swimming and diving competitions. At the 1920 Antwerp Games, the then 14-year-old from Brooklyn Heights, New York, won the first women's Olympic springboard diving competition. Four years later, in Paris, she won a silver in the springboard and a bronze in the 100-meter backstroke.

In the 1924 Paris Olympics, the U.S. team won nine gold medals in the 11 events. Johnny Weissmuller, who would later play Tarzan in the movies, won two individual golds as well as gold in the relay. Gertrude Ederle won two bronze medals and a relay gold.

It was 1926, 22 years after Kellerman's unsuccessful attempts, that Gertrude Ederle not only became the first woman to swim the Channel, but smashed the record set by a man by more than two hours. No woman beat her time until 1950!

Ederle became an American hero, welcomed home with a ticker-tape parade in New York City before an estimated two million people. Ederle's fame came at a huge personal cost as she lost her hearing because of water damage to her eardrums during the channel swim. Ederle had a nervous breakdown in 1928 and a severe back injury put her in a cast for more than four years. When she recovered in 1933, Ederle became a swimming instructor for deaf children.

In the 1932 Los Angeles Games, the Japanese men won five gold, four silver, and two bronze out of 18 possible medals. Only Buster Crabbe won a gold for the U.S. in the 400-meter freestyle. The U.S. women did far better, with four gold medals. Eleanor Holm won the 100-meter backstroke. Helene Madison, who had been named the AP Female Athlete of the Year for swimming in 1931, became the first woman to swim the 100-meter freestyle in a minute at the Los Angeles Games.

We could have written chapters on all these women but we chose Eleanor Holm, Florence Chadwick, Janet Evans, Tracy Caulkins, Debbie Meyer, Mary Meagher Plant, Nancy Hogshead-Makar, Diana Nyad, and Donna de Varona as our swimmers and Micki King and Pat McCormick as our divers.

Eleanor Holm is remembered by many as the "Champagne Girl," a swimming prodigy out of Brooklyn, New York, who had a taste for the good life. Then 14 years old, she made her Olympic debut at the 1928 Amsterdam Olympics, where she finished fifth in the 100-meter backstroke. In 1932, at the Los Angeles Olympic Games, she won the gold by nearly two seconds with a time of 1:19.4. Her nickname came after Holm married singer and orchestra leader Art Jarrett, exposing her to a different lifestyle in which she was hanging out with a Hollywood crowd and performing in many of her husband's nightclub shows.

Holm wanted to defend her gold medal in Berlin. She had not lost a race in seven years and had become the first American woman to be chosen to swim for three Olympic teams. But American Olympic Committee (AOC) President Avery Brundage removed her from the team, despite having 200 American athletes sign a petition to reinstate her. She was removed because she had too much to drink on the ship taking the athletes to Germany.

Ederle's record swim of the English Channel in 1926 fell on August 21, 1950, when Florence Chadwick finished the 19-mile swim in 13 hours and 23 minutes, finishing ahead of the previous record of 14 hours and 34 minutes. On September 24, 1951, Chadwick again swam across the Channel, this time taking the more arduous route from England to France, a 21-mile route that had never been accomplished by a woman and up to that time had been completed by nine men. Chadwick swam the English Channel four times and the Catalina Channel three times.

It was 1968 and the 16-year-old Debbie Meyer knew that by qualifying for the U.S. National Team, she would win Olympic medals. She did more than that and became the first swimmer to win three individual gold medals at one Olympics. Up to her retirement in 1972 at age 20, Meyer set 15 world records and 27 American records, and was named World Swimmer of the Year from 1967 to 1969. In 1968, on the cusp of her Olympic triumph, she was awarded the 1968 Sullivan Award as the top amateur athlete.

Like many others, Mary Meagher Plant was expected to medal in the 1980 Olympics, but did not compete because of the U.S. boycott of the Olympics in the Soviet Union. Meagher Plant would make the most of her opportunity at the 1984 Los Angeles Olympics by winning three gold medals in the 100-meter and 200-meter butterfly and the women's medley relay. In 1985, she was again named the women's World Swimmer of the Year, a title she had won in 1981 with her world record-setting performances in the 100-meter and 200-meter butterfly. Her record in the 100-meter butterfly lasted more than 19 years and her record in the 200-meter event lasted more than 20 years.

By the end of her career, in addition to her Olympic records, Meagher Plant had set seven world records and won 24 U.S. national titles.

Tracy Caulkins captained the U.S. swimming team at the 1984 Los Angeles Olympics while winning individual gold medals in the 200-meter individual medley and the 400-meter individual medley, and swimming the breaststroke on the 400-meter medley relay. Like so many others, she had been primed to win big in 1980 before the United States decided to boycott the Moscow Games. During her swimming career at the University of Florida, Caulkins won 16 national championships, including 12 individual championships, the most ever by any swimmer or diver. In 1982 and 1984, Caulkins received the Broderick Cup, given annually to the nation's top collegiate female athlete. Caulkins burst onto the international swimming scene at the 1978 World Championships in Berlin by winning five gold medals and one silver medal. That performance earned her the 1978 James E. Sullivan Award as the most outstanding amateur athlete in the United States; at age 15 she was the youngest winner of the award to date. Then the United States pulled out of the Moscow Games and Caulkins had to wait.

Janet Evans may have helped create one of the greatest Olympic moments ever when she carried the torch through the stadium in the Atlanta opening ceremonies and handed it to Muhammad Ali. Her Olympic career started in Seoul at the 1988 Olympics, where she won her first gold medal in the 400-meter individual medley and broke her own world record while winning gold in the 400-meter freestyle. Her 400-meter freestyle record stood for more than 17 years. Evans would later add another gold medal by capturing the

800-meter freestyle. Evans's 800-meter freestyle record, later set in August 1989, was one of the longest-standing records in swimming history until it was broken in the 2008 Beijing Olympics. At Barcelona, Evans defended her gold medal in the 800-meter freestyle and won a silver medal in the 400-meter freestyle.

The three swimmers in our book that I know are Nancy Hogshead-Makar, Donna de Varona, and Diana Nyad. I know them more because of their lifelong commitments to social justice, especially in the area of the right for women and girls to compete in sports.

I met Nancy Hogshead-Makar in 1984 after the Los Angeles Olympic Games and was immediately struck by more than the amazing accomplishments of this great swimmer, to which her three gold and one silver medals attest. Nancy immediately displayed intelligence, confidence, poise, and leadership skills that would propel her to be one of the most influential people in the world of sport, especially on the issue of gender equity. As an athlete, she was undefeated in high school and college. She was named Florida's Outstanding Athlete and the best all-around swimmer nationally. I now live in Florida and realize how important sports are here so it was no small feat that Nancy was named as one of the 13 greatest athletes of the 20th century in the State of Florida by *Sports Illustrated* in their Millennium Issue.

Donna de Varona was the youngest swimmer to compete at the 1960 Summer Olympics in Rome. In the 1964 Tokyo Olympics, she won gold medals in the 400-meter individual medley and as a member of the 400-meter freestyle relay. In all, she set 18 different swimming records before she retired after the 1964 Olympics. A year later, she became the first female sportscaster in television history when she signed a contract with ABC. De Varona was a serious activist in support of Title IX and helped to establish the Women's Sports Foundation, where she served as their first president from 1976 to 1984.

Diana Nyad was recognized as the greatest long-distance swimmer in the world throughout the 1970s. In 1979, she completed the longest swim in history, making the 100-plus-mile journey from the island of Bimini to Florida in more than two days of constant swimming. Nyad set numerous world records. In 1975, she smashed the 50-year-old record for circling Manhattan Island in 7 hours and

57 minutes. She is a regular commentator for National Public Radio. Like Hogshead-Makar and de Varona, Nyad is a passionate advocate for social justice and is a staunch supporter of the Women's Sports Foundation.

Pat McCormick failed to make the 1948 U.S. Olympic diving team by $1/100$th of a point. She never looked back and won a "double-double" at the 1952 Helsinki Olympics and the 1956 Melbourne Olympics, McCormick was *Sports Illustrated*'s "Athlete of the Year" and the AP's "Woman Athlete of the Year." Her daughter, Kelly, won a silver medal in the 1984 Los Angeles Olympics and a bronze in the 1988 Seoul Olympics. The McCormicks are the only mother-daughter medal winning combination in Olympic history.

In the Mexico City Games, Micki King led the diving competition until she broke her arm on the ninth of her 10 dives. She finished a devastating fourth. At age 28, the Air Force lieutenant won the gold in Munich. Feeling the athletes were not being treated right, King helped organize the Athletes' Advisory Council (AAC) as a standing forum of the U.S. Olympic Committee. At the inaugural meeting of the AAC, King was elected its first chairman and led the group for the first four years. To this day, it is enormously influential. The Air Force assigned King to the Air Force Academy (AFA) athletic department, where she became the first woman to teach physical education and coach at any military academy. In her first stint as coach from 1973 to 1977, she became the first and only woman to ever coach a man to an individual NCAA championship. In 1992, she retired from the Air Force as a full colonel to accept an assistant athletic director position at the University of Kentucky, where she held the post through 2006.

These swimmers and divers set the way for today's greats. Fifteen U.S. women won medals with seven winning at least two medals in Beijing in 2008. The U.S. team totaled 31 medals, including two gold, 18 silver, and 11 bronze. Natalie Coughlin won a gold, a silver, and three bronze medals. Rebecca Soni won a gold and two silvers. Dara Torres won an amazing three silvers, giving hope to all aging athletes that there is more in them even in their 40s.

Eleanor Holm

American Star of the Women's International Sports Hall of Fame

by Horacio Ruiz

Many will forever remember her as the "Champagne Girl," the swimming prodigy out of Brooklyn, New York, who had a taste for the good life. Aboard the German-bound SS Manhattan en route to the 1936 Olympics, the "Champagne Girl," after a young night's worth of drinking in the ship's first-class section, was found staggering along the ship's deck by the U.S. Olympic team chaperone. Upon being returned to her room in the ship's third-class section reserved for athletes—an indignity to her—she stuck her head out of a window screaming obscenities to no one in particular. Her roommates pulled her in and by midnight she was soundly asleep.

The ship and U.S. Olympic team doctors entered her room and found her to be "in a deep slumber which approached a state of coma" and diagnosed her with "acute alcoholism." The members of the American Olympic Committee (AOC) held a meeting to discuss what sanctions to take against her. The next morning, she was informed by the team manager that she had been removed from the team.

"This chaperone came up to me and told me it was time to go to bed. God, it was about 9 o'clock, and who wanted to go down in that basement to sleep anyway? So I said to her: 'Oh, is it really bedtime? Did you make the Olympic team or did I?' I had had a few glasses of Champagne," she said. "So she went to [AOC President Avery Brundage] and complained that I was setting a bad example for the team, and they got together and told me the next morning that I was fired. I was heartbroken."[1]

That's how the "Champagne Girl" was born. Eleanor Holm was the kind of athlete-celebrity that would have been at the front and center of today's paparazzi. She not only would have been unapologetic about the attention, but would have openly embraced it. Yet for all her celebrity and controversy, she was one of the greatest swimmers of her generation. Holm made her Olympic debut at the

1928 Amsterdam Olympics as a 14-year-old and finished fifth in her specialty, the 100-meter backstroke. In 1932 at the Los Angeles Olympic Games, she set a world record during the qualifying heats with a time of 1:18.2 and won the gold by nearly two seconds with a time of 1:19.4. In between Olympics, Holm married singer and orchestra leader Art Jarrett. Marrying Jarrett exposed her to a different lifestyle now that she was hanging out with a Hollywood crowd and performing in many of her husband's nightclub shows. At times she would appear in a white bathing suit and white cowboy hat while strutting in high heels singing "I'm an Old Cowhand from the Rio Grande."

Even so, she stayed in shape and continued to train for the 1936 Olympics in Germany, hoping to defend her gold medal. She had not lost a race in seven years and had become the first American woman to be chosen to swim for three Olympic teams. But Brundage took the opportunity away from her, despite having 200 American athletes sign a petition to reinstate her. Holm would forever remain angry at the AOC president for denying her the opportunity at repeat gold medals. By all accounts, she was not the only Olympian drinking on the boat and she felt that Brundage held a grudge against her.

"I was everything that Avery Brundage hated," Holm said in *Tales of Gold*, by Lewis H. Carlson and John J. Fogarty. "I had a few dollars, and athletes were supposed to be poor. I worked in nightclubs, and athletes shouldn't do that. But he rained on my parade for only a very short time. He did make me famous. I would have been just another female backstroke swimmer without Brundage."[2]

Upon arriving in Germany and without a meet to swim in, Holm became a correspondent for the Olympics, contributing ghostwritten articles for the International News Service. She also attended many of the receptions hosted by Hitler and the Nazi Party, many of them amazed that she had been kicked off the team for drinking. Herman Goering, a leader of the Nazi Party, gave Holm a silver-plated swastika off his uniform. Americans followed Holm's saga with great interest and intrigue and welcomed her as a celebrity upon her return from Germany. When Holm married second-husband Billy Rose, who was Jewish, she made a gold copy of the swastika and placed a Star of David in the middle set with diamonds in it.

Looking back, Holm said, "I did all right after I won in 1932, but 1936 made me a star—it made me a glamour girl! Just another gold medal would never have done that!"[3]

In 1938, she would star in her lone major motion picture in the 20th Century Fox Movie *Tarzan's Revenge*, starring alongside Glenn Morris, the gold medal-winning decathlete of the 1936 Olympics. She also performed in 39 shows a week co-starring with fellow swimming greats Johnny Weismuller and Buster Crabbe at Rose's Aquacade in the New York World's Fair of 1939–40.

Holm entered the International Swimming Hall of Fame in 1965, becoming known as the Hall's "Great Dame."

"Life owes me nothing—I've had a ball!" Holm said to author William O. Johnson.

Indeed, she had a ball. In 1999, she appeared at a White House screening of HBO's *Dare to Compete: The Struggle of Women in Sports*, and casually stepped to the side of former President Bill Clinton and gave him an easy compliment on his looks. Clinton, somewhat startled, could only ask "What?" to which Holm again complimented him on his looks. Clinton laughed and said that Holm, ever the show woman, had just made his day.

Holm passed away in 2004 at her home in Miami at the age of 91. In a 1984 interview with Dave Andersen of the *New York Times*, the "Champagne Girl" said she no longer swam but played some tennis, and she no longer drank champagne cither, having replaced that with a bit of dry white wine.

Notes

1. William O. Johnson, *All That Glitters Is Not Gold* (New York: G. P. Putnam's Sons, 1972), p.188.

2. Richard Goldstein, "Eleanor Holm Whalen, 30's Swimming Champion, Dies," *New York Times*. February 2, 2004.

3. Goldstein, "Eleanor Holm Whalen."

Florence Chadwick

American Star of the Women's International Sports Hall of Fame

by Horacio Ruiz

On August 21, 1950, Florence Chadwick walked without much fanfare off the beach of France and into the waters of the English Channel. She swam quickly to escape the inshore current, and once out in open water, she slowed her pace. Chadwick had applied to a London newspaper's half-century contest to swim across the Channel, but the newspaper rejected her application because they did not know who she was. Instead, the press accepted the application of a 17-year-old swimmer named Shirley May. Six boatfuls of reporters waited for May to begin her swim across the English Channel, having financed her trip and swimming attempt, while letting Chadwick swim away first without fanfare. Chadwick made it a point to show up on that day, to achieve the goal she had been so focused on in front of those whom had snubbed her. She had won several long-distance swimming competitions in California, having won a two and a half-mile race in La Jolla, California, 10 times in 18 years. But the London newspaper did not know about her successes across the Atlantic.

Chadwick had keyed in on her goal months before applying to the London newspaper. She was granted a transfer by her employer, the Arabian-American Oil Company, to Saudi Arabia that paid her way abroad. Once overseas, she saved money from her job as a comptometer operator, a type of mechanical adding machine, and would go on training swims before and after work in the rough waters of the Persian Gulf. In June 1950, Chadwick quit her job and moved to France to train for her first swim across the Channel in July. In France, she applied to be sponsored by the *Daily Mail*, the London newspaper, but was not accepted. Chadwick, though, had saved enough money from her job in the Arabian-American Oil Company to rent a boat and hire a trainer for her August swim.

At about 11:30 a.m., more than eight and a half hours after she first began her swim, her father, who was trailing on a boat just behind her, wrote on a blackboard: "Only three miles to go." It would be a grueling three miles. Her protective grease coating had worn off so that the chilly waters of the Channel were cruelly numbing. Her swimming appeared to resemble more of a paddling motion, but just 500 yards off the coast of England, as she was urged to take a rest before reaching total exhaustion, Chadwick said, "Don't worry, I've got it made now."[1] She made it up to shore, climbing up rocks off the coast that gashed her feet. Chadwick had finished the 19-mile swim in 13 hours and 23 minutes, finishing ahead of the previous record of 14 hours and 34 minutes set 24 years earlier by Gertrude Ederle. Only 40 minutes later, the other swimmer, Shirley May, gave up to exhaustion and was pulled out of the water in tears. "Everyone's going to think I'm a flop,"[2] May said.

Perhaps it was meant as a joke when Chadwick reached the shore and said, "I feel fine, I am quite prepared to swim back."[3] But only 13 months later, on September 24, 1951, Chadwick was again swimming across the Channel, this time taking the more arduous route from England to France, a 21-mile route that had never been accomplished by a woman and up to that time had been completed by nine men. Three hours into her swim, Chadwick was vomiting every three strokes until it was discovered that fumes from one of the boats trailing her were the cause of her nausea. Her father, again accompanying her, took pill after pill to calm his weak heart, but 16 hours and 22 minutes after she had begun to "swim back," Chadwick dragged herself up on the shore of France to be greeted by boys who ran up to her to cheer her becoming the first woman to swim the English Channel from England to France.

Chadwick could have given up years before stepping into the Channel. She wanted to be a speed swimmer. The first race she ever entered, a 50-yard race as a six-year-old, resulted in her coming in last place. Chadwick continued to practice on her speed, but she could never finish first. At the age of 14, she competed in the national backstroke championship, but came in second to future gold-medal Olympian Eleanor Holm. At age 18, Chadwick missed out on making the Olympic swimming team and decided to give up competitive swimming. As time passed by she remembered her success as an endurance swimmer, and realized where her talent lay. As an 11-year-old, she entered a San Diego Bay endurance swim and gained praise and attention when she finished the six-mile swim. Her swimming career was soon revived.

Her conquest of the Channel sparked a five-year period of swimming brilliance. In 1952, she became the first woman to swim the Catalina Channel (a stretch of water from Catalina Island off the coast of California to mainland California), and only the 10th individual ever. No woman would complete the Catalina Channel swim for another three years after Chadwick first accomplished the feat. In 1953, she would go on to become the first woman to swim the Straits of Gibraltar and the Bosporus one way, and also the first woman to swim the Dardanelles round trip.

Chadwick's swimming career would lead to a number of public appearances in which she promoted swimming and encouraged people to push themselves and to test their physical limits. At the age of 51, in 1969, she embarked on a new career as a stockbroker and would later become vice president of First Wall Street Corporation in San Diego, California. In 1970, she was inducted into the International Swimming Hall of Fame. Chadwick passed away on March 15, 1995, at the age of 76 after a lengthy illness, having swum the English Channel four times and the Catalina Channel three times.

Notes

1. "Two Girls in Swimming," *Time*, August 21, 1950.
2. Ibid.
3. International Swimming Hall of Fame. http://www.ishof.org/honorees/70/70f chadwick.html (accessed March 15, 2008).

Debbie Meyer

American Star of the Women's International Sports Hall of Fame

by Horacio Ruiz

When Debbie Meyer was 12 years old in 1965, her father moved the family 3,000 miles from New Jersey to Sacramento, California, because of a job transfer. For Meyer, the move across the United States was a traumatizing experience. She had to make new friends and adjust to a different city. Even more so, she left a YMCA program, where she swam three times a week during the summer, to a swim program at the Arden Hills Swim and Tennis Club in Sacramento that swam six times a week for an entire year. Her father had been in touch with swim coach Sherm Chavoor before moving to California and arranged for Meyer to begin swim classes once she arrived. She was at her new home on a Saturday and was at her first swimming class two days later.

At her first swim practice, Meyer swam four laps and got out of the pool in frustration. She was not as fast as the other swimmers and was embarrassed because she was not used to swimming as long or for as many days as her counterparts. Chavoor asked where she was going, and she replied she did not think she belonged in the swim program. But before she left, Chavoor told Meyer that he would be at the swimming pool the next day and at the same exact time. Meyer went back the next day, determined to be as good as the other swimmers and to finish the 5,000-yard practices. It would take her three months to get there.

"My dad was a Marine and you've got those qualities in you whether you want to or not," Meyer said. "He's not a lifer Marine, but he's still a Marine at heart. We just didn't give up at that time."[1]

Meyer also credits her mom, a physical education teacher, for encouraging her. All of which led to her becoming one of the greatest swimmers in the world, but she was never really aware of where her swimming abilities could take her.

"I didn't know about the Olympic Games until 1966," she said. "I swam because I loved the water. I loved the challenge of swimming faster times. I wasn't swimming to make the Olympic team. The winter of 1967 I really had the concept of, 'Wow, you really have a chance to make it to the Olympics.'" At the 1967 Pan American Games in Winnipeg, she set world records in the 400-meter and 800-meter freestyle events. In 1968, the U.S. swim team was the best in the world. Even a 16-year-old Meyer knew that by qualifying for the U.S. National Team, as she did, that she would come away with a stash of Olympic medals. But Meyer did more than haul a stash—she became the first swimmer to win three individual gold medals at one Olympics. She also was suffering from "Montezuma's Revenge"—another name for diarrhea in Mexico. But her focus in practice was such that it did not affect her performances at the Olympics.

"I was very focused when I was in the water," Meyer said. "[NBC Sports chairman] Dick Ebersol said to me, 'You know Debbie, I recall you telling me that you never got nervous before a meet. Do you know why that happened?' Because I knew I worked hard, and I knew what I could do. Maybe I didn't know any better. I was anxious to swim because I wanted to know how fast I could go. I wasn't worried about somebody beating me. I just wanted to see how fast I could go."

Meyer would continue swimming until January 1972, when only months before the Munich Olympics, she retired from competitive swimming. The sport was no longer fun for her, even as she was still setting world records after her fabulous 1968 Olympics.

"I just kind of wanted to get on with my life," Meyer said. "I knew being in the pool for four and a half hours a day was not part of my plan. I have no regrets whatsoever about quitting when I did. I had a wonderful life in the swimming pool." Meyer credits swimming with giving her the opportunity to make many friends and to travel extensively around the world. Soon after her retirement, she worked for Speedo in public relations, where she would travel across the West Coast of the United States, up to Canada, and as far east as the Mississippi River. The career switch had an impact on Meyer, who was painfully shy up to when she retired from swimming. The new job forced her out of her shell, where she had to make sales presentations and conduct cold phone calls to promote the Speedo brand. At the 2008 U.S. Swimming Olympic Trials, where the 1968 U.S. swim team held a reunion for its 40th anniversary, Meyer's former teammates could not believe how extroverted she had become. "I just wouldn't stop talking," she said. Meyer also enjoyed endorsement deals as a spokeswoman for M&M's and Mars bar. Meyer went back to her swimming roots and took up coaching jobs with Stanford and Cal-Berkeley. In 1992, Meyer was head coach of both the men's and women's swim programs at California State University, Sacramento, when the school cut the program. In addition to losing her job, in a four-week period Meyer was divorced, her grandmother passed away, and her former coach, Sherm Chavoor, also passed away. "It really was devastating," she said.

Courtesy of Debbie Meyer.

Meyer moved back home with her parents to recover. Soon, she found a place where she could start a swim school. Meyer received a loan from a bank and also from a number of friends and family to put a down payment for the facility in 1993. She vowed to repay everyone back in five years, but she was able to do so in only two and a half years. The swim school also has a special place in her heart because two weeks after opening up the Debbie Meyer Swim School, she met her second husband, Bill Weber. Meyer currently specializes in teaching children with disabilities to swim. The conditions vary and include cerebral palsy, autism, spina bifida, and paraplegic and quadriplegic conditions. "It can be a challenge but they will learn and they can learn," she said. "That's what keeps me going. You have to learn their personality. You have to learn what their disability is. You have to put yourself in that situation and try to figure out how you're going to make it work."

Up to her retirement in 1972, Meyer set 15 world records and 27 American records, and was named World Swimmer of the Year from 1967 to 1969. In 1968, on the cusp of her Olympic triumph, she was awarded the 1968 Sullivan Award as the top amateur athlete. In 1987, she was inducted into the U.S. Olympic Hall of Fame, and in 1997, she was inducted into the International Swimming Hall of Fame. In 2004, Meyer was inducted into the National High School Hall of Fame. Looking back on her career, each induction and recognition has its own place in Meyer's heart. "Each one came at a different stage in my career and my life so they're each highlights," she said. "Every time I get something it's at a different point in my life and it means just as much."

Meyer has thoughts of opening another swim school in Truckee, California, where she holds residence. For the 1972 Munich Olympics, instead of swimming, Meyer worked with the AP, and she still has aspirations of visiting Greece, the birthplace of the Olympic Games. "Some people say they can read people's minds and psychics can speak to the dead, well, water is my sixth sense," Meyer said. "I'm not afraid of it but I respect the heck out of it. There was a purpose for me in this world, and I think it was for me to teach kids to understand and respect the water. The Olympics were part of my journey to get to where I am right now. It taught me a work ethic. It taught me that I can overcome adversity. I got sicker than a dog down there [Mexico City] with 'Montezuma's Revenge,' but I learned to work through pain and become a better person because of it."

Note

1. All of the quotes in this article are by Debbie Meyer, from an interview with the author on July 14, 2008.

Mary T. Meagher Plant

American Star of the Women's International Sports Hall of Fame

by Horacio Ruiz

In 1981, Mary T. Meagher spun the swimming community on its heels with her world record-setting performances in the 100-meter and 200-meter butterfly. Her record in the 100-meter butterfly would last more than 19 years and her record in the 200-meter would last more than 20 years. In 1990, *Sports Illustrated* listed Meagher's 200-meter record as the fifth greatest "single-event" record ever in any sport. Affectionately and appropriately referred to as "Madame Butterfly," her accomplishments in 1981 earned her the women's World Swimmer of the Year Award. Meagher, known by her married name of Mary Plant after marrying speed skater Mike Plant, set her first world record as a 14-year-old at the 1979 Pan Am Games in San Juan, Puerto Rico.

"When I set my first world record I didn't know I had done it," Meagher Plant said. "It was great and it was wonderful, but honestly I hadn't set out that day to do that. It was more of a byproduct of wanting to win and having good coaches and being blessed with talent."[1]

She was expected to medal in the 1980 Olympics, but did not compete because of the U.S. boycott of the Olympics in the Soviet Union. Even as Meagher Plant was reaching the zenith of her swimming career, she considered retiring from swimming after 1980 because she was no longer having fun. But she made some changes to her training schedule to make it more balanced, and by 1981 she was making swimming history. Meagher Plant would make the most of her opportunity at the 1984 Los Angeles Olympics by winning three gold medals in the 100-meter and 200-meter butterfly and the women's medley relay. "Winning the gold medals in '84 was really a nice accomplishment," she said. " '84 was just full exhilaration. It was the highlight of my career and I'm glad some things came together—emotionally and physically." In 1985, she was again named the women's World Swimmer of the Year.

"In her prime, Mary had no weaknesses," said Dennis Pursley, one of Meagher Plant's coaches. "Motivation, technique, physical attributes—I don't know that I've ever seen an athlete who didn't have a weakness on that list—except Mary."[2] Meagher Plant swam at the University of California, Berkeley (Cal), where she received her bachelor's degree in social sciences. At Cal, she won five individual national championships, and in her final collegiate 100-meter butterfly swim in 1987, she set a National Collegiate Athletic Association (NCAA) and U.S. Open record. Following her triumph at the NCAA Championships, Meagher Plant moved from California to her hometown in Louisville, Kentucky, where she continued training for the Olympics. But Meagher Plant was not training up to her potential.

She contacted Bill Peak, her childhood coach who had worked with her for years in Louisville. Peak, then living in Norfolk, Virginia, extended an invitation to Meagher Plant to train with him full-time. Peak wanted to make sure Meagher Plant still had her heart in training and her love for swimming prevailed. "Two days after I got there," she said of arriving at Norfolk, "I knew I was doing the right thing. I'm happier than I've been in a long time. My attitude has improved 1,000 percent and my training has improved 1,000 percent."[3]

At the 1988 Seoul Olympics, still pushing herself at the highest level of competition, Meagher Plant earned a bronze medal in the 200-meter butterfly. After the Seoul Olympics, Meagher Plant retired from competitive swimming and focused on her marriage. She briefly considered swimming professionally on a European tour to earn money, but internally, she knew she was tired of being Mary T. Meagher the swimmer and was ready to enter a new phase in her life.

"It was a tough time," she said. "There was just an inkling of a thought in me that I should continue swimming just to travel. There was money I could make if I swam another year and at that point I assumed I could win if I put my mind to it. My friends were all moving to these cool jobs and I still had to call my dad to support me with money. I just never seemed to be able to get close to where I was. [The record] was neat even though when I was swimming it was a frustration. I swam for seven more years and never swam faster."

By the end of her career, in addition to her Olympic and collegiate success, Meagher Plant had set seven world records and won 24 U.S. national titles. "It was a very conscious decision to leave it all behind," Meagher Plant said. "My husband and I have seen so many athletes that never make that transition into real life. And to have what I have now, I consider myself very lucky."[4]

In 1993, Meagher Plant was elected to the International Swimming Hall of Fame. At the 1996 Atlanta Olympics, Meagher Plant was one of eight athletes to carry the Olympic flag into Olympic Stadium. In 2000, *Sports Illustrated for Women* included Meagher Plant as the 17th greatest women's athlete of all-time in a list of 100. Then, the records that had endured for so long started to fall. In 1999, American swimmer Jenny Thompson broke Meagher Plant's 100-meter record. Thompson said she gained insight on how to break the world record by watching taped footage of Meagher Plant's stroke. "It helped me focus on what I needed to do, and it's made a difference,"[5] Thompson said. Less than one year after the 100-meter record went down, Australian swimmer Susan O'Neill broke Meagher Plant's 200-meter butterfly record. "It's one of the greatest moments of my life. I've dreamed about it for a long time,"[6] said O'Neill, who bested Meagher Plant's record by .15 seconds. Meagher Plant was quick to praise O'Neill for her accomplishment. "I feel great, there couldn't have been a nicer or harder worker than Susie and she really deserves it,"[7] Meagher Plant said. "As I get further away, I appreciate the record more. At this point in my life I'm flattered that for whatever reason, God chose me to swim at that level."

Currently, Meagher Plant lives in a suburb outside of Atlanta with her husband and two children, Maddie and Drew. The adjustment from being an Olympic champion and world-record holder to life outside of athletics was a learning process for Meagher Plant. At one of her jobs, she would have contact with her boss once a week as opposed to having a coach standing over her shoulder every day telling her what she was doing right and wrong. After work, Meagher Plant would drive home knowing she had competently fulfilled her tasks, but wonder whether she was doing it the right way.

"It's just hard to come off a glamorous lifestyle, one where I got a lot of pats on my back," Meagher Plant said. "I was made to believe I was a good person because I swam fast. Luckily, I had parents that taught me you're a good person because you're a good person, not because you swim fast. There were times when I wanted to go back and do things as Mary T. Meagher and do clinics and give speeches. I credit my husband with helping. He told me, 'You had a great career, but now it's time to move on. If you keep one foot in your old life, you'll never walk into your new life.'"

Now, Meagher Plant spends her energy raising Maddie and Drew, holding down the fort at home when her husband is traveling, and cultivating her friendships. She also has been a long-time volunteer for the Girl Scouts as a service unit director; her responsibilities include finding troops for girls and coordinating their efforts. At every U.S. Olympic Swimming Trials, the national swim team has a reunion, and at the trials for the 2008 Beijing Olympics Meagher Plant attended the gathering with her children.

"I thought I'll take them with me this time and introduce them to friends," she said. "I was introduced on the deck during the meet at one point and got a standing ovation and got to sign some autographs. I don't really know what was going through their minds," she said of Maddie and Drew. "How did they interpret that? I talked a little bit to my daughter about the good and bad about being famous. I'm happier now as a mom than I ever was when I was swimming."

Notes

1. Unless noted otherwise, the quotes in this article are by Mary T. Meagher, in an interview with the author, July 7, 2008.

2. *Sports Illustrated for Women*. Mary T. Meagher. http://sportsillustrated.cnn.com /siforwomen/top_100/17/.

3. Frank Litsky, "Meagher Making New Commitment," *New York Times*, March 24, 1988.

4. James Pilcher, "Envy as Swimming Record Is Broken," *AP*, August 23, 1999.

5. Ibid.

6. Julian Linden, "Oldest World Record Broken by O'Neill," *The Independent— London*, May 18, 2000.

7. Ibid.

Tracy Caulkins

American Star of the Women's
International Sports Hall of Fame

by Horacio Ruiz

The story goes that at eight years old, the woman considered to be the greatest all-around swimmer in American history agreed to join the neighborhood swim club on the condition that she would only do the backstroke so that her face would not get wet. Nearly 40 years since joining the swim club, the accolades keep coming in for Tracy Caulkins, who proved to be skilled far beyond just the backstroke. In 2006, she was named the Division I's most outstanding swimmer in women's championships over the previous 25 years. During her swimming career at the University of Florida, Caulkins claimed 16 national championships, including 12 individual championships, the most ever by any swimmer or diver. In 1982 and 1984, Caulkins received the Broderick Cup, given annually to the nation's top collegiate female athlete. Caulkins burst onto the international swimming scene at the 1978 World Championships in Berlin by winning five gold medals and one silver medal. That performance earned her the 1978 James E. Sullivan Award as the most outstanding amateur athlete in the United States; at age 15 she was the youngest winner of the award to date.

At the 1980 Moscow Olympic Games, Caulkins was supposed to showcase her talents to the world, but the United States boycotted the Games because of political disagreement with the Soviet Union. Caulkins was hit hard. At the 1982 World Championships, Caulkins failed to finish higher than third in any event, and even while winning the gold medal at the 1983 Pan American Games, her times were much slower than they had been at the 1978 World Championships. There were whispers that she could no longer compete at an elite level. But Caulkins regained her swimming dominance in January 1984 while winning the 200-meter and 400-meter individual medleys at the U.S. Swimming International meet. "I think a lot of people have counted me out," she said after the meet. "They better watch out."[1]

At the 1984 Los Angeles Olympics, Caulkins captained the U.S. swimming team while winning individual gold medals in the 200-meter individual medley and the 400-meter individual medley, and swimming the breaststroke on the 400-meter medley relay. Her swimming career had come full circle, and she retired following the Los Angeles Games. "It [the 1984 Olympics] was the realization of a dream," Caulkins said. "After all, swimming had always been a focus. Now, after all the work, there are great opportunities."[2]

All told, Caulkins set five world records. Her 63 American records and 48 national titles are both the most by any swimmer, and she is the only swimmer to set U.S. records in every stroke. Caul-

Courtesy of University of Florida Athletic Association Communications

kins's swimming legacy was as a master of all four strokes, and according to the Sullivan Award website, "Caulkins was respected and admired by her teammates for her understanding and compassion as well as for her talents." Following her retirement, Caulkins used her broadcasting degree to take several television analyst positions for swim meets and she became an advisory board member for the Women's Sports Foundation (WSF). In 1985, she actively promoted a survey commissioned by the WSF that found more young women and girls were choosing to compete athletically with men, and girls who grew up competing with boys or in mixed groups were more likely to continue sport activities as adults.

"When I read the report, I felt it really hit on the things that I had experienced in sports," Caulkins said in 1985. "It [co-ed competition] is a social issue that people are going to have to deal with. But I know that I have competed with guys every day since I was eight. And I know at Florida it was good for both the men and the women in the swimming program."[3]

The 1984 Games brought more than gold medals to Caulkins; the Games also brought her a husband. Australian sprint swimmer Mark Stockwell jumped into the warm-up pool in Los Angeles to introduce himself to Caulkins. That move sparked a relationship that led to their marriage in 1991 in Nashville, Tennessee, Caulkins's hometown. The wedding was a cross-cultural affair, with a barn dance with southern cooking serving as the backdrop for the rehearsal dinner, a sit-down dinner at the wedding with the reading of telegrams from all over the world, and the following day, with Stockwell's friends and family teaching the Americans how to play cricket. Despite her disappointment with the boycott of the 1980 Olympics, Caulkins looks back and thinks there may have been a purpose. "If there hadn't been a boycott in 1980, I might not have gone on to 1984, where at 21, I was the 'old lady' on the team," she said. "Then I might never have met my husband."[4]

Caulkins moved to Australia with Stockwell in 1991 and settled in Brisbane. Together, they have four children, all of whom are involved in swimming. In Australia, Caulkins has worked part-time for a construction and development company that both she and her husband own. She also has served as the executive officer for the Queensland Academy of Sport, which provides support to elite and identified developing athletes. In 2006, Caulkins added yet another medal to her vast collection when she was awarded the Medal of the Order of Australia "for service to sport as an administrator and proponent of sporting opportunities for women."

Notes

1. AAU Sullivan Award, "Tracy Caulkins," http://www.aausullivan.org/winners_1978.html.

2. Brian Hanley, "Caulkins Becomes a Trail Blazer," *Chicago Sun-Times*, June 25, 1986.

3. Ibid.

4. Phillip Whitten, "Still Kicking," *Swimming World Magazine*, April 2005.

Janet Evans

American Star of the Women's International Sports Hall of Fame

by Horacio Ruiz

It is the opening ceremony of the 1996 Atlanta Summer Olympic Games, eight years removed from when Janet Evans first captured the world's attention at the 1988 Seoul Olympic Games when she won three gold medals, two of them in world-record time. She stood on the track of Centennial Olympic Stadium as a torch bearer, waiting half-excitedly, half-anxiously, to have her torch lit by American boxer Evander Holyfield and Greek track runner Voula Patoulidou, and at the moment she received the Olympic flame, Evans jogged around the stadium waving at the people in the stands and at the athletes congregated in the infield. She ran up a ramp to where the unlit Olympic cauldron stood, and as she reached the top of the ramp, it was "The Greatest," Muhammad Ali, who took the flame from Evans to light the Olympic cauldron. Evans stepped to the side and took the moment in.

"It was the neatest thing being up there, to see in [Ali's] eyes how thrilled he was . . . I can't speak for him, and I know he has done amazing things in his life, but this was probably pretty, pretty cool," Evans said. "It has to rank right up there with all the great things he's done. If you could have been up there and heard the crowd when he came out. They were cheering loudly when I was up there, but when he came out I thought the stadium was going to fall down."[1]

Ali had received the flame from one of the greatest. Evans is considered to be the best long-distance swimmer in women's history. She had earned the spot to stand next to Ali and share in his excitement. The Atlanta Games were a different kind for Evans, and though only 24 years old at the time, her athletic career had come full circle in Atlanta. She was no longer the bubbly teen in Seoul who would become the face of swimming after winning three individual gold medals, or the ultra-focused veteran at the 1992 Barcelona Olympics who had carried the pressures of defending two of her gold medals in the four years between Olympics. In Atlanta, when she ran up the ramp to stand next to Ali, even after all her records and titles, it was as if she had truly arrived.

At 5 feet, 4 inches, Evans carried her thin and petite frame to become the most dominant swimmer of her time. Her windmill stroke was unorthodox, but it gave the impression she was attacking the water. "It's not a classic style you might expect a world-record holder to have," said coach Bud McAllister. "But underwater, her technique is almost flawless. Above the water, when she's going fast, her arms are almost straight. That's because she has such tremendous acceleration that at the end of her stroke her arms come almost straight out of the water."[2]

Evans was born to swim. She started when she was one year old, literally still in her diapers, when her grandmother thought Evans's mother was wasting her money by putting baby Janet in swim classes. Her parents had a pool in the backyard, and they felt that all the kids in the house should be able to swim in case they fell into the pool. By the time she was three years old, Evans knew how to do all four swim strokes: the breast, butterfly, freestyle, and backstroke. At the age of 17, Evans was on her way to the Seoul Olympics as a senior in high school and the holder of three world records. At the 1988 Olympics, she would win her first gold medal in the 400-meter individual medley and would break her own world record while winning gold in the 400-meter freestyle. Her 400-meter freestyle record would stand for more than 17 years. Evans would later add another gold medal by capturing the 800-meter freestyle. Evans's 800-meter freestyle record, later set in August 1989, was one of the longest-standing records in swimming history, standing 19 years until it was broken in the 2008 Beijing Olympics.

Her bubbly personality resonated through the sporting landscape and the world was in awe of how such a tiny girl could dominate her sport against physically imposing women who towered over little Janet. "The other night Janet was sitting between the two East German women she'd beaten on her way to a world record in the 400-meter freestyle," wrote Tony Kornheiser in a piece on Evans shortly after the 1988 Olympics. "These women were big, and almost identical with their curled ringlets of blond hair, ice-cold blue eyes and broad shoulders. Silent and rather dour, they resembled great stone lions guarding a library. And between them, this little slip of a giggly thing with short brown hair that doesn't even come over her ears, this little pixie."[3]

The next four years would heighten the expectations of the young Olympian. People had begun buzzing in her ear, some suggesting she would have been better off retiring from swimming after her monumental showing at the 1988 Olympics to prosper in the endorsements that were flooding her way. Evans declined these suggestions and instead enrolled at Stanford University, where she would continue to train for the 1992 Olympics. Her body was also changing as she was making the transition from teenager to adult. Evans grew three inches and added on 15 pounds, making it difficult for her to duplicate her swimming feats from just a few years before. By the 1992 Olympics, when Evans was 20 years old, it became apparent that Evans the woman was not quite as fast as Evans the girl, but there was no mistaking she was still the fastest in the world. Evans had not lost a 400-meter race since 1986, and she was the favorite heading into both the 800-meter and 400-meter freestyle races. Evans raised the stakes on her own success. "Who's going to remember whether you set a world record or not?" she said just days before competing in 1992. "They'll just remember what you did at the Olympics."[4]

At Barcelona, Evans would defend her gold medal in the 800-meter freestyle, but it would be her second-place finish in the 400-meter freestyle event that overshadowed her success. Her teary post-swim press conference magnified her disappointment, no matter how much she tried to hide it with her smile. After the race, she told reporters she was happy because she had tried her best and that was the only thing she could ask of herself. No one doubted that she had given her best effort; it was just tough to believe that Evans was truly happy.

"There's a lot of pressure placed on Americans," a teary Evans said to the media after her second-place finish. "You all don't understand the pressure placed on every athlete here, especially those expected to medal. But I think it will help me later in life to get through job interviews and things like that. You learn a lot about yourself. You overcome disappointment."[5]

Evans decided to race in the Olympics once more, certain that the Atlanta Olympics would be the last of her career. It was her desire to represent the United States in Atlanta that spurred four more years of training. Evans's desire to win still burned as wildly as ever, but she was different in Atlanta. This time around, the 24-year-old Evans was the underdog and she understood the importance of taking in all of the Olympic experience.

"Of course, I went to Atlanta wanting to win," Evans wrote in an article looking back on her career. "Who doesn't want to win? But I'd put a lot of miles on my shoulders by then. I just didn't have it when I got there, for a variety of reasons. In Atlanta, I really learned it was okay not to win. It was okay to represent my country, do my best, and be satisfied with the results. And I was."[6]

In her final Olympic race and in the same event where she was the world record holder for so long, the 800-meter freestyle, Evans came in sixth place and 11 seconds behind the winner. Evans walked away with a degree of disappointment, but she was ready for her life after athletics. "I'm happy but I'm sad," Evans said after the race. "It's been a great experience for me and I'm going to miss it. It wasn't exactly a great way to go out, but I'm still happy to be me."[7]

It has been good to be Evans. After her retirement, she became a highly requested public speaker for corporations, where she has worked for Olympic sponsors. She has stayed involved in swimming by conducting her own swim clinics and branding swim meets under the Janet Evans Invitational name. In 2007, she released her book, *Janet Evans' Total Swimming*, as a guide with different training programs for swimmers at different levels. In 2001, she was inducted into both the International Swimming Hall of Fame and the International Women's Sports Hall of Fame. In 2004, she was inducted into the U.S. Olympic Hall of Fame. In all, she won 45 U.S. National titles, set seven world records, and is the only woman to hold three world records concurrently. She has also served as the chairman of FINA's (the worldwide governing body of swimming) Athlete's Committee.

It is true that people remember what you do in the Olympics, as Evans once said, but as she came to realize, they also remember so much more than that.

Notes

1. Jon Wilner, "Evans to Ali—A Glowing Experience," *Daily News*, July 23, 1996.

2. Christine Brennan, "Janet Evans Hits the Pool, Then the Books," *The Washington Post*, September 16, 1988.

3. Tony Kornheiser, "To Beat Janet Evans, Get Up Early," *The Washington Post*, September 24, 1988.

4. John Powers, "Janet Evans Finds Herself Free at Last," *The Boston Globe*, July 24, 1992.

5. Dan Shaugnessy, "Evans' Silver a Crying Shame," *The Boston Globe*, July 29, 1992.

6. Janet Evans. March 26, 2008. http://www.america.gov/st/sports-english/2008/March/20080326163241cmretrop0.6073986.html.

7. Sam McManis, "Janet Evans Goes Out with Head Held High," *Knight-Ridder Newspapers*, July 25, 1996.

Nancy Hogshead-Makar

American Star of the Women's International Sports Hall of Fame

by Richard Lapchick

I met Nancy Hogshead-Makar in 1984 after the Los Angeles Olympic Games. We were in Boston at Northeastern University's Center for the Study of Sport and Society shortly after it opened. I was immediately struck by more than the amazing accomplishments of this great swimmer to which her three gold and one silver medals attest. She immediately displayed intelligence, confidence, poise, and leadership skills that would propel her to be one of the most influential people in the world of sport, especially on the issue of gender equity.

In the immediate months after the Olympics, she was highly sought after as a speaker and an endorser of commercial products. However, her passion for social justice led her quickly to move into the area of supporting Title IX.

But that amazing athletic career gave her the platform. She spent eight years as a world champion swimmer, culminating in the 1984 Olympics, where she won more medals than any other swimmer. She was undefeated in high school and college. She was named Florida's Outstanding Athlete and the best all-around swimmer nationally. To date, she has been inducted into the International Swimming Hall of Fame and the International Women's Sports Hall of Fame in addition to nine other halls. I now live in Florida and realize how important sports are here so it was no small feat that Hogshead-Makar was named as one of the 13 greatest athletes of the 20th century in the State of Florida by *Sports Illustrated* in their Millennium Issue.

While a student-athlete at Duke University, she set Duke records for all nine events she swam. One remains on the books more than two decades later. Nancy Hogshead-Makar was the first female inducted into Duke's Sports Hall of Fame in 1997.

She became a regular commentator for the networks as a swimming analyst, but then became a commentator on social justice issues more than swimming.

When she retired from swimming, she started speaking to more than 100 groups each year about asthma management and sports. She wrote the highly acclaimed *Asthma and Exercise* in 1990 and became the national spokesperson for the American Lung Association. Her book was the first about the relationship between asthma and sports.

Hogshead-Makar earned her law degree at Georgetown University. She served as the president of the Women's Sports Foundation (WSF) between 1992 and 1994, and still serves the WSF as a legal advisor. She has spoken and testified before numerous important gatherings, including Congress and in the courts. The media has turned to her as a regulator commentator on social issues in sport.

After getting her law degree, Hogshead-Makar moved to Jacksonville, Florida, and started representing student-athletes regarding Title IX. She was named by *Sports Illustrated* as one of the most influential people in the 35-year history of Title IX. Her voice is loud and strong. She has always faced down those challenging Title IX. CBS did a special on it for *60 Minutes.* She was ready for what turned out to be a two-hour interview. When Hogshead-Makar saw the final product, she wrote a letter to CBS about its biased reporting. She believes in standing up for justice and does not back down. One of the reasons she feels so strongly about Title IX is how it will help little girls develop character. She advocates that children's participation in exercise of all kinds not only builds character, but also develops leadership skills and enriches the health of all children. She did not need to become a mother to be such an advocate but now has twin daughters who may motivate her on an even more personal level.

She married Scott Makar in 1999. At the time they were both lawyers at the firm of Holland and Knight. Scott is currently Florida's solicitor general while Nancy is a professor of law. They have a son in addition to their daughters.

Hogshead-Makar's new book, *Equal Pay: Title IX and Social Change*, came out in 2007, written with the distinguished scholar, Andrew Zimbalist. On Title IX, not only has she testified in Congress, but she has also presented amicus briefs in the U.S. Supreme Court. She became a law professor in the 1990s, trying to transmit her courage and passion for social justice to the next generation. She is a professor of law at the Florida Coastal School of Law, where she teaches torts, amateur sports law, and a seminar on gender equity in athletics.

When I started the DeVos Sport Business Management graduate program in 2001, the first person I asked to teach our sport law course was Nancy Hogshead-Makar. She instantly became one of our students' favorite professors. She has been a speaker in our program many times since then and the students always love her. Hogshead-Makar has been named to the International Scholar Athlete Hall of Fame and received an honorary doctorate from Springfield College in 2002. There are too many other honors to mention, but it must be said that this extraordinary swimmer took the platform she had as a high school and college student-athlete and later as an Olympian to be able to give her the grounding to use sport as a vehicle for social change in ways that will have an everlasting impact even though it has been 25 years since she took her last stroke in an Olympic competition.

Hogshead-Makar had a life-changing experience that she shared with our students. She was raped in the early 1980s as a sophomore at Duke where she did her undergraduate degree. She told the students, "Before I got raped, my thinking was that I understood there was sexism out there, that people didn't think very highly of women in certain contexts but I didn't think it was ever going to affect me because I was a great athlete and I was smart. After the rape, I went into Women's Studies and have been trying to make this a better world for men and women ever since. I applaud the efforts of organizations like the National Consortium for Academics and Sports that take such a pro-active stand on the issue of men's violence against women."

As part of a settlement of a controversial case where numerous rape and sexual assault charges were brought against Colorado University football players and recruits, Hogshead-Makar was appointed as a Title IX advisor to the university. People who are concerned with the case at the University of Colorado were pleased that somebody with Hogshead-Makar's commitment, passion, and drive to do the right thing was appointed in this role to influence a campus that had serious problems over a long period of time on the issue of men's violence against women.

I consider it a blessing that Nancy Hogshead-Makar has been associated with our program at the DeVos Sport Business Management Graduate School. I am especially grateful that she is a close personal friend.

Donna de Varona

American Star of the Women's International Sports Hall of Fame

by Horacio Ruiz

For a few years in the mid-1960s, Donna de Varona was one of the most recognizable faces in the world. She first made headlines at age 13 as the youngest member of the U.S. Olympic team at the 1960 Rome Olympics. Four years later at the Tokyo Olympics, she captured a gold medal in Olympic record time in the 400-meter individual medley and a gold medal in world record time in the 4 × 100-meter free relay. Soon after the Tokyo Olympics, de Varona retired from competitive swimming with 37 national titles in the backstroke, butterfly, and freestyle and had broken 18 world records. In between her two Olympic appearances and shortly after her retirement, de Varona was the most photographed woman athlete, appearing on the covers of *Life*, *Time*, and twice on *Sports Illustrated*. For the International Swimming Hall of Fame's first international meet in 1965, de Varona was recognized as the "Queen of Swimming." But her success as a gold medalist in swimming is only a small prologue to the impact she would have in fighting for women's rights on the professional side of sports as well as on the playing field.

As a 17-year-old, de Varona became the first woman sports broadcaster to appear on network television when she covered the 1965 men's Amateur Athletic Union (AAU) swimming championships alongside Jim McKay. While she was typecast as a swimming expert early in her career, de Varona was able to move up the broadcasting ranks to eventually become an on-air analyst, commentator, host, writer, and producer. In 1991, she earned an Emmy Award for producing a feature on a Special Olympian and in 1998, she received an Emmy nomination for co-producing, writing, and hosting *Keepers of the Flame*, a television special on the Olympics. While de Varona pioneered the way for women in broadcasting, her impact has been felt just as strongly in her advocacy for creating and protecting opportunities for girls and women in sport.

De Varona was active in advisory positions as early as 1966, when she served on the President's Council on Physical Fitness and

Sport. By 1973, she was a co-founder of the Women's Sports Foundation, the preeminent organization in the United States for the advancement of girls' and women's lives through sport and physical activity. She served as the Foundation's first president from 1979 to 1984 and is currently an honorary trustee for the Foundation. "I felt that women needed an organization that represented just us,"[1] de Varona said. Under de Varona's leadership, the Foundation established an annual fundraising dinner and takes annual visits to Washington, D.C., to speak about the impact Title IX has had on providing opportunities for women in sport. Nearly 30 years after de Varona lobbied for the passage of Title IX, she served on the U.S. Secretary of Education's Commission on Opportunity in Athletics. The Commission was formed to study the effect of Title IX on men and women. When the majority of the Commission had created proposals to change Title IX to preserve opportunities for men, de Varona and Julie Foudy, then-captain of the U.S. soccer team, objected in a minority rebuttal. While they staunchly supported both men's and women's sports, de Varona and Foudy felt that the new proposals would not have helped preserve any more men's sports and would have damaged opportunities for women.

"I am disturbed by the Commission's failure to ask for or consider any data on the impact of its proposals—such as the effect of the recommendations on participation opportunities and scholarships for female athletes," de Varona wrote to the Opportunity in Athletics Commission. "In fact, the impact is likely to be devastating; one estimate calculates that under one of the proposals, women at a typical Division I-A school would lose 50,000 participation opportunities and $122 million in scholarships. This is simply unacceptable. Indeed, as a member of President Ford's Commission on Olympic Sports, I had the privilege of participating in a procedure that was open, fair, and comprehensive and I felt when the process was completed that I had been given the opportunity to fully examine the facts and the impact our recommendations would have on the Olympic community. Therefore, regretfully, because this report does not allow me to meet these responsibilities, I must decline to sign on to it and will be participating in the filing of a separate minority report."[2]

As a result of both de Varona's and Foudy's minority report, Secretary of Education Rod Paige did not alter any of the Title IX legislation because a consensus was not reached by the task force, and in July 2003, the Bush administration announced that the law would remain unchanged. In 1996, de Varona was appointed as the chair of the 1999 Women's World Cup, which would be hailed as the most successful women's sporting event ever. "Soccer is the most popular sport around the world," de Varona said during an interview following the World Cup. "And one of the tests that we've fought in trying to gain acceptance in supporting women's sports is the test of can you fill stadiums, can you get the ratings? Well, we sold over 650,000 tickets. We had a rating of 13, which I guess translates into 40 million homes. And we met people on every standard. And it was a global celebration as well."[3]

Her role as chair of the Women's World Cup was so successful that she now serves on the board of the U.S. Soccer Foundation. Throughout her career, she has received several of the highest honors that can be bestowed to an individual from a number of organizations. In 2000, the International Olympic Committee awarded her with its highest distinction—the Olympic Order for contributing to the Olympic movement worldwide. In 2003, the National Collegiate Athletic Association (NCAA) honored her with its highest individual honor, the Theodore Roosevelt Award, which is awarded annually to "a distinguished citizen who is a former college student-athlete and who has exemplified the ideals and purposes of college athletics by demonstrating a continuing interest and concern for physical fitness and sport." de Varona has been inducted into the U.S. Olympic Hall of Fame, the International Swimming Hall of Fame, and the Women's Hall of Fame.

Dating back to her Olympic roots in 1960, when she first introduced herself as an upbeat teenager, the 2008 Beijing Olympic Games marked de Varona's 18th coverage of the Summer and Winter Olympic Games as a broadcaster for both radio and television. True to both her Olympic spirit and continual fight for women's sports, she is currently the co-chair of the Back Softball campaign to have the sport restored to the Olympics by 2016.

Notes

1. Carline Bennett, "Seven Who Changed Their World," *WeNews*, December 23, 2003.

2. Donna de Varona, letter to Title IX Commission, February 20, 2003.

3. Donna de Varona, interview with Jim Lehrer, *Online NewsHour*, July 12, 1999. Retrieved from http://www.pbs.org/newshour/bb/sports/july-dec99/soccer_7-12.html.

Diana Nyad

American Star of the Women's International Sports Hall of Fame

by Horacio Ruiz

I prepared myself for an interview with Diana Nyad. She wrote through e-mail that she was a fast talker and I probably would have a difficult time keeping up with her if I chose to type our interview, instead of recording it, which I did not have the capacity to do. The preparation was simple. Every week, Nyad has a segment called "The Score" on the Los Angeles-based radio station KCRW. The Score is a four-minute piece put together by Nyad that discusses current events in sports and examines the deeper issues behind those events. I logged onto the KCRW website and listened to archives of Nyad's pieces. Her quick voice seemed to make a point with every word she spoke. I prepared, but she was right. During our interview I could not keep up with her energy and bounty of words, and anyway, in my preparation I got lost in the beauty of her stories. Nyad does tell wonderful stories—a mixture of both dark and light observations unique to the human experience, not least of which is the one about her life.

She first became famous for being the greatest marathon swimmer during a 10-year period spanning from 1969 to 1979 that reached its peak and finality when she recorded the longest swim ever, a 102.5-mile, two-day journey that spanned from the island of Bimini in the Bahamas to Florida. What followed were numerous appearances on talk shows and phone calls from celebrities like movie director Woody Allen, who asked her out on a date. Her story appeared on the front page of the *New York Times* and Walter Cronkite profiled her in his nightly newscast as a woman doing something that nobody had ever done before. Her feat was an inspiration to both men and women.

In 1974, she was the first person to swim the 32 miles across Lake Ontario from north to south and in 1975, she broke a 50-year-old record for the fastest swim around Manhattan Island, which she accomplished in seven hours and 57 minutes.

"You're never like, 'Oh this is a wonderful way to spend a couple of hours,'" she said. "But you learn to handle the pain. It's your desire that keeps saying to you, 'You wanted to do this, you knew this would happen. Manage the pain.' When you see that other shore that's what it's all about . . . the emotional euphoria, the sense of pride. I always do think that those swims are a little metaphor for life."[1]

After powering over waves in the open ocean, losing consciousness in freezing temperatures, crying out of exhaustion and sea-salt sickness, dealing with jellyfish, and losing 20 to 30 pounds throughout some of her swims, what would drive somebody to do something like that and how does it become an attainable goal? For Nyad, there was never a path that logically or conveniently laid itself out and asked her to follow it. Rather, it was a path that took many turns, in some instances jutting into parts where nothing was clear and blind faith alone was the best compass, and turning back out into parts of sheer joy and exhilaration for accomplishments that defied all rationale.

As Nyad says, she lived under the same roof as a con artist, her father, who intimidated her with his larger than life persona that was necessary for a person making a living by lying and stealing. She wrote a *Newsweek* article after her father died, detailing how one time he took her and her two siblings to a mansion in Key Largo, Florida. A few days later they were running out of the mansion and into her father's car when the homeowners arrived earlier than planned and threatened to call the police. It was, her father insisted, a misunderstanding, but Nyad had caught on by then. "As you get older you look back and I was terrified of him in some ways," she said. "My mother knew that he was a liar and a thief and she finally got the courage to divorce him."

As a 10-year-old sitting in geography class, Nyad remembers her teacher promising anyone in class an A if they would join the swim team. The next day she was at practice and after swimming for 10 minutes, Nyad's teacher, a former Olympian, said to her, "Kid, you're going to be the best swimmer in the world." The compliment meant everything to her and swimming became her escape from home. So she turned to the water and dreamed of becoming an Olympian, just like her coach.

But four years would pass before the same man was the source of heart-breaking disillusionment. On the eve of the Florida state swim championships, Nyad was molested by her swim coach—the man she adored the most. The next day, she lost her first swim meet in two years. In both competitive and emotional anguish, the swimmer sank to the bottom of the pool and screamed. The 14-year-old Nyad vowed to herself that the incident with her coach would not ruin her life. The molestation would last four years until she was 18 years old and had graduated from high school, but Nyad never reported it to law enforcement for fear that it would cause her mother a great deal of embarrassment. Those four years of terror, Nyad says, had ramifications that she still deals with today. She continued swimming under her molester's eye, hoping that she could make it to the 1968 Olympics in Mexico City, but she did not qualify at nationals in either the 100-meter or 200-meter backstroke.

She knew her speed was trailing off and her competitive career in the pool was coming to an end. Yet, her desire to forget the traumatic memories of her coach led to the finding of another escape. Nyad still had fantasies of being the best in the world and a desire to compete that became the genesis of her marathon swimming career. She would travel across the world swimming for miles with hundreds of men and women in places like the Nile River and the Bay of Naples. "I was 18 years old, my Olympic dreams were not going to be a reality, and I figured what the heck, I'm going to give this a try," she said.

Then, on a trip back to the United States from one of her overseas swims, a friend suggested to her that there were many daring swims she could attempt at home. Nyad's friend pointed out to her she was from New York and that she should give a swim around Manhattan Island a try, which she did in 1975, capturing the imagination of the likes of Jacqueline Kennedy Onassis, who called Nyad "My hero" on the front page of the *New York Post*. From that point on, Nyad concentrated on fewer swims of longer distances. One particular swim captured her memory—it was one she did not complete. It was a swim from Havana, Cuba, to Key West, Florida, in 1978 that was called off in mid-swim because of weather that was veering Nyad off course. After 41 hours and 49 minutes of relentless effort, the expedition was shut down.

The next year, the crew came together again and Nyad successfully stroked her way into the record books with that 102.5-mile feat, the longest swim ever done by either a man or woman until 1997. Friends and well-wishers would meet her on the shores, and Nyad happily soaked it all in. She enjoyed the attention and the teamwork that came from collaborating with a crew of 50, including Jacques Cousteau and NASA experts. But she also looks back at her swims with a different purpose. "Like a lot of kids that go through molestation they find a way to escape," she said. "I really think, now, the safest place I felt was in the water. When I could be in the water for six hours a day swimming laps I felt like nobody could get me. There was that factor of safety."

After one of her appearances on the *Tonight Show* with Johnny Carson in 1980, the president of ABC Sports, Roone Arledge, noticed Nyad and her penchant for story telling. He offered her a position as an announcer for ABC's *Wide World of Sports*. Her new job took her around the world to cover everything from table tennis championships to triathlons. "Every week I would work a different event and it was fantastic," Nyad said. "There was a great learning curve because the cameramen, the engineers, and the editors were all top flight in the business."

Nyad became famous once more for her journalistic endeavors. She worked at ABC from 1980 to 1990 and has also worked as a columnist for NPR since 1988. While working with NPR she was also the host of the *Savvy Traveler*, where she visited exotic places around the world and, as host of all foreign documentaries for the Outdoor Life Network, swam with whales and kayaked over 40-foot waterfalls. In 1996, she joined FOX Sports as an investigative reporter and covered such topics as the use of performance-enhancing drugs by athletes. Currently, she is heard by millions of people on NPR with her sports commentary on *The Score* and she is also the sports business columnist for the radio show *Marketplace*. It is a dream of hers to be able to host a show where she can invite athletes and speak to them about issues not related to their accomplishments, where she can get to the heart and soul of the athletic experience as she does on her radio shows. "I slowly but surely decided I didn't want to go out and cover events anymore," she said. "I wanted to be one of the people that told stories about sports to the non-sport audience. I wanted to be a storyteller more than an events coverer."

In 1998, as a board member of World T.E.A.M. Sports, an organization that puts able-bodied and disabled athletes together for unique sporting adventures around the world, Nyad and her teammates bicycled 1,200 miles from Hanoi to Ho Chi Minh City in Vietnam. It was an important moment in reconciliation between war veterans from both sides of the Vietnam War. Along with Tour de France champion Greg LeMond and Congressmen John McCain and John Kerry, both Vietnamese and American veterans, many of whom had been blinded and maimed during the war, rode up mountains and ate dinner together while sharing their terrible war stories. Nyad has also started an enterprise with a business partner called bravabody.com, whose mission is for women over 40 years old to not be ashamed of their bodies and to develop pride and confidence through fitness. Also in development is a one-woman show where people would buy a ticket to listen to Nyad tell stories and entertain them for 90 minutes. "I think I have a talent for standing on stage and going for 90 minutes of storytelling that goes in an arc, hopefully making people laugh so hard they will cry and cry so hard they will laugh," she said. "If I have enough guts to do it, I'm going to get it done."

When Nyad was five years old there was somebody telling her stories. It was her father, the con artist, who she remembered would read *The Odyssey* to her late at night, a story about the great Greek mythological figure Odysseus who traveled for 10 years after the Trojan War to get back home. It was one of the good memories Nyad had of her father; maybe he was foretelling her future. Nyad has had her own odyssey by traveling the world, reaching celebrity, and swimming distances that had been unimaginable.

Note

1. All of the quotes in this article are by Diana Nyad, from an interview with the author on July 29, 2008.

Pat McCormick

American Star of the Women's International Sports Hall of Fame

by Horacio Ruiz

I share a difficult moment in my life with Pat McCormick, an "ouchy" as she calls it, because she asks that I share with her after she shared a few of hers with me. She is the only woman and only one of two divers to win two gold medals from the springboard and platform in consecutive Summer Olympics, and yet, McCormick talks about the importance of getting through the difficult times. She says she would be very disappointed if I wrote about everything she told me. No worries, our "ouchies" are meant to be trusted secrets. But, what McCormick has accomplished in and out of athletics should never be kept secret.

"Failures are our blessings," McCormick says. "You have to get through it. Some way, you have to."[1]

It was one of McCormick's earlier disappointments that catapulted her into becoming one of the most decorated American athletes in Olympic history. McCormick fell $^1/100$th of a point short of making the 1948 U.S. Olympic Diving Team, recalling how she sat in the showers crying, and how in her disappointment she dedicated herself to becoming the best diver in the world. She is modest in saying that she had so much support around her that it would have been impossible for her to not be good.

Sammy Lee, a two-time gold medal-winning Olympian and one of McCormick's trusted mentors, said he didn't think McCormick had the ability to be a great diver. He mentioned how she could not point her toes and recalled the thunderous noises McCormick would make on failed dive attempts.

"Pat—she has a lot of guts, and she crashed," Lee said of her painful flops during practices. "Pat was not a natural diver. She had to work at it."[2] Lee underestimated McCormick's determination and her relentless work ethic. McCormick was a wonder from an early age, having strongmen in Los Angeles's Muscle Beach flip her up in the air where she would perform her acrobatics. There is a picture of her when she was no more than 10 years old holding up a well-built man who is standing on her shoulders, with well-defined muscles popping from her little arms and shoulders. She spent her youth at the beach and in the water, sometimes daring to jump off bridges.

After completing her "double-double" at the 1952 Helsinki Olympics and the 1956 Melbourne Olympics, McCormick was *Sports Illustrated*'s "Athlete of the Year" and the AP's "Woman Athlete of the Year." What she vowed to do while wiping away her tears in 1948 had become a reality.

"It becomes a very personal thing," McCormick said. "That was my passion and my goal and anytime you accomplish something like that there's a sense of peace."[3]

And then? McCormick hit a depression, finding herself with an emptiness that had not been there before. Accustomed to training eight to 10 hours a day for the Olympics, sometimes with lacerations and bruised ribs, the life she had known as an athlete for so long was suddenly gone. After a life's worth of preparation, McCormick reached the apex of her athletic career. The rest of her life lay before her, a life she had not prepared for. But just as she said, she found a way to press on and get through her post-Olympic blues.

"The trick is to stay on that victory stand," McCormick told journalist Jim Murray. "Never step down from it."[4]

After making Olympic history, McCormick stayed busy raising her family, being a mother and wife, and standing behind her daughter, Kelly, as she developed into a world-class diver of her own. Kelly would win a silver medal in the 1984 Los Angeles Olympics and a bronze in the 1988 Seoul Olympics. The McCormicks are the only mother-daughter medal winning combination in Olympic history.

In 1984, McCormick was chosen to be a member of the Los Angeles Olympic Organizing Committee. It would change her life. She was picked to speak at Wing Lane Elementary in La Puente, just a few minutes southeast of Los Angeles. After she had given a 45-minute speech, a teacher told McCormick that more than 100 students at the school were failing. The teacher asked McCormick if there was anything she could do, but McCormick couldn't think of what to do to help. Another teacher said the kids were "nothing but a bunch of losers."

McCormick was struck by the comment. She made a commitment to 25 third graders, visiting the school twice a month to work with them. The first three months were a disaster, but then she enlisted a mentor, boxer Paul Gonzalez. Gonzalez, a Southern California native who was training for the Los Angeles Olympics, was a hit with the students as he recalled his involvement with a gang and how he would surely be dead if not for the help of a Los Angeles policeman. He would go on to win a gold medal later that summer. McCormick continued her program, hopeful with every bit of progress she was making, instilling confidence and love in the children. She tracked the progress of the 25 students she began her work with. Her program included aspects of inspiration, mentoring, parenting classes, nutrition education, and tutors. Eighteen of the children graduated from high school and some went on to colleges and universities. Her program would eventually come to be known as "Pat's Champs," set upon the foundation of her own Olympic success. Her program currently has six steps: dream, work, "ouchies," being with good people, helping others, and staying healthy and fit.

"Pat has taught me that there are people that do care about me and those people have taught me to care about myself,"[5] said Sandy Hernandez, a student in McCormick's program.

Over the years, McCormick's work has spread through the Pat McCormick Educational Foundation, which has also included the Life Skills Training Program, which is focused on tobacco, alcohol, and drug use education for adolescents. Her programs have been implemented in several school districts in California and also are in the states of Washington and Vermont. She recently pledged a 10-year commitment for the continued implementation of her programs throughout the California school districts and beyond. The work has been a grind for McCormick, who these days is trying to find enough time to golf and to do some gardening in her yard, but it's a labor of love that has kept her on the victory stand all her life.

"God love you, and I know you're going to be a success," she tells me.[6] It makes me feel good hearing that as we finish our conversation.

Notes

1. Pat McCormick, interview with author, February 8, 2008.
2. Women Who Won Gold—Pat McCormick Bio. Video.
3. Pat McCormick, interview with author, February 8, 2008.
4. Jim Murray, "Diving in from the Highboard," *Los Angeles Times*.
5. Women Who Won Gold—Pat McCormick Bio. Video.
6. Pat McCormick, interview with author, February 8, 2008.

Micki King

American Star of the Women's International Sports Hall of Fame

by Horacio Ruiz

It was a nightmare; the kind that could linger the rest of one's life. Olympic diver Air Force lieutenant Micki King was leading the competition in the 3-meter springboard after eight of ten mandatory dives in the 1968 Olympic Games in Mexico City. It happened on the ninth dive. King's arm hit the springboard as she executed her second to last dive. The accident happened so quickly and innocently, very few people watching even realized she hit. Only two judges caught the mistake and judged her low, but it was missed by the other five judges. She remained in first place with one dive left. Ignoring the mistake, pretending there was not a "bump" on her arm, and fighting off doubts that tried to flood her mind, she performed her last dive—her best dive—a reverse one and a half somersault with one and a half twists. Her arm hurt more than she thought it would, and her poor attempt dropped King off the winner's podium from first place to fourth. The next day, X-rays showed the "bump" on her arm that she did the last dive with was actually a broken ulna bone.

"I was in shock. I was devastated. I couldn't believe I blew it," King said. "I was 24 years old in Mexico City and I had an Air Force career ahead of me. How could I make a stupid mistake like this when the medal was all but mine? I was lost and depressed for a long time afterward. And, at that point, I had no plans to make a comeback."[1]

King took 30 days' leave from Air Force duties after her Olympic nightmare and returned to her hometown to visit her parents while she recovered from the broken arm and depression over the ordeal she had just experienced. As close as she had come to being an Olympic champion, it hurt even more to have lost the way she did. King's parents worried about her, seeing her Olympics tarnished by injury. One day she and her father had a long talk and he reminded her that she was one of the best athletes in the world at Mexico City; that she had met exciting new people from across the globe; and that it was those unique experiences as an Olympian that would always remain special despite missing the medal. But the nightmare still haunted her. "I simply believed I would have to live with my Mexico mistake,"[2] she said. King was certain her time had come and gone.

But in 1969, University of Michigan diving coach Dick Kimball, who had coached King while she was a student at Michigan, convinced her he could get her back into top form. Kimball would sneak King through the backdoors of the diving facilities to get past the administrators who were located at the front door because women were not allowed to compete for Michigan athletics. That year, she made her comeback when she captured the U.S. national diving championship in the 3-meter springboard. It was then that King decided to put the 1968 Olympics behind her and try for the gold once again. She knew exactly what was ahead of her over the next three years leading to the 1972 Games. No one would hand her the gold medal in 1972 because of the accident in 1968. The Air Force supported her request to continue diving and stationed her at an Air Force base near Olympic-caliber facilities, where she practiced diving when she was off duty. She did hundreds of dives a week leading up to the 1972 Munich Olympics. Four years older, King focused solely on the gold medal. "When I headed to Munich I had a whole different attitude. This was my second Olympics, I was 28, I extended my commitment in the Air Force and had begun a career path, but I still had this Olympic goal," King said. "I was a whole new personality type. The glamour and pageantry in Mexico was certainly there in Munich too, but I was looking beyond that and had one mission, to win the gold."[3]

After the preliminary dives, King was in third place, behind two Swedish divers. Prior to the beginning of the competition, Kimball shocked King by telling her that while he would love for her to be 15 points ahead going into the final dives, it would be alright if she found herself two or three points behind the leaders. "I was confused at first," she said. "My coach had been with me at meets for 10 years. I knew him, he knew me. We had kind of a pattern so we were comfortable with each other. He never gave me a license to not finish first in the prelims."

After finding herself in third place and three points behind the leader heading into the final dives, King, surprised that Kimball had predicted everything, asked him why he was okay with her being in third place. Kimball pointed across the pool where the two Swedish divers were being interviewed on worldwide television. Dealing with television interviews after her event would be a new experience for King and Kimball did not want her distracted by reporters asking about the broken arm incident from four years prior. By not being first in the prelims, he felt the reporters were less likely to question her. Kimball also knew the other two divers had used their best dives to get to where they were—King was saving her best for last. "He reminded me they used up their best dives while I was coming in with my strongest dives. Besides, they also knew I had my strongest dives left; and I knew they knew I knew."

The reverse one and a half somersault with one and a half twists that knocked her out in Mexico City was the same dive that catapulted her to the gold in Munich four years later. The nightmare of Mexico was no more.

The 1972 Munich Olympics proved to be an impetus for major changes in U.S. sports. Following her triumph on the 3-meter springboard, King found herself among Olympic teammates who were largely demoralized. There were instances of disappointing performances, disqualifications, the first-ever loss by the U.S. men's basketball team in Olympic competition, and the tragedy of 11 Israeli athletes killed by terrorists. King remembered the tall basketball players sitting in the back of the U.S. Olympic team plane with their knees nearly up to their chins, while the wives of Olympic Committee officers sat in the front in more spacious seats. The tension was close to spilling over; athletes had no voice in matters that affected them directly. On the plane trip home from Munich, several outspoken athletes sat together and made a list of problems that needed attention. King sat among these athletes from several different sports and took notes. Within months after the Munich Games, a handful of these self-appointed members of the 1972 team set a meeting with the U.S. Olympic Committee (USOC) president Phillip O. Krumm. Krumm, sensing the athletes' frustration, recognized the need to include athletes in the Olympics' decision-making process. Krumm, along with USOC executive director Colonel F. Don Miller, formally recognized the Athletes' Advisory Council (AAC) as a standing forum of the U.S. Olympic Committee. At the inaugural meeting of the AAC, King was elected its first chairman and led the group for the first four years.

"Micki was a terrific chairman," original AAC member Ed Williams said. "She was the perfect person for the job. She charmed people. She was a logical choice to be the first president. She was a hard worker, but she was a pleasure to work with."[4]

"If it were not for Micki, we might not have had the AAC for a second four years,"[5] Miller said.

In large part due to King, the AAC established a solid relationship with the USOC in which the two branches developed a mutual respect. It was this charter AAC under King's leadership that hammered out the issues of team selection, coach selection, and 20 percent athlete representation on all USOC committees. President Gerald R. Ford appointed King to his Commission to Study Olympic Sports in 1975. This Presidential Commission studied the entire spectrum of amateur sports in the United States. The recommendations from the Commission's two-year study were incorporated into the federal law known as the Amateur Sports Act (ASA) of 1978. The USOC, as it is known today, is the model recommended by the Sports Commission and included in the federal law. The ASA also incorporated most AAC concerns, including those derived from the athletes' list on the Munich flight home.

After the Olympics, the Air Force assigned King to the Air Force Academy (AFA) athletic department, where she became the first woman to teach physical education and coach at any military academy. In her first stint as coach from 1973 to 1977, she became the first and only woman to ever coach a man to an individual National Collegiate Athletic Association (NCAA) championship. She was sent on assignments to Arizona, Washington, and Germany, before returning to the AFA in 1984 as an assistant athletic director as well as the diving coach. During this second stint, she was named

NCAA Division II Coach of the Year three times and her divers won 11 All-American honors and claimed three individual national titles. In 1992, she retired from the Air Force as a full colonel to accept an assistant athletic director position at the University of Kentucky, a post she held through 2006.

In 1974, Congress passed a law to allow women to attend the then all-male military academies. As the only woman assigned to the AFA at the time, she played a key role in the athletic department transition from men-only to co-ed. She helped develop curriculums for physical education classes, design women's locker rooms from the former men's facilities, and plan for the new women's varsity teams. Her daughter, Michelle Hogue, a 2004 graduate of the Air Force Academy, became a beneficiary of her mother's work decades before. In appreciation, Michelle sent her mother a miniature AFA graduation ring as a gift with a note King will never forget.

"When she chose to go to the Academy it blew me away," King said. "Her father and I didn't push her. The truth is it didn't occur to us that she would go there. It was her junior year when she wrote me that special note. It said, 'Mom, if anyone deserves an Air Force Academy class ring—you do! You helped make it possible for me and all the other girls to be here and I don't think I've ever thanked you. I hope this ring reminds you how special you are—not only to me but to so many people.' Until her note, I never knew if she really understood my role in the co-ed transition, and if she knew how special it was to see my own daughter follow years later as a cadet herself. After I read the note, I knew she knew."

In 1976, King was among the first members of the advisory board for the Women's Sports Foundation. She was inducted into the Women's Sports Foundation Hall of Fame in 1983 and served on its board of trustees from 1988 to 1990. She has served on the board of stewards since 1990. King was elected president of U.S.A. Diving from 1990 to 1994 and in 2005 was selected to serve a four-year term as vice president of the U.S. Olympians Association. Looking back at her career, King recalls milestones and achievements that had not crossed her mind in years, not least of which were her contributions toward advancing opportunities for women in sport.

"I won the ultimate prize in sport, but never once did I represent my high school or my college in an athletic competition," she said. "It wasn't there for my generation and it was wrong. Now I can watch women's national championships on television and say, "'Damn, we did it.'"

Notes

1. Unless noted otherwise, the quotes in this article are by Micki King, from an interview with the author, May 20, 2008.

2. Ibid.

3. Julie Eversgerd, Springboard champion bounces back from broken arm, http://www.olympic-usa.org/CFDOCS/Munich/feature_king.cfm.

4. Mike Spence, "Hogue Helped Athletes Become Part of U.S. Olympic Process," *Colorado Springs Gazette Telegraph*, February 26, 1989.

5. Ibid.

7

FLYING THROUGH THE AIR WITH THE GREATEST OF EASE: WOMEN GYMNASTS

Introduction by Richard Lapchick

Every four years, gymnastics becomes one of the world's favorite sports. The 2008 Beijing Olympics proved that little girls can still win the hearts of the world. Who will forget the faces and performances of American gold medal winners Nastia Liukin in the women's individual all-around and Shawn Johnson in the women's balance beam? In spite of the age controversy that swirled regarding how old the Chinese girls were, it will be easy to remember the performances of the women's team competition gold medalists Fei Cheng, Kexin He, Yuyuan Jiang, Shanshan Li, Yilin Yang, and Linlin Deng. Even if you were rooting for the eventual silver medalists from the United States, the bronze winners from Romania, or those from any other nation, you had to marvel at the Chinese. Americans, of course, were thrilled that Liukin and Johnson both won medals in the women's individual all-around, floor exercise, and balance beam. It was a great week that will last for four more years.

In a young person's sport, you hope that these athletes have a sense of history about their predecessors. In gymnastics, it is a rich history that has often transcended nationalism. The three women profiled in this section became beloved across borders; Olga Korbut, Nadia Comaneci, and Mary Lou Retton were the sports antifreeze to the Cold War.

As a competitive sport, gymnastics is about 100 years old and first came to the United States about 75 years ago. As an activity sport, gymnastics has been around for over 2,000 years. Mass and individual exhibitions were conducted by various clubs and ethnic groups such as the Turvereins and Sokols.

While it was slow-growing in the club area, it was a fast-growing sport in the Turvereins and Sokols. In the 1830s, the activity of gymnastics was introduced to the United States and its school systems by such immigrants as Charles Beck, Charles Follen, and Francis Lieber.

The International Gymnastics Federation (FIG) was formed in 1881 to govern the sport. It was later called the Bureau of the European Gymnastics Federation. The Amateur Athletic Union (AAU) was formed in the United States in 1883. Along with other amateur sports in the United States, the AAU took over the control of the gymnastics.

Men's gymnastics were in the first modern Olympics in 1896 in Athens, where there were individual events. The first men's team competition was added in the 1904 St. Louis Olympics.

The 1924 Olympics marked a turning point as men started to compete for individual Olympic titles in each gymnastic event. The 1928 Games were the first to have gymnastics for women. American women gymnasts did not compete until the 1936 Olympics in Berlin. The 1952 Olympics featured the first full set of events for women gymnasts.

America's first female all-around champion (1931) was Roberta Ranck Bonniwell, the Babe Didrikson Zaharias of Philadelphia. She was the first American woman to coach an Olympic team (1952). She was prominent in a number of other sports, winning the first national javelin title for women in track and field.

By the 1954 Olympic Games, apparatuses and events for both men and women had been standardized. There were scoring standards with a point system from 1 to 10. Modern gymnastics for men's and women's events are scored on an individual and team basis. For men, the events are the floor exercise, rings, pommel horse, vaulting, horizontal bar, parallel bars, and the all-around, which combines the scores of the other six events. Women's events include balance beam, uneven parallel bars, combined exercises, floor exercises, and vaulting. Traditionally, men's gymnastics emphasized power and strength. Grace of movement was the focus for women. However, in 1972, a 17-year-old Soviet gymnast named Olga Korbut changed all of that.

Munich will be remembered first for the Israeli hostage tragedy in the athlete housing, but also for Korbut's performance and ear-to-ear smile. Television showed her as the human side of the Soviet Union mired deeply in the Cold War with the United States. She wept openly when she fell short of a good score on the uneven bars.

It meant she could not win an all-around title. But Korbut came back with her creative and explosive style to capture the gold on the beam and in the floor exercise. Emotions showing, she won the silver in the individual uneven bar event. Her performances helped the Soviet Union to win the team gold medal performance. ABC donned her the Athlete of the Year. President Richard M. Nixon invited Korbut to the White House while she was visiting the United States. In 1975, the United Nations gave Korbut the "Gold Tuning Fork" for her role in bringing the world together through sport and named her "Woman of the Year."

Four years later, Nadia Comaneci, a 14-year-old Romanian gymnast, captured the hearts of the world with her stunning perfection in Montreal. She stood 4 feet, 11 inches and weighed 86 pounds. Never before had someone scored a perfect 10 in an event. In Montreal she achieved seven perfect 10s, three gold medals, one bronze, and one silver. The world fell in love with this child and she returned home to Romania as a national treasure. But like other national treasures in the Eastern Bloc nations, she was constantly watched to assure that she would not defect, which she eventually did. She had one more Olym pics in her and at the 1980 Moscow Olympics, Comaneci won two gold medals and two silver. That gave her an Olympic total of nine medals, including five gold, three silver, and one bronze. These were the Games that the United States boycotted. The Soviet Bloc turned the tables in 1984 by boycotting the Los Angeles Games.

Mary Lou Retton vaulted onto the world stage with her performance at those 1984 Games. Retton scored a perfect 10 when she landed a flawless vault on an injured right knee. With that performance, she clinched the all-around gymnastics gold medal—an honor never before earned by an American. Her smile said it all in that moment, the pain had vanished, and all the time and hard work she invested had paid off. In that moment, a nation and the world became smitten with this young woman and celebrated her achievements.

Retton earned a silver medal in the vault event at the 1984 Games and two bronze medals in the floor exercise and the uneven bars. She helped the U.S. gymnastics team earn a silver medal in the overall team competition, the nation's first medal performance in gymnastics in 36 years. She was the first American woman to win gold in gymnastics and to win the women's gymnastics all-around title.

We have had other stars since these trailblazers.

At the 1988 Olympics in Seoul, the U.S. women did not win a team medal while Phoebe Mills won silver on the balanced beam, which she shared with Gabriela Potorac of Romania.

In the 1992 Barcelona Olympics, the American women won the all-around bronze while Shannon Miller won the all-around bronze, silver on balance beam (shared with Lu Li of China), bronze on the uneven bars, and bronze in the floor routine (shared with Christina Bontas of Romania and Tatiana Gutsu of United Team [former Soviet republics-Estonia, Latvia, and Lithuania]).

Dominique Dawes won 15 national gymnastics championships in nine years and a spot on the 1988 U.S. national gymnastics team—the first African-American on the squad.

Shannon Miller is called the most decorated gymnast in American history with her total of 16 World Championship and Olympic medals. She just missed the individual all-around gold at the 1992 Olympic Games by 0.012. She was the 1996 Olympics balance beam gold medalist.

Dawes and Miller were two members of the so-called Magnificent Seven in Atlanta who made up the 1996 U.S. Olympic Women's Gymnastics Team. They were the first U.S. team to win the gold in the women's team competition. The other members of the team were Dominique Moceanu, Kerri Strug, Amy Chow, Amanda Borden, and Jaycie Phelps.

There was a huge drop off in the 2000 Sydney Olympics; there were no American team medals and no American woman medaled.

At Athens in the 2004 Olympics, the American women's team won all-around silver. Carly Patterson won gold in the individual all-around and silver on the balance beam, while Terin Humphrey won silver and Courtney Kupets won the bronze on the uneven bars. Annia Hatch won silver on the vault.

Today, gymnasts are household names and many children participate in gymnastics as they grow up. Olga Korbut, Nadia Comaneci, and Mary Lou Retton, along with all those gymnasts since, have helped popularize women's competitive gymnastics, making it one of the most watched Olympic events with stars or potential stars on every continent. But like with every sport, we must acknowledge the role of the trailblazers like Olga Korbut, Nadia Comaneci, and Mary Lou Retton.

Olga Korbut

International Star of the Women's International Sports Hall of Fame

by Stacy Martin-Tenney

Olga Korbut seemed so tiny physically, but her smile was big enough to win the hearts of two nations at the 1972 Olympic Games held in Munich. She was a daring acrobat soaring above expectations for the sport of gymnastics, and her performance landed her in that golden spotlight known by only the world's elite performers. Korbut won three gold medals in Munich and captured a silver medal too. The Cold War era characterized her place in history and why she will be remembered for the impact she had on not only the sport but also a relationship between her native land of Russia and the United States of America. Korbut has remained a central figure in gymnastics throughout the years, but sadly has faced the trials and tribulations that accompany fame.

Korbut's tumbling seemed to begin in her mother's womb and she developed her athletic skills throughout her youth with performances for her neighbors. Korbut was the youngest of four daughters born to Valentin and Valentina in Grodno, Belarus. Olga's sister, Ludmilla, had earned the country's coveted title, Master of Sports, as a gymnast. Olga soon followed in her sister's athletic footsteps, and quickly demonstrated her speed and jumping ability. Her daring posture got her into trouble when she tried her acrobatic tricks climbing trees. She entered a gymnastics class at age eight and became infatuated with the rigorous sport. Her life took a dramatic turn at that moment. It was her adventurous spirit and obsession with the sport that would lead her away from her parents and their guidance.

She joined a sports school operated by a boldly innovative coach, Renald Knysh, and he would become the primary influence in her career and life. Knysh ran one of the Soviet Union-supported sports training facilities. The country's need to establish its powerful presence had led to state-supported development in several notable areas. One was sports training facilities. Young children were selected at an early age for their talents and potential, then tested and pushed to extreme limits, in some cases, to develop the Soviet

Union's next athletic phenomenon. Knysh harnessed Korbut's audacious nature through the development of bold new maneuvers that would challenge the routine climate of gymnastics. She perfected a backward aerial somersault on the balance beam, which she named the Korbut Salto, and a back flip to catch on the uneven bars, subsequently called the Korbut Flip. A backward release move on the bars was unprecedented until Korbut demonstrated it during one of her first senior-level competitions. Due to the nature of the move, it was not as widely accepted among the judges of the sport or the National Soviet Sports Council but it was applauded by the audiences in attendance. Knysh and Korbut embarked on a journey to change the Soviet regime's way of gymnastics by demonstrating that women could be both powerful and graceful.

Korbut's determination would not yield and she continued perfecting her style of gymnastics. By 1971, she equaled her sister, Ludmilla, by earning her own Master of Sport title and she had refined her competitive routines in three national championships. The next year was an Olympic year, and Korbut had emerged as a Soviet star in gymnastics and a seasoned competitor. She focused on completing secondary school early and winning gold at Munich. The journey began with a third-place finish at the Soviet National Championships. She dazzled the judges at her first international competition, the Riga Cup, and they awarded her with a win! After graduation from school, she competed for the USSR Cup and Olympic team selection.

Munich will be remembered first for the Israeli hostage tragedy in the athlete housing, but also for Olga Korbut's performance and ear-to-ear smile. She proved to be the human side of the Soviet Union and its Cold War persona. She wept openly when she fell short of a respectable score in the uneven bars, which crushed her hopes of an all-around title, and the audience seemed to feel her teardrops as if they were their own. She won over their hearts with her comeback performance on the beam and in the floor exercise, earning her the gold medal for both. The emotional young girl exhibited her steel reserve of determination as she competed in the individual uneven bar event—winning a silver medal. Her performance contributed to the Soviet team's gold medal performance. ABC donned her the Wide World of Sports Athlete of the Year for her three gold medals and girlish smile. The Cold War seemed to be disarmed slightly by a pixie with a charming smile. President Richard

M. Nixon even invited Korbut to the White House while she was visiting the United States to receive several of her awards. In 1975, the United Nations bestowed the "Gold Tuning Fork" to Korbut for her role in bringing the world together through sport and named her "Woman of the Year."

Fame and extensive international travel came at a personal cost to Korbut. The Soviet Union used her as a marketing arm of the communist regime. Traveling across the globe left her rich in awards but unable to adequately train for the 1976 Olympics. Throughout those three years of travel the KGB trailed her to ensure that communism and their new jewel, Korbut, remained safe. During that same time, Korbut suffered through secret abuse from her coach, Knysh. She would not reveal the trauma until many years later, but Knysh got her drunk just before the 1972 Olympics and forced her to have sex with him. She lacked the support from her family and could only succumb to his sexual abuse as she did the physical and mental abuse she endured while training. In spite of everything, Korbut managed to make the Soviet team in 1976, but she could only muster an individual silver medal in the balance beam and help her team to one more gold medal at the Montreal Olympic Games. Korbut was replaced by Nadia Comaneci as the queen of gymnastics. However, she is still known as the mother of gymnastics for her daring moves and innovation of the sport. Korbut was removed from the Soviet team the next year.

Away from the demanding nature of the sport, she found a new balance in her life. She met Leonid Bortkevich, a Soviet rock singer, and they soon married. From the strife of gymnastics, Korbut found it difficult to conceive and give birth, but she and Bortkevich finally had a son, Richard. She soon transitioned into coaching for the Soviet team for a salary of approximately $312 per week.

After the Chernobyl disaster, only 180 miles from her family's home in Minsk, they immigrated to the United States to protect their young son from radiation poisoning. Korbut had created the gymnastics market in the United States. Korbut felt compelled to help mothers back home who begged her to use her fame to draw attention to the widespread cancer affecting their children after Chernobyl. She organized the Olga Korbut Foundation to raise money for bone marrow transplants and other resources such as doctors and medicine.

Korbut has tried to transition into the private sector of coaching at several schools across the United States. She has difficulty making gymnastics fun and not as punitive and demanding as her experience in the sport. Her passion for the sport is still vibrant. She has a dream of creating a senior gymnastics level for gymnasts 18 years and older to accommodate the change in flexibility that occurs as women age. That is ironic considering her vigorous routines changed what the public expected from gymnastics: young girls with daring moves. Korbut envisions a sport that displays the grace a woman exemplifies in gymnastics as she ages. With grace and vigor, Olga Korbut changed a sport and brought warmth to a Cold War power struggle between two nations.

Nadia Comaneci

International Star of the Women's International Sports Hall of Fame

by Richard Lapchick

From the covers of *Newsweek*, *TIME*, and *Sports Illustrated* at age 14 to walking six hours in the dead of night for her freedom, the life story of Nadia Comaneci is part fairly tale and part horror story. But now three decades after dazzling the world in the 1976 Montreal Olympics, she is a commanding presence in the world of sport wherever she goes.

I was a member of the delegation for the New York City Bid Committee for the 2012 Games. The final decision was being made by the International Olympic Committee in Singapore in 2006. We were there for three days. Among the New York City delegation was Senator Hillary Clinton, Henry Kissinger, Muhammad Ali, Nadia Comaneci, and her husband, Bart Conner. Everywhere we went, people gravitated to Ali and Nadia first. It was a revelation to see her magnetism after all these years and the tumultuous events in her life.

The world at large discovered her in Montreal when the 14-year-old Romanian gymnast captured the hearts of the world with her stunning perfection. She stood 4 feet, 11 inches and weighed 86 pounds. Never before had someone scored a perfect 10 in an event. In Montreal she achieved seven perfect 10s, three gold medals, one bronze, and one silver. The world fell in love with this child and she returned home to Romania as a national treasure. But like other national treasures in the Eastern Bloc nations, she was constantly watched to assure that she would not defect.

She had one more Olympics in her and at the 1980 Moscow Olympics, Comaneci won two gold and two silver medals. That gave her an Olympic total of nine medals, including five gold, three silver, and one bronze.

Her competitive career ended with what many thought was a reflection of the political times. Relations between the Soviet Union and its previously loyal Romania had chilled by 1980. In judging the all-around gymnastics winner, the judges took an unheard of 28 minutes to choose. When the Soviet judge gave Nadia a lower score than the other judges, she slipped to the silver medal while Soviet gymnast Yelena Davydova won the gold.

Fast forwarding, Nadia defected from Romania in 1989, was inducted into the International Gymnastics Hall of Fame in 1996, and married American Olympic gymnastics champion, Bart Conner, in 1996. They are partners in several business ventures, including the Bart Conner Gymnastics Academy, *International Gymnast Magazine*, and Perfect 10 Productions, Inc. (a television production company). Comaneci also does personal appearances, commercial endorsements, speaking engagements, and charity events. She authored a book called *Letters to a Young Gymnast* in 1993 about her life's journey.

But that journey has so many details worth noting here. It shows how fate can enter in the most unlikely ways.

Gheorge and Stefania-Alexandria Comaneci watched their daughter's birth on November 12, 1961, in Onesti, Romania. Coincidentally, the gymnastics coach of an Onesti sports school was Bela Karolyi, who would become one of the most renowned gymnastics coaches ever.

One day Karolyi visited Nadia's school when she was only six years old. He invited her and a friend to come to his gym and be tested after he observed the two pretending to be gymnasts. Nadia passed the test easily and her parents agreed to let her train at Karolyi's gym.

From the start, Nadia trained tirelessly six days a week, four hours a day. She started competing a year later. At age seven and the youngest in the competition, she finished 13th in the Romanian National Junior Gymnastics Championships. Coach Karolyi gave her a doll and reportedly told her "never to finish 13th again." A year later, doll in hand, she won first place as an eight-year-old. She won two more National Junior titles and started competing outside Romania in a "Friendship Cup" meet with Bulgaria. She returned with medals and Bulgarian dolls.

In 1975, Comaneci won four gold medals and one silver at the European Championships, including the gold medal for the all-around competition, making her the youngest girl to have ever won it. She was clearly ready for the Olympics. The uneven parallel bars was the first event and her performance stunned the crowd. The scoreboard lit up with a 1.00, confusing everyone that she got such a low score. Then it settled in that the scoreboard was not able to post the first perfect 10 ever achieved.

By 1976, she had five Olympic medals and more than 200 dolls, reinforcing her image of innocence and youth.

As another milestone, she was awarded the Hero of Socialist Labor, the highest honor in Romania. Comaneci was the youngest girl to receive it.

After the 1980 Moscow Games, Coach Karolyi defected from Romania, provoking Nadia to contemplate the same. The Romanian government kept a close eye on their superstar and did not allow her to leave the country.

In 1989, she defected from Romania in the dead of night, leaving behind her medals and her little brother, Adrian. She walked for six hours to the Hungarian border in bad weather, always looking back with the fear of being caught. There, Constantin Panait met her and took her to the United States. The story, says Nadia, should have ended there. Panait was a 36-year-old Romanian émigré who had arranged the escape. Nadia, the innocent child, suddenly was seen by the side of this married man. She wore heavy makeup and started to shatter the image of her innocent and brilliant youth as the two traveled and stayed together for months.

Coach Karolyi sensed something was wrong and he asked his friend, Alexandru Stefu, a Romanian rugby coach living in Montreal, to help. Stefu discussed a lucrative endorsement contract to get Panait to take Nadia to Montreal. Comaneci asked for help, telling him that Panait was "a bad guy." When Panait returned, he saw Stefu and Comaneci together and left but not before he had all the money he had negotiated for Nadia—close to $150,000. But Nadia was now free and ready to start again. Because she had been so beloved, it was not hard for the world to resume its love affair with the extraordinary woman.

Comaneci was named by *ABC News* and *Ladies Home Journal* as one of the 100 Most Important Women of the 20th century. In 2000, Comaneci was named as one of the athletes of the century by the Laureus World Sports Academy.

Comaneci travels widely pursuing her interests, which include extensive humanitarian work. She is the vice chairperson of the board of directors of Special Olympics International and vice president of the Muscular Dystrophy Association. She returns often to Romania, where she helps numerous charitable organizations and even donated $120,000 to the Romanian gymnastics team.

Dylan Paul Conner was born on June 3, 2006, to Conner and Comaneci. They live in Norman, Oklahoma, where their gymnastics school is located. But they are truly citizens of the world and I was honored to observe that in conjunction with our travels together in support of New York City's attempt to host the 2012 Olympics.

Mary Lou Retton

American Star of the Women's International Sports Hall of Fame

by Stacy Martin-Tenney

Mary Lou Retton vaulted onto the world stage with her performance at the 1984 Los Angeles Olympic Games. Retton scored a perfect 10 when she landed a flawless vault on an injured right knee. With that performance, she clinched the all-around gymnastics gold medal—an honor never before earned by an American. Her smile said it all in that moment, the pain had vanished, and all the time and hard work she invested had paid off. In that moment, a nation became smitten with this young woman and celebrated her achievement as if it was their own. Her accomplishment symbolized a dream coming true, the American dream.

Retton's journey toward this golden moment began when she was seven years old and she first walked into a gymnastics class in her hometown of Fairmont, West Virginia. In a short time, she excelled and earned a spot on the U.S. junior national team. Retton's enthusiasm for the sport garnered the attention of the famous gymnastics coach, Bela Karolyi. He extended an invitation to the 14-year-old to train at the U.S. Gymnastics Center in Houston, Texas. The dedicated little girl left everything she had ever known to follow her dream.

Romanian-born Karolyi coached the renowned Nadia Comaneci, who scored seven perfect 10s at the Montreal Olympic Games. It was Comaneci's awe-inspiring performance that enthralled Mary Lou Retton. Rarely does an athlete have the opportunity to follow in the footsteps of her childhood hero. Under Karolyi's tough tutelage, Retton followed in Comaneci's steps and honed her skills and perfected her talents.

After only a year of training with Karolyi, Retton attained her first international title. She won the all-around at Japan's Chunichi Cup gymnastics competition, the first American woman to do so. She also earned the all-around title at the American Cup during the next three years. There was a new era in American gymnastics that began with the young Mary Lou, who breathed life and excitement into the sport. Before Retton emerged on the scene, U.S. gymnastics was struggling as the 1948 Olympic Games in London marked the last time an American team had won a gymnastics medal. Due to President Jimmy Carter's boycott of the 1980 Olympic Games in Moscow, the United States had suffered eight years since the last Summer Olympiad. The long layoff, coupled with Retton's previous international success, excited the nation. Sport inherently generates a sense of hope and belief in a common goal, whether one plays on the field or watches from the stands. Enthusiasm and interest blossomed as the date grew closer to the 1984 Olympic Games in Los Angeles. Retton's radiance and charisma delivered the magic of sport back into the nation's consciousness.

Retton earned a silver medal in the vault event at the 1984 Games and two bronze medals in the floor exercise and the uneven bars. She helped the U.S. gymnastics team earn a silver medal in the overall team competition, the nation's first medal performance in gymnastics in 36 years. The gold medal eluded her, but the all-around competition still remained. Going into the final event, Ekaterina Szabo, the favorite, led Retton by five-tenths of a point. Retton looked at Karolyi before the vault, and the coach's steely response was simple, "Now or never!"[1] Only two months from knee surgery, Retton charged the vault with vigor and completed a full twisting layout double Tsukahara. Her pristine landing and graceful smile was truly a moment of perfection. Unanimously, the judges awarded perfect 10s and the American Mary Lou Retton captured the gymnastics all-around Olympic gold medal. She was the first American woman to win gold in gymnastics and to date the only American to win the Olympic all-around title.

No other athlete matched her feat of earning five Olympic medals that summer in Los Angeles. Retton was now America's sweetheart. She joined sports heroes like Michael Jordan as a household name, their likenesses gracing the front of the Wheaties Cereal box. Retton entered the "Wheaties Hall of Champions" in 1984 after her stunning performance and she became the first female athlete featured on the Wheaties Cereal box. Karolyi describes Retton's performance as the sweetest moment in his career, topping Nadia Comaneci's seven perfect 10 scores. It was not just the performance that catapulted her to fame, but Retton's persona and how she was able to relate to everyone. Her energy and determination represented what makes America so great—the pursuit of dreams.

Nearly 10 years after that golden moment an AP poll in 1993 voted her the most popular athlete in America. Mary Lou's performance nearly doubled the enrollment in gymnastics schools across the country. Even today, sometimes up to 10 times a day, women approach her to tell her that their own involvement in gymnastics and their college scholarships are because she inspired them. The down-to-earth Retton accepts the honor with grace and humility. She has spent much of her time sharing her inspirational story with others through speaking engagements across the country. She has written books on her outlook on life and her experiences. She married Shannon Kelly, a financial analyst and a former Texas football player, and the couple currently resides in Texas with their four daughters. The young girl that captured America's heart 24 years ago has grown up but her impact will never be forgotten.

Note

1. Eddie Pells. "America's Still Smitten With Mary Lou," *AP Online*, August 18, 2004. http://www.highbeam.com/doc/1P1-97969599.html. (Accessed January 20, 2008.)

8

SPEED, POWER, AND GRACE: WOMEN IN TRACK AND FIELD

Introduction by Richard Lapchick

Track and field events may have been our first sports events. They are almost completely associated with the Olympic Games by the typical sports fan but they also became extremely popular in high school and college as well as on international circuits. Professional track and field has had limited success. This is at least partially because amateurism has been a major issue for track and field athletes. For many years athletes could not accept training money or cash prizes.

Sprints are the first recorded athletic events, going back to at least to the 776 BC Olympics. Some sources indicate that the stade race (approximately 200 meters) was the only event at the first Olympic Games. Eventually, a two-stade race was added.

There were distance events during the ancient Olympics. Records show they were run in stadiums in distances they called "stades," anywhere from seven to 24 stades, which historians think were between 1,400 and 4,800 meters. The discus, shot put, and javelin throw were part of ancient Greek Olympic contests.

Events that we think of as so common today like the steeplechase and marathons are rooted in history. Cross-country events in Britain were run from town to town, with the starting and finishing points being church steeples, ultimately giving us the term "steeplechase."

Track and field in the United States goes back to the 1860s. The Intercollegiate Association of Amateur Athletes of America (IAAAA) was the nation's first national athletic group. It held the first college races in 1873. The Amateur Athletic Union (AAU), which governed the sport for nearly a century, held its first championships in 1888.

Beginning in the 1920s, track and field's scope widened. The first National Collegiate Athletic Association (NCAA) national championships were held for men in 1921. In a breakthrough for African-American women, the Tuskegee Institute in Alabama formed one of the first women's college track teams in 1929. It offered scholarships to women athletes and added women's events to their widely followed Tuskegee Relays.

Track and field events have been staples of the Olympics since the modern games were started in 1896. The four jumping events—the long jump, high jump, triple jump, and pole vault—were part of the 1896 Games. The shot put and discus were part of the first modern Olympics in 1896.

Those games included the 800- and 1,500-meter runs and the marathon. According to legend, the marathon was inspired by the Athenian military courier Phidippides. It was thought that he ran approximately 26 miles from the plains of Marathon to Athens in 490 BC. The hammer became an Olympic event for men in 1900, followed by the javelin in 1908. The 5,000-meter and 10,000-meter were added in 1912 and the 3,000-meter steeplechase in 1920.

Women joined the Olympics in track in 1928 when they ran in the 800-meter race, threw the discus, did the high jump, and ran the 100-meter run and the 4 × 100-meter relay. The 80-meter hurdles and the javelin were added in 1932, the 200-meter and long jump in 1948, the 400-meter in 1964, the 4 × 400-meter relay and the 1,500-meter in 1972, and the 400-meter hurdles, the 3,000-meter, and the marathon in 1984. For women, the triple jump was added in 1996 and the pole vault and the hammer in 2000.

The Cold War helped popularize track and field even more. The Union of Soviet Socialist Republics (USSR) sent its first Olympic team to the 1952 Helsinki Olympics, where its team won several track and field medals. The U.S. and Soviet teams, along with other Eastern Bloc nations like East Germany, fought in one of the sport's fiercest rivalries.

Track became a more popular sport in the 1970s. There was a short-lived attempt to create a professional track circuit when the International Track Association (ITA) was organized. The ITA went bankrupt after several years because not many athletes wanted to participate in ITA competitions because they were getting even larger illegal payments for appearing at amateur meets. That also let them keep their amateur status so they could still compete in the Olympics. The International Amateur Athletics Federation (IAAF) is the governing body for international competition.

There have been so many superstar women who competed in track and field that it was almost impossible to select whom we would feature here. We certainly could have included Betty Robinson Schwartz, Louise Stokes, Tydia Pickett, and Lillian Greene-Chamberlain.

Betty Robinson Schwartz made history in the 1928 Olympics as the first American woman ever to win an Olympic gold medal and the first woman in the world to win an Olympic medal in track and field when she won the 100-meter run as a 16-year-old. She also won a silver that year as a member of the 4 × 100-meter relay team and won a gold medal on the 4 × 100-meter relay at the 1936 Games. She was the first woman to receive a varsity letter at Northwestern University.

In 1932, Louise Stokes and Tydia Pickett were the first African-American women to be included on a U.S. Olympic team. However, they did not compete in the Games because the coach only chose white team members for the events.

Lillian Greene-Chamberlain, the first internationally recognized African-American woman distance runner, was named as the first woman to be director for Physical Education and Sport Programs for UNESCO.

However, those athletes we did include are Babe Didrikson Zaharias, Helen Stephens, Alice Coachman, Mae Faggs Starr, Wilma Rudolph, Madeline Manning Mims, Wyomia Tyus, Florence Griffith-Joyner, Evelyn Ashford, Valerie Brisco-Hooks, Jackie Joyner-Kersee, Joan Benoit, and Willye White and coaches Nell Jackson, Barbara Jacket, and Bev Kearney.

Athletes

Babe Didrikson Zaharias may have been the greatest athlete of all time. Whether it was hitting home runs, playing golf, shooting basketballs, or competing in track and field, she dominated. Her accomplishments were so incredible that I have discussed her career at length in the introduction to this book. Here I will only write of her track and field triumphs.

She became one of the premier track and field athletes in the world, holding records in five different events. In 1932, Babe Didrikson won six gold medals and broke four world records, totaling 30 points at the AAU national meet. The entire second-place team won just 22 points, eight less than Didrikson. She was named the AP Woman Athlete of the Year for track and field.

Didrikson qualified for the 1932 Los Angeles Olympic Games in five events. However, she was only permitted to compete in three events. She won the first women's Olympic javelin and the first Olympic 80-meter hurdles with ease. Babe tied Jean Smiley's world record high jump performance, but was disqualified by two judges who disagreed with her aggressive head-first approach over the bar. Babe was never warned about her style, but nonetheless she was awarded the silver medal while Smiley took the gold.

Because of her all-around abilities, Babe Didrikson Zaharias was named Woman Athlete of the Year six times.

Helen Stephens became known as "The Fulton Flash." At the 1936 Berlin Olympics, the 18-year-old American competed against her rival, Stella Walsh. Stephens defeated the Polish star in the 100-meter race. She earned another gold medal when she anchored the 400-meter relay. Everyone took notice of the young Stephens, including Adolf Hitler. After seeing Stephens compete, Hitler assumed she must be a pure Aryan with her fair hair, blue eyes, and strong build and he immediately requested to meet her. Helen Stephens was the only American athlete to have a private meeting with Adolf Hitler. Stephens retired from track having never lost a sprint. She then played professional baseball and softball and was the owner and manager of her own semiprofessional basketball team from 1938 to 1952.

The cancellation of the 1940 and 1944 Olympics because of World War II denied Alice Coachman early international acclaim; she had dominated the AAU outdoor high jump championships from 1939 through 1948.

She finally got to the Olympics in 1948 and won the gold medal in the high jump. Coachman was the only American woman to win an Olympic gold medal in 1948.

Coachman competed for the Tuskegee Institute, where she also excelled in the indoor and outdoor 50-meter and the outdoor 100-meter sprints. She also ran on the national champion 4 × 100-meter relay team in 1941 and 1942.

Mae Faggs Starr was called the "mother of the Tigerbelles." She was a mentor to stars like Wilma Rudolph and was responsible for the influx of talent that followed her at Tennessee State University. Besides being a trailblazer and pioneer for track and field, she remains one of most decorated sprinters in track and field history.

The 16-year-old Faggs Starr competed in the 1948 London Olympics as the youngest U.S. team member. She did not win there and was not expected to win in the 1952 Helsinki Games. But Faggs Starr and her teammates Barbara Jones, Janet Moreau, and Catherine Hardy won the gold medal in the 4 × 100-meter relay. Four years later in the 1956 Melbourne Games she teamed up with Margaret Matthews, Wilma Rudolph, and Isabelle Daniels to win the bronze medal. She was one of only a few women to compete in three different Olympic Games.

Wilma Rudolph overcame poverty and polio to rise to be one of the very greatest track and field athletes of all-time. During a high school basketball championship tournament, Tennessee State coach Ed Temple was so impressed by her talent that he asked Rudolph to train at Tennessee State's summer camp. She eventually earned a full scholarship and became a Tigerbelle.

After her bronze medal win as a 16-year-old in 1956, Rudolph took the 1960 Rome Olympics by storm becoming the first American woman to win three gold medals. Rudolph won the 100- and 200-meter dashes and then anchored the U.S. 4 × 100-meter relay to victory despite an ankle injury. She was the first African-American woman to receive the Sullivan Award (1961), the highest award in U.S. amateur sports. Rudolph is a true demonstration of someone who was a trailblazer for racial and gender equality and also for people facing personal hardships.

At the time of the Mexico City Olympics in 1968, the 800-meter run was the longest distance women were allowed to run in the Olympic Games. African-American track athletes were stereotypically thought of as fast, sprint distance athletes. Madeline Manning Mims was the first African-American woman to win a distance race in the Olympics.

Another Tigerbelle for Ed Temple at Tennessee State University, Mims had never dreamed of college. She studied there while starring in track from 1968 to 1972.

Mims was a member of four Olympic track teams (1968, 1972,

1976, and 1980) and was the captain in 1972, 1976, and 1980. She won a silver medal as part of the 4 × 400-meter relay team at the 1972 Olympics in Munich. Mims also won seven national outdoor championships. She has returned to the Olympic stage five more times as a volunteer sports chaplain since her own athletic career ended.

In the Mexico City Games, Wyomia Tyus became the first runner, male or female, to defend an Olympic title in the 100-meter dash. She dedicated the gold medal to John Carlos and Tommy Smith. She won the gold in the 100-meter in the 1964 Games, where she also won a silver medal with the 4 × 100-meter relay team. Ed Temple was a father figure for her at Tennessee State University after Tyus's father passed away.

In 1973, Tyus, tennis star Billie Jean King, and swimmer Donna de Varona became the founding members of the Women's Sports Foundation, which has become the premier advocate and programming source for women and girls in sports.

In 1988, the world finally realized the magnitude of Tyus's accomplishments in 1964 and 1968 when Carl Lewis successfully defended his title in the 100-meter at the Olympics in Seoul. Many thought he was the first to accomplish this feat only to learn it was actually Tyus who had done this 20 years earlier.

Florence Griffith-Joyner, perhaps better known as Flo-Jo, was one of the most renowned American track and field athletes. She performed with power, speed, and style and set world records in the 100-meter and 200-meter races.

Griffith won a silver medal in the Los Angeles Olympics in the 200-meter. She was the heavy favorite for the titles in the sprint events at the 1988 Seoul Summer Olympics. She won the 100- and 200-meter gold medals and then won a gold medal in the 4 × 100-meter and a silver in the 4 × 400-meter relay teams. Flo-Jo received the 1988 James E. Sullivan Award as the top amateur athlete in the United States and then retired. Ten years later she died in her sleep— news that shocked the sports world.

Evelyn Ashford was the first woman to run the 100-meter dash under 11 seconds when she set a world record of 10.79 seconds in 1983. At age 19, after only a year of consistent training and coaching, Ashford qualified for the 1976 Montreal Olympic Games. In both the 1977 and 1978 seasons, she won national championships in the 100- and 200-meter dashes. The following year, she returned to the international scene, competing for the World Championship in 1979 and won the 100-meter with ease. She was favored to win the gold in the 100-meter in the 1980 Olympic Games in Moscow but the United States boycotted. She finally won the gold in the 1984 Los Angeles Olympics.

Ashford then carried the U.S. flag in the opening ceremonies of the 1988 Seoul Olympics. In nearly 100 years of the Olympic Games, Ashford was only the third woman and second African-American to carry the country's flag in the Olympic parade. Ashford made her fifth and final Olympic team for the 1992 Olympic Games in Barcelona, Spain, where she won another gold in the 4 × 100-meter relay.

At the 1984 Los Angeles Games, Valerie Brisco-Hooks was the first woman or man to win the gold medal in both the 200-meter and 400-meter dashes during the same Olympic Games. She also helped the United States win in the 4 × 400-meter relay.

She became an advocate for drug-free schools and actively sought out opportunities to interact with students in the classroom to convey her message. She made time in her training and competition schedule because she felt so passionately about making a difference. She continued to have success on the track, setting the world record for the indoor 400-meter race in 1985. She followed up the next year with a world championship title in the 400-meter outdoors. Brisco-Hooks ran on the 4 × 400-meter relay team in the 1988 Olympic Games held in Seoul, Korea. The team was facing their rival, the Soviet Union team, for the first time since the 1976 Olympic Games in Munich after the boycotts of the 1980 and 1984 Olympic Games. While they set a new American record, the Soviets took the gold and Brisco-Hooks and her teammates won the silver. It was Brisco-Hooks's fourth Olympic medal. She retired from the sport soon thereafter.

Jackie Joyner-Kersee's willpower to compete with asthma enhanced her prestige as one of America's greatest athletes ever. Her collegiate athletic career started her on the path to success when she set the NCAA record for the heptathlon twice. She also continued to play basketball for UCLA and was recognized as the UCLA All-University Athlete for three years.

In 1984, Joyner-Kersee won the silver medal in the heptathlon at the Olympics and finished fifth in the long jump. In 1988, she won a gold medal for both the heptathlon and the long jump events, beating her own world record in the heptathlon and setting an Olympic record in the long jump. In 1992, she won gold once more in the Olympic heptathlon and silver in the long jump. Four years later, Joyner-Kersee won a bronze medal in the long jump after she had pulled a muscle and had to withdraw from the heptathlon. In fact, she did not lose a heptathlon in over 12 years from 1984 until the 1996 Olympic Trials. She has always been a community leader, especially for at-risk children, in East St. Louis.

Joan Benoit Samuelson set the women's marathon world record of 2:22:43 when she won the 1983 Boston Marathon. It was her second marathon win and set the stage for her to chase her dream of Olympic Gold at the inaugural women's Olympic marathon at the 1984 Los Angeles Olympic Games, but it also meant that the rest of the competitive field would be chasing her.

Just two weeks before the 1984 Olympic Trials, Joan had knee surgery, but she continued training with vigor. With her goal in sight, she completed a 17-mile training run just a few days after surgery even though the run slightly damaged her leg further. She did not let the pain stop her and she went on to win the 1984 Olympic Trials and the Olympic gold medal easily. In 1985, she also won the James E. Sullivan Award as the top amateur athlete in the country.

Although Willye White was one of the great pioneers for track and field, her most fulfilling work came after she retired from the sport. Her experience in athletics motivated her to get involved with the community. After her retirement from track and field, she fought to make a difference for Chicago's youth and then taught them important life lessons.

She won a silver medal in her first Olympic Games in Melbourne at the age of 19. She became the first American female to medal in the long jump. White coached herself to every Olympics from 1960 to 1972. She remains the only American to have competed on five Olympic track and field teams. At the 1964 Games in Tokyo, she won her second silver medal as a member of the 400-meter relay team.

One of her proudest moments came when she became the first American to receive the UNESCO Pierre de Coubetin International Fair Play Trophy, the world's highest sportsmanship award.

Coaches

In 1956, Dr. Nell Jackson became the first African-American female to coach an Olympic team. She also coached the 1972 Olympic team.

As a student at the Tuskegee Institute from 1947 to 1951, Jackson was a member of the 1948 Olympic team and also competed in the first Pan American Games in 1951. Her events were the 100- and 200-meter sprints.

Jackson returned to her alma mater in 1953 as the women's track and field coach. She also was the first men's swimming coach at Tuskegee, starting the program in 1958. She later coached at Iowa, Illinois State, Illinois, and Michigan State. At Illinois, her team won the national team championship in the 1970 outdoor season.

Jackson also was an assistant athletic director at Michigan State. When she retired from full-time coaching in 1981, Dr. Jackson accepted a position as director of physical education and intercollegiate athletics and professor in the department of physical education at the State University of New York at Binghamton.

When Barbara Jacket took her first coaching job at Prairie View A&M in 1964, it was clear that women had made little progress in gender equity; Title IX had yet to be passed. African-Americans were still not allowed to eat at some cafes and restaurants.

Ignoring these obstacles, Jacket started as a swim coach in 1964. Two years later, she organized the first track and field team but was still unable to get any funding from the school. In her 25-year reign as head coach, Jacket led her teams to more than 20 national championships. She coached 57 All-Americans and five future Olympians. In 1992, she was named the head coach for the U.S. Olympic women's track and field team, becoming the second African-American woman to do so, following Nell Jackson. She led her team to four gold medals, four silver medals, and two bronze medals.

In 1990, Jacket expanded her role at Prairie View A&M. She was named athletic director, making her the only woman in the Southwestern Athletic Conference (SWAC) with this title.

Beverly Kearney was a National Junior College track and field All-American talent who then attended Auburn University. As an Auburn Tiger, she earned two Association for Intercollegiate Athletics for Women (AIAW) All-American honors, Auburn Athlete of the Year, and team MVP. In 1980, she qualified for the U.S. Olympic Trials in the 200-meter. She then did a two-year stint at the University of Toledo, where she held her first head coach title. From Toledo, Kearney accepted the top assistant coach title at the University of Tennessee. Tennessee was just a steppingstone to the powerhouse Kearney would later build at the University of Texas, after she made another stop as the University of Florida's (UF) head coach. Kearney did not waste any time in reaching her goal, and in just her fifth year at the helm of UF, the Gators won the 1992 NCAA Division I Indoor title.

She became the first African-American female track and field head coach to win an NCAA Division I National Championship and just the third African-American head coach ever to win any NCAA title, following John Thompson's 1984 basketball title with Georgetown University and Tina Sloan Green's 1984 women's lacrosse title with Temple University.

The University of Texas (UT) convinced Kearney to join the Longhorns. The relationship has proven prosperous for both since her first season of 1993. When Kearney started her 16th season at UT in 2007–8, she already had led the Longhorns to six NCAA National Championships and 19 conference titles. Twenty four current UT records have been set under Kearney's tutelage.

The United States women won three gold medals in the Beijing Games in 2008. Dawn Harper won the 100-meter hurdles and Stephanie Brown Trafton won the discus. The 4 × 400-meter relay team of Mary Wineberg, Monique Henderson, Sanya Richards, Allyson Felix, and Natasha Hastings won the gold in stunning fashion.

Hyleas Fountain became only the second American besides Jackie Joyner-Kersee to medal in the Heptathlon by claiming the silver. They also won silver medals in the pole vault with Jennifer Stuczynski and the 200-meter with Allyson Felix, while Sheena Tosta got silver in the 400-meter hurdles.

All of these women need to look back on the history of women who have had so many grand triumphs in the Olympic Games over the course of the 80 years they have competed in the Games. It is a rich history.

Mildred "Babe" Didrikson Zaharias

American Star of the Women's International Sports Hall of Fame

by Stacy Martin-Tenney

Babe was the greatest athlete of all time; whether it was hitting home-runs, playing golf, shooting basketballs, competing in track and field, or even sewing. Babe excelled at it all. This Babe didn't play for the Red Sox or the Yankees, but she did strike out the great Joe DiMaggio when she played for the touring baseball team, House of David. Mildred Ella Didrikson (Zaharias) earned her nickname "Babe" after the famed slugger, Babe Ruth, when she hit five home runs during a baseball game in her hometown of Beaumont, Texas. Her skills were unmatched on almost any playing field and across almost every sport. Sportswriter Grantland Rice once wrote, "She is beyond all belief until you see her perform."[1]

She inherited her athletic talent from her mother, Hannah, who had been a talented skater and skier in her native land of Norway. Her father, Ole, carried himself as a man that knew the meaning of hard work and he labored feverishly as a carpenter to make a living for his family in their new American home. He imparted his natural strength, determined work ethic, and passion for perfection onto his daughter Mildred. Babe was born in 1911, a time defined by women's prim and proper behavior, when society generally preferred that girls did not participate in "vulgar" activities like sports. Babe's preference, however, was to shun "feminine" activities and qualities and to spend her time pursuing athletic endeavors. Tomboy was an understatement, since she wasn't running with the boys—she was leading them. She excelled at volleyball, tennis, baseball, swimming, and basketball, the most popular women's sport of the time.

Her accomplishments on the athletic field and aggressive style of play did not win her any congeniality awards from her high school classmates. While she attended high school in Beaumont, her basketball team never lost a game. Babe's talents were extraordinary in almost every arena, including singing and sewing. She recorded "I

Felt a Little Teardrop" and "Detour" with Mercury records label and even won a state fair championship in sewing, but she chose to focus on her athletic interests.

In her junior year, she dropped out of high school to play for the Golden Cyclone basketball team in Dallas, Texas. The Golden Cyclones were the company basketball team for Casualty Insurance Company. Babe was paid as a stenographer, but she spent her time training and competing on the basketball court. She often scored 30 points a game herself, during an era when entire teams were scoring 20 points in a game. Babe led the Golden Cyclones to a national championship before her interests led her to pursue other sports, such as softball and track and field.

Babe capitalized on the coaching she received from the Golden Cyclones track and field team. She quickly learned the very technical field events and became one of the premier track and field athletes in the world, holding records in five different events. The Golden Cyclones team entered the Amateur Athletic Union (AAU) Championships in Evanston, Illinois, in 1932 to qualify for the 1932 Olympic Games. Babe scored 30 points, won six gold medals, and set four world records that afternoon—she single handedly beat teams comprised of 20 or more. No athlete, male or female, had ever accomplished such an astonishing achievement in the history of track and field.

Babe assured her place in the chronicles of track and field for all time and created an exciting buzz around the 1932 Los Angeles Olympic Games. Despite qualifying for the Olympics in five events, she was only permitted to compete in three events because she was a woman. She won the first women's Olympic javelin and the first Olympic 80-meter hurdles with ease. Babe tied Jean Smiley's world record high jump performance, but was disqualified by two judges who disagreed with her aggressive head-first approach over the bar. Babe was never warned about her style, but nonetheless she was awarded the silver medal while Smiley took the gold.

After her brief adventures touring the country with the House of David baseball team and the barnstorming basketball team Babe Didrikson's All-Americans, she turned to the sport of golf. With the same determination that she approached her other sports, she practiced hitting golf balls until her hands blistered and bled. Within a year she had entered her first tournament and won the Texas Women's Amateur Championship. Soon thereafter, the United States Golf Association (USGA) revoked her amateur status because of her professional endeavors in other sports. Babe could not be deterred, so she played as a professional despite her youth in the game. After financial shortfalls, she joined Gene Sarazen, a professional golfer, in exhibition matches around the country.

In the Los Angeles Open she paired with a gregarious wrestler by the name of George Zaharias, and 18 holes later she was swept off her feet. Babe married Zaharias 11 months later and changed her name to Babe Didrikson Zaharias. Under his guidance, she captured the Texas and Western Open golf championships. After agreeing to abstain from professional athletics and only entering exhibition matches for three years, the USGA restored her amateur status. In two years she had perfected her game on the amateur tour and was named Woman Athlete of the Year, an honor she would earn five more times. Babe could never settle for simply winning, she had to accomplish the athletic feat that no one else could. She won 17 consecutive straight tournaments the next season, an achievement that no man or woman had ever earned before. She also became the first woman to win the prestigious British Women's Amateur. At the direction of George and her manager Fred Corcoran, she turned professional again.

Her 1948 earnings were estimated at nearly $100,000 for promotional endeavors, yet her prize money only totaled $3,700 that same year. She and Corcoran were inspired to organize the Ladies Professional Golf Association (LPGA) so that they could build awareness and prestige in ladies golf, thereby increasing the prize money. The women of today are thankful for Babe's forethought and dedication to equal pay, but the gender gap still exists no matter what sport a woman plays or, in most cases, what profession she chooses. Sadly, her endeavors in the golf world would be cut short because only five years after establishing the LPGA she was diagnosed with cancer.

Babe made a name for herself in sport and in life with a persistent attitude and defiant demeanor. She battled her failing health with the same fortitude and strength. In 1953, surgery for cancer was radical rather than practical, but for Babe it was the only course she was willing to consider—action rather than contemplation. She played in a golf tournament only weeks after surgery and continued her season.

She was aptly named the Ben Hogan Comeback Player of the Year. The next year was no different, as she won tournament after tournament and captured her final Woman of the Year Award. On September 27, 1956, Babe Zaharias met a foe that was more stubborn than her, and the cancer finally overcame her. Her audacity was inspirational to many, but especially women, as she dared to redefine how women should be perceived in society. Through her choices, she defined what a woman could be, which has made the sports world a very different, better place to play for all who follow.

Note

1. Larry Schwartz, "Didrikson Was a Woman ahead of Her Time," *ESPN.com*, 2007 http://www.espn.go.com/sportcentury/features/00014147.html. (Accessed January 20, 2008.)

Helen Stephens

American Star of the Women's International Sports Hall of Fame

by Sara Jane Baker

As time passes, the inequality between men's and women's sports is slowly closing. We currently live in an era of Title IX, the Women's National Basketball Association (WNBA), and other women's professional sports leagues, but it was not so long ago that women had to fight for athletic opportunities. Many of the opportunities that exist now for women were unimaginable dreams for female pioneers like Helen Stephens. She was not only one of the greatest American athletes of her time, but she played a big role in paving the way for women's equality in sports.

Although Stephens saw success in almost every aspect of her life, the path she followed was not an easy road. Born in 1918, a time marked by the women's suffrage movement, Stephens grew up in a society with very few opportunities for women and virtually no opportunities for women in athletics. Additionally, women were constantly fighting gender stereotypes. Any woman involved in athletics was looked down upon and seen as unladylike. Stephens was no exception. She grew up on a farm in the small town of Fulton, Missouri. Although Stephens's mother wanted her to play the piano, she was a true tomboy and enjoyed helping out around the farm. Little did she know this farm work would be great training for her future in track and field. She idolized the great Babe Didrikson and at the age of eight, Stephens dreamed of becoming the fastest woman in the world.[1] Not only was this a big dream for a young girl, but it was seemingly unrealistic given the lack of facilities, athletic teams, and opportunities for women during this time. At Stephens's school, girls were required to take physical education, but they did not participate in high school sports. However, Stephens's six-foot frame and blazing speed quickly caught the eye of her high school gym teacher, Coach W. Burton Moore. Coincidentally, Coach Moore was knowledgeable about the sport of track and field and was eager to explore the depths of her talent.[2]

Coach Moore immediately knew that Stephens was special. At practice one day, Coach Moore clocked her at 5.8 seconds in the 50-meter dash, which would have tied the world record if Stephens was competing in an official track meet. He clocked her again just to make sure her time was accurate. When he confirmed that indeed it was, he immediately began cultivating her talent. Just one year later, Coach Moore took Stephens to her first track meet in St. Louis. The meet would give her the opportunity to run against the reigning Olympic gold medalist, Stella Walsh. Not only did Stephens beat the reigning champ, she set the world record in the 50-meter dash. The press quickly heard about Stephens's success and gave her a new nickname, "The Fulton Flash."[3]

The Fulton Flash now had her sights set on the 1936 Olympics in Berlin, Germany. However, with the rise of Adolf Hitler, many Americans urged her not to compete in protest of the Nazis. Although Stephens sympathized with this cause, she also felt strongly about representing her country in the Olympics and fulfilling her childhood dream of being the fastest woman in the world. On July 15, 1936, Stephens and 382 other U.S. Olympic athletes boarded the SS Manhattan to Berlin. Stephens would again be meeting her rival, Stella Walsh, in a much anticipated rematch. Despite her minor shin-splints and the poor weather conditions, Stephens defeated the Polish star and broke the world record. She earned another gold medal when she anchored the 400-meter relay. Everyone took notice of the young Stephens, including Adolf Hitler. After seeing Stephens compete, Hitler assumed she must be a pure Aryan with her fair hair, blue eyes, and strong build and he immediately requested to meet her. Helen Stephens was the only American athlete to have a private meeting with Adolf Hitler.[4]

When Stephens returned to the United States, she was a celebrity. Her hometown of Fulton celebrated her homecoming and everyone wanted to meet the fastest woman in the world. Unfortunately, her popularity also brought negative attention. *Look* magazine printed a picture of Stephens running with a caption that read "Is this a man or a woman?" Stephens was so hurt and angered by this cover that she sued the magazine and was awarded $5,500. In order to maintain her amateur status, Stephens worked odd jobs to make money. However, a turning point in her professional life occurred when a picture of Stephens as a cocktail waitress surfaced, resulting in harsh criticism by prohibitionists. Shortly thereafter, Stephens hung up her amateur status and finally signed a professional contract for financial reasons. She would later question this decision, as she would never be allowed to compete in another Olympic Games.[5]

Her passion for sports extended beyond track and field, as she tried her hand in caging, now commonly known as professional basketball. Using the remaining amount of her settlement money, Stephens, with the help of her friend, Issy, launched the first female basketball team. Stephens's team, The Helen Stephens Olympic Co-Eds Basketball Team, would play against all-men's teams using all-men's rules. She assembled a talented team, including a ski star, a female wrestler, and a baseball star. Stephens would play until she retired in 1941.[6]

The passage of Brown v. Board of Education in 1954, calling for racial equality in the educational system, motivated Stephens to become increasingly active in politics. Stephens realized how few opportunities there were for women in general, but more specifically in competitive sports.[7] Sports had played such a large role in Stephens's life that she wanted to ensure that men and women across the country would have equal opportunities. However, Stephens was still fighting gender stereotypes. Many believed that women should not play competitive sports and some even believed that women athletes became infertile. Stephens also recognized the lack of coaching and training in female sports. Once again, Stephens took action and began coaching. She elicited the help of area coaches and began holding track clinics and setting up training teams. She hoped to generate excitement about the sport of track and field, while developing potential Olympic hopefuls.[8]

Into her adult years, Stephens continued to be recognized and honored for her achievements as an Olympic athlete. She was inducted into the Track and Field Hall of Fame and the National Women's Hall of Fame. By 1984, she had been inducted into six different halls of fame. She continued to be active in track and proved she still had talent, as she continued to be the top performer in her age bracket during various track meets. Stephens refused to let her age slow her down. She participated in women-in-sports conferences and spoke at numerous engagements. In December 1993, the BBC filmed

Stephens for a documentary titled *The People's Century: Sporting Fever*. Tragically, she would not live to see it. On January 17, 1994, Stephens passed away shortly after undergoing surgery for blocked carotid arteries.[9]

Although the world lost an amazing athlete and pioneer, Helen Stephens had accomplished so much in her lifetime. She lived through the women's suffrage movement, World War II, the civil rights movement, and the passage of Title IX. Her athletic accomplishments were simply an afterthought to the incredible gains she made for women's athletics. She defied gender stereotypes and refused to give in to societal ideals for women. Helen Stephens's courage will not soon be forgotten. In fact, it is seen every day as opportunities for women in athletics continue to increase.

Notes

1. Sharon Kinney Hanson, *The Life of Helen Stephens: The Fulton Flash* (Carbondale: Southern Illinois University Press), 6.

2. Ibid., 21.

3. Ibid., 22–25.

4. Ibid., 61–92.

5. Ibid., 117–36.

6. Ibid., 156–65.

7. Ibid., 187.

8. Iibd., 191–94.

9. Ibid., 243–44.

Alice Coachman

American Star of the Women's International Sports Hall of Fame

by Jessica Bartter

At the start of the 2008 Beijing Olympic Games, former Olympian Alice Coachman had more to smile about than the magnificent Opening Ceremony consisting of 2,008 male drummers who remained entirely in sync and the seemingly gravity-defying gliders who trotted the gigantic elevated globe. Most of the 596 American athletes walked the prestigious "parade of athletes" during what has been acclaimed as the most astounding Olympic Opening Ceremony to date. One hundred and twenty-six of those athletes, close to half of whom were black, were set to compete in track and field events, something the African-American Coachman truly pioneered.

Born in 1923 in Albany, Georgia, she was the fifth of 10 children born to Fred and Evelyn Jackson Coachman. With plenty of brothers and sisters to play with, Coachman was a very active child. Growing up in the segregated South did not allow her many opportunities to participate in organized sports, many of the activities in school, or even at the local YMCAs. She was also discouraged from pursuing sporting activities because of her gender. Needless to say, Coachman's formative years were characterized by a lack of support for her athletic ability. Without a proper training facility, she was forced to train on back roads, on playgrounds, and in open fields. Coachman created her own training routine using whatever materials she could find, including her usually bare feet. Despite the less-than-ideal training conditions, Coachman was a gifted athlete with the work ethic to succeed.

Perhaps because of her work ethic and seemingly endless ability, two women openly supported Coachman's potential, encouraging her to use her gifts and talents as best she could: her fifth-grade teacher at Monroe Street Elementary School and her aunt, who supported and defended Coachman's dreams against her parents' wishes. This support was enough to keep her motivated until she reached high school.

In 1938, Coachman attended Madison High School, where the boys' track coach immediately took an interest in her. Since she had never received formal training, Coach Harry E. Lash was able to teach her and nurture her natural talent from the very basic fundamentals. Because her talent was so raw, even the slightest bit of coaching made a big difference. Just one year later, at age 16, Coachman was offered a scholarship to attend the Tuskegee Preparatory School in Alabama, a big step for her, both athletically and academically.

In her first Amateur Athletic Union (AAU) national championship competition, prior to starting classes at Tuskegee, Coachman broke the AAU high school and college women's high jump records in her usual fashion—barefoot. While competing at Tuskegee from 1940 to 1946, Coachman went on to win national track and field championships in the 50- and 100-meter dashes, the 4 × 100-meter relay, and the running high jump. She also led the Tuskegee basketball team to three consecutive conference championships as a guard.

Coachman's love for sports was matched by her commitment to her education. She earned a degree in dress making from Tuskegee in 1946, before moving on to Albany State College in Georgia. Coachman continued her education and her training at Albany State, where she received a bachelor's of arts in home economics in 1949.

Had the 1940 and 1944 Olympic Games not been cancelled because of World War II, it is likely that Coachman would have competed victoriously in both. Coachman was a dominant high-jumper and sprinter for a decade. The peak of her success came when she qualified for the 1948 London Olympic Games with a 5-foot-4-inch jump, despite experiencing back problems. The previous record had been a 5-foot-3^1/4-inch jump in 1932.

One of Coachman's teammates, Audrey Patterson, was the first African-American to win a medal at the 1948 Olympics, earning a bronze medal in the 200-meter dash. Not to be outdone by her teammate, Coachman jumped 5 feet, 6^1/8 inches in the high jump event. Her biggest rival in that event was Great Britain's Dorothy Tyler, who seemed to be mimicking Coachman's every move. Coachman noticed her copycat and decided to alter her starting position on the runway just a bit; Tyler did the same, but she could not handle the adjustment and she had trouble with the height. Tyler did eventually jump the same height as Coachman, but only after her second attempt, making Coachman the gold medal winner. The king of England personally presented the medal to Coachman at the awards ceremony. She was not only the first African-American woman to win a gold medal, but also the first American woman to bring home the gold in a track and field event. She was also the only American woman to win a gold medal in the 1948 Games.

After receiving her medal from the king in her Olympic debut, Coachman returned to the United States, where she was treated like royalty. There were parties thrown for her and banquets held in her honor. In the end, however, she decided to retire from athletic competition. She was only 25 years old and in peak physical condition, but like many wise athletes before and after her, she decided to go out on top.

In addition to her Olympic gold medal, Coachman won a total of 25 indoor and outdoor AAU championships during her career. In retirement, she would continue to benefit from endorsements, a rarity for African-American athletes of her time. In 1952, Coachman became the first African-American female athlete to sign a product endorsement with a multinational corporation, The Coca-Cola Company.

Coachman also gave back to many of the institutions that had offered her so many wonderful opportunities both educationally and athletically. She began teaching high school physical education in her hometown of Albany, Georgia. She also eventually taught at South Carolina State College, Albany State College, and Tuskegee High School.

Building off of the experiences she had as a young child and as an Olympic athlete, Coachman founded the Coachman Track and Field Foundation, a nonprofit organization that provides assistance to young athletes and helps former Olympic athletes adjust to life after the Games. She wanted to make sure that every child who wants to chase after her or his athletic dreams has the opportunity to do so.

At the 1996 Atlanta Olympic Games, Coachman was honored as one of the 100 greatest Olympic athletes in history, a very fitting honor for a phenomenal athlete and pioneer. She paved the way for many African-American female athletes to follow in her footsteps,

leading to an extremely diverse group of American Olympic com-
petitors today. Her sweat and toil did not go unnoticed, as she has
been inducted into several halls of fame, including the National
Track and Field Hall of Fame, the Black Athletes Hall of Fame, the
Bob Douglas Hall of Fame, the Helm's Hall of Fame, the Georgia
State Hall of Fame, and the Tuskegee Hall of Fame.

Coachman preached a message to people in all walks of life: if
you believe and work hard to achieve, victory is yours to receive.
With her diligent work ethic, dedication, and passion, she was able
to overcome many obstacles and reach her Olympic dreams. Her
accomplishments have allowed others like her to dream big.

Mae Faggs Starr

American Star of the Women's International Sports Hall of Fame

by Sara Jane Baker

In an era of track and field superstars like Wilma Rudolph, it was easy to overlook Mae Faggs Starr. However, many people do not realize that a lot of Wilma Rudolph's success can be attributed to Faggs Starr. The "Mother of the Tigerbelles," as Faggs Starr was lovingly called, was a mentor to Rudolph and was responsible for the influx of talent that followed her at Tennessee State University. Besides being a trailblazer and pioneer for track and field, she remains one of most decorated sprinters in track and field history.

Perhaps Faggs Starr was willing to help others because she had been given a big break when she was younger. "When I was in elementary school a policeman came to school, and he was looking for some boys to run in a track meet for the Police Athletic League (PAL)," Faggs Starr recalls.[1] A true tomboy, she ignored the boys-only invitation and joined them in the yard after school. Despite the policeman's skepticism, he humored this small, young girl and lined Faggs Starr up to race against the boys. She easily beat the field. Although this impressed the policeman, he did not need a girl runner, but Faggs Starr did not care. She immediately began running with the PAL, and it was not long after that she caught the attention of an Irish sergeant named John Brennan.

Sergeant Brennan took Faggs Starr under his wing and began developing her talent and she quickly became the pride of the PAL and Brennan's "ace in the hole." His role in Faggs Starr's life soon began to take shape, as it extended from simply serving as a coach to assuming the roles of being a father figure, mentor, and friend. Despite all the obstacles for an African-American woman during this period, Sergeant Brennan believed in Faggs Starr. In fact, during the summer of 1947, Faggs Starr recalls Brennan telling her, "Next summer they are going to have the Olympics and you're going to make the Olympic team."[2]

Sure enough, Brennan's prediction was right. The next year Faggs Starr boarded the SS *America* to the XIV Olympiad in London as the youngest U.S. team member. The 16-year-old left behind her family and the person who had always been by her side, Coach Brennan, but even without that stability, she was unaffected. Even when she was placed in the same heat as the reigning gold medalist, she was unfazed, handling the pressure like a seasoned veteran. Despite placing third in her heat and failing to make the finals, Faggs Starr was not the least bit disappointed. She knew this would not be her last Olympic Games.

After seeing the intense international competition, Faggs Starr and Sergeant Brennan trained harder than ever. She competed in countless races to prepare for the 1952 Olympics in Helsinki, Finland. Before long, the 5-foot-2-inch, 100-pound Faggs Starr was competing against girls twice her size and twice her age. In one race, Brennan put her up against the current world record holder and reigning bronze medalist. He was not surprised when she defeated them both, but Faggs Starr exceeded his expectations by setting a new American record.

Faggs Starr again qualified for the Olympics, but the United States had very low expectations for the U.S. women's track team competing in Helsinki. Many of the stars from the 1948 Olympics withdrew from competition, leaving a deflated team with low spirits and motivation. Faggs Starr, however, refused to give in to this negative outlook; instead, she used this determination as a motivational catalyst. After she placed sixth in the 100-meter, Faggs Starr's last hope for a medal rested with her relay team. Realizing that winners and losers are only separated by mere seconds, Faggs Starr encouraged—and sometimes threatened—her team to practice handoffs. "Mae used coercion with her teammate Barbara [Jones]; she would refuse to do Barbara's hair if the she would not come out for practice."[3] The practice helped seal the American team victory as Faggs Starr and her teammates Jones, Janet Moreau, and Catherine Hardy went on to win the gold medal in the 4 × 100-meter relay.

Fresh off of her Olympic success, Faggs Starr caught the attention of Coach Ed Temple at Tennessee State University. After being one of Coach Temple's first recruits, she once again left her family and coach in Bayside, New York, and began a new chapter in her life. Once she arrived at Tennessee State, she quickly realized the track program was in dire condition. Not only was Faggs Starr one of two girls on the team, but the school did not have any money for travel and there were limited funds to cover expenses. To make matters worse, Faggs Starr was exposed to the segregation of the Deep South for the first time in her life.

However, Faggs Starr approached these obstacles just as she had all the others—with motivation and perseverance. Eventually, the team expanded and Faggs Starr, an Olympian and national champion, was the target for her young teammates. "My teammates, all they cared about in practice was running past Mae Faggs Starr. You couldn't let your guard down." Despite this increased competition, Faggs Starr was the stability of the Tigerbelles, reaching out to the others offering coaching tips, and sharing her experience.

When Faggs Starr qualified for the 1956 Melbourne Olympics, she became the first woman to compete in three consecutive Olympic Games. Nevertheless, in keeping with her nurturing personality, Faggs Starr spent time with one of her fellow teammates, rising star Wilma Rudolph, who entered the 1956 trials full of nerves and jitters. It was Faggs Starr who was partly responsible for helping Rudolph qualify for the Olympic Games:

> I remember Wilma was nervous because she was so young, so I told her to do everything I did. Wilma agreed. So you see me, this 5-foot-2-inch person standing there and you see her, this 6-foot-tall girl, doing everything I did. If I bent over to touch my shoes to limber up, she bent over and did the same thing. If I raised my arm, she raised her arm. It quickly took her mind off her nerves as she tried to watch everything I did. That was the whole idea and it worked![4]

Together with Margaret Matthews and Isabelle Daniels, they earned a bronze medal in the 4 × 100-meter relay. Four years later, Wilma Rudolph would become the first woman to win three Olympic gold medals. Although Faggs Starr was often overshadowed by Rudolph, the selfless Faggs Starr was always happy to help her young teammate.

Soon after Melbourne, Faggs Starr retired from the sport of track and field, but she continued to serve as a mentor. She earned her teaching certificate and embarked on a career that would last over 40 years. In addition to teaching, she also served as an athletic director and track and field coach at Princeton High School in Cincinnati.

In 2000, Mae Faggs Starr lost her battle to breast cancer. Her decorated career and impact on the sport of track and field will not soon be forgotten. She was inducted into the National Track and Field Hall of Fame and she is the holder of more than 150 medals, trophies, and ribbons. Mae Faggs Starr's greatest contribution to the sport, however, is the impact she had on Tennessee State University. Although Mae Faggs Starr is often overlooked due to former teammates like Wilma Rudolph, it was Mae Faggs Starr who set the groundwork for these future stars.

Notes

1. Michael D. Davis, *Black American Women in Olympic Track and Field* (Jefferson, N.C.: McFarland & Company, Inc., 1992), 50.

2. Ibid.

3. Ibid., 55.

4. Lynn Sears, Suite101com, "Mae Faggs Starr," http://www.suite101.com/article .cfm/running/5214 (accessed May 30, 2008).

Wilma Rudolph

American Star of the Women's International Sports Hall of Fame

by Richard Lapchick and Marcus Sedberry

When I was a 14-year-old boy in 1960, Wilma Rudolph and Muhammad Ali helped change my life. I had just visited the Nazi concentration camp in Dachau, Germany. My image of the world had been shattered. While I knew about racism, seeing the bold face of it in its most horrible form made me grow up fast. How were people capable of committing such mass murder against other people? It made me realize that for me in my lifetime, I had to fight against racism and sexism. From Dachau, I went to Rome, where the Olympics further changed my life. I saw the suspension of hate and people living in an idealized world where race, gender, and political ideology were irrelevant. I recognized that it was only temporary, but on those fields and in the arenas life was like it should be. The power of sport was real, and for me it was exemplified by the lives of Ali and Rudolph. I am not sure when I realized it but the template for my life's work was being set.

Wilma Rudolph was born prematurely in 1940 in the segregated American South. America was still recovering from the hardships of the Great Depression. Rudolph's parents, Ed and Blanche, were like millions of people who were poor and, sometimes, homeless as they struggled to live. Ed Rudolph worked as a railroad porter and handyman while his wife Blanche was a housekeeper for wealthy white families. In the face of such poverty, Mrs. Rudolph often made their daughter's dresses out of flour sacks.

Wilma Glodean Rudolph, the 20th of their 22 children, was born in Clarksville, Tennessee, weighing only four and a half pounds at birth and needing extra care. As in so many other southern towns, the local hospital was a whites-only facility and there was only one African-American doctor in the city.

Over the next several years, young Wilma was nursed by her mother through measles, scarlet fever, chicken pox, and double pneumonia. However, when her mother discovered her left leg and foot were becoming weak and deformed, Rudolph had to be taken to the doctor. At a very young age, Rudolph was diagnosed with polio, a crippling disease for which there was then no cure. The doctor told Rudolph she would never be able to walk.

After that visit to the doctor, Mrs. Rudolph took Wilma for treatment 50 miles away twice a week to seek treatment at Meharry Hospital, the medical college of the historically black Fisk University in Nashville. After two years, little Wilma was finally able to walk with the assistance of a metal leg brace. To prevent the Rudolph family from incurring the steady cost of traveling miles to get treatment, the doctors taught Mrs. Rudolph how to administer physical therapy at home.

Rudolph was able to attend a segregated school when she was seven years old after being home schooled for the previous years. Five years later, she was able to walk normally without a brace or corrective shoes. While Rudolph was in junior high school, her older sister Yolanda joined the basketball team. Wilma followed but sat on the bench for three years. Wilma earned the starting guard role and set the state scoring record for the most points in a game and led her team to a state championship. During the championship tournament, Tennessee State's legendary track and field coach, Ed Temple, was very impressed by her talent and asked Rudolph to train at Tennessee State's summer camp. She eventually earned a full scholarship as part of the Tennessee State Tigerbelles.

Only four years after she stopped using the leg braces, Rudolph became a track and field star. A 16-year-old in 1956, Rudolph earned a spot on the U.S. Olympic Team in Melbourne, Australia. In spite of her youth, Rudolph won a bronze medal as a member of the 4 × 100-meter relay. Rudolph did not stop there and in 1959, she qualified for the next year's Olympics by setting a world record in the 200-meter. At the 1960 Olympics in Rome, Italy, Rudolph became the first American woman to win three gold medals. Rudolph won the 100- and 200-meter dashes and then anchored the U.S. 4 × 100-meter relay to victory, despite an ankle injury. Because of her success, gender and racial barriers in track and field began to fall.

After returning from Rome, Rudolph began to receive numerous awards. In 1960, she was named the United Press Athlete of the Year and the AP Woman of the Year. The following year, Rudolph became the first woman to receive the James R. Sullivan Award for Good Sportsmanship. She was also the first woman to receive the European Sportswriters' Sportsman of the Year and the Christopher Columbus Award for Most Outstanding International Sports Personality. In 1980, she was named to the Black Sports Hall of Fame and in 1983, she was inducted into the Olympic Hall of Fame.

Rudolph stood up for justice against her segregated roots when she confronted the governor of Tennessee as a 20-year-old by refusing to participate in a parade that the governor had proposed to acknowledge her tremendous accomplishments. Rudolph boldly told him she would not participate unless blacks and whites were allowed to share in the event together. She was granted her wish and Clarksville, Tennessee, had its first racially integrated event. One more example of the power of sport. An integrated banquet followed.

In 1962, Rudolph retired from track and field and returned to Clarksville to teach at her old school, Cobb Elementary School, as well as be a track coach at her alma mater, Burt High School. The following year, she married Robert Eldridge and had four children, Yolanda, Djuanna, Robert Jr., and Xurry. Also in 1963, Rudolph received her bachelor's degree in English from Tennessee State. After a brief stint of teaching and coaching in her hometown, she moved on to coach in Maine and Indiana, along with becoming a sports commentator on national television and co-hosting a network radio show. Rudolph traveled across the country sharing her story of overcoming misfortune by believing in herself and those around her. She would advise her listeners that "winning is great, but if you are really going to do something in life, the secret is learning how to lose. Nobody goes undefeated all the time. If you can pick up after a crushing defeat, and go on to win again, you are going to be a champion someday."[1]

Rudolph is a true demonstration of someone who was a trailblazer for racial and gender equity, but also for people facing personal hardships. She became a living testament that adversity does not have to have the last word, stating: "Never underestimate the power of dreams and the influence of the human spirit. We are all the same in this notion. The potential for greatness lives within each of us." As a child, doctors told her she would never walk. Instead, she ran through pain, discrimination, and racial and gender inequity and became a role model and pioneer for all to follow. On November 12, 1994, at the age of 54, Rudolph was finally caught. After being in and out of the hospital receiving treatment for brain cancer, Rudolph died. Nonetheless, Rudolph's legacy will last forever. Including for the 14-year-old boy in Rome in 1960.

Note

1. Wilma Rudolph, "Wilma Rudolph Quotes," http://www.wilmarudolph.net/more .html (accessed July 10, 2007).

Madeline Manning Mims

American Star of the Women's International Sports Hall of Fame

by Stacy Martin-Tenney

Courtesy of Madeline Manning Mims

Madeline Manning Mims proved to the world during the 1968 Mexico City Olympic Games that women have incredible resilience and endurance. She ran the 800-meter race in an Olympic record breaking time of 2:00.9 and won the gold medal. In 1968, women had not been afforded the liberties and equal treatment that Title IX later granted in 1972. The United States was in the throes of the civil rights movement and the 1968 Olympic Games will always be remembered with the image of black power raised against the backdrop of Olympic glory. As "The Star-Spangled Banner" played in the thin Mexico City air, Tommie Smith and John Carlos each raised a gloved fist into the air as they stood on the Olympic medal platform receiving the gold and bronze, respectively, for their performance in the 200-meter dash. It was a statement that shook the world of sport and definitely left an impression on the minds of the American public. In her quiet way, Manning Mims made a much louder statement supporting women and their abilities in sports. At that time, the 800-meter run was the longest distance women were allowed to run in the Olympic Games. African-American track athletes were stereotypically thought of as fast, sprint distance athletes. Manning Mims was the first African-American woman to win a distance race in the Olympics.

Her career did not begin in the same audacious way; it was a humble and challenging start. At the young, innocent age of three she was diagnosed with spinal meningitis. The doctors gave up on

Madeline, but her mother's determination and faith persevered. Madeline's mother, Queen, promised that her daughter would serve God in her works and life, if he would save her life. Miraculously, Madeline improved the next day when the doctors visited her. The doctors pondered the medicine, but Queen simply trusted her faith and prayer. She explained to her daughter the promise that she had made on her behalf, and Madeline began on her journey.

Her dedication to God was starkly contrasted with her disobedience to the constraints of her illness. She was supposed to come in and stop playing when she started having symptoms to protect her health, but Manning Mims adapted and fought through the illness and returned to the activity, which strengthened her will and endurance. "I figured it out real quick, that if I got sick, don't go in the house and tell mom because she's going to put you to bed and call the doctor and he's going to come with that needle," Manning Mims said. "I would just go behind somewhere, throw up or do whatever I had to do, and come back and finish playing."[1] Her resolve proved useful when she got older and participated in track and field in high school.

Growing up in the inner-city ghetto of Cleveland challenged Manning Mims and encouraged her to find a way out of the poverty. Running was the quickest way out. She could run quickly, but more important she could outlast the other girls. The Presidential Physical Fitness test was introduced to John Hay High School when she was in the 10th grade. Manning Mims was determined, but had never been outgoing by nature, so she did not participate in extracurricular activities. She tested off the charts for the fitness test and at the urging of her instructors she joined the track and field, basketball, and volleyball teams. She ran track for the Cleveland Division of Recreation in the Amateur Athletic Union (AAU) championships and acquired her first taste of victory with the 440-yard run national title. Coaches marveled at her speed. No other girl had ever run the 440 that fast. She was the first in the world to run it in 55 seconds flat. At 16 years old her entire world changed when she was named to the U.S. national team to represent the country at track and field meets in Russia, Poland, and West Germany. Cleveland would never look the same, and while the city was her roots, her feet had given her wings.

One of the coaches enamored with Manning Mims's talents was Ed Temple of Tennessee State University. He was so impressed with her that he offered her a full athletic scholarship to the university. Manning Mims never dreamed of college, but the world seemed to be opening its doors to her and new experiences awaited her. She accepted the scholarship and again applied her same resolute attitude to both her studies and her sport. One professor in particular changed the way she approached learning. At first, he seemed to play the part of the snooty, arrogant professor insulted by the ignorance of these college students and asked the class questions beyond the scope of their assigned reading. It frustrated the class, but Manning Mims accepted his challenge and her competitive nature went into overdrive. She prepared for each class by going the extra mile, and one day her endurance paid off. He asked one of his pompous questions, and Manning Mims demonstrated her knowledge of the subject with a magnificent oratory, including supporting resources. The professor was awe-struck and simply acquiesced to her, but he did take the time to use her as a pristine example to the class about going above and beyond expectations.

Her performance exceeded expectation on the track as well. The 800-meter run combines the best qualities of a sprint and of a distance run, which makes it especially challenging for an athlete to train for speed and endurance. Manning Mims seemed to be innately equipped with both aspects. Manning Mims's freshman year, 1967, was record breaking. She first set the world record and won the AAU championship in the 880-yard run and later turned in an American record of 2:02.3 in the 800-meter run at the international Pan American Games. The next year was characterized by her Olympic gold and yet a faster 800-meter time of 2:00.9. Tennessee State's Tigerbelles had a dominant presence in track and field and are highly regarded for their 34 national titles, 40 Olympians, and 23 Olympic medals. Manning Mims's famed career was only a piece of that history, as the Tigerbelle story really began with Wilma Rudolph in the 1960 Rome Games becoming the first American woman to capture three gold medals in a single Olympics.

Manning Mims's performance eight years later at the 1968 Olympic Games changed the fate of a nation. She ran away from the competition during the 800-meter race and won with an impressive

10-meter lead over the competition. Sometimes it takes a pioneer to lead the way and demonstrate the possibility. Manning Mims was running after a goal and a dream that day, but she actually was changing the dream of many Nigerian women who saw a woman that resembled them running a long distance. A Nigerian leader later stopped Manning Mims to say, "You are the reason why our women run."[2] Her career included numerous American records, indoor and outdoor national championship titles, three world indoor records, four Olympic teams, an Olympic gold and silver medal, a U.S. Olympic Trials title, a Pan American championship, and a World University Games title. She was also the first woman to break the two-minute barrier in the 800-meter run with a 1:57.9. Her accomplishments are staggering and she truly made a difference, but nothing compares to the work that she is doing today.

Manning Mims still has not slowed down years later, and is now vigorously pursuing her work with God. She has returned to the Olympic stage five more times as a volunteer sports chaplain since her own athletic career ended. She strives to offer solace, motivation, and provide understanding to athletes struggling with the pressures of their sport and traveling to an unknown land. She is also feverishly pursuing her master's of divinity at Oral Roberts University and consequently planning her doctorate studies. She hopes to establish a curriculum and licensing requirements for sports chaplains so that the field will become indoctrinated and legitimate instead of volunteer based. Her own work as an ordained minister and passion for gospel singing has led her on several missionary trips. Her husband, Roderick Mims, shares her faith and supports her goodwill and outreach efforts. She has also shared some of her missionary trips with her daughter, Lana Mims. The mother-daughter bond is strengthened by their faith and by their passion for track and field. Lana is quickly following her mother's famous footsteps, running the shorter sprint distances and competing in the jumps at the University of Missouri. Madeline's son, John Jackson, also competed in track and field in the triple jump.

With the support of her family, Madeline Manning Mims is accomplishing her dreams of fulfilling her mother's promise to God and her passion for sports by founding a governing body for sports chaplains. Through her experience as a sports chaplain she knows that there was little preparation before she stepped into that arena. The United States Council for Sports Chaplaincy will educate and outfit these chaplains so that they can fulfill their purpose and be certified as a professional with the teams rather than a volunteer. With Manning Mims leading the operation, the council will be running full speed in no time. Through her athletic career and now her outreach efforts, Manning Mims has demonstrated the infinite abilities of women to excel despite the barriers others construct in their paths. "Pioneers have lonely journeys, and they're breaking barriers and myths that other people have not dared tread upon,"[3] said Madeline Manning Mims.

Notes

1. Mike Organ. "Former Tigerbelle Used Endurance Well," *The Tennessean*, February 20, 2008.

2. Jodie Valade, "Turning Gold into Inspiration." *Cleveland.com*, January 21, 2008, http://www.cleveland.com/cavs/index.ssf/2008/01/turning_gold_into_inspiration.html.

3. Mechelle Voepel, "Largest Percentage of Women in Olympic History to Compete," *Kansas City Star*, August 10, 2004.

Wyomia Tyus

American Star of the Women's International Sports Hall of Fame

by Sara Jane Baker

Wyomia Tyus was there to witness one of the most memorable events in Olympic history. She watched as Tommie Smith and John Carlos bowed their heads, raised their fists, and silently protested the country that had shown such incredible racial injustice.[1] Tyus was so moved by these actions she dedicated the gold medals for which she had worked so hard to Smith and Carlos. "What I did . . . was win a track event. What they did lasted a lifetime, and life is bigger than sport."[2] Tommie Smith and John Carlos were not the only athletes to make history at these 1968 Olympics. Tyus became the first runner, male or female, to defend her title in the 100-meter dash.

The prestige and steep competition associated with the 100-meter dash has made it one of the most anticipated Olympic races. The winner goes home with not only a gold medal, but the title of "fastest woman in the world." To accomplish this honor once was amazing, but to accomplish it twice was unheard of. However, with all the controversy surrounding these Olympics, Tyus's triumph was overlooked. It would not be until decades later when she would finally be recognized.

In the time period leading up to these Olympic Games, Tyus faced adversity and challenges as many people questioned whether or not she still had the skills to remain competitive. "I was not encouraged to stay in the sport. There were people saying even before 1968 that I was too old to be running. That just goes to show the state of mind of people at the time."[3] Tyus, however, ignored this discouragement and continued with the sport, not because it brought her fame or money, but because she loved it. And what is even more impressive is the fact that not only did she compete in the Olympics, but she ran at record-breaking speed.

This state of mind needed to overcome adversity was nothing new to Tyus. From a young age, Tyus was battling race and gender issues surrounding her participation in sports. Not only did societal ideals tell her women should not play sports, but her own mother believed athletics were unladylike. Additionally, growing up in Griffin, Georgia, provided many other challenges rooted in racial prejudice. Tyus was forced to take a one-hour bus trip to school each morning because the school closest to her house was for white students only. Despite these obstacles, Tyus fell in love with sports, and she believed athletics was a means to break away from these inequalities.

One major reason for her growing passion in sports was due to her father's influence. Much to the dismay of her mother, Tyus's father encouraged his daughter to play sports. In fact, he forced Wyomia's older brothers to include her in the neighborhood games of basketball and football.[4] As a result of these interactions, Tyus's first love became basketball. It was not until she attended a clinic in 1960 that she became interested in track and field. Ed Temple, the legendary coach from Tennessee State University (TSU), invited Tyus to their camp. Temple would not only become her coach, but he would take on a much more significant role when Tyus's father passed away that same year. "Coach Ed Temple came into my life after my father died. A man of integrity, Coach Temple had many sayings to encourage us during the rough times."[5]

With the special bond Coach Temple and Tyus shared, it was no surprise when she attended TSU on a track and field scholarship. TSU had a reputation of producing talented track and field athletes, as former Olympic medalists Wilma Rudolph and Mae Faggs preceded her on the team. Additionally, TSU was one of the few schools that offered athletic scholarships for women. Throughout college, Tyus continued to show improvement and was consistently winning races. This success earned her a spot on the 1964 Olympic team headed to Tokyo, Japan. Although Tyus was the underdog to her teammate, Edith McGuire, Tyus prevailed and took home the gold medal in the 100-meter race.

Leading up to the 1968 Olympics in Mexico City, the United States was at the peak of racial disorder. Many African-Americans encouraged Tyus to protest the Games because it seemed absurd that Tyus would support a country that was not supporting her. Despite these concerns, Tyus felt strongly about defending her 100-meter title. She would not only win the gold medal but in doing so, she set the world record with a time of 11.08 seconds. She earned a second gold medal in the 4×100-meter relay. In her own way, Tyus protested the lack of civil rights in the United States by wearing all black to her awards ceremony.

Upon returning to the United States, Tyus received little recognition for her accomplishments, which came as no surprise to Tyus. "Coach Temple always told us that we could break world records and win gold medals, but we probably still wouldn't be recognized because we were women and we were black."[6] Ironically, this lack of recognition would be the motivation behind her life's work after track.

In 1973, Tyus, tennis star Billie Jean King, and swimmer Donna de Varona became the founding members of the Women's Sports Foundation. This nonprofit foundation's mission is to "advance the lives of girls and women through sport and physical activity." Since its establishment, the Women's Sports Foundation has increased high school sports opportunities for girls by 847 percent and college sports opportunities by 411 percent. Additionally, the Foundation has inspired millions of women to become active by increasing physical education opportunities for over 400,000 girls in lower socio-economic areas.[7]

Tyus's fight for equality in women's sports does not stop there. Tyus has toured over 60 cities to speak and encourage athletics and physical fitness for women. She was a spokesperson for the Active and Ageless, which encouraged those over 50 years old to stay physically active. Tyus also played an integral part in the United States Olympic Committee's Project Gold 2000. Project Gold, which stands for Guaranteed Olympic Leadership Development, attempted to place underrepresented groups, like women and minorities, in leadership roles in sports.[8]

Sadly, it would not be until 1988 when the world finally realized the magnitude of Tyus's accomplishment. Carl Lewis successfully defended his title in the 100 meters at the Olympics in Seoul. Much of the world mistakenly thought he was the first to accomplish this feat only to learn it was actually Tyus, who 20 years earlier had done the same.

Wyomia Tyus is more than a tremendous athlete. She truly embodies humility and altruism as she has never expected praise for her accomplishments on or off the track. Although Wyomia Tyus has never received the attention she deserves, she has ensured that future women pioneers will.

Notes

1. "Wyomia Tyus," The New Georgia Encyclopedia," http://www.georgiaencyclo pedia.org/nge/Article.jsp?id=h-836.

2. "Wyomia Tyus—Olympic Success," http://sports.jrank.org/pages/4987/Tyus-Wyomia.html.

3. Ibid.

4. "Wyomia Tyus—Early Training," http://sports.jrank.org/pages/4987/Tyus-Wyo mia.html.

5. "Wyomia Tyus—A Coach's Influence," http://sports.jrank.org/pages/4987/ Tyus-Wyomia.html.

6. "Wyomia Tyus—Olympic Success."

7. Women's Sports Foundation, "About Us," http://www.womenssportsfounda tion.org/cgi-bin/iowa/about/more.html.

8. "Passing the torch: Women's commission updates," USAT Women's Commission, http://www.smfsport.com/USATWomen/wcnews01.htm.

Florence Griffith Joyner

American Star of the Women's International Sports Hall of Fame

by Sara Jane Baker

Most people recognize Florence Griffith Joyner, famously known as Flo-Jo, as the fastest woman of all time. After all, she holds two world records and earned three Olympic gold medals. Many also remember her unconventional and flamboyant style. She was easily recognizable with her six-inch-long fingernails, long flowing hair, and brightly colored outfits. She, in many ways, brought beauty and femininity to the world of sports. On the other hand, her critics may remember her alleged drug use or untimely death. Very few, however, recognize her accomplishments off the track, her involvement in the community, and the obstacles she overcame to become one of the most influential figures in track and field history.

From the moment she was born, on December 21, 1959, Griffith Joyner was determined to be successful. Born in the poor neighborhood of Watts in Los Angeles, California, she was the seventh of 11 children. Her natural speed and aptitude for track and field were discovered while Griffith Joyner was partaking in one of her favorite childhood activities, chasing jackrabbits outside of her home in the Mojave Desert. When she was five, her father dared her to catch one, and when she easily accomplished this task, it was clear that she had a gift. It was only two years later when she began running track. At age 14, she won the Jesse Owens National Youth Games. When she graduated from Los Angeles Jordan High School in 1978, she had set the school's long jump and sprint records.[1]

In 1979, Florence headed to California State University at Northridge to work with the renowned coach, Bob Kersee, the future husband of the great Jackie Joyner-Kersee. However, she had to drop out after her first year and accept a job as a bank teller to provide for her struggling family. Fortunately, Kersee was eventually able to find financial aid for Griffith, so she was able to reenroll in school the following year. In 1980, Kersee accepted a coaching job with UCLA and Florence followed him there, thus beginning her decorated career at UCLA. She was a national champion in both the 200- and 400-meter dashes and was also a member of the 4 × 100-meter relay that broke the collegiate record in 1981.

After graduating in 1983 with a degree in psychology, Griffith focused on training for the 1984 Olympics in Los Angeles. Her hard work earned her a silver medal in the 200-meter. Following the Olympics, Griffith took a small break from track, and she, once again, worked as a bank teller and often braided hair at night for extra money. In 1987, she married Al Joyner, the 1984 Olympic long jump champion and the older brother of Jackie Joyner-Kersee. Al immediately acted as her training partner and assisted in coaching duties with Bob Kersee. With the help of her husband and coach, Griffith Joyner was quickly back to her old form and ready for the 1988 Summer Olympics.

All of Griffith Joyner's hard work and dedication proved to be a success at the U.S. Olympic trials in Indianapolis. In a single race, she went from a world-class athlete to the "fastest woman of all time." She ran a blistering 10.49 seconds in the 100-meter dash, breaking Evelyn Ashford's previous world record by 0.27 seconds. Her amazing success continued into the 1988 Olympics in Seoul, South Korea, where she would add another world record by running a 21.34 in the 200-meter. She left Seoul with three gold medals, one silver medal, and a new nickname, "Flo-Jo."

Unfortunately, all the success and attention from Seoul brought rumors of steroid use. She was ultimately drug tested 11 different times and never failed once, but her incredible comeback, muscular physique, and record-breaking performances ignited controversy. Despite these rumors, Florence Griffith Joyner's accomplishments continued to be recognized. She was voted Female Athlete of the Year by the AP and earned the Sullivan Award as the nation's top amateur athlete.

As Griffith Joyner drifted away from the sport of track and field, the doping rumors seemed to settle down. Flo-Jo was involved in numerous activities, including writing children's books, designing uniforms for the Indiana Pacers, modeling, and broadcasting sports. In 1991, Griffith Joyner and her husband had a daughter, Mary. Griffith Joyner was quickly proving that she could be just as successful off the track.

Then suddenly, on September 21, 1998, Florence Griffith Joyner died in her sleep at the age of 38. This unexpected tragedy immediately sparked up rumors and was blamed on everything from chronic steroid use, to allergies, to homicide. Her autopsy eliminated these theories, revealing that she had died of asphyxiation from an epileptic seizure. The autopsy results were also unable to prove or disprove whether drugs, steroids, or human growth hormones contributed to her death.

Unfortunately, Florence Griffith Joyner's untimely death overshadowed her incredible impact on the community and world of sports. With all the attention centered on her mysterious death, very few people realized that she founded a children's organization. The Florence Griffith Joyner Youth Foundation is a nonprofit program that serves disadvantaged youth. Also, at the time of her death, Griffith Joyner was serving as a co-chair for the President's Council on Physical Fitness and Sports. President Bill Clinton honored her work by saying, "Though she rose to the pinnacle of the world of sports, she never forgot where she came from, devoting time and resources to helping children—especially those growing up in our most devastated neighborhoods—make the most of their own talents."[2]

Florence Griffith Joyner remains a hero to many people, not only for her record-breaking performances, but for her inward and outward beauty. Her legacy lives on, as her two world records remain and are considered by many to be untouchable. Although young sprinters aspire to be like Florence Griffith Joyner someday, she would want them to dream bigger. She inspired children to fulfill their dreams and constantly strive for greatness. When speaking to America's youth, she always told them, "Don't try to be me. Be better than me."[3] So far, no one has been.

Notes

1. Biography. "Florence Griffith Joyner," www.FlorenceGriffithJoyner.com (accessed November 2, 2007).

2. CNN. "Florence Griffith Joyner," http://edition.cnn.com/2008/SPORT/04/30/florencegriffithjoyner/ index.html (accessed November 2, 2007).

3. Answers.com. "Florence Griffith Joyner," http://www.answers.com/topic/florence-griffith-joyner (accessed November 2, 2007).

Evelyn Ashford

American Star of the Women's
International Sports Hall of Fame

by Stacy Martin-Tenney

Evelyn Ashford was the first woman to run the 100-meter dash under 11 seconds when she set a world record of 10.79 seconds in 1983. Her storied career began years before when the young Evelyn found herself leading a group of boys in a foot race. She is the daughter of U.S. Air Force Sergeant Samuel Ashford and wife Vietta and in typical military fashion, the family was never able to plant their feet for long in one city because duty called. By Evelyn's sophomore year of high school, her family had moved to Roseville, California. She had proven her swift-footed skills in Alabama the previous year on the track, but once they arrived in California there was no girls' track and field team in which she could compete. Not bound by society's divergence of gender for the sport, she turned heads as she raced with the high school boys' track team. Pure athletic talent usually opens doors, and her stunning speed certainly opened the door for her to run with the boys.

Evelyn Ashford matured competitively and became respected by her peers, and those young, high school boys honored her by naming her captain during her senior year. She garnered so much attention that she was offered an athletic scholarship by Coach Pat Connolly at UCLA that year. From her lightning start the first day of practice, she impressed Connolly and he quickly began planning a golden future for Ashford. After only a year of consistent training and coaching, Ashford qualified for the 1976 Olympic Games in Montreal at 19 years old. Placing fifth in the 100-meter dash final, she registered a time that was faster than that of many seasoned veterans of the sport. The tide was turning in women's track and field, and another great era was approaching with Evelyn Ashford stepping onto the track.

With just a taste of international competition, Ashford returned to dominate the women's collegiate competition. In both the 1977 and 1978 seasons, she accomplished the illustrious double-double national championship for a sprinter—a win in the 100-meter dash and in the 200-meter dash. The following year, she returned to the international scene, competing for the World Championship in 1979, and won the 100-meter with ease. Everything was starting to align for the young sprinter and she was favored to win the gold in the 100-meter during the upcoming 1980 Olympic Games in Moscow. Her childhood dream of winning a gold medal for her country, like her hero Wilma Rudolph, was so close that she could taste the victory. However, like so many U.S. athletes, she faced almost unbearable disappointment when her Olympic dreams were crushed due to the U.S. boycott of the 1980 Olympic Games. President Jimmy Carter decided to boycott the Moscow Games in protest of the Soviet Union's invasion of Afghanistan. Ashford then found herself at a crossroads in her career when she injured her hamstring in a race later that summer. As a result, she chose to take a year off to evaluate her goals in track and in life.

She could have let the disappointment conquer her golden dreams, but instead she returned to the track with a renewed sense of purpose and vigor. Her speed improved as the hamstring recovered, and the fleet-footed Ashford returned to the sport to prove her talent to the world's competition. She earned the notable double-double just out of her starting blocks at the 1981 World Cup. During the peak of her career, Ashford collected 20 of the 23 fastest times in the women's 100-meter. Ashford had become the face and the hope of her country in the battle on the track between her native United States and the competitive East German sprinting regime. Her rival in this epic sprinting duel was Marlies Gohr of East Germany, and the two phenoms traded wins in the 100-meter. Gohr defeated Ashford at a Los Angeles meet in 1983, but just one week later Ashford delivered a tremendous performance at the Sports Festival in Colorado with a world-record 10.79 seconds. That same year, Ashford repeated her remarkable double-double performance at the World Cup. As she prepared for the 1983 World Championships in Helsinki, she was focused on beating Gohr in the final. After breezing by the competition in the quarter- and semifinals, her previous hamstring injury resurfaced in the final, crushing her dreams of beating her old foe. Gohr won the battle.

Ashford had faced this same kind of adversity before, but this time she would have to push harder to return from the injury because the 1984 Los Angeles Olympic Games were only months away. And push she did, as she ran away from the field with her coveted Olympic gold medal in the women's 100-meter dash while setting the Olympic record. Ashford delivered a second gleaming performance in the 4 × 100-meter relay and brought home a second gold medal. The victory left a bittersweet taste in her mouth as the games concluded because Gohr, the East Germans, and Soviet Union had boycotted these Games as a result of President Carter's boycott in 1980. Later that summer, she caught up with Gohr in Zurich and overcame her rival in a stunning world-record performance of 10.76 seconds. Ashford was pregnant at the time of the race and took the next 17 months off to have her baby, a daughter she named Raina.

Speculation and doubt circled her return to the sport, as many wondered if this world-class sprinter would return to a competitive level, let alone regain her championship reign. Ashford faced her critics by persevering and her competition and the media quickly recanted their hesitation as Ashford proceeded to win all but two races in 1986. She continued her pursuit of excellence and made her fourth Olympic team in 1988. Ashford immediately made her mark on the 1988 Seoul Olympics, as she was selected by the U.S. team captains to carry the U.S. flag in the opening ceremonies. In nearly 100 years of the Olympic Games, Ashford was only the third woman and second African-American to carry the country's flag in the Olympic parade. It was an honor bestowed on a well-respected athlete by the nation's best to recognize the impact she has had on her sport and the nation. A seasoned competitor, Ashford made the 100-meter final but knew that her teammate, the youthful Florence Griffith-Joyner, would be difficult to beat for the gold. Youth passed experience by 0.29 seconds that day on the track and Ashford was awarded a silver medal in the 100-meter dash. She quickly dug deep into her experience and heart, and came back in the 4 × 100-meter relay to deliver a come-from-behind victory as the anchor leg for the U.S. team. Experience and perseverance was victorious.

Ashford defied the odds yet again, making her fifth and final Olympic team for the 1992 Olympic Games in Barcelona, Spain. The last was similar to the first with wide eyes and breathing the atmosphere in with every breath, but the fifth time poise replaced nervousness. Ashford ran the lead leg on the 4 × 100-meter and as she stood on the podium holding her final gold medal, she took her final breath of Olympic air. Ashford told Flip Bondy of the *New York*

Times in 1992, "I think maybe I'm a pioneer . . . When I started, the Eastern European women had a stranglehold on sprinting. I wanted to prove that Evelyn Ashford could run fast and win a gold medal. Maybe I contributed something good."[1] Ashford was honored for doing something good for track and field in 2006 with her induction into the U.S. Olympic Hall of Fame. She was also awarded the Flo Hyman Award by the Women's Sports Foundation. Ashford has worked for General Motors as an Olympic advisor, made appearances for the U.S. Olympic Committee, commentates for track and field occasionally, but mostly she is the proud mother of her two children and wife of Ray Washington.

Note

1. Flip Bondy, "BARCELONA: TRACK & FIELD; Ashford Hands Off And Then Signs Off," *New York Times*, August 9, 1992. , http://query.nytimes.com/gst/full page.html?res=9E0CEFDA1E3FF93AA3575BC0A964958260. (Accessed January 20, 2008.)

Valerie Brisco-Hooks

American Star of the Women's International Sports Hall of Fame

by Stacy Martin-Tenney

Valerie Brisco-Hooks was the first woman to win the gold medal in both the 200-meter and 400-meter dashes during the same Olympic Games. Her accomplishment during the 1984 Los Angeles Games was not only a first among women, but it also had never been accomplished by a man. Brisco-Hooks also captured the gold as part of the 4 × 400-meter relay team during the 1984 Olympics.

As a young girl she moved with her family from the rural south to the urban Watts neighborhood in Los Angeles. She was inspired to run by her older brothers, Robert and Melvin Brisco. Robert and Melvin were finishing a hard workout at their high school track late one day, when the violence of the neighborhood struck and a stray bullet shot from a gun held by a ninth-grader killed Robert. Valerie was a disobedient 14-year-old and the incident altered her life. She had a new purpose to her athletic career, to finish the run that her brother never would. Robert's track coach encouraged her to come out for the team and carry on their family name, and she carried it proudly throughout her career and into the greatest athletic arena, the Olympic stadium.

Valerie's outstanding high school performance led her to the collegiate level of track and field at California State University, Northridge (CSUN). She continued to excel, winning the 200-meter title at the Association of Intercollegiate Athletics for Women (AIAW) Championships and earning a spot on the U.S. team for the 1979 Pan American Games, where she helped her 4 × 400-meter relay team win the gold medal. Cal State Northridge brought her success in her athletic career and her personal life. She met Alvin Hooks, an equally successful track athlete for CSUN who became a wide receiver for the Philadelphia Eagles. They were married in 1981 and a year later she gave birth to their son Alvin Jr.

Women experience significant changes to their body during pregnancy, and for a track athlete the changes can be truly detrimental. Valerie gained a great deal of weight with the pregnancy and consequently lost her motivation to be physically active, never mind training at an elite level. Her husband encouraged her and even asked Coach Bobby Kersee to try to instill the competitive drive in her once more, but it took Valerie herself to decide that she wanted to pursue her track career. Once she made that choice it took time and patience to get back into shape after 18 months of inactivity. Coach Kersee kept coaxing her into believing in herself and she kept picking up speed. Her husband cared for Alvin Jr., which allowed her time to dedicate to her talent and pursuit of a dream. Though women's bodies are affected greatly by pregnancy, there have been several female athletes who have experienced staggering performance improvements after they return to their sport. Brisco-Hooks was one of them.

By 1984, she was in the best shape of her life and her athletic career was flourishing. She began the year winning the 200-meter indoor national championship and by the summer she added the 400-meter outdoor national championship to her successes. Sprinters have very selective training regimens to hone their fast-twitch response and the appropriate amount of strength for their particular race. If a sprinter decides to double in events, then it is usually the 100-meter and the long jump or the 100- and the 200-meter; if they are really talented, maybe all three events. But it is rare to see an athlete excel in the 200-meter and the longer 400-meter race because the 400-meter requires a certain level of anaerobic endurance not common in the shorter distances. Brisco-Hooks was primed for a victory in both events by the time the Olympic Trials occurred in 1984, and breezed through qualifying in each event.

The political climate surrounding the 1984 Olympics was at best strained as a result of the U.S. boycott in 1980 and the Soviet's retaliatory boycott of 1984. Neither country was secure in sending their athletes into their Cold War enemy's boundaries. At the time the Soviet Union was thought to have the best sprint athletes in the world, so Brisco-Hooks would be running against the rest of the world instead of the best. She focused on what she could control and took solace in the rest of the world coming to her backyard to compete. Her performance proved she was the best during the 1984 Games. Her domination on the track in the 400-meter, the 200-meter, and finally the 4 × 400-meter relay left the crowd inspired by this driven young woman. Her coach, Bobby Kersee, husband and coach of the great heptathlete Jackie Joyner-Kersee, was so overcome with emotion that he leaped over walls and Olympic security to congratulate Brisco-Hooks in a bear hug of excitement and emotion. Brisco-Hooks collapsed on the track from the exhaustion and emotion, and it was a moment remembered as one of those great Olympic achievement stories celebrated by coach and athlete. Her career came full circle from Robert's tragic fall on a Los Angeles's high school track to three Olympic Gold Medals in the Los Angeles stadium. Brisco-Hooks dedicated her 400-meter victory to Robert and the 200-meter win to the rest of her family for their unconditional support.

Brisco-Hooks did not experience the typical leap to stardom that usually accompanies one gold medal, let alone three, but she did have the unique opportunity to appear on the popular Cosby Show and test her speed against Bill Cosby himself in the episode "Off to the Races." Brisco-Hooks chose to leverage her popularity in the Los Angeles community instead of exploiting it for financial endorsements. She became an advocate for drug-free schools and actively sought out opportunities to interact with students in the classroom to convey her message. She made time in her training and competition schedule because she felt so passionately about making a difference. She continued to have success on the track, setting the world record for the indoor 400-meter race in 1985. She followed up the next year with a world championship title in the 400-meter outdoors. Brisco-Hooks ran on the 4 × 400-meter relay team in the 1988 Olympic Games held in Seoul, Korea. She was in the twilight of her career and looking beyond what track and field had to offer, but her competitive nature was in overdrive. The team was facing their rival, the Soviet Union team, for the first time since the 1976 Olympic Games in Munich. The boycotts of 1980 and 1984 Olympic Games had simply fueled the fire. The U.S. women's 4 × 400-meter relay team was ready to run, and they ran fast enough for a new American record. But, sadly the Soviets took the gold medal that day. Brisco-Hooks earned her fourth Olympic medal and her first taste of silver. She retired from the sport soon thereafter.

Most people hope to leave a place better than they found it, but Brisco-Hooks revolutionized the sprint world of track and field. She proved that impossible feats are in fact possible with hard work and dedication. Michael Johnson later accomplished the same feat as Brisco-Hooks, winning Olympic Gold in the 200-meter and 400-

meter sprints, and he did it with sponsor support and specially designed gold spikes to run those fateful races. She accomplished the feat with grace, class, and pure emotion that encapsulated everything she had given of herself to the sport. She began her athletic career out of tragedy, struggled through the effects of her pregnancy on her career, set Olympic records, won numerous championships, and captured four Olympic medals. She is a woman of strength, passion, and drive and a true champion. Today, Valerie Brisco-Hooks resides in Los Angeles and trains disadvantaged children for the Special Olympics.

Jackie Joyner-Kersee

American Star of the Women's International Sports Hall of Fame

by Stacy Martin-Tenney

Jackie Joyner Kersee pictured with Richard Lapchick at the National Consoritum for Academics and Sports' 2003 Giant Steps Awards Banquet and Hall of Fame Inductee Ceremony.

Jackie Joyner-Kersee has always had "a kind of grace" as an athlete because while she is a tough competitor she has always demonstrated poise and charm on and off the track. Her race in life has been filled with obstacle after obstacle, but she breezed past each one with her head held high as if each was just another hurdle on the track. Her maternal grandmother, Evelyn Joyner, named her Jacqueline after former First Lady of the United States, Jacqueline Kennedy Onassis, a woman known for her elegance. Evelyn knew that Joyner-Kersee would also be a first lady.

Joyner-Kersee quickly secured the title of "Greatest Woman Athlete of the Twentieth Century," assuring her place as the first lady of track and field for quite some time. She competed in the heptathlon, a two-day event comprised of the 100-meter hurdles, high jump, shot put, and 200-meter on the first day, and the long jump, javelin, and 800-meter on the second day. Her place in history would not be secured simply because she was the first female to become so decorated in track and field, for as time passes her records will be surpassed by future generations of runners. Rather, Joyner-Kersee will remain in our memories because of the way she conducted herself with such class.

Joyner-Kersee grew up in East St. Louis, Illinois, and spent most of her time at the Mary Brown Community Center, which offered sports to young people as well as story time and painting.

Joyner-Kersee's neighborhood was plagued with violence and drug abuse, so the community center was as much a safe haven as it was an opportunity for personal growth. Al and Mary, Joyner-Kersee's parents, had married young and were barely out of childhood themselves when Jackie was born. Mary Joyner was extremely conscientious about her daughter's future and so she pushed her in the classroom and on the athletic fields to break the cycle of babies having babies that seems so compelling in a poor community. Her daughter was to know greatness, not poverty. Joyner-Kersee's trek to the top would start when she joined the track club at age nine without any financial resources. She sold candles to her elementary classmates to raise money for track meet travel expenses. She ran in a pair of shoes until the rubber wore out or they fell off. Joyner-Kersee had it all from a young age—she steadily ran past her competition on the track and excelled in the classroom.

Evelyn Joyner doted on Joyner-Kersee by playing dress up with her and painting her tiny fingernails so they would match her own. Joyner-Kersee felt like the first lady when her grandmother was around. She was the adult who always made her feel special as a child. Evelyn planned a trip from Chicago to visit her darling granddaughter, and Joyner-Kersee could rarely contain her excitement any time her grandmother planned a visit. The trip was only a few days away when the family received a call that Evelyn would be visiting the angels instead. Joyner-Kersee's step-grandfather was a destructive alcoholic. He had come home drunk from the bar and shot Evelyn with a 12-gauge shotgun while she was sleeping. Joyner-Kersee had it all, except her loving grandmother. She never drank or used any recreational drugs because she saw how their use often leads to violence. She is proud of the fact that her family never became victims of violence because they continued to expect great things from one another and encouraged one another's hopes and dreams, just as Evelyn encouraged Joyner-Kersee to be the first lady of whatever her heart desired.

Joyner-Kersee became a talented high school athlete in track and field and basketball. She was so successful that she was offered a scholarship to UCLA, consistently one of the top track and field programs in the country. She was so talented that she is one of the few athletes who could handle the demands of two sports and her coursework. Her mother asked her to come home for Christmas her freshman year, but she declined and promised to come home in the spring. Unfortunately, she would return home sooner than she intended. Joyner-Kersee's mother died suddenly from meningitis just a short time after the Christmas invitation she had declined. Joyner-Kersee went home to attend her mother's funeral. Her three siblings were terribly grief stricken. As the eldest child, Jackie Joyner-Kersee had to remain strong. She held her head high above the abyss of emotion drowning everyone else. Returning to school, she remained strong for nearly a year but the wave of grief found her in Los Angeles the next Christmas when Joyner-Kersee realized that she wouldn't be getting a call to come home that year. The tears flowed and she momentarily lost the resilience that she so elegantly displayed on the athletic fields. Her indestructible façade may have cracked, but it would not crumble. She endured the almost insurmountable pain and did not veer from the path that her mother had set for her all those years ago. She continued her education to set an example for her family, showing them life would go on and they would not become victims of tragedy.

It is often said that when a door closes, there is an open window. However, one can get seriously scraped climbing through. Joyner-Kersee saw her open window as an open lane on the track, but in 1982 she developed a condition known as exercise-induced asthma. As a woman who characterized herself as invincible, she was shaken to the core when told that she had limitations. Jackie Joyner-Kersee denied that she had a disease, but today she admits that she was simply too scared to acknowledge it. She went so far as to hide her inhaler from people, even when her breath escaped her and she needed to use it. Eventually, she couldn't deny its existence any longer; she didn't take her inhaler with her to practice one day and ended up in an emergency room feeling suffocated and losing control. When she woke up, she awakened with an awareness of her disease and realized that her medication was life-sustaining. She then altered her routines and workouts, acknowledging that she would not become weak and vulnerable to the disease.

Once again, doors seemed to be closing on her and her escape from life's anxiety seemed to be slipping away. Someone special stepped in and helped her manage her disease as well as her track and field career. Bob Kersee, the assistant coach at UCLA, had experienced the loss of his mother and he offered his support to Joyner-

Kersee and then helped her gain control of her asthma. He encouraged her to continue in track and field as the same fierce competitor that she had always been, and helped her realize that the asthma was not a limitation, just another competitor. His compassion and reinforcement were invaluable to Joyner-Kersee and a friendship began to blossom. Four years later, this friendship was solidified when they became husband and wife. Bob has the same fire in him that Joyner-Kersee does when it comes to competition. He is her biggest critic and her biggest fan on the track. He will scream at her on the track and cook her dinner the same evening. They truly complement each other and their relationship has proven successful in life and in sport.

Joyner-Kersee became a household name because of her remarkable athletic achievements. Her willpower to compete with asthma enhanced her prestige. Her collegiate athletic career started her on the path to success when she set the National Collegiate Athletic Association (NCAA) record for the heptathlon twice. She also continued to play basketball for UCLA and was recognized as the UCLA All-University Athlete for three years. In 1984, Joyner-Kersee won the silver medal in the heptathlon at the Olympics and finished fifth in the long jump. She would go on to win numerous heptathlon titles at the World Championships and Goodwill Games. She graduated from college, married Bob, and then in 1988, struck gold. She set the world record in the heptathlon at the U.S. Olympic Trials and won the long jump. She traveled to the Olympics and won a gold medal for both the heptathlon and the long jump events, beating her own world record in the heptathlon and setting an Olympic record in the long jump. In 1992, she won gold once more in the Olympic heptathlon and stole silver in the long jump. Four years later, Joyner-Kersee won a bronze medal in the long jump after she had pulled a muscle and had to withdraw from the heptathlon. In fact, she did not lose a heptathlon in over 12 years from 1984 until the 1996 Olympic Trials.

Her success in track and field built the pedestal on which she so gracefully speaks from today. She was a star female athlete during a time when girls who competed in sports were commonly referred to as tomboys. She challenged that perception by exuding what she calls "a kind of grace." She describes her definition of grace in her autobiography, which appropriately is titled *A Kind of Grace*. She continues to promote women in athletics and encourages young girls to follow in her footsteps.

Her career came full circle around the track and finished at her starting line in East St. Louis. The community center that she enjoyed so much as a child had closed while she was traveling the world for track meets and publicity appearances. Wanting to give the children of East St. Louis the same opportunities that had placed her in such an advantageous position, she took a percentage of all of her endorsements and raised $40,000 to reopen the center. She wanted to give more and explored ways to finance a brand new 37-acre facility that boasts indoor and outdoor tracks, basketball courts, and state-of-the-art computer rooms. She is determined to create opportunities for children who are facing the same tough decisions and turbulent lifestyles that she did when she was their age. One such experience that she provided was a trip to New York City for the Macy's Thanksgiving Day Parade for 100 children through her Jackie Joyner Kersee Community Foundation. The inspiration that she received at the Mary Brown Center when she was nine was so profound that all of her efforts are focused on her Foundation today.

She also speaks out about asthma as her next great opponent. She says that she approaches fighting the disease as if it is one of her competitors and her treatment is the training she needs to be competitive. According to Letterlough of the *Philadelphia Tribune*, African-Americans "only represent 12 percent of our population, [but] they comprise 26 percent of the deaths related to asthma." Joyner-Kersee was fortunate enough to have the proper medical treatment for her disease, but she realizes that not everyone is fortunate enough to receive sound medical care that is needed to manage the disease properly. She knows that African-Americans are more likely to simply attempt to live with asthma, and she wants to use her status to draw attention to how tragedy can happen without treatment and how one can live a full and complete life with it.

She also speaks about the importance of goal setting and violence prevention. She challenges her audience to think about what could happen at their school even though they have not experienced a violent act as of yet, and how they could prevent it. The loss of her grandmother had a profound influence on her life. She now wants to provide a positive influence for today's youth. She had goals and dreams that carried her out of an impoverished neighborhood and that brought her back to that same town with a renewed purpose. She emphasizes that having goals is a real antidote to violence. Her audience may have come to hear Jackie Joyner-Kersee, the world's greatest female athlete, but they left hearing a message that challenged them to be serious about their future.

Joyner-Kersee has experienced the power that sport can have, and she has done everything she can to utilize that power. She has even entered the business of sports, first and foremost through her endorsement money that she has funneled into the Jackie Joyner-Kersee Community Foundation. She ventured outside her sport to become certified as a sports agent with the National Football League Players Association from 1998 to 2001, a role that only five females had filled prior to that time. Her company, Elite International Sports Marketing Inc., is designed to help athletes prepare for a career in athletics as well as preparing them for life after their career is complete. She has been extraordinarily successful in the heptathlon in track and field, and she is becoming an exceptional leader in the heptathlon of life.

Joan Benoit Samuelson

American Star of the Women's International Sports Hall of Fame

by Stacy Martin-Tenney

Joan Benoit set the women's marathon world record of 2:22:43 when she won the 1983 Boston Marathon. She was a blossoming 25-year-old runner with many miles behind her and a plan to run many, many more. Winning the famed Boston Marathon was not new for Benoit; she conquered that barrier at age 21. However, winning the 1983 Boston Marathon at a world record pace meant a whole new world of running and athlete stardom for Benoit. Her victory meant that not only was she chasing her dream of Olympic Gold at the inaugural women's Olympic marathon at the 1984 Los Angeles Olympic Games, but it also meant that the rest of the competitive field would be chasing her. Joan Benoit is one of those great athletes whose talents place her among the greatest, but her unassuming nature keeps her in humble company. She made a vow just before she finished the Inaugural Olympic marathon to be herself and remain grounded despite the momentum of her success.

Benoit started a family shortly after she won the Olympic Gold, when she married Scott Samuelson. She took the Olympic victory in stride and beautifully grew into a career that had a place for both a family and athletic stardom. Joanie, as she is affectionately known across the sport of endurance running, built a life in her home in Freeport, Maine, an ideal setting for a distance runner with all of nature's beauty surrounding her. It is her home that helps her keep the promise she made to herself shortly before crossing the Olympic finish line. The serenity of the water as it breaks across the point and the garden that she obsessively cares for create a peaceful calm. A long-distance runner is, by nature of the sport, patient and dedicated. These two traits suit Joan's interest in gardening perfectly. Her dedication extends past distance running and gardening, as she has been the exemplary committed mother to her two children, son Anders and daughter Abby. Each sponsor and race director knows that her children's athletic endeavors always took precedence over her own.

Courtesy of Bowdoin College Sports.

Joan Benoit Samuelson, as a 21-year old senior at Bowdoin, winning the 1979 Boston Marathon. It was the first of two Boston Marathon victories for the eventual 1984 Olympic marathon winner.

Keeping a variety of interests seemed to ease the strain of a career in an endurance sport. Marathons take their toll on a body over the grueling 26.2 miles, but what can be even more draining is the mileage that a runner puts in each week to prepare for a race. Benoit Samuelson has faced her fair share of exhaustion and pain throughout her career. Injury was never really a hurdle to her, but rather motivation to train more. In fact, she was introduced to distance running in her youth when she was recovering from a broken leg she suffered in her first sport of skiing. It seems implausible to most, to recover from a broken leg by running miles and miles, but Joan was motivated to do whatever it took so she could be strong on the slopes. Her path throughout her career did not stray much from that auspicious start. Joan could not be deterred from any goal that she was striving toward. Just two weeks before the 1984 Olympic Trials, Joan had knee surgery, but she continued training with vigor. With her goal in sight, she completed a 17-mile training run just a few days after surgery even though the run slightly damaged her leg further. She did not let the pain stop her and she went on to win the 1984 Olympic trials and the Olympic gold medal easily.

The very next year Benoit Samuelson won the Chicago Marathon in record-breaking time, 2:21:21, a new American record that lasted until 2003. In 1985, she also won the James E. Sullivan Award as the top amateur athlete in the country. Throughout her career, she struggled with various injuries, but Benoit Samuelson continued to live a very balanced life, spending time gardening, skiing with her family, and running. Her speed was impressive in non-marathon-distance races as well. She won six prestigious Falmouth Road Races, a 7.1 mile race, with four course record-breaking performances. Benoit Samuelson was also victorious in other major races, such as Bay to Breakers 12K, Bobby Crim 10-miler, Quad City Times Bix 7-Miler, and the Tufts 10K for Women. She has also won seven major marathons throughout her storied career.

In May 2007, Joan Benoit Samuelson celebrated her 50th birthday and although some people look for a more relaxed pace later in life, the years surrounding her birthday were lived at an accelerating pace. Just like the previous years of her life, she continued to set lofty goals for herself. The loftiest, quite literally, was to climb Mt. Kilimanjaro in Tanzania before she turned 50, and she reached the top with ease. Benoit Samuelson sets goals and quite regularly achieves them but it is not with the same motivation with which others set out; she climbs mountains simply because they are there. She entered the Oklahoma City Half Marathon in April 2007 but half way through the race, her old injury flared up in her calf and her foot. Joan's determination and stubbornness would not permit her to give up, so the woman who runs a full marathon in 2:46:27 limped the remaining six and a half miles to finish a half marathon in 1:54:52. The injury did hamper her goal of running 50 miles on her 50th birthday a month later, but instead of giving up she set out for a 60-mile bike ride with a 70-year-old friend—splitting their ages was the simplest way to settle the distance.

Her overcommitted lifestyle makes it hard to fit 60-mile bike rides in on a regular basis. She keeps busy by supporting environmental causes, organizing her own road race, Beach to Beacon 10K, following her children's endeavors, skiing with Scott, maintaining her garden, running 60 miles a week, and constantly giving back to the sport that gave her so much. It is enough to make anyone feel tired, but that is just a slice of Joanie's life. Her life has been so rich in experiences and people that adore her. She begged her husband not to throw a 50th birthday party, but he could not let this milestone pass without recognition. Scott secretly asked Joan's circle of friends and colleagues to send "seeds for her garden with a few thoughts."[1] He organized the "seeds" in seven large keepsake albums. Some sent roasted coffee beans with encouragement for the miracle gardener to grow something from them, and others sent intricate drawings of something inspiring about Joan. In her hurried state, Joan has only had time to look through the abundance of pages in two of the albums, but she still makes time for correspondence and thank you notes to her crowds of friends.

She invests most of her time in the Beach to Beacon 10K in Cape Elizabeth because it is a symbol of what she has given the sport and what the sport has given her in return. The B2B, as it is affectionately known, is laborious at best for Joan, but it is a labor of love. She signs countless posters for thank you gifts, makes at least a dozen appearances on television shows and at volunteer and sponsors' parties, but the most important thing she does every year is run the B2B with her two children and husband. Seeing Benoit Samuelson run this race is a sight the crowd yearns for while they wait, and the finish line erupts with applause as she crosses the line. Benoit Samuelson kindly thanks everyone again at the final gathering every year.

Joan's final career race was the Women's Olympic Marathon Trials held in Boston in April 2008. Joan says running at Boston "isn't about making it to Beijing. It's about finishing in a respectable time." For Joan Benoit Samuelson that means that for her last professional running goal, she wants to run a full marathon in 2:50:00 at 50 years old. As usual, she not only succeeded but she also surpassed her goal and turned in a time of 2:49:08 and finished 90th of 124 competitors. Her character, passion, and commitment have led her through many full marathons and a full life. Joanie has already finished in a respectable time and in a more than respectable way in most people's minds.

Note

1 Susan Rinkunas, "The Last Go 'Round," *Runner's World*, January 1, 2008, 99.

Willye White

American Star of the Women's International Sports Hall of Fame

by Sara Jane Baker

Willye White has given so much to the sport of track and field. However, if she was still alive, White would tell you how much more the sport gave to her. The multiple Olympian credited track and field for not only helping her overcome obstacles, but more important, for teaching her important life lessons.

Although White was one of the great pioneers for track and field, her most fulfilling work came after she retired from the sport. Her experience in athletics motivated her to get involved with the community. White loathed the selfish athletes who did not do anything to help the less fortunate, so after her retirement from track and field, she fought to make a difference for Chicago's youth. She established a sports program for young girls; however, White's goal was not to teach them the fundamentals of sports. Rather, she only used sport as a vehicle to reach her students, and then taught them important life lessons. It was through sports that White learned these same valuable life lessons.

White faced racism at a very young age while growing up near a cotton field in Money, Mississippi. After seeing her bright-green eyes and reddish-light brown hair, White's father insisted that White could not possibly be his child, and he left shortly after her birth.[1] Overcome with the difficulties of being a single parent, White's mother soon entrusted White to her grandparents. Her grandfather, whom she considered her hero, would wake her up at 4 or 5 every morning to drive 60 miles to pick cotton. He used this labor to teach White important life lessons.[2] Like most places in the Deep South, racism was prevalent in Money. White described cross burnings and lynchings as an everyday part of her life. She was not allowed to play with the girls in her neighborhood, so instead she would play Cowboys and Indians with the boys. Ironically, this is where her athletic ability first surfaced.

At the age of 10, White and her cousin tried out for the high school track team. The coach quickly took notice when White was beating many of the girls on the varsity team. Although White had tremendous speed, she started long jumping because the team already had enough sprinters. Even at such a young age, White exhibited passion, drive, and commitment. All her hard work paid off as she qualified for the Olympic Games in Melbourne, Australia, at the age of 19. She won a silver medal and became the first female American to medal in the long jump. Upon White's return home, Tennessee State, under the leadership of Ed Temple, offered her a scholarship. Temple was highly regarded in the track and field world as he also coached Olympic champion Wilma Rudolph and the great Mae Faggs. White, however, quickly realized that Temple was too controlling for her, so she left after only six months and transferred to Chicago State University.

Despite no longer having a coach, White's amazing success continued. White coached herself to every Olympics from 1960 to 1972. She remains the only American to have competed on five Olympic track and field teams. At the 1964 Games in Tokyo, she won her second silver medal as a member of the 400-meter relay team. Despite competing in five consecutive Olympics, White never won a gold medal, which she contributed to helping her keep her motivation and drive. Competing internationally in the Olympic Games also taught her an important lesson: racism and hatred do not exist everywhere in the world. Upon reflection on her Olympic experience, she said, "The Olympic movement taught me not to judge a person by the color of their skin but by the contents of the heart."[3]

This life lesson motivated White to succeed long after her retirement from track and field. When White moved to Chicago in 1960, she became a nurse and public health and administration quickly became another one of her passions. Five years later, in 1965, she became a public health administrator at the Chicago Health Department. In 1976, White graduated from the University of Chicago with a degree in public health administration.

In addition to working in public administration, White continued to play an active role in sports. She served as the president of the Midwest chapter of U.S. Olympians for 12 years. White also served as a coach for athletes competing in the National Sports Festival and the World Cup Track and Field Championship Games. In 1990, she founded WBW Hang on Productions, a sports and fitness consulting firm.

White used her years of experience as an athlete, administrator, and coach to reach the youth of Chicago. She chose to remain in the inner city of Chicago, where she felt the most needed. She used her close proximity to mentor and teach Chicago's south side. In 1990, she founded the Willye White Foundation in Chicago. This Foundation helped raise money and develop self-esteem for underprivileged children. One big initiative for her Foundation was the Robert Taylor Girls Athletic Program, which reached the children living in the nation's largest housing project. In addition to teaching children sports and important teamwork skills, it also provided them with a summer day camp and healthcare services like immunizations, dental check-ups, and medical check-ups.

White received a lot of recognition for her success in track, as well as her movements off the track. One of her proudest moments came when she became the first American to receive the UNESCO Pierre de Coubetin International Fair Play Trophy, the world's highest sportsmanship award. She was inducted into 11 halls of fame, and she was named one of the greatest athletes of the century by *Sports Illustrated for Women* and *Ebony Magazine*.[4]

On February 6, 2007, Willye White passed away from pancreatic cancer. Although White lost this battle, she overcame so many barriers throughout her lifetime. Her legacy as a track and field star will remain for decades to come, but her impact as a teacher and mentor will live on forever.

Notes

1. Frank Litsky, "Willye B. White, the First 5-Time U.S. Track Olympian, Dies at 67," *New York Times*, February 7, 2007.

2. Kenny McReynolds, "Willye White," *Chicago Sun-Times*, September 19, 1988.

3. "Olympic Track Star Willye White Dies," *AP*, February 7, 2007.

4. "Willye B. White Biography," *The History Makers*, http://www.thehistorymakers.com/biography/biography.asp? bioindex=190 (accessed July 10, 2008).

Nell Jackson

American Star of the Women's International Sports Hall of Fame

by Sara Jane Baker

Coaching at any level requires patience, strong listening skills, and extensive knowledge of the sport. Coaching at the Olympic level, however, brings additional pressure and extremely high expectations. Because of these high standards, it is truly an honor to be selected as a head coach of an Olympic team. When Nell Jackson was named as the head coach for the track and field team, she added to this honor by breaking an incredible barrier for African-American women.

A native of Athens, Georgia, Jackson ignored the obstacles and lack of opportunities for an African-American woman born in 1929. From a young age, Jackson excelled in track and field and at only 15 years old, she competed in her first national championship. The following year she had the opportunity to race against the reigning Olympic champion, Stella Walsh, in the 200-meter dash. Although she placed second to Walsh, Jackson showed incredible potential. At age 17, she was named to the U.S. All-American team.

Her accomplishments caught the eye of head coach and Hall of Famer, Cleve Abbott, at the Tuskegee Institute, where Jackson had the opportunity to train with other amazing athletes like Mary McNabb, Catherine Johnson, and Evelyn Lawler. In addition to being the star on Tuskegee's team, Jackson was a leader serving as a captain and providing constant support for her younger, less experienced teammates. In fact, fellow teammate and future Olympian, Mary McNabb, credits Jackson for helping with her slow start.[1] In 1948, the 19-year-old earned a spot on the U.S. Olympic team. Jackson ran the 200-meter and teamed up with Mae Faggs on the 400-meter relay. Although she did not earn a medal in the London Games, her career was just beginning to blossom.

Upon returning home, Jackson did not waste any time in expanding her impressive resume. In 1949, Jackson etched her name in the record books as she set a new American record in the 200-meter dash with a time of 24.2 seconds. The following year Jackson would have a rematch with her rival, Stella Walsh, at the national champi-onships. With her newfound confidence from her record-breaking performance, Jackson would, this time, be victorious. In 1951, Jack-son was invited to compete in the inaugural Pan American Games. She once again showed her dominance by winning the sprint team relay and placing second in the individual 200-meter dash.

Although Jackson was still a competitive force in the track world, she opted not to compete in the 1952 Olympics in Helsinki, Finland. Instead, she shifted her focus to coaching. She began at her alma mater, but would later have coaching stints at Illinois State, the University of Illinois, and Michigan State. Showing her incredible impact as a coach, Jackson was given the ultimate opportunity—coaching the 1956 Olympic team. Not only was this a true testament to Jackson's influence as a coach, but it also broke a major barrier for African-American women as she became the first to be named head coach of any U.S. Olympic team. Jackson held this position again in 1972 at the Munich Olympics. She was a true trailblazer, as she paved the way for many other African-American female coaches.

Her influence did not stop at coaching from the sidelines. In addition to serving as an administrator for the U.S. Olympic Com-mittee (USOC) and the International Association of Athletics Feder-ations (IAAF), Jackson spent many years with The Athletics Congress (TAC), now known as USA Track and Field (USATF). Jackson served as vice president of the organization for many years, but held the role of secretary until the time of her death in 1988.

Nell Jackson's legacy will continue on, as each year, one ath-letics administrator is awarded the NACWAA Nell Jackson Award. In addition to being an active member of the National Association of Collegiate Women Athletics Administrators (NACWAA), the recip-ient must demonstrate leadership, courage, compassion, conviction, tenacity, and vision—all qualities shared with the late Nell Jackson.[2] This award is a prestigious honor for the annual recipient, but more important, it is a tribute to a true pioneer and role model.

Notes

1. Michael D. Davis, *Black American Women in Olympic Track and Field* (Jeffer-son, N.C.: McFarland & Company, Inc, Publishers, 1992).

2. National Association of Collegiate Athletic Administrators, "Nell Jackson Award," http://www.nacwaa.org/aw/awards_nj.php.

Barbara Jacket

American Star of the Women's International Sports Hall of Fame

by Sara Jane Baker

Live life to the fullest. Be grateful for what you have. Nothing is promised to you. These are the principles by which Barbara Jacket has lived.[1] These principles, along with her naturally competitive nature, have shaped one of the most successful, influential, and famous coaches in track and field history. More important, the thousands of students and athletes under her influence have come to share Jacket's philosophy of living and her competitive nature.

From the beginning, Jacket was a competitor. Growing up in an era when a girl competing in athletics was frowned upon, she remembers playing "shirts and skins" with the boys in the neighborhood. But whether competing against girls or boys, Jacket was sure to win. Growing up in a single-parent household in the small Texas town of Port Arthur, Barbara, her brother, and her mother all shared a single-room house. In fitting with her grateful nature, Jacket never viewed her childhood poverty as a hardship. "When I was a kid, I didn't know that we were poor because we always had something to eat."[2] In fact, Jacket credits these experiences for making her the amazing competitor she still is today.

Not your average tomboy, Jacket was fearless and did not hesitate to stand up to anyone, including her 200-pound brother. Growing up, she remembers seeking out fights. "I'd fight for my sister. I'd fight for my cousin, I'd fight for everybody,"[3] Jacket admits. Fortunately, sports became a more appropriate outlet for her competitive and aggressive nature. At only 10 years old, Jacket started on the area high school softball team.

Like other African-American women of her time, Jacket faced obstacles that were more ominous than childhood poverty. Jacket remembers mischievously drinking out of the "whites only" water fountain to see how it differed from the "colored" water fountain.[4] Attending a segregated school, Jacket's basketball team had to receive special permission to play against the white high schools. In addition, the sexist attitudes of the era discouraged her from playing sports. Since there were limited girl's teams to play on, Jacket often ended up as the only female on the boys teams. These obstacles, rooted in two things she had no control over, her race and her gender, would not soon disappear.

Nevertheless, sports became her ticket to college. "If it hadn't been for sports, I could not have gone to college because my mama had no money to send me,"[5] Jacket remembers. She attended the Tuskegee Institute in Alabama. Because Jacket had always been so focused on athletics, most people who knew her assumed she would struggle academically. Jacket persevered with the same drive and determination she exhibited in her sporting career. Despite her accomplishments in athletics, graduating from college in 1958 remains one of Jacket's greatest lifetime achievements. Her degree in physical education provided the foundation for her life's work.

When Jacket took her first coaching job at Prairie View A&M in 1964, it was clear that women had made little progress in gender equity as Title IX had yet to be passed. Furthermore, African-Americans were still experiencing racism as many of the major conferences, like the Southeastern Conference (SEC), still did not allow black athletes to participate. Female athletes were also not given scholarships, they played in poor facilities, and they had limited opportunities. For many people, the mere thought that women should even participate in sports was still being questioned. Jacket explains, "When they built the gym [at Prairie View A&M] in 1964, they didn't include dressing facilities for women."[6] Additionally, African-Americans were still not allowed to eat at some cafes and restaurants. "We had to tell them what we wanted at the back, even though they had a black cook," Jacket remembers. "The cook fixed your hamburger and you got it to go."[7]

Ignoring these obstacles, Jacket started as a swim coach in 1964. Two years later, she organized the first track and field team but was still unable to get any funding from the school. As a coach, she was demanding, always pushing her athletes to reach their full potential and capabilities. "I raised hell with them; I pushed them to do what they were capable of."[8] This strategy paid off for Jacket—in a big way. In her 25-year reign as head coach, Jacket led her teams to more than 20 national championships. She coached 57 All-Americans and five future Olympians. Jacket's greatest athletic lifetime achievement came in 1974, when she led her very first team to a national championship. This accomplishment set the tone for the rest of Jacket's successful career.

All of Jacket's accolades caught the attention of the United States Olympic Committee. In 1992, she was named the head coach for the U.S. Olympic women's track and field team, an honor only previously held by one other African-American woman. This high-pressure experience turned out to be the best experience she would never want to do again. Working with professional athletes gave Jacket a new appreciation for the purity of college athletics. "Coaching elite athletes becomes a business . . . That cold business aspect makes high-level coaching much less fun than coaching your own team and seeing it develop."[9] Nevertheless, Jacket continued her pattern of success when she led her team to four gold medals, four silver medals, and two bronze medals.

Although coaching became Jacket's legacy, few know that teaching was her true passion. In fact, teaching is the reason she has remained at Prairie View so long. "I never wanted my job to depend on how well my students could jump or throw, or how fast they could run."[10] Jacket's role as a teacher extends far beyond academics. She attempts to teach them life lessons to better prepare them for the real world. As a child who came from nothing and overcame hardships along the way, Jacket can easily relate to her students. "I let them know that the world doesn't owe them anything—that they have to go out there and get it for themselves, but that they shouldn't be afraid to ask for help."[11]

In 1990, Jacket expanded her role at Prairie View A&M. She was named athletic director, making her the only woman in the Southwestern Athletic Conference (SWAC) with this title. She remains in this position today. She also serves on the Division I Men's and Women's National Collegiate Athletic Association (NCAA) Track and Field Committee. Jacket is showing no sign of slowing down. She exercises daily and hopes to continue helping Prairie View's track team when she retires.

Throughout her career, Barbara Jacket never strayed far from her Texas roots. Through her loyalty and dedication as a coach, teacher, and mentor, Jacket is responsible for putting the small town of Prairie View, Texas, on the map. Jacket's numerous honors, awards, and championships are simply an afterthought to her most significant accomplishment: influencing and developing the lives of so many young people.

Notes

1 P. J. Pierce, *Texas Wisewomen Speak: Let Me Tell You What I've Learned* (Austin: University of Texas Press, 2002), 134.

2. Ibid., 129.

3. Ibid.

4. Ibid.

5. Ibid.

6. Ibid., 131.

7. Ibid., 130.

8. Ibid., 131.

9. Ibid., 133.

10. Ibid., 132.

11. Ibid., 132.

Beverly Kearney

American Star of the Women's International Sports Hall of Fame

by Jessica Bartter

After she slowly made her way up the steps and across the stage, each foot carefully placed in front of the next with the help of a cane on either side, she finally arrived at the podium. She leaned over to the microphone and said, "I want you all to know that I have two canes, but I really only need one . . . deep down inside I'm a diva and I couldn't wear my sneakers so I had to kind of compromise a little in order to wear my dress shoes."[1] The 450 guests, each on edge as they watched the star of the evening struggle to the stage to accept her award, roared with laughter. It wasn't just Beverly Kearney's gorgeous smile that warmed their hearts, but the resiliency that resounded as soon as she spoke to them. A tear rolled down my smiling face as I sat in the very back of the banquet hall, enthralled by the emotion a perfect stranger could bring to me.

A perfect stranger is perhaps a bit of an exaggeration. For the previous 10 months I had repeatedly read Kearney's story and watched the heart-wrenching television specials that introduced her to me. Kearney was the recipient of the National Consortium for Academics and Sports' Coach Award in honor of National Student-Athlete Day in 2005. As one of the event coordinators, the anticipation of meeting her was overwhelming and to my great pleasure and emotion, she did not disappoint my expectations.

The preeminent coach hails from Bradenton, Florida. While life for Kearney didn't come easy, even as a child, she has made the most of every situation, capitalizing on expecting nothing but the best from herself. Though carefree she wasn't. Kearney was the sixth of seven children her mother had with five different men. As the situation would suggest, her father was not a big contributor in her childhood. However, Kearney refused to let her absent father, alcoholic mother, and surroundings of drugs and prostitution determine her fate. Instead, Kearney blazed her own path—and quickly!

In high school, the track and field athlete was recruited to the basketball team for her speed. Girl's basketball began in 1974 at her high school and by 1975, Kearney was a member of the team. Her high school basketball coach said the guard's speed gave her the ability to steal the ball and make easy lay-ups but her shooting skills left something to be desired.

During her senior year, Kearney had to deal with the sudden death of her mother. She turned to Joan Falsone, a former assistant athletic director for county schools, who encouraged Kearney to enroll at Florida's Hillsborough Community College in 1977. The National Junior College track and field All-American talent was then welcomed at Auburn University. As an Auburn Tiger, she earned two Association for Intercollegiate Athletics for Women (AIAW) All-American honors, Auburn Athlete of the Year, and team MVP. In 1980, she qualified for the U.S. Olympic trials in the 200-meter.

Upon earning her bachelor's degree in social work, Kearney sought work as a social worker until Falsone suggested the coaching field. Kearney's athletic talent was unquestionable, but her coaching success was only a vision of Falsone's. Kearney's later coaching success would prove Falsone to be a visionary.

Kearney put in the time to learn the in's and out's of the coaching profession while she earned her master's degree in adapted physical education at Indiana State University, where she served the track team as a graduate assistant. She then did a two-year stint at the University of Toledo, where she held her first head coach title. From Toledo, Kearney accepted the top assistant coach title at the University of Tennessee because the track powerhouse was irresistible, despite the step backward in job titles. Tennessee was just a stepping-stone to the powerhouse Kearney would later build at the University of Texas, after she made another stop as the University of Florida's (UF) head coach. Again Kearney did not waste any time in reaching her goal, and in just her fifth year at the helm of UF, the Gators won the 1992 National Collegiate Athletic Association (NCAA) Division I Indoor title. Kearney became the first black female track and field head coach to win a NCAA Division I National Championship and just the third black head coach ever to win any NCAA title, following John Thompson's 1984 basketball title with Georgetown University and Tina Sloan Green's 1984 women's lacrosse title with Temple University.

The University of Texas couldn't help but take notice of the thriving coach and quickly wooed Kearney to join the Longhorns.

Courtesy of the National Consortium for Academics and Sports.

Beverly Kearney at the National Consortium for Academics and Sports' 2005 Giant Steps Awards Banquet and Hall of Fame Inductee Ceremony.

The relationship has proved prosperous for both since her first season of 1993. When Kearney started her 16th season at UT in 2007–8, she already had led the Longhorns to six NCAA National Championships and 19 conference titles. Twenty-four current UT records have been set under Kearney's tutelage. Several of her student-athletes have gone on to win nine Olympic medals since 1992; the 2008 Beijing Olympics were represented by more Longhorn talent and Kearney protégés.

While 2008 marks a big birthday for Bev, as she is endearingly called, it was not age that kept her from quickly entering the stage that evening in 2005. The 50-year-old, who could easily pass for someone in her 30s, was critically injured in a car crash that left her one of three survivors in a five-person, single-car crash. While headed to Disneyworld on December 26, 2002, the vehicle Kearney was riding in crossed the median of Interstate 10 before rolling several times. Alcohol was not involved. Kearney, who was not wearing a seatbelt, was thrown from the vehicle. She suffered a critical back injury and underwent five hours of surgery to repair her vertebrae. Nonetheless, Kearney was lucky to be alive. She was traveling with two friends, Ilrey Sparks and Michelle Freeman, Freeman's mother Muriel Wallace, and Sparks's two-year-old daughter Imani. Sadly, Ilrey Sparks and Muriel Wallace did not survive the accident. The accident left Kearney with paralyzing injuries and a huge responsibility; Bev became the legal guardian and caregiver for Imani Sparks. They both live with fellow survivor Michelle Freeman.

After two more surgeries in a month's time, Kearney coached from her hospital bed, watching tapes, and writing notes and orders for her assistant coaches to pass along to the team.

Like everything else in which she participates, Kearney gave 100 percent to her physical therapy and has steadily improved since early 2003. She joined the team on the field in a wheelchair just three months after the accident. Her character and leadership was already inspiring to her young student-athletes, but without words, her presence inspired them immeasurably more. Though doctors worried Kearney would never use her legs again, she boldly stood on April 5, 2003, to the amazement and joy of the 20,000 athletes and spectators of the Texas Relays. After steadying herself with one arm, she flashed that gorgeous Bev smile and raised the other arm with a classic Longhorn hand signal. Marcus Sedberry, a University of Nebraska sprinter who was competing that day, delayed his warm-up in anticipation of what she promised she would do three months prior. The sight of her standing nearly brought Sedberry to tears. "The 2003 Texas Relays was a remarkable event," he remembers. "The competition was great as usual, but the competition was overshadowed by the anticipation of Coach Bev standing for the first time since her accident. When she stood up, it sent a deafening roar across the entire Mike A. Myers Stadium. Regardless of what school you were affiliated with or cheering for, you were on your feet cheering and applauding the courage and determination Coach Bev showed at that moment."[2]

Kearney steadily progressed from the wheelchair to a walker, then two canes, until she was down to just one cane in 2005, a feat that encouraged her to give away her wheelchair. While her balance is still not what it used to be, Kearney finds it easiest to get around in her scooter for long hauls. She credits Michelle Freeman, fellow survivor and the driver of the car that crashed, for her on-going care and support. In addition to living with Kearney and Sparks, Freeman is a volunteer coach with UT and has been a constant caregiver to Kearney since 2002.

While Kearney's coaching accomplishments are stand-alone amazing, the personal tragedy she has faced makes her success even more astounding. Most important, Kearney has hundreds more student-athletes to influence and titles to win in her years to come. Two goals remain unconquered on Kearney's list: professionally, to win the triple crown (winning an indoor and outdoor track and field title and the cross country title in a single year) and, personally, to wiggle her toes. Something tells me, when she does wiggle her toes for the first time in years, her student-athletes will be so inspired, they will easily bring home the triple crown. Or perhaps, it will happen the other way around. Either way, Beverly Kearney has already proven she can accomplish anything she puts her mind, heart, and faith into.

Notes

1. Beverly Kearney, Acceptance Speech, The National Consortium for Academics and Sports' 7th Annual Giant Steps Awards Banquet and Hall of Fame Induction Ceremony, Orlando, Florida, February 21, 2005.

2. Marcus Sedberry, interview with author, April 30, 2008.

9

THE EXPLOSION OF WOMEN'S SOCCER

Introduction by Richard Lapchick

Women's soccer is now so popular in the United States that sometimes we forget this such popularity is quite new. While women's leagues existed in Europe in the 1930s, organized women's soccer was one of the outgrowths of Title IX and thus did not start to really develop until the late 1970s. College teams started in the 1980s and the national team was first established only in 1985. How fast things moved from there!

The gold medal U.S. women's victory at the 2008 Beijing Olympics reestablished the long dominance by U.S. women with two World Cup titles, three Olympic gold medals, and one silver medal since 1991.

The Craig Club Girls Soccer League was the first organized women's league in the United States. It was established in 1951 in North St. Louis by Father Craig of St. Matthew's Parish, had four teams, and lasted for two years. Prior to the Craig Club, women's soccer was limited to gym classes, pickup, and some intramural games.

Title IX changed everything in soccer as in other sports for girls and women. A decade later there were 100 college women's soccer programs established. The Association for Intercollegiate Athletics for Women (AIAW), which organized women's college events before the National College Athletic Association (NCAA) took over (see the section on administrators), immediately began sponsoring women's varsity programs. Cortland State won an informal national championship in 1980. North Carolina hosted the first official national championship in 1981 and won the event. They have remained a perennial powerhouse for women's soccer since.

By 1985, there were more than 200 women's college teams. Five years later, nearly 40 percent of colleges had a women's team, a fourfold increase from 1980.

The colleges became a pipeline for the development of the women's national team. Among the top college programs are North Carolina, Santa Clara, Notre Dame, Portland, UCLA, the University of Central Florida, George Mason, Connecticut, and Penn State.

At the same time, there was an explosion in girls youth soccer. All of this led to the growth of women's club soccer, allowing women to play beyond college or even if they did not play in college.

The national team, now so synonymous with women's soccer, did not win even one of the four matches it played in 1985. But the first goal scored was by Michelle Akers, then a player at the University of Central Florida. She was later named the Women's Player of the Century!

A year later North Carolina coach Anson Dorrance took over and brought April Heinrichs, a future Hall of Famer, and NCAA All-American Debbie Belkin. In the next two years, additions included Joy (Fawcett) Biefield, Kristine Lilly, Mia Hamm, Carin Jennings, Julie Foudy, and Shannon Higgins.

The pace of development at the elite level quickened when the world's governing body of soccer, Federation Internationale de Football Association (FIFA), established the Women's World Cup to be held in China in 1991. Dorrance added Brandi Chastain and Wendy Gabauer. The U.S. team swept a five-game tournament in Bulgaria without allowing the opposition a single goal. There were 20,000 fans at each game in China and the U.S. women beat Norway in the final to win the first Cup.

But the women finally became icons after they won the gold medal in the Atlanta Olympics in 1996 before 76,000 fans in the University of Georgia's football stadium. I saw Vince Dooley, the legendary Georgia football coach and then athletic director, and he told me that it was greatest game in their stadium since his star Herschel Walker played there in the 1980s.

The 1999 Women's World Cup was held in the United States and was a smashing success. The U.S. team broke a scoreless tie with a penalty shot by Brandi Chastain to defeat China. The team made the covers of national magazines and the front pages of most of the major newspapers. There had been an average of 38,000 fans per game and more than 650,000 attended in total. The final game was attended by more than 90,000 in the Rose Bowl. Television ratings were also excellent.

This seemed like the time to establish a professional women's league. In 2001, John Hendricks, CEO of Discovery Corp., launched the Women's United Soccer Association (WUSA), with a partnership agreement between WUSA and Major League Soccer. Fan attendance averaged 8,000 per game and was above projections.

The 2003 Women's World Cup saw the world catching up to the American women who finished third. The traditional powers were still strong and Brazil, Japan, and Mexico were coming on fast.

The WUSA ceased operations before the 2004 Olympics began. The U.S. women won the gold medal in Athens and, of course, did the same in Beijing.

In this section, we have chosen to highlight the careers of three women: Michelle Akers, Mia Hamm, and Julie Foudy. The popularity of the sport is so new that the soccer trailblazers are more contemporary than most of those in the other sports highlighted in this book.

As stated earlier, Michelle Akers was voted the Female Soccer Player of the Century by FIFA. In 2004, Akers and Mia Hamm were the only two women named to FIFA's list of the 125 greatest living soccer players named during FIFA's 100th anniversary. She was a four-time All-American at Central Florida. She was a scoring machine for the women's national team after scoring its very first goal in 1985. Between 1985 and 1990, she scored 15 goals. In 1991, she set a record with 39 goals. She scored 10 goals in the 1991 Women's World Cup. Akers scored both goals in the 2-1 championship game against Norway. When she retired before the 2000 Olympics in Sydney, she was the U.S. National Team's second all-time leading scorer with 105 goals, 37 assists, and 247 points. Mia Hamm was the No. 1 scorer.

Hamm was fittingly born in 1972, the year that Title IX was passed. She is arguably the greatest women's soccer player to ever play the game and broke almost every record on the national and Olympic teams. Hamm has become one of the most recognizable females in sports, a cultural icon, and a hero for men and women around the world. Her popularity has brought attention to the sport of soccer, as well as creating other opportunities for women in sports.

Hamm played for the University of North Carolina at Chapel Hill, where she led the Tar Heels to four NCAA women's championships. She was an All-American and was so dominant that she was nicknamed "Jordan" after fellow UNC student-athlete, Michael Jordan. She is still the all-time record holder in the Atlantic Coast Conference (ACC) for goals, assists, and total points and is the world's leading scorer in international competition among both men and women with 158 goals.

Julie Foudy made the U.S. National Team as a 16-year-old. In 1991, she was named Soccer Player of the Year and was also a four-time All-American at Stanford. Foudy played and was co-captain for the U.S. National Team for 18 years. She played in four Women's World Cups and three Olympic Games and retired after the 2004 Olympics. Foudy played in 271 international games, ranking her third all-time among men and women soccer players.

Her post-playing career has established her national leadership role as she has been a political and social activist for issues that include women's rights, child rights, and fair labor standards. Foudy challenged the labor practices of her sponsor, Reebok, for using young children to stitch their soccer balls. Reebok built a new factory without child labor. This led to the FIFA Fair Play Award. She was the first woman to win it. Foudy served as the president for the Women's Sports Foundation (WSF), where she focused her energy on the preservation of Title IX, which was under attack from the Bush administration. In 2005, when the Commission on Opportunity in Athletics threatened to weaken Title IX, Foudy was one of the first to protest. Her efforts paid off, as many of the commission's recommendations were never implemented. In 2007, she created the Julie Foudy Sports Leadership Academy to teach girls, ages 12–18, how to be leaders on and off the field through the sport of soccer.

Akers, Hamm, and Foudy have been giants in the game of soccer and all the other greats who have and will follow will forever be in the debt of these trailblazers.

Michelle Akers

Future Hall of Famer

by Sara Jane Baker

With three gold medals and two World Cup Championships to date, the U.S. Women's National Soccer Team has experienced tremendous success. These accomplishments are especially amazing considering it was only 1985 when the United States launched its first women's team. Michelle Akers had been with the U.S. team since its beginning and deserves much of the credit for growing and increasing the popularity of soccer. Now retired, she set an example and standard for today's top players as someone who never gave up and who always played with passion and heart.

Courtesy of UCF Athletics Communications.

Although Akers's parents divorced when she was in sixth grade, she was never without strong role models in her life. Akers's mother broke a barrier for women when she became the first female firefighter in the city of Seattle, Washington. Like her mother, Akers had big dreams, a competitive spirit, and lots of energy. "My dream was to play for the Pittsburg Steelers like 'Mean' Joe Greene and one day win the Super Bowl by catching the 'Hail Mary' pass as the last second on the scoreboard ticked down," Akers remembers.[1] She was completely unaware of societal norms and expectations of women and cried when her teacher told her girls do not play football. Instead, Akers's mother enrolled her in softball, basketball, volleyball, and soccer. Soccer quickly became her passion and by high school, she was the starting center midfielder. She was so good that the men's coach asked her to train with his team.

After high school, her talent took her all the way to Orlando, Florida, where she was offered a scholarship to the University of

Central Florida (UCF). Not surprisingly, Akers's incredible work ethic, passion, and focus made her the most decorated soccer player in UCF's history. In addition to earning All-American honors four times, Akers was twice named UCF's Athlete of the Year, and she led the team to three National Collegiate Athletic Association (NCAA) tournament appearances. Akers left UCF as the all-time leading scorer, and her No. 10 jersey was retired.

In 1985, at only 19 years old, Akers joined the first-ever U.S. National Team. It did not take long for Akers to establish herself as the star of the team. In the second-ever full international game against Denmark, Akers scored the first goal in the history of the program. For the next five years, Akers continued to lead the team in scoring with 15 goals in 24 games. In 1991, the inaugural FIFA Women's World Cup was held in China. Akers led the U.S. team to its first world championship as the top scorer and winner of the Golden Boot, a prestigious award given to the leading scorer in European League matches. Her international fame brought about the opportunity to sign an endorsement deal and thus, she became the first female soccer player to have a paid sponsor. Akers even pursued her childhood dream of playing in the National Football League (NFL) by trying out as a place kicker for the Dallas Cowboys.

Akers was recognized internationally and had established herself as the top female soccer player in the world. She was at the top of her game. Then, suddenly in 1993, Akers collapsed during a match at the Olympic Sports Festival in San Antonio. What appeared to be mononucleosis advanced into a diagnosis of Epstein-

Courtesy of UCF Athletics Communications.

Barr Virus, or Chronic Fatigue Syndrome. If this illness was not enough, a year later, Akers divorced her husband of four years, Roby Stahl. The once dominant player and incredible competitor quickly seemed to be losing confidence and motivation. In a 1996 journal entry, Akers wrote:

> I can honestly say these few years were pure hell for me. I went through a divorce. I struggled to get through the day or hour, depending on how bad I was feeling. I desperately searched for medical answers and help but found very little. I frequently asked myself, what happened to that strong, dynamic, tireless Michelle Akers? Will I ever see her again? And who am I now? I was alone. I was scared. I was in agony.[2]

While most players would have used this illness as an excuse to retire, Akers, once again, proved why she was the top player in the world. Through her perseverance, dedication, and strong faith in God, Akers worked to get back to her old form. However, it was no easy task. Akers struggled to take a five-minute walk without getting out of breath, and after a game, Akers required two liters of intravenous fluid to rehydrate. To add to these circumstances, Akers had 13 knee surgeries, countless stitches, broken facial bones, and concussions. In fact, Julie Foudy, another standout on the U.S. National Team calls her one of the most unlucky players in the game. "She plays a very physical game and things happen, but it's just so unfortunate that it happens to her so often."[3]

Despite the many obstacles, Akers's play on the field never deteriorated. After winning a gold medal at the Atlanta Olympics in 1996, Akers looked toward the 1999 World Cup. However, she was uncertain whether or not her body would hold up. While her team mates were doing media interviews and photo shoots, Akers kept to herself focusing solely on the World Cup. "The tension of 'do-or-die' produces steel-minded strength. I could feel myself sharpening mentally, focusing deep inside me. Still I was bracing myself for the [physical] cost of going 90 minutes,"[4] Akers remembered of her preparation.

Finally, at the Rose Bowl in front of 90,187 fans and 40 million TV viewers—the highest number for a women's sporting event—the World Cup stage was set. Battling 110-degree heat, Akers played almost the entire 90 minutes of the championship match. However, when the game went into overtime, Akers was unable to participate. While Akers was in the locker room hooked up to a heart monitor and IVs, Akers's teammates battled to the end, winning the game in a shootout. Although Akers was still recovering during the immediate team celebration, her passion and heart did not go unnoticed. U.S. coach Tony DiCicco said, "We all witnessed one of the greatest women athletes in history—a true champion leaving it all on the field, fighting for her teammates."[5]

Akers officially retired in 2001. It was an emotional departure for her teammates and fans, but the fatigue had become too much for her to handle. Although soccer had always been Akers's passion, she wasted no time in finding a new one. Akers launched Soccer Outreach International (SOI) with a goal "to seek out and inspire kids of all nations to become leaders of quality character, faith, and clear purpose through the game of soccer." Akers's love for animals and intuition for horses also motivated her to start the Michelle Akers Sundance Horse Rescue and Outreach. In addition, she has authored three books: *The Game and the Glory*, *Standing Fast*, and *Face to Face*. Akers's most important role, however, is one of a mother and wife. In 2003, Akers married attorney Steve Eichenblatt, and together they have a son, Cody.

Recently, Michelle Akers was named to the FIFA 100, a list dedicated to the greatest living soccer players. This is an amazing accomplishment considering Mia Hamm was the only other American honored. It also attests to her level of talent; however, it cannot begin to depict her incredible contribution to the game of soccer. As one of the biggest trailblazers in the sport, she laid the foundation for the future of U.S. women's soccer, and she illustrated, better than anyone else, what it means to play with tremendous courage and heart.

Notes

1. Judith A. Nelson, "Michelle's Higher Goal," *Today's Christian*, http://www.christianitytoday.com/tc/2000/ 002/1.18.html. March/April 2000.

2. Pocantico Hills Central School, "Michelle Akers," http://www.pocanticohills.org/womenenc/akers.htm (accessed September 11, 2008).

3. Nelson, "Michelle's Higher Goal."

4. Ibid.

5. Ibid.

Mia Hamm

Future Hall of Famer

by Sara Jane Baker

Courtesy of the UNC Athletic Communications Office.

Mia Hamm is arguably the greatest women's soccer player to ever play the game. She made numerous appearances on the national and Olympic teams, and she broke almost every record imaginable. Although her name will probably remain in the record books indefinitely, her records alone cannot describe everything she has done, not only for the sport of soccer but for all women's sports. Hamm has become one of the most recognizable females in sports, a cultural icon, and a hero for men and women around the world. Her popularity has brought attention to the sport of soccer, as well as creating other opportunities for women in sports.

Friends and family remember her athleticism from a very young age. Born in 1972, the same year Title IX was passed, Hamm spent most of her childhood trying to keep up with her older brother, Garrett. She played every sport, particularly basketball, soccer, and football. Although her athletic talent was prevalent across all sports, at the age of 14, she decided to focus solely on soccer. Hamm was so gifted at soccer that she moved from her home in Wichita Falls, Texas, to Virginia to finish high school and play on a superior soccer team. At age 15, Hamm made the record books for the first of many times as the youngest player to be named to the U.S. National Soccer Team.

Hamm took her talents to perennial powerhouse, the University of North Carolina (UNC) at Chapel Hill. She led the Tar Heels to four National Collegiate Athletic Association (NCAA) women's championships, earning multiple All-American, All-Atlantic Coast Conference (ACC) player, and ACC Female Athlete of the Year honors

along the way. Hamm was so dominant on her soccer team and on
UNC's campus that she was nicknamed "Jordan" after fellow UNC
student-athlete, Michael Jordan.
Her legacy at UNC still remains, as
she is the all-time record holder in
the ACC for goals, assists, and total
points. Realizing that there will
never be another person quite like
Mia Hamm, the University of North
Carolina retired Hamm's number,
19, in 1994.[1]

Her incredible soccer career
did not stop after college, as she
continued to play on the U.S. National Team. Although Hamm plays
the position of forward, she is often
considered the best all-around
player due to her versatility on the
field. In fact, she has even played
goalie. Over the course of her career, she participated in four World
Cups and three Olympic Games and
played a major role in the United
States' World Cup victories in 1991
and 1999 and the Olympic gold
medals in 1996 and 2004. Seeing as
she has scored goals in 13 countries
against 25 different national teams,
it is not surprising that she is the
world's leading scorer in international competition among both men
and women with 158 goals. Her
success has earned her numerous
awards, including U.S. Soccer's
Female Athlete of the Year, Team
MVP, and ESPY's Female Athlete
of Year. Hamm retired after the

Courtesy of the UNC Athletic Communications Office.

2004 Olympics, spending a remarkable span of 17 years on the U.S. National team.

Her achievements on the soccer field have catapulted her to celebrity status off the field. *People Magazine* named Hamm one of the 50 most beautiful people in 1997 and Nike, a long-time sponsor of Hamm, named the largest building on its corporate campus in Oregon after her.[2] She also authored a book entitled *Go for the Goal: A Champion's Guide to Winning in Soccer and Life*. With all this success and attention, many would believe Hamm would overshadow her incredible teammates, but that was not the case. Hamm was quoted in the *Boston Globe* saying, "There's no 'me' in Mia and no 'Ham' in Hamm."[3] Hamm and her teammates have symbolized the essence of team unity. Although Hamm may be the cover girl of soccer, she realizes that much of her success came with the help of her teammates. Her appreciation of teamwork extends to bettering society and her dedication to various causes.

In 1999, Hamm started the Mia Foundation, which focuses on raising funds to cure bone marrow diseases and developing programs for young women in sports. With the help from founding partners Nike, Mattel, and Gatorade, the Mia Foundation is able to focus on two very different missions, but they are similar in that they are both issues that Hamm is passionate about.[4]

In 1996, Hamm's best friend, hero, and older brother, Garrett, died of aplastic anemia, a rare blood disorder. As Hamm was preparing for the 1996 Olympics, she stood by her brother when the doctors told Garrett that there was nothing more they could do. With the pain of this news in her heart, Hamm went to Atlanta to compete in the Olympic debut of women's soccer. Garrett watched from the sidelines, as even his illness could not stop him from supporting his sister and her teammates as they went on to beat China to win the Olympic gold medal. Since his death, Hamm has been committed to the research and fundraising efforts of bone marrow diseases. In 2001, the Mia Foundation held the first Garrett Game. The Garrett Game is an exhibition game that features all-star players as well as All-American college players. It has since become an annual event that raises awareness and funds for bone marrow disease research and causes.

Hamm also realizes how fortunate she has been in her life, and she wants to be able to provide young women everywhere with the same opportunities. Hamm credits the pioneers in her sport for the opportunities, and she wants to ensure that the progress of women continues to grow.

Now that Hamm is retired from soccer, she faces a new challenge: motherhood. In 2007, Hamm and her husband, baseball player Nomar Garciaparra, became the parents of twin girls. Since her retirement from soccer, she is anxious to devote her life to something else. Hamm admits that she will miss playing the game, but she will contribute to the sport in new ways. Not only will she be a spectator, but she plans on being involved in the women's professional soccer league that will be launched in 2009.[5] Although soccer saw an incredible player and pioneer for women's sports hang up her cleats, Mia Hamm's impact both on and off the field will be seen by generations to come.

Notes

1. "About Mia," *Mia Hamm Foundation*, http://www.miafoundation.org/about mia.asp (accessed April 4, 2008).

2. Landon Hall, "Mia Hamm Deals with Celebrity Status," *AP Online*, June 5, 1999.

3. John Powers, "No 'me' in Mia. She's her sport's most recognizable-and perhaps best-player, but for US star Hamm, the team comes first," *The Boston Globe*, June 18, 1999.

4. "Our Mission," *Mia Hamm Foundation*, www.miafoundation.org (accessed April 4, 2008).

5. Billy Witz, "Momma Mia facing the best women's soccer teams was nothing compared to Hamm's latest endeavor—being the mother of 9-month-old twin daughters," *Daily News*, January 5, 2008.

Julie Foudy

Future Hall of Famer

by Sara Jane Baker

On July 10, 1999, fans from around the world watched as the U.S. Women's National Soccer team defeated China in the World Cup. The 11 players on the field proved that with focus, perseverance, teamwork, and sportsmanship, a team could accomplish anything. Men and women from all over the world admired these women for their amazing soccer skills and ability to perform under pressure. One of these players, midfielder and co-captain Julie Foudy, is giving fans another reason to cheer for her.

From a very early age it was clear that the San Diego native had a gift for soccer. In high school Foudy earned All-American honors and was named Player of the Year in Southern California for three straight years. Her first appearance on the U.S. National Team came at the young age of 16.[1]

This early success earned her a scholarship to Stanford University. While in college, the impressive awards continued. In 1991, she was named Soccer America Player of the Year. For three consecutive years, she was named the team MVP. She was also a four-time National Collegiate Athletic Association (NCAA) All-American. Despite all this success in soccer, Foudy was never solely defined by her athletic abilities at Stanford. In college, Foudy epitomized the true meaning behind the term "student-athlete," earning a biology degree and then being accepted to Stanford's prestigious medical school. Yet, she decided to forgo medical school to pursue her dream of playing professional soccer. She would later be inducted into the Stanford Hall of Fame for her contributions as a student-athlete, and she was recently named one of the "100 Most Influential NCAA Student-Athletes."[2]

Foudy would go on to play for the U.S. National Team for 18 years, serving as a co-captain during her entire tenure with the team. Playing in four Women's World Cups and three Olympic Games, Foudy, along with her teammates Mia Hamm, Joy Fawcett, and Brandi Chastain, were often said to represent "the golden era" of women's soccer. Many people credit them for bringing popularity and attention to the sport. When Foudy retired from soccer in 2004, she had played in 271 international games, ranking her third all-time among men and women soccer players.

Her impact does not stop there. Besides embodying everything a student-athlete truly should be, Foudy used her notoriety to bring attention to important, yet controversial issues. She has been a political and social activist for issues ranging from women's rights, to child rights, to fair labor standards. In the late 1990s, Foudy questioned the labor practices of her sponsor, Reebok, for using young children to stitch their soccer balls. Her work earned her the FIFA Fair Play Award, an honor never previously bestowed on a female. Additionally, Foudy served as the president for the Women's Sports Foundation (WSF), a nonprofit organization designed to change the lives of girls through sports. With the WSF, Foudy focused a lot of her energy on Title IX. In 2005, when the Commission on Opportunity in Athletics threatened to weaken Title IX, Foudy was one of the first to protest. Her efforts paid off as many of the Commission's recommendations were never implemented.

One of Foudy's biggest contributions to society came after the birth of her first daughter, Isabel Ann, on January 1, 2007. Having a daughter of her own gave Foudy a special interest in opportunities for women. She wanted to make sure her daughter would grow up in a society where she could do and be anything. Not only did Foudy want this for her daughter, but she wanted it for every daughter around the country. This belief was the inspiration behind creating the Julie Foudy Sports Leadership Academy.

The Leadership Academy was created in 2007 by Foudy and her husband, Ian Sawyers. The goal of the academy is to teach girls, ages 12–18, how to be leaders on and off the field through the sport of soccer. Among other topics, the curriculum focuses on leadership values, community involvement, public speaking, and team building. Additionally, the academy addresses diversity. In the past, Billie Jean King has served as a keynote speaker, as well as other leaders from diverse backgrounds. The Leadership Academy always addresses Title IX, and the impact it has on women.[3]

In a world where athletes are defined by simply their athletic abilities, Julie Foudy is an exception. Foudy is not only an athlete, but a political and social activist, scholar, mother, and leader. Foudy has made an impact in nearly every aspect of her life. With Foudy's leadership academy, she hopes to "build tomorrow's leaders and to use soccer as a vehicle to do it."[4] What better person to teach this to young girls? After all, she is and has been a leader in every sense of the word.

Notes

1. Julie Foudy Soccer Camps, "Staff," http://www.juliefoudysoccercamps.com/soccer_camp_core_staff_for_2006.htm (accessed July 10, 2008).

2. Ibid.

3. Julie Foudy Leadership Academy, "Academy Philosophy," http://www.juliefoudyleadership.com (accessed July 10, 2008).

4. Ann Killion, "Former Soccer Star Julie Foudy Passing on Her Life's Work to Youth," *San Jose Mercury News*, May 31, 2007.

10

WOMEN'S SOFTBALL AND WOMEN IN BASEBALL: STANDING TALL FOR FEMALES FOR DECADES

Introduction by Richard Lapchick

The year 1996 is often talked about as the year of women in the Olympics. Women's soccer and basketball were expected to be huge and they were. There were high expectations but no way to know what the new sport of softball would bring. It turned out to be huge, especially for the dominant team from the United States. These Olympic athletes became instant global celebrities as 120,000 fans packed the stadium to watch the games in person. A short nine years and two more gold medals later, the International Olympic Committee (IOC) pulled softball—and baseball—as Olympic sports at the IOC meetings in Singapore in 2005. I was at those meetings as part of the delegation for the New York City bid for the 2012 Olympics. To say that the anti-George Bush sentiment was strong is an understatement and I believe it affected the vote on softball. A majority was needed to keep the sport and the vote was 52-52!

The Olympics were not so important for baseball, which lost 54-50. It seemed like a blow to women's sport in general and the fight began to get softball back. As of this writing, the battle is still on and is being waged by a movement called Back Softball.

Softball has been a rich source of athletic competition for American women and was enormously popular even before the passage of Title IX.

The modern era of softball took off during the Chicago World's Fair in 1933, when a Chicago newspaper and a local business man got 55 teams to compete at the Fairgrounds. There were three divisions: men's fastpitch, men's slowpitch, and women's softball. The male and female champions were honored equally.

More than 350,000 people packed the stadium for the competitions and the branding of the sport began and enabled it to move away from its Midwestern roots. Sports historians estimated that within a decade five million Americans were playing softball. Many were women.

Women were also playing—and excelling—in baseball. Major League Baseball Commissioner Judge Kenesaw Mountain Landis banned women from professional baseball in 1931 after 17-year-old pitcher Virne Beatrice "Jackie" Mitchell struck out Babe Ruth and Lou Gehrig in an exhibition game for the Chattanooga Lookouts. Landis voided Mitchell's contract, saying baseball is "too strenuous" for women.

The Negro Leagues also kept women out, but not Toni Stone who eventually worked her way through the Negro minor leagues to sign with the Indianapolis Clowns in 1953. She replaced their previous second baseman whose contract had just been sold to the Boston Braves for $10,000 after he batted .380 for the Clowns. The player Stone replaced was Henry "Hank" Aaron. But women playing men's baseball was far from the norm.

We have included the story of Effa Manley because she played such a unique role in baseball. Effa and her husband Abe, were the owners of the Brooklyn Eagles (which would later gain fame as the Newark Eagles), which joined the Negro National League (NNL) in 1935. Effa was white and Abe was African-American. She could best be described as the team's business manager—which essentially put her in charge of nearly everything concerning the Eagles except for the actual playing of the games. Effa was responsible for the schedule, travel, publicity, advertising, purchasing, concessions, negotiating player contracts, ball park operations, marketing, ticket sales, and community relations programs. There are few if any women in 2008 with responsibilities of this magnitude with any sports franchise. Manley was definitely one of a kind 60 years ago.

Toni Stone, born Marcenia Lyle, became the first woman to play professional baseball when she broke the gender barrier in 1953. She learned to play the game on the playgrounds of St. Paul, Minnesota, with the boys in her neighborhood, and later in the Catholic Midget League. As a child, determined to participate in the sport she loved, she collected Wheaties cereal box tops to exchange for a chance to be in a baseball club the cereal was sponsoring. Unlike most women, she did not get her start in softball.

But softball has produced so many stars, including the women we highlight in this section. Lisa Fernandez, Joan Joyce, Margie Wright, Sharon Backus, Michelle Akers, and Dr. Dot Richardson are the pantheon of stars. Donna Lopiano could have been in this section but her advocacy efforts for Title IX and leadership at the Women's Sports Foundation have her elsewhere in the book. Joyce, Wright, and Backus have become legendary coaches.

Lisa Fernandez is the youngest of the five. In high school she amassed 12 perfect games, 69 shutouts, 80 career victories, 1,503 career strikeouts, and an amazing 0.07 ERA.

She then went to UCLA, where she led the Bruins to the National Collegiate Athletic Association (NCAA) Women's College World Series four times. They won the national title in 1990 and 1992. Fernandez was a three-time Honda Award winner, an honor given to the nation's best softball player and won the 1992–93 Honda-Broderick Cup for being the nation's top collegiate female athlete.

Fernandez had an NCAA record winning percentage of .930 (93-7). She broke seven school records and led the nation in hitting and pitching her senior year with a .510 batting average and an ERA of 0.25. Her career ERA of 0.22 still stands second in the NCAA history books.

She helped the U.S. win three Olympic gold medals. Lisa was both the top pitcher and hitter in the 2004 Games in Athens, where she set a new record for batting average in Olympic history with a .545 average.

Two-time Olympic softball gold medalist Dr. Dot Richardson was much more than just a star shortstop. Richardson, who hit the first homerun ever in Olympic softball, became an orthopedic surgeon while training for the U.S. Olympic team. In addition to being a star softball player, Dot played basketball for UCLA her freshman and senior year. She considers her greatest moment in sports to be hitting the game-winning homerun to win the gold medal in the 1996 Olympic Games, the year softball debuted. She is currently vice chair of the President's Council on Fitness and a hero to girls aspiring to all kinds of new heights.

At age 16, Joan Joyce had become good enough to join the Raybestos Brakettes, the most legendary and powerful team in women's softball. An injury to the Brakettes' starting pitcher in 1958 launched Joyce into the spotlight as the team's new hurler. Just 18 years old, she led the team to a national championship, pitching a no-hitter in the title game.

During her time with the Brakettes, Joyce won 429 games while losing only 27. She struck out 5,677 batters in 3,397 innings pitched, and threw 105 no-hitters and an incredible 33 perfect games. In 1974, she led the Brakettes to a world title in the third International Softball Federation (ISF) Women's World Championship. Joyce holds a career pitching record of an astonishing 753 wins and 42 losses, including 150 no-hit, no-run games and 50 perfect games.

Joyce played on 12 national championship teams, was an 18-time American Softball Association (ASA) All-American, and won or shared the MVP award in the Women's National Championship eight times.

She did not limit her time to softball. Joyce was a three-time Amateur Athletic Union (AAU) basketball All-American at Chapman College (now Chapman University), setting a national tournament single game scoring record with 67 points. Joyce was also a four-time Women's Basketball Association All-American and played on the U.S. National Team in 1965.

Joyce was a 19-year member of the Ladies Professional Golf Association (LPGA) from 1977 to 1995, recording a low round of 66.

In 1994, Joyce established the women's softball program at Florida Atlantic University, where she has amassed nine A-Sun Conference Championships and one Sun Belt Conference Championship.

As a student-athlete at Illinois State University, Margie Wright cherished her time and graduated with 11 varsity letters spread across the sports of basketball, softball, and field hockey and, more important, a defined purpose for her life. Inspired by her interactions with a former coach, Wright decided that she too would coach female athletes in order to help provide them with hope, direction, and the best opportunities possible.

Wright took the reins at her alma mater in 1980, leading the Redbird softball program to the 1981 Association for Intercollegiate Athletics for Women (AIAW) Softball College World Series. In six years as head coach, Wright won 163 games with a .638 winning percentage and two conference titles. That was for starters.

After 24 seasons as the coach of the Fresno State Bulldog softball team, Wright is the winningest coach in NCAA softball. She is one of two coaches in any collegiate sport to have ever won over 1,300 games and was the only coach at Fresno State to have brought home a National Championship (1998) until the men's team won the 2008 College World Series. She has coached 53 All-Americans, 15 Olympians, 16 Academic All-Americans, and four NCAA Postgraduate Scholarship Award winners. The Bulldogs have averaged 50 wins a season and are among the leaders in Women's College World Series trips with 10 appearances, including three third-place and three runner-up finishes in addition to its national title.

Sharron Backus played softball in the pre-Title IX era, so she never became a college player. But what a college coach she made, becoming the women's equivalent of John Wooden as the Wizards of Westwood at UCLA. She spent her college years playing for the powerful Orange (California) Lionettes, winning a national championship and earning All-American honors. She was picked up by the Raybestos Brakettes. As a Brakette, Backus's shortstop play contributed greatly to the team's success, which included five consecutive national championships from 1971 to 1975.

But it is her coaching career which will always be remembered. Over 22 seasons at UCLA (1975–96), Backus amassed a career record of 854-173. The Bruins captured eight national championships. The team's NCAA glory years included three consecutive national titles (1988, 1989, and 1990), 10 Pac-10 titles, 18 postseason appearances, and 15 national top-four finishes.

During Backus's era, Bruin softball produced nine Olympians, including Dot Richardson and Lisa Fernandez, 53 All-Americans, and 24 U.S. National Team Members. Thus three of the six softball figures in this section were Bruins. All six and the two baseball figures were amazing.

Marcenia Lyle Alberga a.k.a. Toni Stone

American Star of the Women's International Sports Hall of Fame

by Ryan Sleeper

Upon first glance, there was nothing unusual about the 1953 Negro League baseball game taking place in Omaha, Nebraska, that Easter Sunday afternoon. Legendary pitcher Satchel Paige was on the mound throwing a no-hitter for the St. Louis Browns. As another probable strikeout victim entered the batter's box, Satchel, as he often did just to give the opposition a chance, asked where the batter wanted him to throw it. "You want it high? You want it low? You want it in the middle? Just say. How do you like it?" The batter responded, "It doesn't matter."[1] The batter then proceeded to lace a single right over Satchel's head into center field. Overjoyed by this rare occurrence, the batter barely made it to first base and fell while rounding the bag. The batter would later describe this as the happiest moment in her life. Not surprisingly, this was the only hit Satchel allowed that day. In fact, there was really only one surprise that day when it was revealed the batter was actually a woman.

Toni Stone, born Marcenia Lyle, became the first woman to play professional baseball when she broke the gender barrier in 1953.[2] She learned to play the game on the playgrounds of St. Paul, Minnesota, where she was raised by her father, a barber, and her mother, a beautician. "They would have stopped me if they could," Stone recalls, "but there was nothing they could do about it."[3] Unlike most women, she did not get her start in softball. She played pickup games of baseball with the boys in her neighborhood, and later in the Catholic Midget League. As a child, determined to participate in the sport she loved, she collected Wheaties cereal box tops to exchange for a chance to be in a baseball club the cereal was sponsoring. She realized from an early age that she was different from the other girls and described herself as an "outcast" because she was not interested in adopting traditional roles reserved for women.[4] Gabby Street, the big league catcher and later manager of the world champion St. Louis Cardinals, was a huge influence on

Stone in her early playing days. After he was demoted to managing the minor league team, the St. Paul Saints, he established a baseball school near Stone. After she pestered him enough to play, she was finally given a chance to participate. When Gabby saw of what Stone was capable, he sponsored her by buying her a pair of cleats and admitting her into his school.

When Stone was 15 years old, she moved to San Francisco with less than a dollar in her pocket to find an ailing sister. This move would prove propitious for Stone's career in professional baseball. After bouncing between jobs, doing everything from making salads in a cafeteria to operating forklifts in the shipyards, she discovered Jack's Tavern, a popular social-gathering place for African-Americans. There she met tavern-owner, Al Love, who helped her get a spot on an American Legion team.[5] From there she earned a roster spot on a semiprofessional team called the San Francisco Sea Lions. However, she soon began to feel like the owner was not paying her what he had promised. As she became accustomed to a career in a male-dominated society, Stone learned to stand up for herself.

Upon receiving a better offer from another team while on a road trip through New Orleans, she decided to stay and play for the New Orleans Black Pelicans, a Negro League farm team. She would eventually move to the New Orleans Creoles, another farm team for the Negro League, where she made up to $300 a month.[6]

Stone's big break in baseball would come in 1953, when Syd Pollack, owner of the Indianapolis Clowns, signed her to her first major league contract. The Clowns, a major Negro League team, were often referred to as the Harlem Globetrotters of baseball. They earned this reputation because of their frequent publicity stunts, but the Clowns' owner insisted that hiring Stone was a legitimate baseball move. In his defense, the Clowns had toned down their antics, and were actually one of the top-rated teams when she was signed, having won the league championship in 1950. Also, the team really did need to fill a void at second base. After all, their previous second baseman's contract had just been sold to the Boston Braves for $10,000 after he batted .380 for the Clowns.[7] The player Stone replaced was Henry "Hank" Aaron.

It is interesting to note that Stone might not have had the opportunity to break the gender barrier in baseball if Jackie Robinson had not broke the color barrier in baseball just six years earlier in

1947. As a result, many of the best African-American players defected to Major League Baseball, and therefore, the Negro League owners had to look toward new avenues to compete on the field and at the gate. The irony is, Stone originally sought out to break the color barrier in women's baseball in the All-American Girls Baseball League, but upon being turned away because of the color of her skin, she went back to what she was accustomed to, playing on teams with all men and defied history. She really had no interest in being the first woman to play in men's baseball, only that she had an opportunity to play at all. "I come to play ball," she declared after signing with the Clowns. "Women have got just as much right to play baseball as men."[8]

While some players and fans were receptive to this pioneer, she also gracefully endured a great deal of sexist treatment. One of the first things requested of her upon her move to the major leagues was that she wear a skirt while playing to add sex appeal to the games for male spectators. Again, being the strong woman that she was, she refused to do so saying, she would quit before accommodating that particular idea. Stone was also frequently the victim of "spikes-up" slides at second base from male players who resented having to share the field with a woman. Sliding with the spikes on the bottom of the cleats "up," or toward the fielder, is an unsportsmanlike action with the intention of physically harming the opposition. Once, one of her own teammates even lobbed the ball to her for a play at second base in order for the play to take longer to develop, increasing the probability of a collision. Stone prided herself on standing in to take the unwarranted punishment and still make the plays, even bragging about the scars on her legs from her playing days.

Beyond the unequal treatment from her co-workers was the routine emotional abuse from the fans. "They'd tell me to go home and fix my husband some biscuits, or any damn thing. Just get the hell away from here,"[9] remembers Stone. The press was also often unkind. Doc Young of the *Chicago Defender* once wrote, "Girls should be run out of men's baseball on a softly padded rail for their own good. This could get to be a woman's world with men just living in it."[10] Being the humble and forgiving woman that she was, she reacted by saying, "They didn't mean any harm and in their way they liked me. Just that I wasn't supposed to be there."[11] That last point is arguable, as Stone was touted as a solid infielder who frequently made unassisted double plays at second base and batted a respectable .243 in her 50 games with the Clowns before being traded to the Kansas City Monarchs.

Following an unpleasant year in Kansas City where she did not receive a lot of playing time, Stone retired after the 1954 season. She moved back to Oakland, California, with her husband, Aurelious Alberga, who was a pioneer in his own right, being credited as the first black officer in the U.S. Army.[12] She worked as a nurse in Oakland for many years, but continued to play recreational baseball until the age of 60. Toni Stone passed away in 1996 of heart failure at the age of 75. She was honored before her death when St. Paul, Minnesota, declared March 6, 1990, as "Toni Stone Day." She would later have an athletic field and a play named after her in St. Paul. The play, Tomboy Stone, paid homage to her chosen nickname, Toni, which she picked because it sounded like "Tomboy." Tributes to Toni Stone can be found in the Baseball Hall of Fame in Cooperstown, New York, as well as in the Negro League Baseball Museum in Kansas City, Missouri. Stone once told a teammate, "A woman has her dreams, too."[13] Being such a modest human being, grateful just to play baseball, I would have to doubt that even in her wildest dreams she could imagine her story being such a lasting inspiration to female athletes all over the world.

Notes

1. Gai Berlage, *Women in Baseball* (Westport, Conn.: Praeger, 1994), 128.

2. Barbara Gregorich, *Women at Play: the Story of Women in Baseball* (San Diego, Calif.: Harvest, 1993), 173.

3. Ibid., 169.

4. Judy Hasday, *Extraordinary Women Athletes* (Danbury, Conn.: Children's Press, 2000), 46.

5. Martha Ackmann, "Baseball Was Her Game," *SFGate*, March 12, 2006, http://www.sfgate.com/cgi-bin/article.cgi?file=/chronicle/archive/2006/03/12/ING4THK SUN1.DTL (accessed February 9, 2008).

6. Gregorich, *Women at Play*, 171.

7. Ibid., 173.

8. Ibid.

9. Ibid., 174.

10. Ackmann, "Baseball Was Her Game."

11. Gregorich, *Women at Play*, 174.

12. Ibid., 175.

13. Hasday, *Extraordinary Women Athletes*, 45.

Effa Manley

A Racial and Gender Pioneer

Special Contribution by William A. Sutton

The accomplishments of Effa Manley would be noteworthy regardless of the enterprise in which she worked. The fact that she worked in the business of sport in the 1930s and 1940s, which at the time was almost exclusively a male endeavor, is remarkable—and given she was a woman in an interracial marriage to an African-American entrepreneur whose biggest interests were gambling and baseball makes her story that much more intriguing and inspirational.

Effa Manley and her husband Abe, the owners of the Brooklyn Eagles (which would later gain fame as the Newark Eagles), joined the Negro National League (NNL) in 1935. Abe spent most of his time recruiting and acquiring players for the team, which meant Effa was left running the business of the baseball club—an area in which she would excel. As Effa learned more and more about the business of baseball, she became an outspoken advocate and defender of black baseball. The Eagles moved to Newark for the 1936 season, thus beginning an intriguing relationship between black baseball, the city of Newark (which had a much larger black population than Brooklyn), and the marketing and management skills of Effa Manley.

While always chasing the perennial champion Homestead Grays, the Newark Eagles fielded a winning team almost every year and had some of the most high-profile players in the NNL. Players like Monte Irvin, Ray Dandridge, Willie Wells, George "Mule" Suttles, Larry Doby, and Don Newcombe helped the Eagles attract large crowds of up to 10,000 spectators, causing a writer to remark that the Eagles were to (black) Newark what the Dodgers were to Brooklyn. Effa Manley was one of the first owners to understand the link between popularity on the field and popularity in the community. While Abe built a solid foundation on the field, it was Manley who developed the complementary relationship in which Newark helped the Eagles and the Eagles helped Newark. She made sure that the team had an image of upholding the black community's best standards—and was heavily involved in using the Eagles as a platform for cause marketing initiatives for the NAACP, career opportunities for blacks in medicine, social organizations such as the Black Elks lodges, and fundraisers for various local schools and other community-based organizations.

Effa Manley, like contemporary Cleveland Indians Owner Bill Veeck, also realized the value of a ticket and the importance of price integrity—neither was interested in giving away free tickets—but both promoted the idea of selling tickets (and in turn, having people from the benefiting organization sell the tickets) and donating a portion of the proceeds to some type of cause marketing initiative. One of the more interesting examples of this type of endeavor occurred in 1941, when Manley and the Eagles were enlisted to help raise funds for the local Jewish community center by playing an exhibition game against the well-known white barnstorming team, House of David.

The one thing that set Manley apart from many of her contemporaries was her ability to see the value of long-term marketing initiatives—those initiatives with more of a future impact on financial fortunes rather than an immediate return. Sponsoring youth baseball teams in order to teach young people about the game and to create an ongoing relationship between the youth and the game was a viable long-term growth strategy—growing and developing a market to ensure the long-term stability of the team. Perhaps if more people would have thought like Effa Manley, there would be more African-Americans playing and watching baseball in 2008 than the current levels, which have been dropping annually.

Manley's role could best be described as the team's business manager—which essentially put her in charge of nearly everything concerning the Eagles that occurred in Newark except for the actual playing of the games. This meant that Manley was responsible for the schedule, travel, publicity, advertising, purchasing, concessions, player contract negotiations, ballpark operations, marketing and ticket sales, as well as the aforementioned community relations programs. There are few, if any women, in 2008 with responsibilities of this magnitude with any sport franchise—so imagine how unique this was when it occurred more than 60 years ago.

As Effa was met with more and more success, Abe Manley began turning more and more of the operations of the Eagles over to her until it grew to the point that she had final say in everything—including hiring managers and ultimately overseeing the sale of players to the now integrated major leagues. As the NNL and the Eagles were disbanding, Manley battled with the likes of Branch Rickey over the fate of Monte Irvin and she made her point and was able to sell Irvin to the New York Giants. How ironic is it that the widely anticipated integration of Major League Baseball in 1947 would lead to the ultimate devastation of one of the most visible black enterprises in the United States, the Negro baseball leagues?

The demise of the NNL and the Newark Eagles meant that she did not have any day-to-day baseball responsibilities—but Manley's baseball related work was not complete. She worked tirelessly, until her death in 1981, to gain recognition for great Negro League players like Satchel Paige, Josh Gibson, Biz Mackey, and many others by the Baseball Hall of Fame. Manley was also involved in oral baseball histories and film documentaries about the Negro Leagues such as Craig Davidson's film *The Sun was Always Shining Someplace*. Manley's dream would become a reality in 1971—and she would have been even more pleased in 2008, when all of the surviving Negro league players were "drafted" by major league teams as a gesture to compensate for overlooking these players and excluding them from the mainstream version of the game they loved.

Effa Manley was a driven force when she found challenges and satisfaction in the management of a men's game. Sadly, there are few women pioneers who worked in the sports industry at the levels and with the accomplishments of Effa Manley—but more than 60 years later she is still a source of pride, accomplishment, and aspiration for the women of today.

Sharron Backus

American Star of the Women's International Sports Hall of Fame

by Catherine Lahey

There will only ever be one John Wooden, a respected, modest legend who is considered by many to be the greatest athletic coach of all time. In 27 seasons as head men's basketball coach at UCLA, Wooden led his Bruins to 10 National Collegiate Athletic Association (NCAA) championships, seven of them consecutive. His teams captured 19 conference crowns and he coached four perfect, undefeated seasons. He is the mastermind of the Pyramid of Success and the originator of some of the most eloquent and intelligent advice for sports and life. ESPN named him the "Greatest Coach of the Twentieth Century" and he has been inducted into the National Basketball Hall of Fame as both a player and a coach.[1] The name "Wooden" is universally synonymous with humble success. Although Wooden is cemented firmly at the apex of the coaching profession, many would be surprised to know that there is an equally successful, female Wizard of Westwood.

Born in 1946, Sharron Backus became interested in sports as a girl growing up in a neighborhood full of boys. Backus says, "I loved the outdoors and I loved physical activity. Playing sports was a way for me to fit and be accepted by my peers. When I went out to play with or against the boys, I had to be just as good as they were."[2] Backus soon developed into an excellent athlete, a fact that was not lost on local California coaches. At the time, opportunities for females in athletics were largely spread by word of mouth and by the ages of 12 and 13, Backus was getting offers to play on teams in a number of different sports. Although her parents never pushed her toward athletic achievement, they encouraged her by providing her with the opportunity to play and follow her own dreams.

During her high school years, Backus was playing softball with the Whittier Gold Sox in addition to competing in basketball, golf, swimming, and volleyball, among other sports. In 1961, Backus helped the Gold Sox to a national title while earning second team All-American recognition. Since Backus's college, Cal State Fullerton, did not offer women's athletics, she spent her college years playing for the powerful Orange (California) Lionettes, winning another national championship and again earning All-American honors. By that time Backus had developed into one of the most gifted and dedicated players in the sport and was picked up by an equally legendary and successful team, the Raybestos Brakettes. As a Brakette shortstop, Backus contributed greatly to the team's success, which included five consecutive national championships from 1971 to 1975.[3] Much like John Wooden, Backus elevated herself to the top of her sport as an athlete before beginning an incredible career as a coach.

In 1975, Backus received an incredible offer. Although she had never coached softball, Backus was hired by UCLA to lead the Bruin softball team into a new era in women's athletics. Backus is still in awe by the offer. "The mere fact that UCLA would give me that opportunity still amazes me. Even though I played for great coaches like Margo Davis and Ralph Raymond, all of my personal coaching experiences were in something other than softball."[4] The chance that UCLA took on an incredible athlete and unproven coach paid unimaginable dividends. A decorated champion herself, Backus immediately went about inspiring a champion's drive and discipline in her student-athletes. Together, Backus and her Bruin teams achieved a level of success mirroring that of their counterparts in UCLA men's basketball during the Wooden era.

Over 22 seasons at UCLA (1975–96), Backus amassed a career record of 854 wins, 173 losses, and three ties, numbers which equate to a Wooden-esque winning percentage of .831. During her tenure the Bruins captured eight national championships, one under the auspices of the Association for Intercollegiate Athletics for Women (AIAW) and the other seven through the NCAA. The team's NCAA glory years included three consecutive national titles (1988, 1989, and 1990), 10 Pac-10 titles, 18 postseason appearances, and 15 national top four finishes.

During Backus's era, Bruin softball produced nine Olympians, including Dot Richardson and Honda-Broderick Cup Winner Lisa Fernandez, 53 All-Americans, and 24 U.S. National Team members. In addition to leading the Bruins to these incredible heights, Backus has been inducted into numerous halls of fame for her outstanding talents as both a player and a coach.[5] Looking back, Backus calls her years at the helm of Bruin softball an "unbelievable ride."[6]

Backus began and ended her collegiate coaching career as a Bruin. She would later go on to coach professionally and also serve as director of player personnel for the women's professional league. As a coach, she revisited her previous successes by leading the Orlando Wahoos to a League Championship in her first year season with the league. Her legend only grew stronger.

Although their excellence as UCLA coaches links them together, what is most similar about Sharron Backus and John Wooden is their insistence on growing and encouraging the whole person and their humility about their own achievements. Athletic achievement was important to both coaches, but never at the expense of greater life lessons and the discovery of the true meaning of success. Backus continues to follow that philosophy today, giving these encouraging words to young athletes. "Follow your dreams" she says, putting the emphasis on the individual. "The dreams have to be yours—not your cousin's dreams, or your uncle's dreams or your mother's dreams. You have to really know what that dream is within yourself and then you must work hard to achieve it."[7] This is the greatest gift, the greatest teaching, that both Wooden and Backus have instilled in their student-athletes. It is the gift of opportunity, the gift of courage, the gift of belief. It is the gift of the Wizards of Westwood.

Notes

1. "John Wooden: A Coaching Legend," Men's Basketball, UCLA Athletics, http://uclabruins.cstv.com/sports/m-baskbl/spec-rel/ucla-wooden-page.html.

2. Sharon Backus, telephone interview with Catherine Lahey, May 27, 2008.

3. Nena Rey Hawkes and John F. Seggar, *Celebrating Women Coaches: A Biographical Dictionary* (Greenwood Publishing Group, 2000) 9–15.

4. Sharon Backus, telephone interview with Catherine Lahey, May 27, 2008.

5. "Head Coach Sharron Backus," UCLA 2008 Softball Media Guide.

6. Sharon Backus, telephone interview with Catherine Lahey, May 27, 2008.

7. Ibid.

Margie Wright

American Star of the Women's International Sports Hall of Fame

by Catherine Lahey

Like so many other women in sports, Margie Wright's first experiences with athletics were marked by disappointment. As a 10-year-old in Illinois, Wright was banned from playing Little League because of her gender. After she had been crying inconsolably for days, Wright's father finally convinced her to play for him on an all-girls team.[1] Although Wright was the one immediately saddened, it was the Little League Association that should have been crying. Through the dedication of her parents, the little girl the Association turned away became one of the most talented athletes the area had ever seen. Today, Wright is thankful for the opportunities that came of her initial denial, saying, "My experiences as a player and coach in the sport of softball have been phenomenal. Not only did I have the opportunity as a young girl to play at the highest level available because of my mom and dad, but that led me to a career that has allowed me to accomplish every possible goal a player or coach would ever dream to accomplish."[2] Despite, or perhaps because of, the adversity she faced, Wright dedicated her life to the promotion of athletic and professional opportunities for young women.

Contributing to this personal calling were Wright's experiences as a college athlete. Even though facilities and amenities for female athletes were often scarce, Wright cherished her time as a student-athlete at Illinois State University. She graduated with 11 varsity letters spread across the sports of basketball, softball, and field hockey and, more important, a defined purpose for her life. Inspired by her interactions with a former coach, Wright decided that she too would coach female athletes in order to help provide them with hope, direction, and the best opportunities possible.[3]

Wright immediately became head softball, basketball, volleyball, track, and bowling coach at Metamora High School in Illinois, mentoring a number of young women. Soon, she returned to collegiate athletics as a volleyball and softball coach at Eastern Illinois University. Wright found her way back to her alma mater in 1980, taking the reins of the Redbird softball program and quickly leading them to the 1981 Association for Intercollegiate Athletics for Women (AIAW) Softball College World Series. In six years as head coach at Illinois State, Wright amassed 163 wins, a .638 winning percentage, and two conference titles, just a glimpse of the great success to come.

Wright brought her winning ways to California's Fresno State University for the 1986 season when she was chosen from 74 applicants to become the Bulldogs' next head coach.[4] Upon her arrival, Wright began to mold Fresno State into a successful and disciplined fastpitch program. Not only were Wright's athletes expected to perform on the diamond, they were also pushed to excel in the classroom. As stated on Fresno State's softball website, the philosophy of the Bulldogs' program is simply to be "the very best you can be, both as a softball player and as a person."[5] From the beginning of her tenure, Coach Wright set the bar high for her student-athletes.

Now in her 24th season at the helm of Bulldog softball, Wright is the winningest coach in National Collegiate Athletic Association (NCAA) softball. She is one of two coaches in any collegiate sport to have ever won over 1,300 games and was the only coach at Fresno State to have brought home a National Championship (1998) until the men's team won the 2008 College World Series. In softball, Wright is a coaching legend, respected at every level of the game. She has coached some of the most talented and intelligent athletes to ever play the sport, including: 53 All-Americans, 16 Academic All-Americans, 15 Olympians, and four NCAA Postgraduate Scholarship Award winners, just to name a few distinctions. During her tenure, the Bulldogs have averaged 50 wins a season and are among the leaders in Women's College World Series trips with 10 appearances, including three third-place and three runner-up finishes in addition to its national title.

Along with all of the team success, Wright has also been honored numerous times for her personal contributions to the game and to women's athletics. She has twice been inducted into the Hall of Fame at her alma mater (once as a player and once as the member of a specific team) and is a member of the Fresno Athletic Hall of Fame. Wright is a five-time winner of Western Athletic Conference Coach of the Year and seven-time winner of West Region Coach of the Year and was named 1998 National Coach of the Year for softball. Additionally, she has been inducted into the Illinois Amateur Softball Association (ASA) and National Fastpitch Coaches Association (NFCA) Halls of Fame. Wright has also acted as a coach in the United States Olympic System, serving as a U.S. National Team coach for the 1996 Quadrinium, a period that included her time as an assistant during the team's 1996 Olympic gold medal victory in Atlanta. In 2005, Wright was inducted into the International Women's Sports Hall of Fame for her contributions to women and women's athletics, an honor that she considers very meaningful.

Although she has dedicated her life to achievement and expects excellence, it is not awards, public recognition, or wins that motivate Wright. For Wright, the true goal of coaching is to lead young women to expect the individual best from themselves while always promoting the continued improvement of the climate of women's athletics. In 2006, one of Wright's "kids" (she considers her team to

Courtesy of Fresno State University Athletics.

be a family) was diagnosed with cancer.[6] The young woman is now in remission, but the diagnosis and ensuing battle reminded Wright that her coaching philosophy is the right one. Winning in collegiate softball is important, but winning at life is the true quest.

When asked to consider the entirety of her dynamic career as a player and a coach, Wright commented, "The support of my parents and family made all of the difference in the world and the fact that I had to put myself through college on a bank loan, has driven me to fight for Title IX and the future for young women in athletics. My 34-year playing career allowed me to play with and against some of the best female athletes ever and my 34-year coaching career has given me the opportunity to coach some of the best athletes ever in my sport. Representing my country in the Olympics and all areas of international competition, winning a gold medal, and winning an NCAA National Championship is more than I could have imagined. And bigger than that, having a positive effect on the growth and development of so many athletes, my life as a coach has been very rewarding. I truly owe it all to my parents, family, and all those athletes I have had the opportunity to be around."[7]

Coach Wright might be surprised to find out how many of those current and former female athletes feel that they owe it all to her.

Notes

1. Sheila Mulrooney Eldred, "For Wright, Some of Best Coaching Moves Made Off Field," Sports, *The Fresno Bee*, April 3, 2004.

2. Margie Wright, email interview with Catherine Lahey, May 27, 2008.

3. Sheila Mulrooney Eldred, "For Wright, Some of Best Coaching Moves Made Off Field," Sports, *The Fresno Bee*, April 3, 2004.

4. Jeff Davis, "Wright Gets Her Day—and It's by Proclamation," Sports, *The Fresno Bee*, May 15, 2005.

5. Margie Wright, "A Message From Coach Wright," Softball, Fresno State Bulldogs Website, http://gobulldogs.cstv.com/sports/w-softbl/spec-rel/011701aab.html.

6. Karrin Luce, "A Day in the Life of a Coach," *The Yelp*, Fresno County Women's Chamber of Commerce, April 2007.

7. Margie Wright, email interview with Catherine Lahey, May 27, 2008.

Joan Joyce

American Star of the Women's International Sports Hall of Fame

by *Catherine Lahey*

Known as "the finest women's softball player of all time,"[1] Joan Joyce not only excelled on the diamond, but on the courts, the links, and the lanes as well. A former teammate from the Connecticut Falcons, Kathy Neal, said Joyce "really was the Babe Didrikson Zaharias of her era."[2]

Born August 1, 1940, in Waterbury, Connecticut, Joan Joyce was introduced to sports by following her father, Joe, to the ball fields. Interested in baseball, young Joan began honing her skills by throwing a ball against a wall of her family home, which her mother soon outlawed. Undeterred, Joan built herself a backstop with chicken wire strung across two trees. At the tender age of 16, Joyce had become good enough to join the Raybestos Brakettes, the most legendary and powerful team in women's softball. An injury to the Brakettes' starting pitcher in 1958 launched Joyce into the spotlight as the team's new hurler. Just 18 years old, she led the team to a national championship, pitching a dominant no-hitter in the title game.

Joyce's dominant pitching career had just begun. Her pitching philosophy was simple and effective: "keep the umpires out of it. That meant to pitch to the area where the batter didn't want to swing."[3] During her time with the Brakettes, Joyce won 429 games while losing only 27. She struck out 5,677 batters in 3,397 innings pitched, and threw 105 no-hitters and an incredible 33 perfect games. In 1974, she led the Brakettes to a world title in the third International Softball Federation (ISF) Women's World Championship. Joyce holds a career pitching record of 753 wins and 42 losses, including 150 no-hit, no-run games and 50 perfect games.

To the dismay of her opponents, Joyce was as great a hitter as she was a pitcher, carrying a career batting average of .327. She led the Brakettes in batting average six times and once achieved a single season average of .406. Joyce played on 12 national championship teams, was an 18-time Amateur Softball Association (ASA) All-

American, and won or shared the MVP award in the Women's National Championship eight times. She has been inducted into the ASA National Hall of Fame (1983) and the ISF Hall of Fame (1999).[4] The legend continues.

The moment that Joyce considers the most notable and favorite of her career came in August 1961 at Municipal Stadium in Waterbury, Connecticut. In front of a record crowd, Joyce was set to face off against the greatest hitter of all time, Ted Williams, to benefit The Jimmy Fund. The battle began. Some people claim that Williams hit a few to the outfield but Joyce disagrees. She recalls, "Ted was at bat for 10 to 15 minutes, he fouled off three. Dom DiMaggio came down with Ted and I let up on him so he could hit a few, but Ted? No. He swung and missed a lot. He finally got so disgusted he threw the bat down and walked away."

The two legends met again five years later. Just as she had done the first time, Joyce threw rise balls, exploiting the fact that baseball players have never seen a pitch that moves upward. After Williams struck out, he went to the mound and gave Joyce a hug, waving to the crowd as he left. At the age of 81, when asked about facing the great Joyce, Williams confirmed that "the story is all true. Joan Joyce was a tremendous pitcher, as talented as anyone who ever played." Joyce was able to add another baseball legend to her no-hitter list when she struck out Hank Aaron in an exhibition in West Hartford in 1978.[5]

As if her achievements on the softball diamond weren't enough, Joyce excelled at volleyball, bowling, basketball, and golf. As a teenager, she carried a 180 average on the bowling lanes. In basketball, she was a three-time Amateur Athletic Union (AAU) All-American at Chapman College (now Chapman University), setting a national tournament single game scoring record with 67 points. Joyce was also a four-time Women's Basketball Association All-American and played on the U.S. National Team in 1965. Following her playing career, she served as an official for 15 years, officiating three collegiate national championship games. As a volleyball athlete, Joyce served as a player/coach on the Connecticut Clippers of the United States Volleyball Association. She competed in four National Tournaments and was named to the All-East Regional team. Adding to this already lengthy list of achievements are her golf accomplishments. Joyce was a 19-year member of the Ladies Professional Golf Association (LPGA) from 1977 to 1995, recording a low round of 66. She was once listed in the Guinness Book of World Records for the lowest number of putts in a single round (for both men and women) with 17. In a tribute to her overall athleticism, Joyce twice participated in the popular "Superstars" television specials, competing and succeeding against some of America's best male and female athletes.[6]

In 1994, Joyce began a new chapter in her athletic career when she was hired by Florida Atlantic University (FAU) to build a softball program from the ground up. The Owls achieved success immediately, earning Joyce her first Atlantic-Sun Conference Coach of the Year award. In only their third season, the Owls captured their first A-Sun Championship, also the first for the FAU athletic program. Joyce was again honored as A-Sun Coach of the Year. In 1999, the National Collegiate Athletic Association (NCAA) awarded an automatic bid to the A-Sun Conference champion for the NCAA tournament. The Owls won their third championship in a row and with it their first ever NCAA tournament appearance. Joyce and her staff were named the Southeast Region Coaching Staff of the Year by the National Fastpitch Coaches Association. Since she began the program in 1994, she has amassed nine A-Sun Conference Championships and one Sun Belt Conference Championship.

In addition to her duties as the skipper of the softball team, Joyce also serves as the head coach of the women's golf team. During her tenure she has coached three A-Sun Golfers of the Year. As she has done throughout her career, Joyce excelled in many areas outside of softball, in the same year she took on the golf team she also stepped up to the plate to take on the position of senior women's administrator. She held the latter position until 2001.[7]

Joan Joyce is truly a legend in women's sport. Her versatility and natural athleticism are largely unrivaled, regardless of gender. Although she has been inducted into a total of seven Halls of Fame, including the International Women's Sports Hall of Fame, it is difficult to encapsulate and fully honor her athletic prowess. She has contributed significantly to women's athletics through her play, her officiating, and now her coaching. Regardless of all her achievements, Joyce will always be best remembered as the "girl" who struck out two of Major League Baseball's greatest.

Notes

1. Robert Condon, *Great Women Athletes of the 20th Century* (Jefferson, N.C.: McFarland & Company, 1991).

2. Tom Yantz, "The Missing Legend; Tom Couldn't Touch Joan." *The Hartford Courant*, December 30, 1999.

3. Ibid.

4. Joan Joyce, ASA National Softball Hall of Fame Member, ASA.

5. Tom Yantz, "The Missing Legend; Tom Couldn't Touch Joan."

6. Joan Joyce, Biography, Florida Atlantic University Softball Media Guide, 2008.

7. Ibid.

Dr. Dorothy "Dot" Richardson

Future Hall of Famer

by Catherine Lahey

The Energizer Bunny, the advertising icon famous for his boundless supply of exuberant energy, has nothing on two-time Olympic softball champion and orthopedic surgeon Dr. Dot Richardson. Richardson worked to complete medical school and an orthopedic residency, a notoriously taxing task, while simultaneously training to maintain the skill and conditioning of an elite, international athlete. Even more impressive was that she always did so with her trademark smile and contagious enthusiasm for the challenges and blessing that each day brings. Her father Ken confirms that she's always been extremely energetic. As evidence, he recounts the story of a trip that the family took from Orlando to California when Dot was just nine months old. Sitting still seemed virtually impossible for little Dot and she crawled endlessly around the car, driving her mother Joyce to look for an alternative solution. In a final effort to contain her, says her father, "we put her in a box in the backseat. That's how she got across the country—in a box."[1] From that point forward, Dot's enthusiasm for exploration was virtually uncontainable.

Even as a young child, Richardson was tremendously athletic. A talented baseball player, Richardson desired to join a Little League team like her brother at a time when Little League baseball was reserved for boys. After being pleasantly shocked by the skill level of 10-year-old Richardson, one enterprising coach finally offered her a chance to play on his Little League All-Star team—as long as Dot would promise to cut off her hair and dutifully answer to the name "Bob." Disappointed, the Richardson family politely declined. Just three years later, Richardson would be recognized as a prodigy in the world of women's softball, becoming the youngest player in the Women's Major Fast Pitch League at the tender age of 13. Richardson became immersed in the game, learning its nuances from players who were older and more experienced, although sometimes not as talented. When it came time to choose a college, Richardson soon found her way to UCLA, a school with a rich and decorated softball history, after a brief stint at Western Illinois University.

During her time at UCLA, Richardson cemented her place as a star in the Bruin constellation and as one of the greatest softball players of all time. She was named the team's MVP and an All-American in each of the three seasons she played at UCLA. Aside from being a gifted shortstop, Richardson led the team in batting during all three seasons and was a key player during the Bruins' 1982 National Championship season. In recognition of her stellar physical talents and contributions to the collegiate game, Richardson was named National Collegiate Athletic Association (NCAA) Player of the Decade for the 1980s and has also been inducted into the prestigious UCLA Hall of Fame. She also found the time and energy to play basketball at UCLA during her freshman and senior years, a testament to her athleticism and seemingly bottomless well of energy.

Her accolades and accomplishments in the sport of softball are almost too numerous to mention. Richardson is a 15-time American Softball Association (ASA) All-American selection, a seven-time winner of USA Softball's MVP award (over three decades no less) and was named the 1996 Athlete of the Year by the United States Olympic Committee. She has been lauded for her athleticism, her volunteerism, her inspirational speaking ability, and her guidance as a role model to young people. She is a four-time Pan American Games gold medalist, again over three different decades, and a two-time gold medalist with the highly decorated U.S. Olympic Softball team. Among her most emotional accomplishments was hitting the game winning home run in softball's inaugural gold medal game in the 1996 Olympics. While many people would be content to claim these achievements as their contribution to the world, Richardson has always been an advocate of reaching for ones dreams and exploring one's passions with enthusiasm.

Beyond the diamond, Richardson powered toward her goal of becoming an orthopedic surgeon by obtaining a bachelor's degree from UCLA, then a master's degree in exercise physiology/health from Adelphi University, and finally a doctorate from the University of Louisville. She then completed an orthopedic residency program and an orthopedic fellowship all while training and competing as one of the world's elite softball players. She and former teammate (and all-time great) Lisa Fernandez constructed a makeshift batting cage in their third-floor apartment in order to facilitate a way for Richardson to practice while maintaining the grueling schedule of a medical student in residency. The morning after a middle of the night hitting session, a sarcastic note appeared on her door "If you're going to train for the Olympics," it read, "please do it at a decent hour." Fernandez and Richardson were amused. "Nobody knew we really were training for the Olympics," said Fernandez.[2]

Today, Richardson combines her passions for athletics and medicine as the executive and medical director of the USA Triathlon Training Center in Clermont, Florida, and as the founder and commissioner of the ProFastpitch X-treme Tour. Since two major projects could never be enough, she also finds the time and energy to serve as the vice chairman of the President's Council on Physical Fitness and Sports. As always, she continues to perform inspirational speaking engagements and actively involves herself in encouraging young people to follow and achieve their dreams. The best representation of Dr. Dot can be found in the encouragement and guidance that she shares with others. "A true champion is someone who wants to make a difference, who never gives up, and who gives everything she has no matter what the circumstances are. A true champion works hard and never loses sight of her dreams."[3] Richardson is certainly a true champion.

Notes

1. Austin Murphy, "Dot Richardson," *Sports Illustrated*, July 18, 1994.

2. Steve Rushin, "Playing with Heart," *Sports Illustrated*, July 29, 1996.

3. Dot Richardson Quote, Heroes & Heroism, QuoteLady, http://www.quotelady .com/subjects/heroes.html.

Lisa Fernandez

Future Hall of Famer

by Catherine Lahey

Courtesy of UCLA Sports Information.

Undoubtedly the most recognized name in the sport of women's softball, Lisa Fernandez is often referred to as the greatest player to ever take the field. When asked about her athletic prowess and her innumerable pitching records, Fernandez is likely to respond with an unexpected story. She will tell the tale of an eight-year-old making her competitive debut. In her first game on the mound, international softball legend Lisa Fernandez lost, 28-0. "I mean, I walked the bases loaded. I was hitting people. I'd never pitched to a batter, never pitched to an umpire; I'd only pitched to my mom in the back yard." In her next game she only walked 18, setting into motion a cycle of improvement, dedication, and perseverance that shaped Fernandez into the pinnacle of international softball talent.[1]

As a teenager, Fernandez attended St. Joseph High School in Lakewood, California, where she played in the most celebrated high school game in softball history. Fernandez was a freshman facing Gahr High School and ace pitcher De De Weiman. The game became a true pitcher's duel as Fernandez and Weiman battled for 21 innings before the game was suspended on account of darkness. After another eight innings the following day, Lisa Fernandez and St. Joe's came out on top, winning 1-0 on a Fernandez run. That legendary game was just the beginning of an incredible high school career in which she amassed 12 perfect games, 69 shutouts, 80 career victories, 1,503 career strikeouts, and an amazing 0.07 ERA.

Fernandez continued on to play softball for a storied UCLA program. During her time there as a four-time All American, she led the Bruins to the National Collegiate Athletic Association (NCAA) Women's College World Series four times, earning the national title twice (1990 and 1992). Fernandez was a three-time Honda Award winner, an honor given to the nation's best softball player. She also earned the NCAA Top VI award, which is presented to the top six senior student-athletes in all divisions. To top it all off, she was presented with the 1992–93 Honda-Broderick Cup for being the nation's top collegiate female athlete. Fernandez's incredible career at UCLA boasts an NCAA record winning percentage of .930 (93-7). She broke seven school records and led the nation in hitting and pitching her senior year with a .510 batting average and an ERA of 0.25. Her career ERA of 0.22 still stands second in the NCAA history books. In 2003, Lisa Fernandez became the eighth UCLA softball player inducted into the UCLA Athletics Hall of Fame.

After her time at UCLA, Fernandez continued to play on the national and international circuits. She accrued many accolades throughout her national playing career, including three-time Olympic Gold Medalist, United States Olympics Committee (USOC) Top 10 Athlete of the Year Award, two-time Women's Sports Foundation Athlete of the Year Nominee, Amateur Softball Association (ASA) Player of the Year, eight-time ASA All-American, six-time Major Fast Pitch National Champion with the Raybestos Brakettes and California Commotion, and five-time ASA Women's Major Fast Pitch National Championship MVP. Her list of achievements and honors is long and prestigious.

Internationally, Fernandez is a three-time Olympic gold medalist. Fernandez was one of five former Bruins to play on the 1996 gold-medal winning U.S. Olympic team and one of six former Bruins on the 2000 roster. In the 1996 final, Fernandez recorded the final three outs to secure victory for the United States. In the 2000 Games, she pitched the United States to gold in the semifinal game over the Australians and in the final over Japan. During the "Central Park to Sydney" tour in 2002, Fernandez tossed five consecutive perfect games, striking out all 21 batters in one of those contests. Fernandez then led the way to a third consecutive gold medal as the top pitcher and hitter in the 2004 Games in Athens. She set a new record for batting average in Olympic play by hitting .545.

Over the course of her illustrious athletic career, Lisa Fernan-

Courtesy of UCLA Sports Information.

dez has been an inspiration to young women all over the world. They have watched her dominate the sport of softball not only as a pitcher, but as third baseman and a hitter. Fernandez now looks to be an inspiration to another group of people, mothers. After the 2004 Olympics, Fernandez decided she was ready to begin a family with her husband, Michael Lujan. Antonio Mayo Lujan was born on December 19, 2005. Since then she has carefully balanced her family life, professional life, and playing career with the help of many friends and family members. Fernandez hopes "to be a role model to future moms, who can know that there is a way to do it all and still be good to all that you need to be good to, and still put the child at the front." She admits it takes a lot of support and she has been blessed to have it.[2]

Lisa Fernandez is the most recognized name in the sport of softball, a tremendous athlete who has fought her way to the top through hard work and dedication. A Little League coach once told her she would never be a good pitcher because her body was not built right for the job. She responded by eclipsing "good" to become the best ever. Her motto is "Never be satisfied."[3]

Fernandez continues to impact the sport of softball as an assistant coach at her alma mater, UCLA. In addition to her favorite and most important role, being a mom, she also works as a national clinician and motivational speaker. A true leader and role model, Lisa Fernandez is not just a world class athlete. She is, simply, world-class.

Notes

1. The Official Website of Lisa Fernandez, "The Early Years," LisaFernandez16 .com, http://www.lisafernandez16.com/earlyyears.htm.

2. Jill Lieber Steeg, "Fernandez Has Plenty of Support in Comeback," *USA TODAY*, November 27, 2007.

3. Real Women in Sports, "Lisa Fernandez," Real Women in Sports: Athletes, http:// www.realwomeninsports.com/fernandez.php.

11

WOMEN BASKETBALL PLAYERS:
LEAVING FOOTPRINTS ON THE HARDWOOD

Introduction by Richard Lapchick

Women started playing basketball within months after James Naismith invented the game. The first team was organized in 1892 at Smith College by Senda Berenson, who would join Bertha Teague and Margaret Wade as the first three women inducted into the Basketball Hall of Fame. But that was 92 years later and is too big a leap for now.

New Orleans is not only the home of American jazz; women's college basketball was introduced there in 1895 by physical educator Clara Gregory Baer at Sophie Newcomb College. Baer also published the first set of basketball rules for women in the same year.

The first college game was played in 1896 between Stanford and the University of California, Berkeley. Men were not allowed to attend because the women were dressed "inappropriately" after they gave up wearing floor-length dresses. Women began to break out of the Victorian era prudery and stereotypes about what women and girls could and could not do. Stanford won that first game, 2-1! Because of the controversy over dress, college basketball for women didn't really catch on early in the 20th century.

In those early days, women played a six-player, three-court game with stationary guards and forwards. You couldn't hold the ball for more than three seconds or dribble more than three times. Women could not leave their area on the floor. Halves became 15 minutes instead of 20 in 1903. All of this was intended to make sure basketball was not too strenuous for women. It is easy to forget that when basketball was invented, women were three decades away from getting to vote and the notion of gender equity was not on the table.

The game became international when the International Women's Sports Federation was formed in 1924 and hosted its version of the Olympics with basketball included in the competition.

By 1925, 37 states held high school varsity basketball state tournaments. The driving force behind the increasing popularity was the Amateur Athletic Union (AAU), which sponsored amateur and industrial leagues. The AAU sponsored the first national women's basketball championship in 1926.

The game evolved during the 1950s and 1960s when a "roving" game was adopted with two stationary guards and forwards and two "rovers." The five-player, full-court game was embraced in the 1970s. A lot happened between 1892 and 1970.

There was the great athlete, Babe Didrikson Zaharias, who was the first famous woman to play in the 1920s. Didrikson Zaharias led her team, the Golden Cyclones, to the 1931 AAU Championship. Didrikson Zaharias is featured elsewhere in *100 Trailblazers*.

Nera White was the star female basketball player of her time. A great ball handler, she easily could also drop in shots from behind what is today's three point line. She was named AAU All-American from 1955 to 1969 and was the first female player inducted into the Basketball Hall of Fame in 1992.

One of the earliest women's basketball teams was the All-American-Redheads formed in 1936. Their formation highlighted the tension between being an athlete and being a woman. Team members had to dye their hair red or wear red wigs, wear makeup, look beautiful, and play well. The Redheads played exhibitions against men's teams.

In addition to the Redheads and the Golden Cyclones, sponsored by the Casualty Insurance Company and led by Didrikson Zaharias, other early teams included the Hazel Walker Arkansas Travelers and the Canadian Edmonton Grads who played a total of 522 games in Canada, the United States, and Europe. They played both men's and women's teams and won an amazing 502 games and lost only 20!

During these days, the three-court game changed to two with six players on each team. As the global popularity of the game increased, the U.S. women's basketball team won the 1953 World Championships.

There is little doubt that the most important thing to happen for women's basketball, as well as all women's sports, was the 1972 enactment of Title IX, which required that all schools receiving money from the federal government allocate equal funds for women's teams, especially regarding recruitment, scholarships, and program funding. As it became implemented, the rise of women's high school and college basketball was dramatic.

On the college level, the Commission on Intercollegiate Athletics for Women (CIAW) hosted the first "national championship" of women's college basketball won by West Chester State College in 1969.

In 1971, women finally adopted the five-player, full-court game and introduced the 30-second shot clock.

The Association for Intercollegiate Athletics for Women (AIWA) was founded in 1971 to govern collegiate women's athletics and to administer national championships including basketball. The AIAW held its first women's collegiate basketball championship in 1972 when Immaculata College defeated West Chester State, 52-48. The following year witnessed the introduction of athletics scholarships for women in AIAW programs. In 1974, the AIAW basketball championships were televised and broadcast on the radio.

The year 1975 was a huge year when a regular season game between Maryland and Immaculata was on national television for the first time while Immaculata played the first women's game in Madison Square Garden before 12,000 fans. Kodak became the first sponsor of women's basketball.

Delta State's Luisa Harris won the first Broderick Cup as the most outstanding athlete in AIAW in 1977. A year later, the inaugural Margaret Wade Trophy, named after Delta State's coach who led her team to three consecutive AIAW titles, went to Montclair State's Carol Blazejowski.

The National College Athletic Association (NCAA), which had not been a huge advocate for women's sports, saw the increased popularity and seized the reins from the AIAW, which lost a court battle with the NCAA. Much more is said about this in the administrators section.

After the 1981–82 academic year, the AIAW discontinued sponsorship of national championships and later was legally dissolved. At this time, the NCAA assumed sole sanctioning authority of its member schools' women's sports programs. The Women's Basketball Coaches Association was formed in 1981 in the midst of the changes in control.

The first NCAA women's championship game was played in 1982, with Louisiana Tech defeating Cheney State, 76-62. Within three years the NCAA introduced innovations with a smaller ball and the three-point shot.

Women's basketball was introduced in the Olympics at the 1976 Montreal Olympics. Nancy Lieberman was brought onto the world stage and helped the United States win a silver medal. It was not until the Los Angeles Olympics in 1984 when the U.S. women began to make the gold seem like their own. They won in L.A., Seoul, Atlanta, Sydney, Athens, and Beijing, losing only in Barcelona when they won the bronze medal.

The history of women's professional basketball featured a series of starts and stops until the formation of the Women's National Basketball Association, better known as the WNBA.

In 1978 the Women's Professional Basketball League, or WBL, began with eight teams and lasted three seasons.

Ann Meyers Drysdale, Lynette Woodard, and Nancy Lieberman tried to play in the men's pro leagues. In 1979, Meyers Drysdale, the four-time All-America at UCLA, signed a $50,000 contract with the National Basketball Association's (NBA) Indiana Pacers but failed to make the team. In 1985, guard Lynette Woodard, who had starred for the University of Kansas, became the first woman to play for the Harlem Globetrotters. In 1986, the 28-year-old Lieberman was the first woman to play in a men's pro basketball league when she joined the United States Basketball League's (USBL) Springfield Fame. The next year she played for the Washington Generals on their tour with the Harlem Globetrotters.

In 1991, the Liberty Basketball Association lasted for only one exhibition game.

A year later, the Women's World Basketball Association was launched in the Midwest with six teams, but it soon folded also.

The American Basketball League, known as the ABL, was founded five years later. The number of teams grew from eight to 10. It lasted three seasons, two of which had the rival WNBA grabbing far more attention after it started its first season in 1997.

Then in 1996, the WNBA was established with the backing of the NBA. Television contracts were signed with ESPN, NBC, and Lifetime. By the end of 2000, the league had grown to 16 teams. With the Final Fours, pre-season National Invitational Tournaments (NITs), the WNBA, and Olympic championships, the game of women's basketball grows in popularity with each passing year. There have been so many great figures in the game as players and coaches that it was a major challenge to pick those we would feature in the section of *100 Trailblazers*.

I could have written about all the trailblazers mentioned above but we have decided to present more in-depth profiles on Vivian Stringer, Pat Summitt, Tara VanDerveer, Margaret Wade, Cheryl Miller, Nancy Lieberman, Sheryl Swoopes, Lisa Leslie, Ann Meyers Drysdale, and Betty Jaynes.

Pat Summitt is basketball's winningest college basketball coach for men or women. She has been the head coach of the Tennessee Lady Vols basketball team since 1974. She was an All-American player at the University of Tennessee-Martin and co-captained the 1976 Olympic basketball team.

Her record is staggering: 14 Southeastern Conference regular season titles, 13 Southeastern Conference (SEC) tournament titles, 18 Final Four appearances, and eight NCAA championships. Her teams have been in every NCAA tournament. She is a seven-time national coach of the year. She is respected as a mentor, coach, teacher, and civic leader.

By the time Coach Vivian Stringer joined Rutgers she had established herself as a coach who turned struggling teams into national powerhouses. In 1971, Coach Stringer made her coaching debut at Cheyney State, a historically all-black college. Stringer's Iowa team had the first-ever advanced sellout of a women's basketball team, proving that women's basketball had the potential to be as successful as men's basketball.

Stringer has one of the best records in the history of basketball, men's or women's. She was the first coach in NCAA history to lead three different women's programs to the NCAA Final Four: Cheyney State College (now Cheyney University of Pennsylvania) in 1982, the University of Iowa in 1993, and Rutgers in 2000 and 2007. She is the third winningest coach in women's basketball history, behind only Tennessee's Pat Summitt and the recently retired University of Texas coach Jody Conradt.

Stringer tried out for the cheerleading squad, and although she was the most talented, she was cut from the team because of her race. With the help of an NAACP leader, Stringer fought this ruling and later became the first black cheerleader at her high school. She has stood up for justice ever since, including her handling of the controversy with radio host Don Imus, which is detailed in her story in this section.

She also faced a series of terrible personal tragedies, but has shown courage, class, and dignity throughout her coaching career to inspire so many younger people.

Stanford Head Coach Tara VanDerveer's record since 1985 is also amazing. In her first 22 seasons, she compiled a 571-137 record for a .806 winning percentage. She has led her team to two NCAA Championships, three title game appearances, six Final Four appearances, 16 Pac-10 Titles, and 20 consecutive trips to the NCAA Tournament. She started coaching at Idaho, where she led the Vandals to a 42-14 (.750 winning percentage) record in her two seasons there. She moved to Ohio State, which she then led to a 110-37 record (.748 winning percentage) in five seasons. The Buckeyes had four consecutive 20-win seasons, had four Big Ten Championships, and made three NCAA Tournament appearances. She also coached the U.S. women to gold in the 1996 Olympics.

Summitt, Stringer, and VanDerveer all stand on the shoulders of Margaret Wade.

Wade is often called the "mother of modern women's college basketball." She contributed to the sport of basketball in almost every capacity, and without her, women's basketball would not enjoy the recognition it does today.

Although Wade was a skilled college and professional player, she is best remembered for contributions to the sport of basketball as a coach. She created a dynasty at Delta State University, leading the Lady Statesmen to three consecutive AIAW National Championships and racking up a .789 winning percentage, a percentage that few coaches—men's or women's—have matched.

Her accomplishments are even more impressive given the obstacles Wade faced. When she started coaching at Delta State in 1972, women were still fighting for equality in sports. In fact, 1972 was the first year Delta State had even fielded a women's basketball team since 1931—ironically, a team that Wade was a member of while a junior at Delta State.

The memory of Margaret Wade retains a prominent place in the world of college athletics. Each year, the best female player in NCAA Division I Basketball is awarded the Margaret Wade Trophy.

Betty Jaynes is like the thread that runs through the modern story of women's basketball. She was the long-time director and CEO of the Women's Basketball Coaches Association (WBCA). In 2006, she received the Bunn Lifetime Achievement Award from the Basketball Hall of Fame for lifetime achievement in basketball.

Jaynes was the women's coach at Madison College (now James Madison University) from 1970 to 1982, leading her team to a 142-114 record. After coaching, she took over the leadership of the WBCA, where she has been a leader in women's basketball for over 25 years. During her reign, the WBCA grew into a 5,000-plus-member organization. The WBCA serves as an advocate, an information source, and a base of support for all levels of the women's basketball game.

Then there have been the players. There have been so many great ones and there will be so many to include in the future. Among the 2008 U.S. Olympic team members not highlighted here were now three-time Olympic gold medalist Katie Smith (Detroit Shock), now two-time gold medalists Sue Bird (Seattle Storm), Diana Taurasi (Phoenix Mercury), and Tina Thompson (Houston Comets). Seimone Augustus (Minnesota Lynx), Sylvia Fowles (Chicago Sky), Candace Parker (Los Angeles Sparks), and Cappie Pondexter (Phoenix Mercury) all won their first medals in Beijing.

Lisa Leslie won an unprecedented fourth gold medal in Beijing. It continued her amazing career. In a high school game she scored 101 points in the first half before the opponents forfeited. She chose to attend USC, where she was a four-time Pac-10 All-Conference player, and she was the seventh player chosen in the WNBA draft, which brought her to the Los Angeles Sparks. In 2002, she became the first player to score with a dunk in a WNBA game. She later dunked in the 2005 All-Star game. In 2006, she scored her

5,000th WNBA point and won her third MVP crown. She sat out the 2007 season to have a child but was back for the 2008 season and a Beijing gold.

Not on the Olympic team for the first time in 16 years was Sheryl Swoopes, who is often called the "female Michael Jordan." In high school, she led Brownfield High to its first Texas State Championship for girls' basketball in 1988. In college, she led the Texas Tech Lady Raiders to its first NCAA National Championship in 1993. In the pros, she led the Houston Comets of the WNBA to victories in the first four championships in the league's existence from 1997 to 2000. In the Olympic Games, she led Team USA to three straight gold medals in 1996, 2000, and 2004.

Cheryl Miller may have been the most recruited female high school player ever after she led her high school to four straight California State Championships while averaging 32.8 points and 15.0 rebounds per game. Her team finished with a 132-4 record during her high school career, an average of just one loss per year. During her senior season, Miller scored a record 105 points, a girl's high school basketball record that would stand for more than 20 years. In that same game, Miller dunked the basketball, which was an unprecedented feat for a female in organized play.

She chose to stay home and play for USC. She led the USC Lady Trojans to back-to-back national championships in her first two years and was the tournament's MVP both years. Miller won a gold medal in the 1984 Summer Olympic Games and finished her career with USC with a 112-20 record. She was also a four-time All-American and a three-time recipient of the Naismith Award. In 1993, at just 29 years old, she returned to her alma mater as the head coach of USC. In two seasons, Miller led the Lady Trojans to a 44-14 record and a 1994 Pac-10 conference title. In 1995, she joined her current employer, Turner Sports, where she does basketball commentary for TNT and TBS.

Nancy Lieberman helped change how we view women in college ball after she chose Old Dominion University (ODU) for her collegiate career. They called her "Lady Magic" for her flashy passes and brilliant scoring drives. She built ODU's program into a national powerhouse as she led them to a National Women's Invitational Tournament Championship in 1977–78 as well as back-to-back AIAW National Championships in 1978–79 and 1979–80. In her final two seasons at Old Dominion, the team achieved a 72-2 record. She was a two-time winner of the Wade Trophy along with the Broderick Award, which awards the nation's best collegiate female athlete.

Before getting to ODU she had already won an Olympic silver medal as the youngest basketball player in Olympic history to ever win a medal. Lieberman played in the various women's pro leagues and on men's pro teams before becoming a noted television analyst for women's basketball.

Like Lieberman's, Ann Meyers Drysdale's basketball bio spans over four decades. Meyers was the first woman to receive a full athletic scholarship from UCLA, where she was a four-time All-American, set 12 of 13 school records, and helped UCLA win a national championship in 1978. Meyers Drysdale also was on the volleyball team and won a track and field national championship in 1975. She earned a silver medal with Lieberman at the Montreal Games in 1976.

Meyers Drysdale is still the only female ever to sign a free-agent contract with an NBA team. She was the first player drafted in the WBL, where she played for the New Jersey Gems and was named MVP after averaging 22.2 points. Meyers had a distinguished career as a broadcast journalist before becoming the general manager of the WNBA's Phoenix Mercury in 2007.

So now all this great history, achieved when there was less opportunity, has opened the doors wide for today's great women's basketball players. Now we can cheer for Smith, Bird, Taurasi, Thompson, Augustus, Fowles, Parker, Pondexter, and so many more in the future because of the likes of Lieberman, Drysdale, Swoopes, Miller, and Leslie.

Margaret Wade

American Star of the Women's International Sports Hall of Fame

by Sara Jane Baker

Margaret Wade's legacy will always be as the "mother of modern women's college basketball."[1] The title is not the least bit hyperbolic. After all, she contributed to the sport of basketball in almost every capacity, and without her, women's basketball would not enjoy the recognition it does today.

Although Margaret Wade was a skilled college and professional player, she is best remembered for contributions to the sport of basketball as a coach. She created a dynasty at Delta State University, leading the Lady Statesmen to three consecutive Association for Intercollegiate Athletics for Women (AIAW) National Championships and racking up a .789 winning percentage, a percentage that few coaches—men's or women's—have matched.[2]

Former players have described Wade as relentless in her demands of her players. Sue King, a standout player at Delta State, described the intensity of the calisthenics regimen Wade dictated with one simple statement: "She all but killed us."[3] King's teammates and, in fact, everyone who ever played under Wade, would most likely echo similar sentiments. When every last bit of mental and physical energy was exhausted, Wade would find a way to get her players to reach deeply within themselves and somehow find even more.

While all would agree that her high performance expectations were integral to her teams' successes, her ability to personally inspire each player was, perhaps, even more significant.[4] Pat Summitt, the winningest coach in basketball history stated, "Anyone who knew Margaret was touched by her life. She had a passion for teaching and a desire to win that was hard to quench."[5]

Her accomplishments are even more impressive given the obstacles Wade faced. When she started coaching at Delta State in 1972, women were still fighting for equality in sports. In fact, 1972 was the first year Delta State had even fielded a women's basketball team since 1931—ironically, a team that Wade was a member of while a junior at Delta State. The next year Delta State cut women's basketball, depriving Wade of the opportunity to play her senior year. Declaring that the sport was "too tough" on women in the 1932 statement defending its decision, Delta State officials stated that an intercollegiate basketball program for women "could not be defended on sound grounds."[6]

Decades later, when Wade was asked to lead the reinstated program, she quickly turned attention away from any lingering stereotypes about women and made an instant impact. A former Delta State sports information director described her first year as "one of the most amazing accomplishments in sports history."[7] This successful first year turned out to be only a precursor to many more triumphant seasons.

Through coaching, Wade was able to finally accomplish many of the goals she was unable to attain as a player since the star forward's career was suddenly cut short at the start of Wade's senior year. Basketball had been the focus of Wade's life since her youth, and she described this time as "especially tough." Filled with anger and despair, Wade and her teammates burned their college uniforms as a form of protest again the administration's sexist decision.

Several years later, Wade had another opportunity to play basketball. She played two seasons with a semi-pro team, the Tupelo Red Wings. Unfortunately, her career was cut short again, this time with a knee injury.

Nevertheless, Wade was determined to find another way to be involved with the game she loved so much. Coaching became her way to stay connected. She enjoyed a successful reign as the coach for the Cleveland (Mississippi) High School girls basketball team. When Wade stepped down from this position in 1954, she had led her team to the North Mississippi tournament 14 out of 15 seasons.

Before accepting the coaching job with Delta State, Wade served as the director of women's physical education for the school. This job, along with her success at the high school level, made her the obvious prime candidate for head women's basketball coach when the program was reinstated in 1973. Wade was eager about this opportunity. It brought back the great memories of her college career and also served as a way for her to bring emotional closure to the pain of her terminated 1932 senior season.

The current administration at Delta State stills credits Wade for putting the small college in Cleveland, Mississippi, on the map. Margaret Wade impacted the school not only as a coach, but also as a player and administrator. The current women's basketball coach at Delta State, Sandra Rushing, credits Wade with making her job easier. "Her legacy of winning, and the way she went about it, will never be forgotten on this campus."[8] Rushing says that giving her recruits and players the opportunity to wear the same immortal green and white and to play in the same venerable facility that Margaret Wade made famous has made coaching basketball at Delta that much easier.

Margaret Wade passed away in 1995 but not before being recognized for her achievements. She became the first woman, coach or player, ever to be inducted into the National Basketball Hall of Fame. She was also enshrined in both the Delta State University and Mississippi Sports Halls of Fame.

The memory of Margaret Wade retains a prominent place in the world of college athletics. Each year, the best female player in National Collegiate Athletic Association (NCAA) Division I Basketball is awarded the Margaret Wade Trophy. The trophy is not only the oldest and most prestigious award in women's basketball, but its annual presentation serves as a way to assure that the greatest players of today and tomorrow will never forget this great pioneer. With the establishment of the trophy in 1978, Margaret Wade's name has already been associated with the some of the greatest names in college basketball, including Rebecca Lobo and Diana Taurisi. This connection only seems appropriate. She is, after all, a major reason why these women had the opportunity to play and excel in college basketball.

Prior to her death, Margaret Wade commented on the honor of this trophy: "My last will and testament to the 'Margaret Wade Trophy' will be the satisfaction that prospects of the award will create and stimulate desires in young women athletes throughout the country which will propel them to their greatest achievements in athletics; if their athletic accomplishments can be recognized by the award, then my life has been worthwhile."[9]

Notes

1. 2004–05 Lady Statesmen Media Guide, "Lily Margaret Wade." Delta State University, http://www.gostatesmen.com/sports/wbasketball/WBB-PDFs/Section7-WBB-0607-MargaretWade40to41.pdf.

2. Ibid.

3. "Margaret Wade, 82, basketball Coach," *New York Times*, http://query.nytimes.com/gst/fullpage.html?res=990CE5DA1138F934A25751C0A963958260.

4. Ibid.

5. "Lily Margaret Wade." Delta.

6. Ibid.

7. Ibid.

8. Ibid.

9. Ibid.

Nancy Lieberman

Future Hall of Famer

by Richard Lapchick with Brian Wright

I was speaking at a luncheon in Dallas in 1986 introducing the National Consortium for Academics and Sports (NCAS) to a group of business and educational leaders in the Dallas-Fort Worth area. I talked about the difficulty of balancing athletics and academics for the student-athlcte and how the NCAS was going to give athletes who did not finish their degrees a second chance to return to school.

The idea of the NCAS was new then and the audience listened politely. Then a woman in the audience raised her hand and asked to intervene. I instantly recognized that it was Nancy Lieberman, the great basketball star. It was an E. F. Hutton moment as everyone turned to listen. She said, "I wish this program was available when I played at Old Dominion University. College athletes have so many demands on them that it is hard to finish the degree in four years. The NCAS will be a great complement to what student-athletes need." Nancy was an iconic figure then and ended up getting us a great deal of support, which helped build the success of the NCAS.

I was lucky enough to be in Virginia when Nancy Lieberman played for Old Dominion University (ODU). As a New Yorker myself, I knew of her legendary accomplishments in high school and in international competition. At a time when Title IX was new and the National College Athletic Association (NCAA) had yet to take over women's sport, Nancy Lieberman was a headline act who lit up the landscape with her game and her New York attitude. You knew that there was change about to happen and it was exciting to be around it. I was a real fan but did not get to know her until that day in Dallas. We have been good friends ever since.

Born in the basketball-crazed environment of New York, Lieberman developed a deep love and passion for the game. Although she had obvious talents on the court at an early age, stereotypes about women's sports were everywhere. Women and girls alike were discouraged from playing competitive sports, and those who decided to play sports were perceived as "tomboys." The stereotypes did not stop Lieberman's goal of becoming a professional basketball player. Her confidence kept her on task.

She took her game to the outdoor courts and gyms of Harlem and competed with some of the best young players in the city. Lieberman dominated the competition with a rugged and tough style of play that differentiated her from other players in the city. Playing hard and playing tough became second nature for Lieberman. Standing at 5-foot-10-inches, Lieberman was able to tower over her smaller opponents and use her physical style of play to outmatch and overpower them. By her sophomore year of high school, Lieberman was one of the best basketball players in the city and was invited to the American Basketball Association USA's National Team trials. As a 15-year-old high school student, Lieberman was named to the U.S. National Team. She helped the U.S. National Team win gold and silver medals in the World Championships and Pan American Games of 1975 and 1979, respectively. She was the youngest basketball player in Olympic history to ever win a medal when she helped the U.S. team win the silver medal even before she ever set foot on a college campus.

Lieberman became known as "Lady Magic" for her flashy passes and brilliant scoring drives. She helped grow ODU's women's basketball program into a national powerhouse. She led them to a National Women's Invitational Tournament Championship in 1977–78 as well as back-to-back Association for Intercollegiate Athletics for Women (AIAW) National Championships in 1978–79 and 1979–80. The team went 72-2 in her final two seasons at Old Dominion. She was a two-time winner of the Wade Trophy, which honors the nation's best women's basketball performer for their academic, community service, and on-court performances, along with the Broderick Award, which awards the nation's best collegiate female athlete. After college, Lieberman was regarded not only as one of the best female athletes to ever play college basketball, but also one of the best collegiate basketball players ever on a men's or women's team.

Lieberman hoped to play on the U.S. women's team in the 1980 Olympics in Moscow but was stopped by the boycott of President Jimmy Carter. Although she was disappointed about the missed opportunity, Lieberman agreed with the decision to withdraw from the Games because of the Soviet Union's invasion of Afghanistan. In 1980, Lieberman entered the Women's Professional Basketball League (WBL) draft and was selected by the Dallas Diamonds. In her first season with the Diamonds, Lieberman lead them to their first and only championship series appearance.

Lieberman took a leave of absence from the Diamonds to train tennis-great Martina Navratilova. Lieberman returned to the Diamonds in the 1984 season as a member of the newly formed Women's American Basketball Association (WABA). In the 1984–85 WABA season, Lieberman led the team to the championship while earning MVP honors, averaging 27 points per game.

Lieberman was again leading by example on the court for women playing at the highest levels of sport. She wanted to show women, young and old, that they could make a good living in sports. In 1986, Lieberman made history once again by becoming the first woman to join a men's professional basketball team. She played an entire season with the Springfield Fame of the United States Basketball League (USBL) and then played for the Long Island Knights the following season. In 1988, Lieberman made her final move as she joined the Washington Generals on a World Tour with the storied Harlem Globetrotters. Such sports career decisions were unprecedented and played a very significant role in promoting the visibility of women playing professional sports in the United States.

In 1988, Lieberman became the color commentator for NBC during the Olympic Games in Seoul covering the Women's Olympic basketball team on their way to winning a second Olympic gold medal. Lieberman would later go on to write two books, one on her life story as an athlete, and the other on the evolution of women's basketball with Robin Roberts of ESPN and ABC. As a player, Lieberman was a pioneer for women's sports. As an analyst at the Olympics Games, Lieberman promoted women's sports and in 1993 she was rewarded by becoming the first woman inducted into the New York City Basketball Hall of Fame. Not long after, Lieberman was inducted into the Naismith Basketball Hall of Fame for her great accomplishments on the court.

In 1997, with the conception of the Women's National Basketball Association (WNBA), Lieberman felt that this was the league that she had dreamt of as a child and wanted to be a part of the inaugural season. At age 38, Lieberman decided to return to the court and take part in the historical opening season of the WNBA. She was the 15th overall selection in the WNBA draft by the Phoenix Mercury and entered the season as the oldest player in the league. Her experience and leadership on and off the court paid dividends for the Mercury as she helped lead them to the regular season Western Conference Championship and the semifinals of the WNBA playoffs. The home fan attendance of the Mercury also was evidence of Lieberman's ability to attract fans to women's sports just as she had done her entire life. The Mercury achieved a league high average of 13,000 fans per game. The following season, Lieberman decided to move into the front office as general manager and head coach of the expansion WNBA Detroit Shock franchise. Lieberman was very successful in this endeavor as well, leading the Shock to a winning record in its first season and a coveted trip to the WNBA playoffs.

Throughout her illustrious career as an athlete, analyst, coach, and executive, Lieberman has been very successful, not only for herself, but for the advancement of women's sports as a whole. The growth of women's sports, particularly basketball, can be directly linked to her courage and desire to achieve more for women within the world of sports.

Nancy Lieberman has continued her role as a broadcaster for ESPN during WNBA and NCAA women's collegiate games. Lieberman also hosts basketball camps and clinics for young girls trying to improve their athletic abilities and teaches them they can make a career of playing the sport they love. Through her lifetime of success on the court, as well as her commitment to women's opportunities off the court, Lieberman has fulfilled her early age promise of making history in sports.

Her game on the court was eye-popping. But Nancy Lieberman never stopped speaking up for what she believed in, whether it was for expanded opportunities for women and girls in sport, social justice for people of color, or balancing academics and athletics. I was the lucky beneficiary that day in Dallas, but thousands of people have benefited from her speaking out. Her voice was amplified by the greatness of her game, but I have no doubt that she would have been a force in this world if she had never picked up a ball. Lucky for us that she picked it up and spoke out.

Ann Meyers Drysdale

American Star of the International Women's Hall of Fame

by Sara Jane Baker

In high school, Ann Meyers Drysdale had a chance to try out for the men's basketball team. However, after strong discouragement from others, the fear of injury, and the intimidation of the increased competition, she chose not to try out. When she was approached by the Indiana Pacers in 1979, she would not let this second opportunity to play on a men's team elude her—again.

Meyers Drysdale's incredible athletic ability surfaced from a very young age. Ann's father, who played in the American Basketball Association (ABA), and her mother fought for Ann to participate in athletics. In high school, after forgoing her chance to play on the men's team, she became a star on the women's team. She was named an All-American and Team MVP for each of her four years. In 1974, Ann broke the first of many barriers when she became the first high school student to play on the U.S. National Team.

This would not be the last time Meyers Drysdale would break a barrier and defy societal ideals for women. She received the first women's full athletic scholarship from UCLA in 1974, which was especially amazing given that schools were not yet required to fund athletics for women. It did not take long for her to live up to these high expectations. In her freshman season, Meyers Drysdale led the team in almost every category: field goal percentage, rebounding average, free throw percentage, assists, steals, and blocked shots. She was also named a Kodak All-American. Her success earned her a spot on the first-ever Women's Olympic Basketball team in 1976. In her senior campaign, she led her school to the Association for Intercollegiate Athletics for Women (AIAW) championship.

Meyers Drysdale left a legacy at UCLA. She became the first player, male or female, to be named an All-American in each of her four years, and when she graduated, she ranked third all-time in scoring and led the schools in assists and steals.

Her college success made her one of the most coveted athletes for the new Women's Professional Basketball League (WBL). Not surprisingly, Meyers Drysdale was selected as the number one overall draft pick in 1978, the same year the league had been established. She enjoyed a short stint in the league, playing from 1978 to 1980 for the New Jersey Gems. Meyers Drysdale showed her dominance by being named the co-MVP for the 1979 and 1980 seasons.

Because she was such a dominant player in the WBL, she eventually caught the attention of the men's league. The Indiana Pacers offered Meyers Drysdale a free agency contract for $50,000, marking the first time a female had signed a National Basketball Association (NBA) contract. Not only was it unheard of for a female to make such a large amount of money playing sports, it was even more implausible that a woman play in the NBA. With the memory of her high school experience, Meyers Drysdale was ready for the challenge ahead of her.

"Physically and mentally I was the best prepared I had ever been to play the game of basketball,"[1] said Meyers Drysdale about the tryout. She knew she had some weaknesses in comparison to the men; however, she also knew her fundamentals were just as good, if not better. After all, she had been around the sport of basketball her entire life. After an intense, three-day tryout, Meyers Drysdale felt she had given her best performance. The coach, however, felt that her 5-foot-9-inch frame could not sustain the men's physical game. "I was disappointed that the coach didn't keep me on the team at least through the preseason, because I believed I had all the qualifications they expect from the free agents and rookies who go to the next level."[2] Despite not making the team, Meyers Drysdale broke an incredible barrier for women.

Most people would have viewed this as a failure. Not Ann Meyers Drysdale. She simply had to find another path. She began working in the public relations and broadcasting departments for the Indiana Pacers. After attending broadcasting school, she embarked on a career that would last over 20 years. She served as a sportscaster and color analyst and provided commentary for men's and women's basketball, softball, tennis, volleyball, and soccer for ESPN, NBC, and CBS. Meyers Drysdale is arguably best known for coverage of Men's and Women's National Collegiate Athletic Association (NCAA) basketball tournaments during the 1990s. In 2006, Meyers joined an elite group of sports journalists, including Bob Costas and Rupert Murdoch, by winning the USSA Ronald Reagan

Media Award. At a time when female broadcasters were a rarity, Meyers Drysdale paved the way for future female broadcasters.

To add to her distinguished list of honors and accomplishments, Meyers Drysdale was inducted into the inaugural class of the Women's Basketball Hall of Fame. She was also enshrined at the Naismith Memorial Hall of Fame. Meyers Drysdale, and her late husband, Don Drysdale, were the first couple to be hall of famers, as he was a standout pitcher for the Brooklyn and Los Angeles Dodgers.

With all of her experience and background in the sport of basketball, it was no surprise when she was approached by Phoenix to help in their basketball operations department. In 2006, Meyers Drysdale became the third general manager of the Phoenix Mercury and the vice president for the Phoenix Suns. Although Meyers Drysdale was excited about both roles, she was especially eager for the opportunity to advance the popularity of the Women's National Basketball Association (WNBA). The Suns managing partners say that "Ann is someone that has great integrity and a Hall of Fame resume. I believe she will do an excellent job leading this franchise forward."[3] If Meyers Drysdale's past is any indication, she is destined for success.

Growing up in an era before Title IX, Ann Meyers Drysdale seemed unaware of the limits and inequality inflicting women's sports. The country watched in amazement when Ann Meyers was the first high school player to make a U.S. National Team, first female to receive a full scholarship, and the first female to sign a contract with the NBA. Ann Meyers Drysdale is a true trailblazer, and her perseverance and leadership has paved the way for others and has provided new opportunities for women.

Notes

1. Kim Doren and Charlie Jones, *You Go Girl!* (Kansas City: Andrews McMeel Publishing, 2000), 219.

2. Ibid.

3. WNBA, "MERCURY: Mercury names Ann Meyers Drysdale as General Manager," http://www.wnba.com/mercury/news/myers_gm_060912.html.

Pat Summitt

American Star of the Women's International Sports Hall of Fame

by Jessica Bartter

Most basketball coaches hope the "summit" of their careers could match just one mediocre season of Pat Summitt's, but talent like hers is what separates good coaches from exceptional ones.

The responsibility of a coach extends far beyond the bench in Summitt's mind. She embodies the title of a true life educator, caring about her athletes' personal lives and demanding their dedication to academics while building a program at the University of Tennessee (UT) that resembles a family. And that family just so happens to consist of approximately 150 female basketball players because Summitt has held the reins of UT's program for 34 years now, since she was a youthful 22-year-old new to the coaching realm.

Most of Summitt's experience came from being on the court, not the bench. The dominant player started all four years of high school before continuing her dominance at the University of Tennessee-Martin playing basketball and volleyball. Summitt graduated in 1974 as the basketball squad's all-time leading scorer with 1,045 points. Nearby in Knoxville, heads were turning. Summitt received a letter from the physical education department's chairperson, Dr. Helen B. Watson at the University of Tennessee-Knoxville, offering the 21-year-old senior a graduate teaching assistantship and the assistant coaching position for the women's basketball team. Eager to continue her education and have the ability to continue playing in order to train for the 1976 Montreal Olympic Games, Summitt accepted UT's offer. Just two weeks after her acceptance, Summitt was shocked to learn the current head coach was taking a sabbatical and the university wanted Summitt to take full command. For someone who had never planned a practice—let alone ran drills—one can imagine the shock and horror young Summitt felt.

UT probably prepared itself for a few lull years after Summitt's hire, anticipating the new coach may need some time to bring home a .500 season or even a conference championship. But the mountain was one Summitt was built to climb. In just her first year as a coach, UT brought home a 16-8 record and a trip to the finals of the state tournament. All the while, Summitt was working on her master's degree, teaching physical education classes, and working on her own game. She successfully juggled all four tasks and she soon found herself on the 1975 U.S. Women's World Championship team and the 1975 Pan American Games team. And just as she'd hoped, she traveled with the U.S. team to Montreal for the 1976 Olympic Games, where she co-captained the team that brought home the silver medal.

In just her third season at UT, Summitt saw her wins jump to over 20—a number they have never fallen below since. The Lady Vols went 28-5 while making it to the Association for Intercollegiate Athletics for Women (AIAW) Final Four in 1976–77. The next nine seasons saw successful return trips to the national tournament, but that coveted national championship eluded Summitt until 1986–87. The Lady Vols went on to win seven more National Collegiate Athletic Association (NCAA) titles since 1987, most recently in 2007–8, when they defended their 2006–7 title.

Her UT teams of 1996, 1997, and 1998 were the first ever women's basketball squads to win back-to-back-to-back titles. She is hoping her 2008–9 season will bring another three-peat. Summitt will start the 2008–9 season as the all-time winningest coach in NCAA basketball history—men's or women's—with a 983-182 record. En route to UT's eighth NCAA championship, Summitt's basketball programs had produced 14 Southeastern Conference (SEC) Championships (out of 28), 24 trips to the regional finals, and 16 Final Four appearances. Summitt has already been named both the SEC and NCAA Coach of the Year seven times, and her career is not over yet. In 2000, she was named the Naismith Coach of the Century. In honor of her accomplishments, UT officially nicknamed their basketball arena, "The Summitt."

Despite the forceful persona that Summitt now exhibits, she was once shy and timid, which may shock some of her former team members. Though she'd always gone by Tricia or Trish, her hesitation in correcting Dr. Watson and other physical education department officials in her early UT days allowed them to re-nickname her Pat. Subsequently, the name Pat Summitt is the one that has gone down in the history books.

Young Trish was born in Henrietta, Tennessee, in 1952. Growing up, Summitt quickly learned the meaning of diligence firsthand from her strong disciplinarian father, her constant competition with three older brothers and younger sister, and the demands of living on a family farm. In Summitt's family, hard work was not appreciated, it was expected. More so, laziness and excuses were not tolerated. When she was a child, Summitt's routine included attending school and church, and performing her daily chores such as chopping tobacco, plowing the field, or baling hay. After finishing her chores, Summitt found refuge in playing basketball with her brothers in the hayloft.

Summitt's strict father stressed the importance of education to her at a young age. She never missed a day of school from kindergarten through high school. This value stuck with her and is one she has insisted upon her student-athletes, emphasizing the student. All of her players are required to sit in the first three rows of class, pay attention, complete all of her assignments on time, and show respect to everyone. Any player who chooses not to go to class has also made the decision not to play in the next game. The honor of being a Lady Vol comes at a price. A player must be dedicated to her team and academics, and be responsible for her actions at all times. Summitt's tough demeanor has paid dividends to the individual team members and the university; in 34 years, she has graduated 100 percent of her players who have exhausted her athletic eligibility.

In the community, Summitt is an active philanthropist and in 1997 was honored by then-First Lady Hillary Clinton at a White House luncheon for the "25 Most Influential Working Mothers" chosen by *Working Mother* magazine. She has acted as a spokesperson for Big Brothers/Big Sisters and the American Heart Association, and is active with the Verizon Wireless HopeLine program, the United Way, the Juvenile Diabetes Foundation, and The Race for the Cure. Along the way, Summitt has accumulated many awards and recognitions for her contributions. In 1996, she was awarded "Distinguished Citizen of the Year" by the Boy Scouts of America and in 1998 she was named the "Woman of the Year" by both *Glamour* magazine and the City of Knoxville. Most notably, in 2000, Summitt became just the fourth women's basketball coach to be elected into the Basketball Hall of Fame.

After 34 seasons at Tennessee, Summitt is much more than a coach to her Lady Vols. She is a leader, master motivator, champion, educator, role model, and friend. Summitt acts as a mentor to her players, teaching them to believe in themselves and reach their full potential as student-athletes at Tennessee and in life. Most important, though, she leads by example.

C. Vivian Stringer

American Star of the Women's International Sports Hall of Fame

by Sara Jane Baker

Coach Vivian Stringer has proven she can overcome any obstacle she encounters. With adversity from personal struggles, family crises, and negative media attention, she has conquered each one with dignity and class. Despite all this adversity, C. Vivian Stringer is one of the most successful coaches in the history of college basketball. She has also been a role model, mentor, and inspiration to many.

When Coach Stringer took over the Rutgers women's basketball team in 1995, she knew it was going to be a road paved with challenges. Stringer inherited a struggling team that had not experienced a 20-plus win season in four years. For some, this may seem like an overwhelming task, but for Stringer, it was just another opportunity for success. Despite these odds, Coach Stringer was completely confident in the potential of her team. Two recruiting classes later, her team won the Big East Championship and made an appearance in the National Collegiate Athletic Association (NCAA) tournament, eventually making it to the Sweet Sixteen. In the next eight seasons, Stringer led her team to seven NCAA tournament appearances. In 2007, Stringer's team advanced to the national championship game in Cleveland, Ohio. Although the Scarlet Knights were defeated by perennial powerhouse, Tennessee, Stringer proved that hard work, persistence, and a little optimism will eventually pay off.[1]

Stringer's success should not come as a surprise given her past credentials. By the time Coach Stringer joined Rutgers, she had established herself as a coach who turned struggling teams into national powerhouses. In 1971, Coach Stringer made her coaching debut at Cheyney State, a historically all-black college. She started her career in the early 1970s, when women's sports were still struggling to take off. However, Stringer and her team played in front of large crowds and qualified for the first-ever NCAA women's basketball national championship. Despite losing to Louisiana Tech in the national championship game, Stringer had proven herself as a coach. After 11 seasons at Cheyney State, Stringer went to the University

of Iowa. Her success continued as she led her team to nine NCAA tournament appearances and established Iowa as a dominant women's basketball team. Stringer's Iowa team had the first-ever advanced sellout of a women's basketball team, proving that women's basketball had the potential to be as successful as men's basketball.

All her success did not go unnoticed. One of her proudest honors is being voted National Coach of the Year by her peers three times. She has also been named Coach of the Year by *Sports Illustrated*, *USA Today*, *The LA Times*, and the Black Coaches and Administrators (formerly the Black Coaches Association). *Sports Illustrated* named her one of the "101 Most Influential Minorities in Sports" in 2003. On top of countless honors, she has rewritten the coaching history books. She is the first basketball coach, male or female, to bring three different teams to the NCAA tournament. Among Division I women's basketball coaches, she ranks third in wins. In 2001, she was inducted into the Women's Basketball Hall of Fame.

These statistics, awards, and honors are enough to impress anyone. However, her success is even more amazing given the obstacles and struggles she had to overcome along the way. Very few know the details of her personal and family struggles. The adversity for Stringer started at a very young age. Stringer, one of five children, was born in the small town of Edenborn, Pennsylvania. Her parents instilled the values of hard work, perseverance, and a strong work ethic. She was required to do various chores around the house on a daily basis while her father supported the family by working in the coal mines. With all of the financial constraints, Stringer never heard her father complain. Even after both of his legs were amputated due to gangrene, he continued to do his best to support the family.

In high school, there were very few opportunities for women in sports, especially for an African-American woman. There was a cheerleading squad at her high school, but there were no other girls' sports team at her high school. Stringer tried out for the cheerleading squad, and although she was the most talented, she was cut from the team because of her race. With the help of an NAACP leader, Stringer fought this ruling and later became the first black cheerleader at her high school. This struggle had a huge impact on her life, and she could have never known how much it would help her overcome the adversities she would later face.[2]

Stringer saw true strength in her mother when her father passed away during her childhood. Instead of dwelling on the loss, her mother immediately took over the family responsibilities, found a job, and supported the family.

The strong family values that Stringer learned in her upbringing helped her with her own family. Vivian married William D. Stringer and they had three children. However, once again, Vivian faced another challenge. After her middle child, Janine, suffered from meningitis, she was left with special needs. Stringer and her husband strived to give their daughter the best medical attention available and, once again, she thrived in the face of adversity. During this time, Stringer was coaching at Iowa, and it was clear that she did not let this challenge affect her coaching duties as she guided her team to the Final Four.[3]

Then on Thanksgiving Day 1992, another tragedy struck. Her husband unexpectedly died of a heart attack.[4] This was arguably the most devastating event in her life. Despite struggling to raise her three children by herself, she demonstrated tremendous strength, much like her mother had when her own husband passed away. While some would be unable to recover from such a tragedy, Stringer picked up her family and moved to New Brunswick, New Jersey, to begin her incredible reign at Rutgers University.

With all the success Stringer was experiencing at Rutgers University, it finally seemed as if the adversity had stopped. After an impressive season, the Scarlet Knights upset the No. 1 seeded Duke and reached the NCAA Tournament Final Game. This accomplishment, however, was quickly overshadowed by negative comments from radio show host, Don Imus. Following the tournament, Imus, a nationally syndicated radio host, and his executive producer were discussing Rutger's final game versus Tennessee. Rather than praising the accomplishments of both teams, the hosts made offensive and derogatory comments toward the Rutgers team, referring to them as "rough girls and nappy headed hoes." Stringer called Imus's remarks "racist and sexist . . . deplorable, despicable and unconscionable."[5] She handled this obstacle just as she had the other ones, with dignity and class. With Coach Stringer's leadership, the Rutgers team met with Don Imus and eventually accepted his apology.[6] With Essence Carson, Rutgers's captain, as their spokesperson, Rutgers's entire basketball team embodied all the traits of Stringer—courage, eloquence, and strength. They ensured that Rutgers basketball will not be remembered for Imus's ignorant comments, but for their amazing accomplishments on and off the basketball court.

Recently, in early 2008, Vivian Stringer and her Rutgers basketball team received the first ever Eddie Robinson Leadership Award from the National Consortium for Academics and Sports. This award is presented to those who exemplify courage and stand up for justice. Under Stringer's amazing leadership, the Scarlet Knights were able to make this negative situation into a positive learning experience. Coach Stringer is not only teaching these players basketball skills, she is also instilling in them important values and lessons that they will utilize for the rest of their lives.

Notes

1. Rutgers Women's Basketball, "C. Vivian Stringer." *Scarlet Knights*, http://scarletknights.com/basketball-women/coaches/stringer.html (accessed July 10, 2008).

2. Kelly Whiteside, "Rutgers Coach Has History of Standing Firm," USA TODAY, April 11, 2007.

3. Kathy Crockett, "Sports Hero: C. Vivian Stringer" http://www.myhero.com/myhero/hero.asp?hero=stringer (accessed July 10, 2008).

4. Melanie Jackson, "Stringer's Dream Come True," http://sports.espn.go.com/ncw/news/story?id=2282959, January 9, 2006.

5. Maria Newman, "Rutgers Women to Meet with Imus over Remarks," *New York Times*, April 10, 2007.

6. "Rutgers Team: We Accept Don Imus Apology," *AP*, April 13, 2007.

Tara VanDerveer

American Star of the Women's International Sports Hall of Fame

by Ryan Sleeper

When Tara VanDerveer arrived at Stanford in 1985 to take over as just the third coach in the school's history, the Cardinals were a mere 9-19 the preceding season, having missed postseason play for the third consecutive year. In just her third season at the helm, VanDerveer had her team completely turned around, finishing the 1987–88 season with an impressive 27-5 record and an appearance in the National Collegiate Athletic Association (NCAA) Tournament's Sweet Sixteen. Even though there was very little room left to improve, VanDerveer did just that during her fourth and fifth seasons at Stanford. She coached her team to the Elite Eight during the 1988–89 season and during the 1989–90 season, VanDerveer led the Stanford Cardinal women's basketball team to its first ever national title. Stanford and VanDerveer quickly rose to elite status in women's collegiate basketball and have never looked back. With a recent contract extension signed, VanDerveer will remain at the helm of the team through the 2011–12 campaign and it should be a while before Stanford even needs to consider hiring the fourth coach in its history.

VanDerveer's list of achievements at Stanford alone is staggering. In her first 22 seasons on The Farm (the nickname given to Stanford's basketball arena), she has compiled a 571-137 record, good for a .806 winning percentage. She has led her team to two NCAA Championships, three title game appearances, six Final Four appearances, 16 Pac-10 Titles, and 20 consecutive trips to the NCAA Tournament.

While these results are quite awe-inspiring, they are of no surprise to the ever-growing list of people who have been affected by VanDerveer's golden touch. She simply wins wherever she goes. In her very first coaching job at Idaho, she led the Vandals to a 42-14 (.750 winning percentage) record in her two seasons there. In her second and final season with Idaho, her team appeared in the Association for Intercollegiate Athletics for Women (AIAW) Tournament, which was the national tournament before the NCAA Tournament was established. She then launched her next basketball team into national prominence when she coached the Ohio State Buckeyes to a 110-37 record (.748 winning percentage) in five seasons. This stint included four consecutive 20-win seasons, four Big Ten Championships, and three NCAA Tournament appearances. She led the Buckeyes as far as the Elite Eight during the 1984–85 season before taking her present job at Stanford.

VanDerveer has also experienced success on the international level. She famously took a one-year leave of absence from Stanford to coach the U.S. Olympic Women's Basketball Team. Her team took home the gold medal at the 1996 Summer Games in Atlanta. During her time as head coach of Team USA, she compiled an overall record of 88-8 (.917 winning percentage), and from 1995 through the Olympic gold in 1996, VanDerveer led the team to a remarkable 60-0 record.

It is often difficult to explain what exactly makes a coach successful or unsuccessful. In VanDerveer's case, throughout her career she has been able to recruit the best talent by connecting with people. She achieves this relationship by being authentic and trustworthy to her players. Perhaps this is a trick she picked up while watching Coach Bob Knight before her practices when she was the starting guard for the Indiana Hoosiers women's basketball team. In her own words from her book *Shooting from the Outside*, VanDerveer explains her coaching style:

> I say what I think, sometimes to the chagrin of my players and bosses. I'm not out to hurt anyone's feelings. In fact, I try to keep in tune with my players' moods and concerns. But being honest is the only way I know, and it's the only way I know how to coach. The most direct route between teaching and understanding, as between two points, is a straight line. Don't make your players guess what you're trying to tell them. Lay your cards on the table. Tell the truth as clearly as you know it.[1]

Her achievements have culminated in spots in the Women's Basketball, Women's Sports Foundation, Greater Buffalo, and Indiana University halls of fame. Her reach on the game of basketball stretches far and wide. Her coaching honors include National Coach of the

Year three times while at Stanford, Big Ten Coach of the Year twice, District Coach of the Year three times, Pac-10 Coach of the Year six times, Northern California Women's Intercollegiate Coach of the Year five times, USA Basketball National Coach of the Year, and the USOC Elite Basketball Coach of the Year. In addition, she has coached two Naismith Player of the Year honorees, 10 Kodak First-Team All-Americans, eight Pac-10 Player of the Year winners, 34 Pac-10 First-Teamers, and 30 players selected to play for Team USA. The impact VanDerveer is making in women's basketball may be endless, as the countless great players that have learned from her will spread her lessons for generations to come.

Tara VanDerveer was born on June 26, 1953. She grew up in upstate New York during a time before Title IX brought equal opportunities for women in sports. In high school, despite her father's lack of support toward her quest to be involved in basketball, Tara proved to herself that a woman can do anything a man can do by being the best basketball player, male or female, at her school. She then developed an interest in coaching while taking notes everyday from Bob Knight at Indiana. Her passion and relentless pursuit to be a part of the game she loved proved to her father that she could indeed have a future in basketball, and she showed the rest of us that any woman can accomplish anything she truly believes in.

Note

1. Tara VanDerveer, *Shooting from the Outside* (New York: Avon Books, 1997), 16.

Betty Jaynes

Administrative Pioneer for Basketball Coaches

by Horacio Ruiz

When the Women's Basketball Coaches Association (WBCA) held its first convention in 1982 just outside of Philadelphia in Wayne, Pennsylvania, the organization was set to pick its first executive director. The organization had been created the year before to address the needs of women's basketball coaches. During the 1982 convention, the WBCA had a membership of 212 coaches and 99 attendees when Betty Jaynes was named its first executive director. She had been the head women's basketball coach at Madison College (later to be renamed James Madison University) since 1970, where she compiled a 142-114 record, including a Virginia (Association for Intercollegiate Athletics for Women [AIAW]) state championship in 1975 and three runner-up finishes. Jaynes first joined the staff at Madison in 1968 as an assistant professor of physical education with primary teaching duties in gymnastics, tennis, and swimming. She earned her master's degree in physical education from the University of North Carolina in 1968 and her bachelor's degree in physical education from Georgia College in 1967. As Jaynes accepted the WBCA's executive director position, she resigned from her post as head women's basketball coach. Jaynes is a basketball lifer, having dedicated her career to advancing the participation, development, advocacy, and opportunities for girls and women in basketball.

During her tenure, the WBCA increased its membership to 5,000, including 98 percent of Division I women's basketball coaches. Jaynes was respected for her leadership position in rules policies. She chaired the United States Girls' and Women's Basketball Rules Committee from 1979 to 1981 and was the tournament director of the 1975 AIAW Large College National Basketball Championships, the first-ever championship game sell-out in the modern era of women's basketball. At the same tournament, Jaynes played a leading role in presenting the first-ever Kodak Women's All-America Basketball Team. "I think that's when I really realized how much I loved administration," Jaynes said. "Eastman Kodak came and they stayed with women's basketball for more than 30 years. As you get more responsibility with administration, you want to move into the administration area. I loved administration—I loved that part of it. I think that's why when the WBCA was created I didn't have any problem at all taking over that executive directorship."[1]

She chaired the Kodak All-American program from 1976 through 1982 and brought in Kodak as one of the first sponsors of the WBCA. Today, being named as an All-American is the most prestigious honor in women's basketball. In 2005, the WBCA celebrated its 25th anniversary. By contrast to the inaugural convention in 1982, the 2006 WBCA Convention held in Boston, Massachusetts, had approximately 2,000 registrants and 120 exhibitors.

"This truly shows the interest that has been developed for the basketball coaching profession and the game of women's basketball," Jaynes said. "The most outstanding changes have been in the marketing of WBCA programs, as well as the wide respect in the athletic world regarding the opinions and visions of the coaches of women's basketball."[2]

Throughout her career, Jaynes has also served on USA Basketball's board of directors and as chair of its Bylaws Committee, as a Women's Sports Foundation trustee and vice president, a Women's Basketball Hall of Fame board member, and as an Atlanta Tip-Off Club board member and its vice president. Jaynes was named the WBCA's first CEO on September 1, 1996. In 2006, Jaynes was the recipient of the Bunn Lifetime Achievement Award from the Naismith Memorial Basketball Hall of Fame, the most prestigious award presented by the Hall of Fame outside of enshrinement. The award honors coaches, players, and contributors whose accomplishments have impacted basketball anywhere from the high school to the international level.

"The dedication and passion Betty has demonstrated for basketball has been instrumental in the growth and success of the women's game at all levels," said John L. Doleva, the Hall of Fame president and CEO. "Her leadership of the WBCA and her service for numerous committees and organizations has helped shape the sport, and her lifelong commitment to basketball exemplifies the spirit of the Bunn Lifetime Achievement Award."[3]

In addition, Jaynes was inducted into the Women's Basketball Hall of Fame in 2000 and the National Association of Collegiate Directors of Athletics (NACDA) Hall of Fame in 2006. A native of

Covington, Georgia, Jaynes founded and served as president of the Georgia Women's Intersport Network (GA WIN), whose mission is to develop and promote public awareness for women's involvement and achievement in athletics and to create a strong network for women and girls involved in sports. GA WIN has championed Title IX legislation at the state and national levels, established the Georgia Girls' High School Soccer State Championship, and hosts the annual SPORTSFEST event to expose girls ages 8 to 13 to sports in which they may not otherwise have an opportunity to participate. The annual sports clinic is free of charge for its participants.

Her involvement in basketball dates back to her high school years, when Jaynes lettered in basketball all four years and was an All-State selection in both her junior and senior years. During her senior year, she led her team to a 33-1 record and a berth in the 1963 Class AA Georgia State Championship Game. "My parents really wanted me to be more of a Shirley Temple type," she said. "They provided me with opportunities to play piano, dance, and play the trumpet. In sixth grade middle school PE class I became very enthralled with basketball. I was very athletic so I picked up on those skills. It was that physical education experience that got me into the game."[4]

Betty Jaynes served as the WBCA's first CEO until 2001. Since then, she has worked as a consultant for the WBCA, acting as chief liaison to affiliated governing bodies and sport organizations, overseeing the WBCA's legislative role with the NCAA, and handling additional advisory affairs.

"Anytime that you start out something—that you have a passion for—you don't know what the ends will be, it's the process," Jaynes said. "That's what I have enjoyed with my life, it's the process trying to make it the very best that I can on behalf of the coaches."[5]

Notes

1. Betty Jaynes, interview with the author, September 16, 2008.
2. Mercyhurst College, "WBCA Celebrates 25th Anniversary," Mercyhurst College, http://hurstathletics.cstv.com/sports/w-baskbl/spec-rel/092705aaa.html.
3. Naismith Memorial Basketball Hall of Fame, "Betty Jaynes Recipient of Prestigious Hall of Fame Bunn Lifetime Achievement Award," Naismith Memorial Basketball Hall of Fame, http://www.hoophall.com/genrel/030707aaq.html.
4. Betty Jaynes, interview with the author, September 16, 2008.
5. Ibid.

Lisa Leslie

Future Hall of Famer

by Stacy Martin-Tenney

Courtesy of the University of Southern California.

Standing 6-foot-5-inches tall, she dominates any room she enters and any basketball court she graces with her presence. Early in life, Lisa Leslie did not even consider playing basketball, the sport she loves today, in fact, she adamantly refused. Like most young girls, she struggled to define herself, but it was more difficult for Leslie given her impressive stature. It was so simple and so clear to everyone around her that her height would equip her with a powerful presence on the basketball court. However, she was not convinced and her willful personality would fuel her opposition to the notion of playing basketball. Finally a friend's determination swayed her to try out for the team in seventh grade. And destiny took over. Of course, Leslie's strong work ethic, commitment, and resolve to better her game didn't hurt either.

She was the consummate athlete, always looking for the next edge and a way to excel. Whether it was improving her fitness level through additional training, perfecting the skills she would need on the court through drills and shooting practice, or even playing pick-up against the boys so that someone could challenge her presence on the court, she was always taking it to the next level. Leslie possessed an inherent fortitude and strength of mind at an early age and those attributes also made her a force to be reckoned with on the court. She credits her mother for those qualities and for teaching her to stand tall in all realms of life. Her mother, Christine Espinoza, instilled those lessons early and often in life despite being gone frequently during Leslie's youth. Her mother worked as a cross-country truck driver to earn a living to sustain her three daughters, since Leslie's father had left the family when she was four.

Leslie continued to mature through life's struggles and make her own way in the world through the sport of basketball. At Morningside High School in Inglewood, California, she earned national attention for her play and by the time she was a junior *USA Today* selected her as a first team high school All-American. Her talents were unbelievable, delivering an average 21.7 points, 12.8 rebounds, and 6.2 blocks per game that year. As a senior, Leslie challenged Cheryl Miller's national record for points in a single game; in a regular season match up with South Torrance High, she scored 101 points before halftime. Her team had contributed one additional point to bring the score to 102-24 against their opponents at the half. Unfortunately, the embarrassment was too much for the South Torrance team and they forfeited the rest of the game, eliminating Leslie's chance of breaking the record of 105 points, still held by Miller today. While her personal victory was cut short, the team triumphed with a California state title in women's basketball later that season. In that championship game, Leslie managed 35 points, 12 rebounds, and seven blocked shots despite suffering from the chickenpox. Her performance earned her the prestigious Naismith Award. She was not only a standout in basketball, as she also earned varsity letters in volleyball and track and served as class president for three years. These collective efforts yielded her the Dial Award for the nation's top high school student-athlete. She could have ventured across the country to any school of her choice to play collegiate basketball, but she chose to remain close to her roots in Los Angeles, California, and selected USC.

The accolades continued in college, further cementing her name into the sport's record books. She earned honors such as Pac-10 Freshman of the Year, Pac-10 first-team all four years (the first freshman to earn the honor), and All-American honors in 1992, 1993, and 1994 when she won her second Naismith Award. Her play continued to dominate the courts and helped her team to four National Collegiate Athletic Association (NCAA) tournaments and two Elite Eight appearances. USA Basketball took notice of the phenom and recognized her as Female Athlete of the Year in 1993. Her future with USA Basketball had yet to unfold and no one could have predicted the impact that Lisa Leslie would have on the sport of basketball, especially the women's game. While she had limited success early in the U.S. basketball arena, trying and failing to make some teams, she led others to gold medals in the World University Games and Goodwill Games.

After she graduated from college with a bachelor's degree in communications, she was left without an opportunity to play in her own country, so she traveled abroad to pursue her passion for basketball in Sicilgesso, Italy. "I think we are cheated as a gender," she told *Entertainment Weekly*. "No one knows what happens to all the great people in our game. It seems like we're written off."[1] In 1996, she garnered the opportunity to play in her home country on the world's stage when the Olympic Games were held in Atlanta, Georgia. Her versatile play as a center could not be matched by the rest of the world and the United States captured Olympic gold. She earned the single-game U.S. Olympic record for most points with 35 in the international bout. After the Games, women's basketball had gained enough momentum to establish its own professional opportunity in the United States, and the Women's National Basketball Association (WNBA) was born. Leslie was selected to play for her hometown team, the Los Angeles Sparks.

Her illustrious career only perpetuated the success of the sport and her own personal fame. Leslie may be one of the most aggressive women to play center and many have compared her seamless, yet aggressive, style of play to Kareem Abdul-Jabbar, but her willowy, model-like appearance has also helped to establish women as beautiful, powerful athletes. Leslie was not only a professional basketball player, but also a model for the renowned Wilhelmina Models agency. When she was not gracing the basketball court with her superb skills, she was gracing magazine covers like *Vogue* with her stunning smile, proving that women can have it all.

Her prowess on the court captured two WNBA Championships for the Sparks and two MVP titles, with both honors coming in 2001 and 2002. On July 30, 2002, she elevated the women's game above the rim, quite literally, as she became the first woman to slam dunk a basketball in a professional game. Her game has always dominated the international stage, including team gold medals in the 1998 and 2002 World Championships and her personal MVP in 2002.

Her golden touch at the Olympics is simply awe-inspiring. She led the U.S. women to gold in Sydney in 2000 and ended the 2004 Athens Olympics as the U.S. all-time Olympic leading scorer with

Courtesy of the University of Southern California.

407 points and another gold medal. Only one female basketball player had earned four gold medals at the Olympics, Teresa Edwards, but no one had ever earned four consecutive gold medals in women's basketball until Lisa Leslie led Team USA to victory in Beijing in 2008. What is even more impressive is that it was her first season back after giving birth to her daughter, Lauren in 2007. Leslie has become an accomplished working mother as well, even running off the court during a pre-game warm up to tend to her daughter's needs. Leslie missed playing with the national team in 2006 due to family circumstances; the team earned bronze at those World Championships. Her spark was definitely missed.

The U.S. women's national team head coach, Anne Donovan, summed up Leslie's omnipresence when she returned to the team: "Just her talent and what she brings to the team both offensively and defensively, but her presence and her leadership and her experience and all those gold medals that she's won, it's just really great to have her back on the court with us."[2] Leslie ended her Olympic career in Beijing this year by fouling out with six minutes and 33 seconds remaining in the game, not uncommon for her aggressive style of play. She walked off the court to a loud ovation for her years of service, the attention she brought to the game on the international and domestic scene, and, most of all for the charisma, style, and dedication with which she played the game.

Notes

1. Gale Schools. Celebrating Women's History: Lisa Leslie, http://www.gale schools.com/womens_history/bio/leslie_l.htm.

2. 2008 NBC Beijing Olympics. Athletes: Lisa Leslie Bio, http://www.nbcolym pics.com/athletes/athlete=547/bio/index.html.

Sheryl Swoopes

Future Hall of Famer

by Ryan Sleeper

Courtesy of Texas Tech Athletic Media Relations.

In high school, she led Brownfield High to its first Texas State Championship for girls basketball in 1988. In college, she led the Texas Tech Lady Raiders to its first National Collegiate Athletic Association (NCAA) National Championship in 1993. In the pros, she led the Houston Comets of the Women's National Basketball Association (WNBA) to an unprecedented "four-peat," winning the first four championships in the league's existence from 1997 to 2000. In the Olympic Games, she led Team USA to three straight gold medals in 1996, 2000, and 2004. It is no wonder Sheryl Swoopes is frequently referred to as the "female Michael Jordan." Perhaps some would suggest calling Michael Jordan the "male Sheryl Swoopes." Like Mike, she even has her own shoe, "Air Swoopes;" the first basketball shoe endorsed by a woman. Being the first three-time WNBA MVP, first three-time WNBA Defensive Player of the Year, and still holding numerous scoring records from every level of play, including the most points ever scored, by a male or a female, in a college championship game (47), she is clearly one of, if not the, best women's basketball players of all time. It's hard to believe all of this was accomplished by a woman who grew up wanting to be a cheerleader.[1]

Swoopes was raised in a single-parent household having never known her father. In order to support her and her three brothers, Swoopes's mother worked three jobs and sometimes had to seek public assistance in order to feed the family. Even though, as a young child, Swoopes would enjoy getting dressed up with her cousin and "cheering" for her two older brothers, she never tried out for the cheerleading squad because she knew her mother could not afford the uniform, pom-poms, and shoes she would need to participate. Instead, she began playing basketball with her brothers, sometimes only being able to do so on a homemade hoop consisting of a bicycle wheel and a plywood backboard. Her brothers resisted her company on the court at first, telling her, "Basketball is for boys. You can't play."[2] They would eventually allow her to play, but would be rough with her in an effort to deter her from wanting to participate. She was often brought to tears from the scrapes and bruises she had to endure, and her mother would recommend staying inside to "play with her dolls." These comments would only serve to motivate her to wipe away the tears and continue to play.

The early merciless competition would begin to shape Swoopes into the basketball player she became. She was already a team leader by the time she started playing organized basketball with other girls her age. In her third year with the Little Dribblers, her team traveled to Beaumont, Texas, to play in the National Championship. After losing by just a couple of points, Swoopes was depressed because she felt she had let the team down, but she did not let this setback deter her from playing basketball. In junior high, she set her sights on becoming a varsity player once she reached high school. In order to achieve this goal, she started playing against all boys during open gym time at the local high school three nights a week. She was rarely picked for a team and when she did get to play, she was often taunted and mocked. Again, this experience toughened her up and her play steadily improved. When she reached high school, she was moved to the varsity team after just one game on the junior varsity team. She would lead her high school to a state title her junior year, scoring 26 points and grabbing 18 rebounds in the championship game. Efforts like this in the biggest games would soon become a pattern in her playing career.

Upon graduating from high school, Swoopes signed with the University of Texas to play for the Lady Longhorns, the best women's basketball program in the state. However, after visiting the campus the week before classes and practices started, she realized she had made the wrong choice after being so far from home for just one day. She backed out of her commitment, forgoing her eligibility to play for any Division I program for at least one year. Still wanting to play basketball, she enrolled at South Plains Junior College, just 30 miles from her home, where she played for two years. She eventually moved back to a major basketball program when she transferred to Texas Tech University, 38 miles from home, her junior year. With her talents finally on a big stage, she brought a great deal of attention to women's basketball. One highlight of her illustrious collegiate career was scoring a career high 53 points against Texas, the program many called her crazy for leaving. She would finish her time at Texas Tech by bringing them its first national championship, while scoring a championship record-high 47 points in her final game.

After graduating in 1993, as arguably the best-known female player, Swoopes was forced to continue her playing career overseas in Italy because the United States did not have any professional basketball leagues for women. After just 10 games, she again was feeling homesick, and returned to Texas, putting her professional basketball career temporarily on hold. Finally, in 1997, due in large part to Swoopes helping increase the popularity of women's basketball, the WNBA was formed, and she was quickly signed by the Houston Comets.

She missed a lot of her first season in the WNBA because she was pregnant with her son, Jordan, named after Michael.[3] After astonishingly returning to play just six weeks after giving birth, she instantly became one of the best players in the league and would lead her team to the first four WNBA championships. She would encounter another setback in 2001, when she experienced a potentially career-ending knee injury. After pondering retirement, she returned to the league and promptly won yet another MVP award in 2002. She credits her son, whom she calls her world, for motivating her to make it back to the game. "Mommy, you're still good," he said, "If you retire, who am I gonna watch?"[4]

In October 2005, Swoopes courageously came out of the closet, announcing she was a lesbian on Good Morning America, making her the first high-profile athlete of the three major sports (basketball, football, baseball) to announce their homosexuality while still playing. In an interview, Swoopes explained, "I don't want to say I've been living a lie, but for the past seven, eight years I haven't been able to be comfortable in my own skin, around my own friends and family."[5] She was nervous that this announcement could

Courtesy of Texas Tech Athletic Media Relations.

potentially cost her thousands of dollars in endorsement deals, but wanted to be a leader for the lesbian community, showing it is okay to be yourself and that being homosexual does not make you any less of a great person. Not only did Swoopes's endorsers not back out of her deals, she actually signed a new six-figure deal with Olivia Cruises and Resorts, a lesbian-based business. Swoopes does not think she was born homosexual, and believes that people cannot help with whom they fall in love.

"My biggest concern is that people are going to look at my homosexuality and say to little girls, whether they're white, black, Hispanic, that I can't be their role model anymore."[6] Influencing young girls in a positive way is so meaningful to Sheryl that she cried the first time she saw a little girl wearing her jersey. "I've worked hard all my life to be the person I am, and to think that my saying who I really am might cause me not to be a role model is a huge concern."[7] Swoopes says she wants people to say, "You see what this woman is doing? She's strong, she's powerful, and she is who she is. And you can be okay with that."[8]

Sheryl Swoopes is strong, powerful, and is who she is. And she is still a role model and is even more of a leader.

Notes

1. Sheryl Swoopes, *Bounce Back*, (Dallas: Taylor, 1996), 4.

2. Christina Lessa, *Stories of Triumph: Women Who Win in Sport and in Life* (New York: Universe, 1998), 115.

3. Amelie Welden, *Girls Who Rocked the World: Heroines from Sacagawea to Sheryl Swoopes* (Milwaukee, Wis.: Gareth Stevens, 1999), 100.

4. Anne Stockwell, "She Is Our Champion," *The Advocate*, November 22, 2005.

5. Ibid.

6. Michael Hirsley, "Swoopes Concerned Her Sexuality Will Affect Her Role-Model Status," *Chicago Tribune*, October 26, 2005.

7. Stockwell, "She Is Our Champion."

8. Ibid.

Cheryl Miller

American Star of the Women's International Sports Hall of Fame

by Ryan Sleeper

Cheryl Miller is a hall of fame basketball player and commentator for Turner Sports. She was born January 3, 1964, in Riverside, California, into a family of very talented athletes. In fact, you may have heard of some of her four brothers. Her older brother, Darrell, played Major League Baseball for the Los Angeles Angels of Anaheim and her younger brother, Reggie, was a National Basketball Association (NBA) superstar for the Indiana Pacers. This inherited athletic prowess does not even mention her oldest brother, Saul Jr., whose father, Saul, felt was the most talented of all the Miller children. Growing up, her gifted brothers were not easy on Cheryl when it came to sports. "They'd throw me a ball, tackle me, pile on, mangle me," Cheryl recalls.[1] She would benefit tremendously from this tough love, and as with many of the athletes found in the pages of this book, the experience of practicing so much with her male counterparts would prepare Miller to dominate her peers. She got so good that she would usually beat Reggie, who was a year younger, in their frequent one-on-one games. However, as the two siblings got older, and taller, little brother Reggie became not so little, or beatable, blossoming to a height of 6 feet, 6 inches. Fortunately, Cheryl grew to a height of 6 feet, 2 inches. The best brother-sister combination in basketball history began benefiting from their skills while they were in high school. The two would hustle on their local playground when Reggie, with Cheryl out of sight, would approach unsuspecting two-somes and ask if they wanted to play him and his sister for $10. Needless to say, the offer was accepted and Cheryl would emerge to their competitors' chagrin. Also needless to say is where the $10 on the table would end up.

Miller was part of the first generation that benefited from Title IX, which led to a never before seen equal opportunity for women in sports, and in turn a realistic future in basketball for Miller. Many of the women athletes who competed before Title IX did not have the advantage of playing in high school or college, receiving an education through an athletic scholarship, or being drafted to any of the numerous leagues for women that emerged as a result of this act. Fortunately for basketball fans, Miller, one of the greatest players of all time, did have this opportunity.

Miller began taking full advantage of her athletic opportunities in high school at Riverside Polytechnic High School, where she had a remarkable career. Miller led her high school to four straight California State Championships while averaging 32.8 points and 15 rebounds per game. Her four state titles, during her four years in high school, coincided with her four straight All- American honors from *Parade* magazine—an unprecedented accomplishment for any player, male or female. Other achievements in high school include setting a California state scoring record averaging 37.5 points per game one season, being named Street & Smith's National High School Player of the Year in 1981 and 1982, receiving the Dial Award for being the high school scholar-athlete of the year in 1981, and leading her team to an incredible 84-game winning streak. Her team finished with a 132-4 record during her high school career, an average of just one loss per year. Unbelievably, these are not even the accomplishments that made Miller most famous. During her senior season, playing against Norte Vista High School, Miller scored a record 105 points, a girl's high school basketball record that would stand for more than 20 years before Epiphanny Prince scored 113 in a game in 2006. Even more newsworthy to many, during that same game, Miller dunked the basketball, which was an unprecedented feat for a female in organized play.

Coming out of high school as, perhaps, the greatest female ever to play the game, Miller was recruited by 250 colleges. She chose to stay close to home and attended USC. Her impact on its women's basketball program was immediate. During her freshman year, she led the Lady Trojans to a 30-2 record and a comeback victory against top-ranked Louisiana Tech in the National Collegiate Athletic Association (NCAA) championship game. Miller had 27 points, four blocks, nine rebounds, and four steals in the game, and was named the tournament's MVP for her effort. Astonishingly, she repeated this feat her sophomore season, picking up her second tournament MVP award while leading her team to back-to-back NCAA championships by defeating the Tennessee Lady Volunteers 72-61 in the title game.

The 1984 Summer Olympic Games were in Miller's college town of Los Angeles, California, and she was recruited to play for the U.S. women's basketball team. She played for none other than the head coach she had just defeated for the 1984 NCAA Women's Championship, Coach Pat Summitt, the winningest NCAA basketball coach of all time. Miller was the team's leading scorer and led them to the gold medal. Quite understandably, she considers this accomplishment one of the greatest in her career.

Miller returned to USC for her junior year, and despite having one of her greatest statistical years, averaging 26.8 points and 15.8 rebounds per game, the Lady Trojans lost nine contests and were unable to "three-peat" by winning the title for the third consecutive year. Miller would lead the team back to the title game her senior season, but this time they were defeated by the top-ranked University of Texas Lady Longhorns. Miller finished her career with USC with a pristine 112-20 record; she was also a four-time All-American and a three-time recipient of the Naismith Award. For her accomplishments, Miller was honored as the first USC basketball player, male or female, to have her number (31) retired. Miller also excelled in the classroom, graduating with a bachelor's degree in sports information.

Upon graduation, Miller was drafted by several basketball leagues, including the United States Basketball League, a men's league. However, with the creation of the Women's National Basketball Association (WNBA) still a decade away and no real strong opportunity for women in professional basketball, Miller began an illustrious broadcasting career with ABC Sports. She returned to the court in 1986 to lead the U.S. women's national team to another gold medal at the Goodwill Games in Moscow. She was also selected to play for the 1988 Olympic team, but just before the Games, Miller suffered a career-ending knee injury.

Despite the injuries, Miller has continued to impact the game of basketball. In 1993, at just 29 years old, she returned to her alma mater as the head coach of USC. In two seasons, Miller led the Lady Trojans to a more-than-respectable 44-14 record and a 1994 Pac-10 conference title. In 1995, she joined her current employer, Turner Sports, where she does basketball commentary for TNT and TBS. In November 1996, she added to her list of firsts for women, becoming the first female analyst to ever cover a nationally televised NBA game. She took a four year leave of absence from in front of the camera to take a position as head coach and general manager of the Phoenix Mercury, a team she led to the 1998 WNBA Finals. She resigned from that post after the 2000 season, returning to Turner, and has never looked back. Cheryl Miller has used her diverse talents to bring positive attention to women's basketball, and has blazed trails for women in not only the sport itself, but sports business as well.

Note

1. J. Kelly, *Superstars of Women's Basketball* (Philadelphia: Chelsea House Publishers, 1997), 38.

12

A SMASH OVER THE NET: WOMEN'S VOLLEYBALL

Introduction by Richard Lapchick

When I think about women and volleyball, I see two shining stars: Flo Hyman and Misty May-Treanor.

Hyman's bright star burned out early when she collapsed and died during a professional volleyball match in Japan at age 31. The sports world was stunned when sadly, on January 24, 1986, her life and career ended in the same instant.

Hyman did not even start playing volleyball until she was 17 years old. In high school, Hyman was on the basketball and track and field teams. When she grew to 6 feet, 5 inches, she took up the game she would come to dominate.

She earned the first female athletic scholarship awarded by the University of Houston in 1974, became a three-time All-American (1974–76), and was named the Most Outstanding Collegiate Player in 1976.

The U.S. women had a poor history in the Olympics where they never finished higher than fifth (1964). The U.S. national team did not even qualify in 1972 or 1976. Led by Hyman, the U.S. team not only qualified, but was the favorite for the 1980 Moscow Olympics. The United States boycotted those Games.

Four years later, Hyman helped lead the U.S. team to its first ever medal, the silver, in Los Angeles. Hyman was also socially and politically conscious and joined forces with civil rights leader Coretta Scott King, democratic vice presidential candidate Geraldine Ferraro, and astronaut Sally Ride to lobby for the Civil Rights Restoration Act and the strengthening of Title IX.

Before her first Olympic medal was placed around her neck, Misty May-Treanor had to involve her mother in the celebration. It was the 2004 Athens Olympics, and May-Treanor was heartbroken not to be able to share the moment with her mother, Barbara May, who had died of cancer in 2002. Instead of having her mother there in person, she shared the moment with her in spirit by spreading some of her mom's ashes on the sand on which she had just cemented Olympic history.

May-Treanor and teammate Kerri Walsh won the gold medals in beach volleyball in both the Athens and Beijing Summer Olympics. They have dominated the sport. Misty May played Division I volleyball from 1995 to 1999 at California State University, Long Beach, where she was a two time All-American and twice was the National Collegiate Athletic Association (NCAA) Player of the Year. They won the national title and went undefeated while she shared the NCAA Championship's Most Outstanding Player award. Finally, she won the Honda-Broderick Cup, which is awarded to the top female college athlete, in 1998.

Misty May-Treanor played her first professional match on the Association of Volleyball Professionals (AVP) tour in May 1999, while still a college senior. She fell in love with beach volleyball and partnered with Holly McPeak. They qualified for one of two U.S. Olympic berths for the Sydney Games but they did not medal and placed fifth.

It was after Sydney that she teamed up with Kerri Walsh and the history of the sport has never been the same. They were the international Fédération Internationale de Volleyball (FIVB) tour champions in 2002. Then they joined the AVP tour in 2003 and went undefeated. In fact, going into the Beijing Games, they had won 101 straight matches and 18 tournaments since June 2007. Ironically, they lost a match shortly after Beijing to fellow 2008 Olympians, Nicole Branagh and Elaine Youngs, at the AVP Shootout in Cincinnati, Ohio.

An American sport, volleyball was 113 years old in 2008. The sport became more popular outside the United States, but now, again, is very popular in the United States, especially after the U.S. men won the gold and the women won the silver indoors while Misty May-Treanor and Kerri Walsh won women's beach volleyball gold and Phil Dalhausser and Todd Rogers won the men's gold on the beach.

Some speculate that the estimated 46 million Americans who play volleyball will increase after the Olympics. Worldwide, there are 800 million players who regularly play volleyball. Those are big numbers. Volleyball ranks second to soccer in participation sports. Shortly after basketball was invented in Springfield, Massachusetts, by Dr. Naismith at the YMCA, William G. Morgan, an instructor at the YMCA in nearby Holyoke, decided to create a game less rigorous than basketball. He blended elements of basketball, baseball, tennis, and handball to create volleyball. The first players were businessmen in a class he was teaching at the Y.

Morgan had called the game "mintonette." Then someone told Morgan that the players seemed to be "volleying" the ball back and forth. The name "volleyball" was christened and on July 7, 1896, the first game of volleyball was played at Springfield College.

In 1922, the YMCA held the first national volleyball championships in Brooklyn, New York, with 27 teams from 11 states.

The United States Volleyball Association (USVBA) was formed in 1928 to govern the sport in the United States. The first U.S. Volleyball Open was held with a field that was open to non-YMCA squads. The first U.S. Women's National Volleyball Championships was not held until 1949.

While many believe the beach volleyball version is new, it actually started with men in 1930. California was the home of the game.

In 1947, the FIVB was founded. Volleyball was introduced at the Tokyo Olympic Games in 1964.

The U.S. National Women's team began a year-round training regime in 1975, followed in 1977 by the U.S. National Men's team.

As it took over women's championships, the NCAA staged the first women's volleyball collegiate championship in 1981. The University of Southern California won the crown.

Professional players united under the umbrella of the American Volleyball Professionals (AVP) in 1983. Three years later in 1986, the Women's Professional Volleyball Association (WPVA) was formed to administer, govern, and protect the integrity of women who were pros. The WPVA was dissolved on April 6, 1998, after 11 seasons.

The U.S. men and women took gold and silver medals in indoor volleyball competition in the 1984 Los Angeles Olympics. The women never made the finals again until the Beijing Games in 2008, when they lost to Brazil but captured another silver. In 1984, they lost to China. In 2008, they were coached by "Jenny" Lang Ping, who was the star of the Chinese team in 1984.

The men took gold again in the 1988 Seoul Olympics.

Beach volleyball was becoming global although the AVP and WPVA were focusing primarily on the United States. A pro circuit was developed in Australia in 1987. In 1990, the FIVB created its own circuit, with tournaments in Brazil, Italy, and Japan. Beach volleyball was a demonstration at the 1992 Olympics in Barcelona. It officially joined the Olympic roster in 1996 for men and women.

The money increased and by 2002, prize money for women was $1,750,000 for 11 tournaments on the FIVB tour. The popularity and apparent financial security of the sport seem set.

So the American women who won the silver medal in Beijing can dream of their first gold medal. The likes of 2008 team members Ogonna Nnamani, Danielle Scott-Arruda, Tayyiba Haneef-Park, Lindsey Berg, Stacy Sykora, Nicole Davis, Heather Bown, Jennifer Joines, Kimberly Glass, and Robyn Ah Mow-Santos can create their own history in the years ahead. And perhaps Nicole Branagh and Elaine Youngs may be ready for a gold themselves in beach volleyball. But the stars of volleyball trailblazers Flo Hyman and Misty May-Treanor will always be visible to inspire them.

Flora "Flo" Hyman

American Star of the Women's
International Sports Hall of Fame

by Jessica Bartter

A bright star burned out early when Flo Hyman collapsed to her death during a professional volleyball match in Japan at age 31. Her friends, family, and fans were distraught over her death and although Flo had nicknamed herself the "old lady" of volleyball, they all believed her life and career were far too premature to come to an end. But sadly, on January 24, 1986, her life and career ended in the same instant.

Though almost certainly on her way to bigger and better things, Hyman accomplished a tremendous amount during her short life and career, becoming the face of American volleyball as it was catapulted from a recreational pastime to the popular college and youth sport it is today. Hyman's own participation in volleyball started recreationally as she and her older sister, Suzanne, would head to the beach from her hometown of Inglewood, California, to look for some pick-up games and tournaments on the sand. Beach volleyball adds several elements of difficulty to the sport of volleyball since simple athletic moments like running and jumping can turn into tremendous feats in the sand. Needless to say, this start greatly prepared Hyman for the force she would become on the indoor courts.

In high school, Hyman played basketball and ran track and field, but she did not play competitive volleyball until she reached her full height of 6 feet, 5 inches tall at age 17. Her lack of competitive volleyball experience did not seem to affect her abilities and she earned the first female athletic scholarship awarded by the University of Houston in 1974. The three-time All-American (1974–76) and Most Outstanding Collegiate Player (1976) managed to double major in mathematics and physical education, but chose to leave college early to capitalize on her volleyball skills. She had always planned to return to school to graduate when her volleyball career ended. Referring to balancing her volleyball career with her education, she once said, "You can go to school when you're 60. You're only young once, and you can only do this once."[1] She unfortunately never had the chance to return to school and graduate; her volleyball career was still blossoming when she died.

Hyman left the University of Houston in 1976 because she saw the great need the national team had for players like herself. After placing fifth and eighth in the 1964 and 1968 Olympic Games, respectively, the U.S. national team did not even qualify for the Olympics in 1972 or 1976; Hyman wanted that to change. With Hyman at the helm, the U.S. team qualified for the 1980 Moscow Olympic Games and was even thought to be the favorite for gold, but like 61 other nations, the United States boycotted the Moscow Games. Determined to put American women's volleyball on the international radar, Hyman remained with the team, pushing them for another four years. They won a bronze medal at the 1982 World Championships in Peru and a silver medal at the 1983 Pan American Games in Caracas. When the 1984 Olympic Games in Los Angeles arrived, the American team was ready and the Hyman family was excited to watch her represent the United States in their very own hometown.

Suzanne, the eldest of the eight Hyman children, recalled watching her little sister and former teammate, Florie—as she was affectionately known to her large family—lose the gold medal match. "The family was up in the stands, crying," she said. "But Florie came by and waved. You could see her smile. She was happy. She had reached her goal. She had played for a gold medal. I thought to myself 'If she is happy, why am I crying?'"[2] The team that had never before medaled in Olympic history earned the silver medal, which is still the highest finish ever for a women's Olympic indoor volleyball team. The 2008 Beijing Olympics saw a repeat silver medal finish when the American women lost to Brazil in the gold medal match.

After those Summer Games, Hyman moved to Japan to play professionally. While abroad, she realized the United States did not give women's sports as much respect as other countries did. She often returned home to advocate for increased opportunities and funds for female athletes. She also joined forces with civil rights leader Coretta Scott King, democratic vice presidential candidate Geraldine Ferraro, and astronaut Sally Ride to lobby for the Civil Rights Restoration Act and strengthening of Title IX.

Hyman had planned to play in Japan for two seasons before returning home to give her full attention to broadcasting and coaching

American volleyball and continuing her advocacy for equal rights. She had already helped bump up her team Daiei from Japan's third division to the first division. Yet, it was during her second season in 1986, while playing a match in Matsue City, when she collapsed on the bench after routinely subbing out of a game. Her death was first attributed to a heart attack, but her family asked for an autopsy upon her body's return to California. The autopsy found that Hyman's death actually pointed to a disease known as Marfan Syndrome, a connective tissue disorder that can affect many body systems, including the skeleton, eyes, heart and blood vessels, nervous system, skin, and lungs. While Marfan is known to afflict more than 1 in 5,000 people, often individuals with long arms, fingers and toes, Hyman's diagnosis had gone undetected. The examining doctor found a three-week-old blood clot near her deadly aortic tear that suggested an earlier rip had already begun healing when the fatal rupture occurred in the same area.

Upon the realization that Hyman had a healthy heart, but suffered from an undetected genetic disease, two of her seven remaining siblings went to a Marfan symposium where they were convinced to get tested for the syndrome. The test results of Flo's brother came back positive and he underwent open-heart surgery to correct the disorder, almost certainly saving his life. Flo Hyman had managed to advocate for the well-being of others even after she passed on.

In 1987, National Girls and Women in Sports Day was established to remember Hyman for her "athletic achievements as well as her philanthropic work to assure equality for women's sports."[3] While the day has grown to recognize more current sports achievements and draw attention to the struggle of gender equality in sports, Hyman is remembered for her positive influence on American civil rights in general and women's volleyball in particular. This Olympic star still shines bright, just from a greater distance now.

Notes

1. Biography of Flo Hyman, "Flo Hyman," Wikipedia.org, http://en.wikipedia.org/wiki/Flo_Hyman, (May 31, 2008, accessed June 18, 2008).

2. George Vecsey, "Sports of The Times; Remembering Flo Hyman," *New York Times*, February 5, 1988.

3. Elizabeth M. Verner, "Seeking Women Donors for National Girls and Women in Sports Day," *The Journal of Physical Education, Recreation and Dance* (September 1, 1998).

Misty May-Treanor

Future Hall of Famer

by Jessica Bartter

Before she watched the flag being raised in her honor while being serenaded by the national anthem or even before her first Olympic medal was placed around her neck, Misty May-Treanor had to involve her mother in the celebration. It was the 2004 Athens Olympics, and May-Treanor had just clinched a spot on the podium by winning the beach volleyball semifinal match. Ecstatic to exceed her previous Olympics where she and teammate Holly McPeak finished fifth during the Sydney Games, May-Treanor was heartbroken not to be able to share the moment with her mother, Barbara May, who had died of cancer in 2002. Instead of having her mother there in person, she shared the moment with her in spirit by spreading some of her mom's ashes on the sand on which she had just cemented Olympic history. She saved half of the ashes from her canister for what she hoped would later be a gold medal celebration.

The next day, May-Treanor's dream came true as she stood atop the Olympic podium with new teammate Kerri Walsh. The stars and stripes were raised and the national anthem blared, but most important, May-Treanor's mom was there in the only way she could be; with a tattoo in her honor on Misty's shoulder, her ashes in the sand, and her memory in the hearts of her daughter and husband, Butch May.

May-Treanor fell into volleyball quite easily, as the Los Angeles native grew up playing beach volleyball at the Santa Monica Pier with her parents. A competitive edge ran through her veins. Her mom played tennis at UCLA and her dad was a member of the 1968 U.S. Olympic volleyball indoor squad. Misty's mother turned to beach volleyball to play with her husband and even enlisted Karch Kiraly, a three-time Olympic gold medalist in volleyball (indoor and outdoor), to baby-sit her daughter. Misty and her father entered her first tournament when Misty was just eight years old.

May-Treanor moved to Costa Mesa, California, for high school, where she dominated Orange County's indoor volleyball from 1991 to 1995. At Newport Harbor High School, her team won two state championships and she was named to the Division I All-California Interscholastic Federation (CIF) team and was honored as the Player of the Year. During her senior year, May-Treanor was named the nation's best girls volleyball player by *USA Today*. These accolades easily earned the attention of nearby Long Beach State.

Brian Gimmillaro, the head coach of "The Beach," as Long Beach State is affectionately known, said, "Misty is the Magic Johnson or Wayne Gretzky of volleyball. She does everything, and she does it with more creativity and imagination than anyone who came before her. She is the center and the future of this sport."[1] But before she became "the center and future" of volleyball, May-Treanor put Long Beach State on the map. In 1997 and 1998, the setter was named the American Volleyball Coaches Association (AVCA) and *Volleyball Magazine*'s national player of the year. However, what was even more remarkable was May's leadership in driving her 49ers to a perfect 36-0 season en route to the 1998 National Collegiate Athletic Association (NCAA) Championship during her senior year. Long Beach State was the first Division I volleyball program to accomplish an undefeated season. That season, May-Treanor was also named the nation's top female collegiate student-athlete when she won the 1998–99 Honda Broderick NCAA Athlete-of-the-Year Award. She became just the second volleyball player to ever garner that honor, following Dietre Collins at the University of Hawaii in 1982–83.

Following the end of her last collegiate volleyball season, May-Treanor debuted on the professional outdoor circuit in a tournament with beach veteran Holly McPeak, while simultaneously wrapping up her senior year classes. After graduating with her bachelor's degree in kinesiology, May-Treanor joined the U.S. Women's National Team. But the indoor game had taken a toll on May's body and love for the game and her interest in the alternate challenge of beach volleyball could not be ignored.

On the beach, May-Treanor and McPeak enjoyed early success during the 1999–2000 season. Though they were a year behind in the Olympic qualifying process, the duo surpassed expectations and rankings, winning three Fédération Internationale de Volleyball (FIVB) tournaments and finishing fifth or higher in the rest. These finishes qualified them for one of the two U.S. Olympic berths to the 2000 Sydney Olympic Games.

These Games were the only Olympic competition her mother was able to watch from the stands. Yet her mother had a huge hand in her future Olympic success. Barbara May met Kerri Walsh's parents at the 2000 Olympics while they were cheering for Kerri Walsh during the indoor competition. The parents started talking and decided Kerri should join forces with Misty on the sand in future competitions. Luckily, both women agreed, and thus, the most unstoppable, dynamic, and dominant beach volleyball team was born.

Misty May-Treanor and Kerri Walsh joined the FIVB tour in 2001 and were the tour champions in 2002. In 2003, they joined the Association of Volleyball Professionals (AVP) tour, where they enjoyed an undefeated 39-0 season and were named Team of the Year. Their domestic and international success had many people buzzing about a possible medal at the 2004 Olympics. To the applause of many, May-Treanor and Walsh earned the gold medal at the 2004 Athens Games and were the first beach volleyball team to defend their Olympic title, taking home the gold again during the 2008 Beijing Olympic Games. And just as she had done in 2004, May-Treanor sprinkled more of her mom's ashes on the sand during her competition to make sure her mom could be a part of the unprecedented Olympic celebration.

The gold medal victory in Beijing marked Walsh and May-Treanor's record 108th consecutive match victory. They held the previous record of 89 consecutive matches before surpassing their own record. The new record stands at 112 straight wins, as the team lost for the first time on August 31, 2008. The dominant duo have been named AVP Team of the Year every season since joining the AVP tour in 2003. As of September 2008, May-Treanor had won more tournaments than any other female player with 103 total victories, had the highest career earnings for any women's player domestically ($844,388) and internationally ($849,520), and held the most international career wins with 38. She was named the AVP's Best Offensive Player in 2004, 2005, 2006, and 2007 despite being a setter indoors. A true all-around force on the court, May-Treanor was also named Best Defensive Player of the Year in 2006 and 2007.

While her awards and accolades suggest eyes are often on her, May-Treanor prefers them not to be. She once said, "I don't like to be the center of attention unless I'm on the dance floor."[2] Fittingly, she made her primetime television debut in the fall of 2008 on

ABC's Dancing with the Stars before an Achilles tendon injury caused her to leave the show.

The next goal for this "star" is to start a family with husband and Florida Marlins' catcher, Matt Treanor. While having children may take precedence over volleyball for the next few years, it is unknown whether the 2012 London Games will find May-Treanor back indoors playing for the national team, out in the sand to challenge for a three-peat, or—much to Walsh's dismay—in the stands watching with her child(ren). Either way, Coach Gimmillaro predicted it: Misty May-Treanor has secured the future of volleyball. Beach volleyball has become one of the fastest growing Olympic sports to be added to the international menu, in both participants and viewers. Such dominance and talent of Misty May-Treanor's is hard to come by and even harder to ignore.

Notes

1. *Sports Illustrated.com*, "Spotlight: Mist May, Volleyball," http://sportsillustrated .cnn.com/siforwomen/news/1999/07/09/spotlight/, July 9, 1999 (accessed September 1, 2008).

2. Mary Buckheit, "Easy livin' with Misty," ESPN.com, July 20, 2007, http://sports .espn.go.com/espn/page2/story?page=buckheit/070720.

13

WOMEN IN THE MOTOR SPORTS INDUSTRY BLAZE A HARD ROAD

Introduction by Richard Lapchick

The motor sports industry historically has seemed to be the most exclusive white male club in sports. Tennis, golf, and swimming, the so-called country club sports, had the same label but slowly—very slowly—barriers began to fall.

But for women and people of color in the motor sports industry, it has been a hard fought battle. Despite NASCAR's Drive for Diversity and other efforts, progress has seemed grudgingly slow. Although motor sports has had a long rich history of racing excitement; it has also carried a strong perception as being a world of white men racing in and running a sport followed by more white men and white women watching. Images of Confederate flags in the stands and parking lots continue to reinforce the perception that officials have worked hard to change. NASCAR's mantra has been that it is "committed to making our sport—on and off the racetrack—look more like America." It has a decade or more of programs to show that it has tried.

Suddenly the name of Danica Patrick on the Indy circuit has hastily changed things. In the 2008 Indianapolis 500, there were three women in the field. Thirty-one years earlier in 1977, there were no less than three female drivers in the field of the Firecracker 400 NASCAR race at the Daytona International Speedway: American Janet Guthrie, Belgian Christine Beckers, and Italy's Lella Lombardi. Hall of Famer Lee Petty presented flowers to all three of them before the start. It was the first time since 1949 that three women had competed in a NASCAR event, and the only time on a superspeedway. None did well that day but they opened the doors. The time has come.

Patrick is a marketing magnet and endorsers are rushing to her. Male drivers got envious while she was good, but had not won and still got the attention. When she won in 2008, their voices were more muted. Although her trajectory seemed so fast, Patrick recognized the shoulders she had been elevated on.

As a young girl she had attended a driving school run by Lyn St. James, a trailblazer herself as a former IndyCar driver and the first woman to win the Indy 500 Rookie of the Year Award. Patrick was fortunate that St. James took a special interest in her and helped her meet owners and other influential people in the racing circuit. St. James made Patrick her intern at the Indy 500.

Patrick sacrificed a great deal by leaving home at the age of 16 to pursue her racing career in Europe where she raced Formula One cars. She finished second in England's Formula Ford Festival, the best finish ever for an American driver. After spending more than three years overseas, she returned to the United States after catching the eye of former Indy 500 champion and team owner Bobby Rahal.

On April 19, 2008, Patrick took her first lead of the race at Twin Ring Motegi in Japan with two and a half laps remaining. When she won, she became the first woman ever to win an IndyCar race. It was a whole new world for women in motor sports.

But there were those big shoulders. There could have been others, but we have focused on St. James and Janet Guthrie.

Another could easily have been four-time Top Fuel Dragster World Champion, Shirley Muldowney, the one often acclaimed as the "first lady of racing." She was recently inducted into the Automotive Hall of Fame. In 1965, Muldowney was the first woman licensed by the National Hot Rod Association (NHRA) to drive a gasoline-burning gas dragster capable of speeds over 150 mph in the quarter mile.

Guthrie had been faced by torrents of sexist abuse by fans, crews, and other drivers. She heard young men wish she would crash and was asked by the national media if she was a lesbian. A fellow Indy driver said he could teach a hitchhiker to be a better driver than she could ever be. Richard Petty, the man they called "The King," said she may be a woman, but she sure as heck was no lady.

But with no prominent women drivers before her, two men in the industry finally stepped forward to help. Junior Johnson, a key figure in the history of NASCAR, took Guthrie under his wing.

Guthrie could not get her car to run faster than 141 mph, so after Johnson and Hall of Fame driver Cale Yarborough tested the car and could not run it any faster themselves, both Johnson and Yarborough decided to give Guthrie their racing setup.

She would qualify for the race in the row just behind Dale Earnhardt Sr. and Bill Elliott, and finished the race in 15th place, having become the first woman to compete in a NASCAR Winston Cup super speedway.

In 1977, she was back at Indianapolis, becoming the first woman to race in the Indy 500 finishing 29th in her debut as the result of engine trouble. She raced twice more at the track. In 1978, she finished ninth, an Indy 500 career-best. In 1977, she became the first woman to race in the Daytona 500. Despite engine problems, she would still finish as the top rookie of the race while taking 12th place. At the Daytona 500 in 1980 she captured an 11th-place finish. Guthrie raced in 33 NASCAR races over four years, recording five top 10 finishes. She would also race in 11 IndyCar races, her most successful race coming in the 1979 Milwaukee 200, when she finished fifth. Ironically, it would also be the last Indy race of her career.

Sponsors dried up when she thought she was at her peak. Many believed that a male driver with her credentials would have been able to secure sufficient sponsorships. It was not to be for this trailblazer.

Almost a quarter of a century later, Guthrie asked for an autograph from 19-year-old Sarah Fisher, the youngest and third woman ever to compete in the Indy 500. Fisher signed it, "To Janet, my idol." It was 2002.

Lyn St. James distinguished herself in other forms of closed circuit races before debuting in her first Indy 500 race in 1992, having held 31 international and national speed records over her 20-year career, while also finding success on road courses.

St. James continued to focus on her racing in the Sports Car Club of America (SCCA) and International Motor Sports Association (IMSA) circuits. One day Dick Simon gave her a call. "'Hey kid, you want to drive an IndyCar? Be at Memphis tomorrow.' And he hung the phone up," St. James said. "I got to drive that IndyCar at that race track and I thought I had died and gone to heaven—it was so cool. It was the most powerful, most precise, most perfect race car I had ever been in." She and Simon worked hand in hand

and St. James finished with a total of seven starts at the Indy 500.

Perhaps because of the help she received, no woman has given back to the sport more than St. James. She started the Lyn St. James Foundation, in conjunction with the University of Indianapolis, to accelerate the agenda of women in motor sports. Her Foundation published the "Time to Drive: Attitudes toward Women in Motorsports" report. It states that "women are knocking louder than ever on the doors of opportunity in motorsports . . . Cultural views of women in racing are changing and today, little girls share boys' dreams about driving racecars."

According to St. James, the mission of the Foundation "is to provide leadership, vision, resources, and financial support in order to create an open environment for women's growth in automotive fields." Its Driver Development Program has trained more than 150 women drivers from 38 states. Danica Patrick and Sarah Fischer are only the most well known so far.

The Driver Development Program propels young girls and women to quickly take advantage of any opportunities available. Her program was the first of what are now several diversity programs designed to provide more opportunities for minority and female drivers. Among the future stars she has coached are Becca Anderson, Allison Duncan, Renee Dupuis, Sondi Eden, Deborah S. Renshaw, Erin Crocker, Jessica Brannan, Kelly Sutton, Jenny White, and Sunny Hobbs.

Male drivers who might have been envious at the attention garnered by Patrick had an easy out before she won at Twin Ring Motegi. Now everyone knows she can win—and others behind her—and the track may be finally leveled. In addition to those St. James helped, watch out for Kathryn Legged, who completed a test in Miranda's Formula One car, and NHRA's Ashley Force. The fans are loving it and media attention has been raised. We have reached a new era for women in the motor sports industry.

Janet Guthrie

American Star of the Women's International Sports Hall of Fame

by Horacio Ruiz

Courtesy of Janet Guthrie.

There was no place to turn, no place to hide for Janet Guthrie, and pretend those people hadn't said those things or behaved the way they did. Maybe it was a bit of a surprise, to have young males wishing she would crash or to be asked by the national media if she was a lesbian. Maybe it hurt when a fellow Indy driver said he could teach a hitchhiker to be a better driver than she could ever be or to have Richard Petty, the man they call "The King," say she may be a woman, but she sure as heck is no lady.

On second thought, there was a place to hide—inside the racecars she loved to drive so much that would let her turn the wheel around the corners of the impossibly hallowed Indianapolis Speedway. But when she brought the car to a halt at Indy's Gasoline Alley, took her helmet off, and got out of the cockpit, there came back the spotlight, showering her as much with rays of light as with the insults she would carry in her memories the rest of her life. But she didn't want to hide, she just wanted to race, and maybe the things all those people said did hurt, but she could easily laugh it all off.

So when Guthrie, in 1976, attempted to qualify for the Indianapolis 500 and failed less because of her ability and more because of a car that just couldn't compete, there's no telling how many people gladly said to themselves or anyone willing to listen, "Told you so." Did they know about her past? That she had been racing for 13 years, first with a Jaguar XK 120 and then with a 140 model while winning in the highly competitive Sport Car Club of America circuit, many times being the mechanic and sleeping in the back of cars to save money? By the time she decided to concentrate on racing full-time in 1972, she purchased a Toyota Celica and converted it into a racing vehicle, continuing her career as a racecar driver. In 1975, as a veteran racer and in the middle of a tough financial situation, she thought to herself, "One day you really must come to your senses and make some provision for your old age."[1] Then came her big break a year later, when car owner Rolla Vollstadt invited her to test-drive a car at the Indianapolis race track. Vollstadt wanted a woman racer, and after doing his research, it was Guthrie to whom he was always referred. Did they know?

Bruton Smith knew. Smith, a track promoter in Charlotte, watched the media circus following Guthrie at Indianapolis. He could see that by inviting her to his track in Charlotte for the World 600, she would become an instant draw. "I think it was jealousy. I was jealous of her being at Indianapolis," Smith said. "I knew in my mind that she should be here. I never met her, but I knew of her 'cause Janet had a lot of experience driving sports cars."[2]

Guthrie had invested herself emotionally and physically to making the field at Indianapolis. She initially did not want to consider an alternative form of racing, but given the choice between watching at Indianapolis and taking a crack at stock car racing, the choice was simple. It seemed as if Guthrie would again repeat the car woes at Charlotte she had experienced at Indianapolis, but it was Junior Johnson, a racing legend as much for his victories as for being a key figure in the history of NASCAR, who took Guthrie under his wing. Johnson was one of the good ole boys and a former moonshiner who first ran fast cars to outrun the police who were chasing him for trafficking homemade whiskey across state lines. Guthrie could not get her car to run faster than 141 mph, so after Johnson and Hall of Fame driver Cale Yarborough tested the car and could not run it any faster themselves, both Johnson and Yarborough decided to give Guthrie their racing setup. "When a newcomer came into the sport, if he was in trouble, my team would help him out," Johnson said. "She wasn't no different. She was a race driver. She needed help. We helped her. We'd do it again."[3]

She would qualify for the race in the row just behind Dale Earnhardt Sr. and Bill Elliott, and finished the race in 15th place. Guthrie was exhausted and suffering from carbon monoxide inhalation by the end, having become the first woman to compete in a NASCAR Winston Cup super speedway.

In 1977, she would be back at Indianapolis, becoming the first woman to race in the Indy 500. She set the fastest time of any driver in the opening day of qualifying, and also set the fastest qualifying time on the second weekend. Guthrie would finish 29th in her debut as the result of engine trouble, but would race twice more at the track. In 1978, she became the first woman owner/driver in Indy racing, responsible for hiring the crew, housing the crew, and purchasing car parts while handling the media and racing duties. She would go on to finish ninth, an Indy 500 career-best. In 1977, she would also become the first woman to race in the Daytona 500. Guthrie was in eighth place 10 laps from the finish at Daytona when engine problems again derailed her. She would still finish as the top rookie of the race while taking 12th place. At the Daytona 500 in 1980 she would turn in an 11th-place finish. Guthrie raced in 33 NASCAR races over four years, recording five top 10 finishes. She would also race in 11 IndyCar races, her most successful race coming in the 1979 Milwaukee 200 when she finished fifth. Ironically, it would also be the last Indy race of her career. The money well had dried up. She could only find top sponsors for three years. She has no answer as to why, coming off a career-best finish, there suddenly was no money. "I wish I had been able to go on, but no money, no race," Guthrie said. "That remains a problem for many women athletes. I was shocked and dismayed. You can compare my record in my 11 IndyCar races with the first 11 IndyCar races of any of the superstars, and I think you would find the comparison quite decent. I had a hard time reconciling myself to that. It was a sport I loved very much."[4]

Maybe it hurt when people said those things and behaved the way they did, but it really hurt when she wanted to race so badly and couldn't. From 1979 through 1983, she was regularly in New York City looking for corporate sponsors, but then "I realized that if I kept looking for sponsors I would jump out a window,"[5] she says.

Guthrie retreated to her home in Aspen, Colorado, and channeled her frustration into what would become a 1,200-page manuscript detailing her racing experiences from the perspective as both a driver and as a woman in the driver's seat. In 1980, she was in the first group of women ever inducted into the Women's International

Sports Hall of Fame. In 2006, she would be inducted into the International Motorsports Hall of Fame. In 2002, she made her way back to the Indianapolis 500, and for the first time ever, asked for an autograph from a 19-year-old woman named Sarah Fisher—the youngest and third woman ever to compete in the Indy 500. Fisher signed it, "To Janet, my idol."

In 2005, she released a book, having edited her 1,200-page manifest into a 300-page autobiography entitled *Janet Guthrie: A Life at Full Throttle*. It was a work of labor 25 years in the making. Her hope was, and still is, to inspire women that follow her footsteps and to let the world know what it was like taking those footsteps. "Someday, a woman will win the Indianapolis 500; someday, a woman will win the Daytona 500," Guthrie wrote in the final paragraph of her book. "I wish I could have been that driver. I hope some reader of this book will be."

Guthrie still follows many of the women in the Indy racing circuit today, analyzing their performances when she gets the chance. For the 2008 Indianapolis 500, Guthrie will take part in a Saturday night fundraiser fashion show, joking that she needs to somehow find a way to lose 10 pounds. On Sunday, when the race is beginning, the woman who helped shape the history of the world's most famous race will be on a plane returning home.

"I really don't like watching it if I'm not racing. It's because I didn't," Guthrie sighs, "quit willingly."[6]

Notes

1. Janet Guthrie, interview with author, April 15, 2008.
2. Janet Guthrie Transcript. http://www.lowesmotorspeedway.com/news_photos/press_releases/507342.html, May 9, 2006.
3. Ibid.
4. Barbara Huebner, "Guthrie: Pioneer Who Was Driven—Her Perseverance Overcame Sexism," *The Boston Globe*, October 20, 1999.
5. Janet Guthrie, interview with author, April 15, 2008.
6. Ibid.

Lyn St. James

Future Hall of Famer

by Horacio Ruiz

Lyn St. James, the oldest rookie to ever qualify for the Indy 500 and the second woman ever to qualify for the race, has heard all the comments from men in racing about women in racing. An automotive factory manager told her that if a team hired a woman as a racer, then it would mean that the team must not be very serious about winning. A top NASCAR executive once told St. James that women just don't have the strength to handle a car. To which she replied—almost making too much sense—that a car does not know the gender of the pilot, and while it takes a number of physical and mental qualities to be a great racer, none of them are exclusive to a specific gender.

"The car doesn't know the difference, so it doesn't go, 'Oh, you know, I've got this woman driving, so I'm going to do [things] differently,'" St. James said in an interview prior to her final Indy 500 race. "So it's finesse, it's feel, it's precision, it's concentration, it's focus, it's eye-hand coordination, it's technical know how, it's competitive drive. None of those things are gender-specific. So it's a gender-neutral sport, and it takes physical strength, it takes physical fitness, but more muscle doesn't make you go faster."[1]

St. James distinguished herself in other forms of closed circuit races before debuting in her first Indy 500 race in 1992, having held 31 international and national speed records over her 20-year career, while also finding success on road courses. St. James twice raced in The 24 Hours of Le Mans in France, the biggest endurance race in the world, and also was a two-time winner in her car division in the 24 Hours of Daytona race. She also won a title in the 12 Hours of Sebring. She was heavily involved in two sports car racing series, the Sports Car Club of America (SCCA), where she participated in 53

Trans-Am races and totaled seven Top-5 finishes, and the International Motor Sports Association (IMSA), where she participated in 62 GT races and totaled six wins, 17 Top-5 finishes, and 37 Top-10 finishes. It was clear that she knew both how to handle a race car and how to win.

Her dream, however, had always been to drive an IndyCar. For years she had been asking former race car driver and team owner Dick Simon to give her a shot. But St. James knew that she needed more experience in order to get her shot at driving an IndyCar. "So I thought if I could go to Talladega and set a record with a turbocharged four-cylinder engine, which I currently was racing with Ford Motor Company, that would give me turbo experience and oval track experience so that I could then talk about doing IndyCar stuff," St. James said. "We set the record as we went over 200 mph in a Ford Pro, but I couldn't get any other doors to open."[2]

St. James continued to focus on her racing in the SCCA and IMSA circuits, and then she decided to go once again to Talladega, where she set another track record with a Thunderbird at an average speed of 212 mph. Still, she couldn't get anyone to listen until Dick Simon gave her a call. "Finally, [Simon] called me one day—it was after the end of the season. And he goes, 'Hey kid, you want to drive an IndyCar? Be at Memphis tomorrow.' And he hung the phone up," St. James said. "I got to drive that IndyCar at that race track and I thought I had died and gone to heaven—it was so cool. It was the most powerful, most precise, most perfect race car I had ever been in. And I did so well that Dick said to me at the end of the day—he said to me, 'We can do this.' And that was the key, he didn't say 'I

Courtesy of Lyn St. James.

could do this,' he said, 'we could do this.' So he bought into the idea and the concept that we could do this."[3]

Her biggest obstacle lay in finding a team sponsor. St. James had been down that path many years before when, in 1981, she was able to secure Ford as a sponsor for her IMSA team after numerous failed attempts. She credits her experience from the late 1970s and early 1980s in dealing with the desperation of convincing potential sponsors for her resolve in not quitting. "At the time I thought, 'I have nothing to lose, I have absolutely no reason to not do this. I've been down this path before of trying to convince people that they needed to say yes,'" St. James said. "I was a little smarter. I was not just selling me as a want-to-be because I now had an established driving record."[4]

Four years and 151 companies later, St. James had found a company willing to be a sponsor for her Indy 500 debut in 1992 when retail store JC Penney got on board. She would go on to earn the highest finish of her Indy 500 career with a 12th-place showing. She also was the 1992 Indianapolis 500 Rookie of the Year. She would compete in seven Indy 500 races, including six consecutive starts from 1992 to 1997. She would go on to race in 15 Indy Races, tallying two Top-10 qualifying spots and one Top-10 finish. In 1994, she qualified in the sixth spot for the Indy 500, the highest ever for a woman at the race until Danica Patrick qualified in the fourth spot in 2000.

"I did a mighty good job with limited amount of seat time in an IndyCar," St. James said. "It would be like going to the Olympics every four years and not competing in between. I am very proud, but also frustrated that I was not able to show what I could do, so-to-speak. I was just kind of coming out of my shell, and for that I'm very proud that I was able to get as far as I could and accomplish as much as I did."[5]

St. James would run in her final Indy 500 in 2000, and then went on to concentrate on her racing foundation, the Women in the Winners Circle Foundation. The Foundation is active in helping women learn the business side of racing, specifically in being able to gain sponsorship dollars. It took St. James four years and 150 companies before JC Penney, on the 151st try, became her sponsor for her first Indy race, and she is currently working to make it easier for future women in racing. She is aware that women are becoming more involved in racing from the grassroots levels to the more organized leagues, but finding sponsorship money has still been an area where women struggle.

Currently, two of the most prominent women in IndyCar racing have been through St. James's program, and she is now a mentor to both. Both Danica Patrick and Sarah Fisher are making strides for women in racing. St. James is proud to have had both of them go through her program, which has attracted more than 250 racers, and is certain about their appreciation for the women who paved the way for them. "I think they're both very honored and appreciative of where they're at," St. James said. "I think they're starting to even understand their own legacy that they're starting to leave in the world of racing."[6]

All the while, St. James is busy cementing her legacy as both a pioneer and ambassador for women in racing. Through her Foundation, she is creating driving opportunities and educating women about the business of racing. "Attitudes prevent people from providing opportunities, but it's getting better—slowly. Not nearly at the pace I think it should," St. James said. "What I want to see is an equal opportunity for an openly competitive environment. I also think that if you pursue something strong enough and hard enough then you can get it done."[7]

Notes

1. Jim Clash, (2000). The Adventurer. http://www.youtube.com/watch?v=ACd-tc Mhqko.
2. Ibid.
3. Ibid.
4. Lyn St. James, interview with the author, June 20, 2008.
5. Ibid.
6. Clash, The Adventurer.
7. Lyn St. James, interview with the author, June 20, 2008

Danica Patrick

Future Hall of Famer

by Horacio Ruiz

There she was on May 29, 2005, with just seven laps to go, not simply contending to win one of the most famous car races in the world. Danica Patrick was seven laps away from beating the boys and winning the Indianapolis 500. The people in the stands watched her go by, hollering and raising their arms for her, some claiming that after decades of attending the race, it was her lead that for the first time ever gave them goose bumps at the track. On television, the announcers' voices were full of excitement—history was being made before a world audience on ABC. But the announcers wondered to the watching world if Patrick had enough fuel in her car to finish the race. Then, in an instant, eventual winner Casey Wheldon passed Patrick, who was indeed racing on fumes and whose tires were badly worn down. Patrick would finish fourth, the highest ever for a woman, while also becoming the first woman to lead a lap at the Indy 500, leading a total of 19 laps for the day. It was a momentous day in sport for women, and it forever changed the racing expectations of a gender. On that day, when the world was ready to celebrate a woman and her race car like never before, Patrick's celebrity skyrocketed.

In the following week's *Sports Illustrated*, it was Patrick and not Wheldon who appeared on the cover. A few weeks after that, Wheldon, apparently stung by the attention given to Patrick, wore a shirt reading "I actually won the Indy 500." At an autograph session, the demand for Patrick was so great that the Indy Racing League, the governing body of the U.S. open-wheel racing circuit, created a separate line for Patrick. Three other racers, including Wheldon, were expected to participate, but boycotted the autograph session because of the special set-up created for Patrick.

The boys she nearly beat late in May were suddenly getting defensive. One driver suggested her 5-foot-2 and 100-pound frame gave her an unfair advantage compared to all the other men in the racing circuit. One magazine article, while defending Patrick from the ridiculousness of her unfair "size advantage" still rang up a headline reading "Why Danica Patrick is Overrated." The article went on to say that while Patrick, in her rookie year in 2005, was indeed attaining a certain amount of success, she was doing so in a watered-down racing league beset by collective bargaining disputes and a lack of quality drivers. The article wondered if Patrick would have been as successful a decade earlier, when it claimed she would have been competing against superior drivers.

The funny thing is Patrick didn't achieve her level of success by accident or because of inferior competition. She started her racing career as most drivers do, by racing go-karts. Patrick won her first Grand National Championship by the age of 12 and progressed to different classifications while winning two more national titles and 10 regional titles. In 1996, she dominated her class, winning 39 out of 49 feature races. She also began attending a driving school run by Lyn St. James, a former IndyCar driver and the first woman to win the Indy 500 Rookie of the Year Award. St. James took a special interest in Patrick, helping her meet owners and other influential people in the racing circuit and taking her to the Indy 500 as her intern.

"Out of 200 that have gone through my program, no more than 10 set themselves apart that I've gone out of my way to help behind the scenes," St. James said in an interview with the *San Jose Mercury News*. "They have to be exceptional. It's not good enough to just be good. The reality is you have to be extraordinary. I saw Danica as extraordinary."[1]

Patrick left her home in Roscoe, Illinois, at the age of 16 to pursue her racing career in Europe. Once overseas, she would race Formula One cars and competed in what she called the Harvard of racing. In England's Formula Ford Festival, she finished second, the best finish ever for an American driver. After spending more than three years overseas, she returned to the United States after catching the eye of former Indy 500 champion and team owner Bobby Rahal, who said Patrick endured "the most intense training ground there is in motor sports" and succeeded. "I saw a girl who was willing to make the most difficult of choices, who had the absolute commitment and desire and willingness to sacrifice," Rahal said. "I saw that and the tremendous strength of hers. I think going to England to race always takes commitment and dedication and sacrifice, but for a girl to do it, it makes it doubly so. Forgetting the fact that she did very well over there, just the fact that she was even there spoke volumes in my mind. That's what really convinced me that it was worth giving her an opportunity."[2]

But since splashing onto the racing scene in 2005, Patrick had been dogged by questions of whether she would ever win. Many of her critics said that because of her gender and commercial appeal she had been given more opportunities to win than is afforded most drivers. For the IndyCar driver, taking on the burden of being the most successful woman ever on the open-wheel racing circuit, the task at hand has not been easy for Patrick. The truth is, when you're racing cars at metal-twisting speeds for your paycheck, nothing ever comes easy. Not even tears of joy.

On April 19, 2008, Patrick took her first lead of the race at Twin Ring Motegi in Japan with two and a half laps remaining. On television, the announcers wondered aloud once again if she had enough fuel to finish the race in first, and this time she did, becoming the first woman ever to win an IndyCar race. "Boys, move over, the lady is coming through," one of the announcers said. "Danica Patrick wins at Twin Ring Motegi!"

Patrick stopped her car, stood up in the cockpit, and took off her helmet and racing mask to wipe away tears. There was no smile. She hugged her husband and mother while shedding some more tears and letting out muffled sobs as she buried her face into her husband's embrace. No doubt the tears she wiped away contained muted amounts of joy, but more than anything, they contained a sense of justification.

"I feel like a wuss crying, but it's a long time coming. Finally," Patrick said on the track. "Thank you to Andretti-Green, thank you to all my teammates, and . . . finally," she said once more with a sigh. If at the Indy 500 she was giving people goose bumps, at Twin Ring Motegi she was giving people a reason to cry with her.

On that day, Patrick proved herself capable of winning, but she has always been attractive enough to capture the spotlight from all the men, by far, even without victory. So even as her professional career develops on an upward slope on the grandest stage, many drivers, possibly envious, wonder whether all the attention is warranted. Patrick has one definite and undeniable advantage over the rest of the field—she is beautiful and fully capable of displaying her beauty. To that, there is no fast-enough car or gutsy-enough maneuver that other racers can perform to either take away her beauty and fame or to capture it. She has appeared in magazines modeling bikinis and other outfits, not shying away from the attention given to a woman succeeding in a sport dominated by men. Patrick also has been a major marketing force for the Indy Racing League (IRL), which has struggled to find a consistent audience but has gained an increasing amount of interest since Patrick joined the league.

Even with the success and publicity she brings to the sport, there will be racers like Formula One driver Jenson Button, who once said in reference to Patrick, "A girl with big boobs would never be comfortable in the car. And the mechanics wouldn't concentrate. Can you imagine strapping her in?"[3]

Patrick once gave a quote of her own relating to drivers like Button: "I need to beat them, belittle them, and make them feel small. Trying to run them off the road at 170 mph isn't sweet and kind."[4]

The male drivers who might have been envious at the attention garnered by Patrick had an easy out before she won at Twin Ring Motegi. Now everyone knows she can win and the track may be finally leveled. The fans are loving it and media attention has been raised. We have reached a new era for women in the motor sports industry.

Notes

1. Danica Patrick, racecar driver, *Current Biography*, October 2005.
2. Tom Gardner, "Danica Patrick Drives a Toyota, Envisions a Ferrari," *The AP*. June 19, 2003.
3. http://en.wikipedia.org/wiki/Danica_Patrick.
4. http://www.askmen.com/women/models_250/292_danica_patrick.html.

14

CONCLUSION

by Richard Lapchick

We celebrate the lives of these amazing women for being trailblazers in their respective categories so that those who follow them with their own great athletic and societal achievements can clearly see who opened, and in some cases smashed, the doors open for them. Many of our trailblazers made their marks between the 1950s and 1980s and have had so many greats follow them. Then there are the few who came in the 1990s who are still opening the doors. How better to honor one's life than to have someone want to follow in your footsteps?

And it is not just women competing against other women. Annika Sorenstam and Michelle Wie have both competed in Professional Golfers Association (PGA) Tour events. The trailblazers have made it possible for women to expect to win in a motor sports race after Danica Patrick won an IndyCar race in Japan in 2008. Candace Parker won the slam dunk contest at the McDonald's All-American game in 2004. She beat five guys. One of them was Josh Smith, who won the National Basketball Association's (NBA) Slam Dunk contest in 2005! Only 20 years earlier, there had never been a woman dunk in a college game before West Virginia's Geogreann Wells ripped the nets in 1984.

The life of each trailblazer should be celebrated for what she accomplished, often in the face of doubt and sometimes legal obstacles before Title IX and even after. It took additional legislation and successful lawsuits to move toward full implementation. The Supreme Court allowed monetary damages to be awarded in the 1992 Franklin v. Gwinnett County case. Cases were soon filed at Brown, Colorado State, and Auburn. That got colleges and high schools moving faster.

To believe in what you cannot see is a powerful and daring feat and is what our trailblazers did. Today, women and girls of all ages and races have role models to emulate and athletes who look like them. Had Babe Didrikson, Althea Gibson, Wilma Rudolph, Billie Jean King, and so many others featured in this book yielded to what society told them, how much longer would it have taken for girls and women to gain access in the world of sports? These trailblazers all demonstrated vision, determination, and courage. Of course, they all had enormous athletic skills to help the vision, determination, and courage.

Now women are in the huddle and feel the miracle of sport where it does not matter if you are African-American, white, Asian-American, Latino, Native American, or Arab-American. It does not matter if you are rich or poor, Democrat or Republican. It does not matter what faith you follow or even if you follow a faith. The team cannot win unless everyone pulls together.

Future Power Sharing for Women and People of Color in Sport?

But there are still huge gaps for women, especially when it comes to power. Who covers the games? More important, who runs them? I helped author a second study on the media for The Institute for Diversity and Ethics in Sport (TIDES) at the University of Central Florida in 2008. It again showed how white males totally dominate the key positions on our newspapers and websites in the United States and Canada.

The AP Sports Editors (APSE) websites and newspapers received a grade of C for racial hiring practices and an F for gender hiring practices in the key positions covered in the 2008 study.

It is important to have voices from different backgrounds in the media. This report showed that in 2008, 94 percent of the sports editors, 89 percent of the assistant sports editors, 88 percent of our columnists, 87 percent of the reporters, and 89 percent of the copy editors/designers were white, and those same positions were 94, 90, 94, 91, and 84 percent male.

The APSE represents almost every sports section of newspapers and online media sources in the United States and Canada. The report included the positions of more than 5,200 people.

The Institute also authors the Racial and Gender Report Cards for each pro and college sport. Who runs our teams? Our leagues? Our athletic departments? Unless there is a keeper of the flame lit by these trailblazers, it is possible that the flame could flicker and be extinguished.

The best in sharing that power in 2008 is the Women's National Basketball Association (WNBA), which received an A+ for gender hiring practices with a 97.5 and an A+ for race with a 94.5. In the combined grade for race and gender, the WNBA earned an A+ with 96 points. This was the highest combined grade for any sport in the history of the Racial and Gender Report Card.

The WNBA received As for race in the WNBA League Office, head and assistant coaches, general managers, team professional administration, and player opportunities. It received As for gender in the WNBA League Office, head and assistant coaches, general manager, team senior administration, and team professional administration. The WNBA only had one category below an A for gender (team vice presidents). For race there were two categories below an A in team vice president and senior administrative positions.

The WNBA had the highest number of As as well as the lowest number of grades below an A in all categories in the history of the Racial and Gender Report Card.

The National Basketball Association (NBA) earned its highest grade ever for gender, tied its highest grade ever for race and had men's pro sports first ever A for a combined grade for race and gender. The NBA had an A+ for race with 96.2 points (the same as the 2006–7 report), a B+ for gender with 84.5 points (up from 82) for a combined A. In the 2006 Racial and Gender Report Card, the NBA had an A+ for race and B for gender, which combined to give the league an overall grade of B+.

Overall, Major League Baseball (MLB) earned an A- for race and a C+ for gender. This gave MLB a combined B. This marked continued improvement over the last two Report Cards. In the 2006 Major League Baseball Racial and Gender Report Card, MLB earned a high B+ for race, a C+ for gender, and a combined B. In 2005, MLB earned a low-range B+ for race, a D+ for gender, and a combined C+.

Major League Soccer (MLS) had a second consecutive solid A

(93.4 points) for racial hiring practices, up slightly from its 93.3 total in 2007. The MLS gender grade increased dramatically from a D+ in 2007 to a high C+ (78 points, up from 64.6) in 2008. In 2007, MLS had no category used to measure gender being above a D+. In 2008, only one category was below a C. MLS had a combined grade of B+ with 85.7 points, up significantly from C+/B- with 79 points in 2007.

The National Football League (NFL) received an overall B+ grade for race (87.1 out of 100). That was down slightly from 88.6 in the 2007 Racial and Gender Report Card. No grade was issued for gender because of insufficient data. The NFL had received a D+ for gender in the 2004 Report. The percentages of women have increased slightly between 1 and 3 percent since then in the categories of team vice presidents, team senior administration positions and in professional administration. Overall, there was little change on gender in the last three reports.

At the college level in the 120 institutions that play Division I-A college football, that is, our biggest sports schools, whites held 335 (91.3 percent) of the 367 campus leadership positions. White women held 57 (15.5 percent) of these positions. There were only two Asian males, one Native American male, and one Latina woman among the 367 people.

As of September 2008, there were four (3.3 percent) African-American men and two (1.7 percent) Latino men serving as presidents. There were no Asian or Native American men as president at Division I-A institutions. There were 16 (13.3 percent) white women, three (2.5 percent) Latina women, and one (0.83 percent) Asian woman serving as president while there were no African-American or Native American women presidents at Division I-A schools.

There were 120 athletic directors in Division I-A who oversee football. Among them there were 11 (9.2 percent) African-American men, four (3.3 percent) Latino men, and one (0.83 percent) Native American man serving as athletic directors. There were no Asian athletic directors. There were seven (5.8 percent) white women in charge of an athletic department that oversees football. There were no African-American, Asian, Native American, or Latina women athletic directors in Division I-A.

Among the faculty athletics representatives (FARs) there were three (2.4 percent) African-American men, one (0.8 percent) Latino man, two (1.6 percent) Asian men, and one (0.8 percent) Native American man. There were 32 (26.0 percent) women, none of whom were African-American, Latina, Asian, or Native American.

All (100 percent) of the 11 Division I-A conference commissioners are white men. Among these 11 men are those that head Bowl Championship Series (BCS) Conferences and hold what are now considered to be among the most powerful and influential positions in college sport.

Just as with people of color, women in front offices lag behind everywhere except in the WNBA regarding running our games and our teams. It will undoubtedly take more pressure and education to further hasten change at these levels.

What I said in the first two books of this series, *100 Heroes: People in Sports Who Make This a Better World* and *100 Pioneers: African-Americans Who Broke Color Barriers in Sport*, is still relevant for *100 Trailblazers*. The 100 women "described in this volume should serve as a light, indeed, as a beacon for us all. They followed their dreams and helped us dream as well. They served others even as they succeeded on the playing field. They found hope where others believed none existed. Let us cheer their accomplishments as we follow their example" and ensure no man, woman, or child is prevented from achieving their dream again.

So in the three years prior to the completion of this book, Pat Summitt became the winningest coach in the history of college basketball, Lorena Ochoa became the first woman golfer to earn $3 million in a year, Danica Patrick won an Indy race, swimmer Natalie Coughlin became the first woman to ever win back-to-back 100-yard Olympic backstroke events, and Lisa Leslie won her fourth basketball gold medal. There are more stories that will be written but all of them will reflect on what these 100 trailblazers did for women and girls in sports. They have proven nothing is impossible.

Like the heroes and pioneers in the first two books, these trailblazers changed teammates, schools, communities, and, ultimately, the nation. In some cases, they made us forget the Cold War. The American women helped speed up the healing process of the wounds of America's history of segregation and denying women equal rights. I am convinced that sports is helping us to stop talking about a white America and a black America, a Latino America and an Asian America, a male America and a female America. Sports can help us see that we are all part of the United States of America. Those of us in sports, and all Americans, are deeply in debt to the heroes, pioneers, and trailblazers whose lives we featured in these books. The examples they gave us should inspire us all to do more for more people in the years ahead.

ABOUT THE NATIONAL CONSORTIUM FOR ACADEMICS AND SPORTS (NCAS)

The National Consortium for Academics and Sports (NCAS) is an ever-growing organization of colleges, universities, and individuals. The mission of the NCAS is to create a better society by focusing on educational attainment and using the power and appeal of sport to positively effect social change.

The NCAS evolved in response to the need to "keep the student in the student-athlete." The NCAS was established by Dr. Richard E. Lapchick and since its inception in 1985, NCAS member institutions have proven to be effective advocates for balancing academics and athletics. By joining the NCAS, a college or university agrees to bring back, tuition free, their own former student-athletes who competed in revenue- and non-revenue-producing sports and were unable to complete their degree requirements. In exchange, these former student-athletes agree to participate in school outreach and community service programs addressing social issues that affect America's youth.

There have been hundreds of people who have worked in NCAS programs over the past 23 years to help us fulfill our mission. Each has helped because of his or her passion for combining academics, sport, and the way we use sport to bring about social change for our children.

The NCAS started with 11 universities in 1985 and now has more than 220 member institutions. Members of the NCAS have brought back 28,594 former student-athletes to complete their degrees through one of our biggest programs. The Degree Completion Program was just a dream in 1985, but more than 28,000 now say that dream has become a reality.

Returning student-athletes participate in outreach and community service programs in exchange for the tuition and fees they receive when they come back to school. They have reached over 16.5 million young people in cities in America, rural America, and suburban America. Wherever there are college campuses, our student-athletes are in the community helping young people face the crises of the past 23 years. Member institutions have donated more than $309 million in tuition assistance to these former student-athletes.

With no athletic participation in return this time around, the biggest return possible is to the student who leaves with the degree he or she was told would be there for them when first enrolling. The NCAS and its members have been able to work with children on issues like conflict resolution, improving race relations, reducing men's violence against women, stemming the spread of drug and alcohol abuse, and emphasizing the importance of education and the importance of balancing work in the classroom and on the playing field.

The NCAS has worked with organizations and schools to help them understand issues of diversity, not only as a moral imperative, but also as a business necessity. The NCAS utilizes the Teamwork Leadership Institute (TLI) to teach our colleges, professional athletes, and all of the people that sport touches the importance and value of diversity which then in turn reflects back on society as a whole. The mission of TLI is to help senior administrators as well as team front office and athletic department staff, through the provision of diversity training services, to apply the principles of teamwork to all areas of athletic departments and professional sports organizations. Challenges that stem from cultural prejudice, intolerance, and poor communication can be aggressively addressed in intelligent, safe, and structured ways. TLI works with staff members to help them anticipate, recognize, and address the problems inherent to diverse teams and staff. Diversity training demonstrates that diverse people have a great deal in common. Rather than being divisive issues, racial, ethnic, and gender differences can serve as building blocks. Just as in sports, these differences can strengthen the group. TLI has provided workshops for over 150 athletic organizations, including college athletic departments, the National Basketball Association, Major League Soccer, Maloof Sports & Entertainment (Sacramento Kings), and the Orlando Magic.

The Mentors in Violence Prevention (MVP) National Program, founded in 1993 by Northeastern University's Center for the Study of Sport in Society, is a leadership program that motivates student-athletes and student leaders to play a central role in solving problems that historically have been considered "women's issues:" rape, battering, and sexual harassment. The mixed gender, racially diverse former professional and college athletes that facilitate the MVP National Program motivate men and women to work together in preventing gender violence. Utilizing a unique bystander approach to prevention, MVP National views student-athletes and student leaders not as potential perpetrators or victims, but as empowered bystanders who can confront abusive peers. The MVP National approach does not involve finger pointing, nor does it blame participants for the widespread problem of gender violence. Instead, it sounds a positive call for proactive, preventative behavior and leadership. MVP National has facilitated sessions with thousands of high school and college students and administrators at dozens of Massachusetts schools as well as with hundreds of student-athletes and administrators at over 120 colleges nationwide. MVP National has also conducted sessions with professional sports leagues including players and staff from the National Basketball Association (NBA), National Football League (NFL), and International Basketball League (IBL) as well as with personnel from the U.S. Marine Corps. MVP has also trained the rookie and free agents of the New England Patriots and New York Jets, minor league players of the Boston Red Sox, and Major League Lacrosse (MLL).

    With the alarming rate of alcohol use and abuse among students, the NCAS, in collaboration with The BACCHUS and GAMMA Peer Education Network, sought a solution through education and developed the Alcohol Response-Ability: Foundations for Student Athletes™ course in 2004. It is a 90-minute, internet-based alcohol education and life skills program designed specifically for student-athletes and those who work with them in the college and university setting. In this first program of its kind, student-athletes receive a customized educational experience that is interactive, interesting, and designed to help them reduce harm and recognize the consequences associated with alcohol abuse in their campus communities. In its first year on college campuses, results came back overwhelmingly positive. Ninety-three percent of the students who took the course said they learned something new, and 95 percent of them said they would try at least one of the strategies they learned to lower their risk. An impressive 83 percent said they would likely make safe decisions as a direct result of the course. These figures prove that much more needs to be done with alcohol abuse education.

    One of the NCAS's most recent program additions is Hope for Stanley. The mission of the Hope for Stanley Foundation is to bring volunteers from all walks of life to the New Orleans area to perform community service. The type of community service includes, but is not limited to, rebuilding homes, creating and landscaping playgrounds, and delivering essential goods and materials to areas affected by Hurricane Katrina. The Hope for Stanley Foundation places a focus on student-athlete, athlete, and sport administrator involvement from across the world in the rebuilding of homes and playgrounds because of its belief in the power of sport for social change.

Each of the 100 heroes whose lives you can read about in the first book of this series, *100 Heroes: People in Sports Who Make This a Better World*, was honored in celebration of another NCAS program, National STUDENT-Athlete Day (NSAD). NSAD is celebrated annually on April 6, providing an opportunity to recognize the outstanding accomplishments of student-athletes who have achieved excellence in academics and athletics, while making significant contributions to their communities. In addition to honoring student-athletes, the Annual National STUDENT-Athlete Day program selects recipients for Giant Steps Awards. These awards are given to individuals on a national level who exemplify the meaning of National STUDENT-Athlete Day. Each year nominations are received from across the country, and the Giant Steps Award winners are chosen by a national selection committee in categories ranging from civic leaders, coaches, parents, teachers, athletic administrators, and courageous student-athletes. *100 Heroes* was a compilation of the inspiring life stories of the first 100 to be chosen in honor of the "giant steps" they have taken in sports, in society, and in life itself.

The NCAS uses former athletes to deliver a message because so many can relate to sport. Many of today's young women as well as athletes of color do not realize how different their field looked 100, 50, or even 25 years ago. The history of race and gender in the United States may be studied by young Americans but too many cannot relate. But young people do relate to sport. By illustrating the history of America's racial and gender barriers through the vehicle of sport, the picture may become clearer. It can be the role of those who lived it to educate the next generation and there will be no better time to do so than now. *100 Heroes*, *100 Pioneers*, and *100 Trailblazers* tell many courageous stories, our history, and how sport positively impacted race and gender relations in the United States.

About the Authors

Richard E. Lapchick

Human rights activist, pioneer for racial equality, internationally recognized expert on sports issues, scholar, and author Richard E. Lapchick is often described as "the racial conscience of sport." He brought his commitment to equality and his belief that sport can be an effective instrument of positive social change to the University of Central Florida, where he accepted an endowed chair in August 2001. Lapchick became the only person named as "One of the 100 Most Powerful People in Sport" to head up a sport management program. He remains president and CEO of the National Consortium for Academics and Sport and helped bring the NCAS national office to UCF.

The DeVos Sport Business Management Program at UCF is a landmark program that focuses on the business skills necessary for graduates to conduct a successful career in the rapidly changing and dynamic sports industry. In following with Lapchick's tradition of human rights activism, the curriculum includes courses with an emphasis on diversity, community service and philanthropy, sport and social issues, and ethics in addition to UCF's strong business curriculum. The DeVos Program has been named one of the nation's top five programs by the *Wall Street Journal*, the *Sports Business Journal*, and *ESPN The Magazine*.

In December 2006, Lapchick, his wife and daughter, and a group of DeVos students formed the Hope for Stanley Foundation, which is organizing groups of student-athletes and sports management students to go to New Orleans to work in the reconstruction efforts in the devastated Ninth Ward. As of the summer of 2008, Hope for Stanley members have spent 15 weeks in the city in a partnership with the NOLA City Council.

Lapchick helped found the Center for the Study of Sport in Society in 1984 at Northeastern University. He served as director for 17 years and is now the director emeritus. The Center has attracted national attention to its pioneering efforts to ensure the education of athletes from junior high school through the professional ranks. The Center's Project TEAMWORK was called "America's most successful violence prevention program" by public opinion analyst Lou Harris. It won the Peter F. Drucker Foundation Award as the nation's most innovative nonprofit program and was named by the Clinton administration as a model for violence prevention. The Center's MVP gender violence prevention program has been so successful with college and high school athletes that the United States Marine Corps adopted it in 1997. Athletes in Service to America, funded by AmeriCorps, combines the efforts of Project TEAMWORK and MVP in five cities across the nation.

The Center helped form the National Consortium for Academics and Sports (NCAS), a group of over 215 colleges and universities that have adopted the Center's programs. To date, more than 27,430 athletes have returned to NCAS member schools. Over 12,200 have graduated. Nationally, the NCAS athletes have worked with more than 15.3 million students in the school outreach program, which focuses on teaching youth how to improve race relations, develop conflict resolution skills, prevent gender violence, and avoid drug and alcohol abuse. They have collectively donated more than 16.6 million hours of service.

Lapchick was the American leader of the international campaign to boycott South Africa in sport for more than 20 years. In 1993, the Center launched TEAMWORK-South Africa, a program designed to use sports to help improve race relations and help with sports development in post-apartheid South Africa. He was among 200 guests specially invited to Nelson Mandela's inauguration.

Lapchick is a prolific writer. His 13th book, *100 Pioneers: African-Americans Who Broke Color Barriers in Sport*, was published at the end of 2007. Lapchick is a regular columnist for ESPN.com and *The Sports Business Journal*. Lapchick is a regular contributor to the op ed page of the *Orlando Sentinel*. He has written more than 450 articles and has given more than 2,700 public speeches.

Considered among the nation's experts on sport and social issues, Lapchick has appeared numerous times on *Nightline, Good Morning America, Face The Nation, The Today Show, ABC World News, NBC Nightly News*, the *CBS Evening News*, CNN, and ESPN.

Lapchick also consults with companies as an expert on both managing diversity and building community relations through service programs addressing the social needs of youth. He has a special expertise on Africa and South Africa. He has made 30 trips to Africa and African Studies was at the core of his PhD work.

Before Northeastern, he was an associate professor of political science at Virginia Wesleyan College from 1970 to 1978 and a senior liaison officer at the United Nations between 1978 and 1984.

In 2006, Lapchick was named both the Central Florida Public Citizen of the Year and the Florida Public Citizen of the Year by the National Association of Social Workers. Lapchick has been the recipient of numerous humanitarian awards. He was inducted into the Sports Hall of Fame of the Commonwealth Nations in 1999 in the category of Humanitarian along with Arthur Ashe and Nelson Mandela and received the Ralph Bunche International Peace Award. He joined Muhammad Ali, Jackie Robinson, Arthur Ashe, and Wilma Rudolph in the Sport in Society Hall of Fame in 2004. Lapchick won the Diversity Leadership Award at the 2003 Literacy Classic and the Jean Mayer Global Citizenship Award from Tufts University in 2000. He won the Wendell Scott Pioneer Award in 2004 for leadership in advancing people of color in the motor sports industry. He received the "Hero Among Us Award" from the Boston Celtics in 1999 and was named as the Martin Luther King, Rosa Parks, Cesar Chavez Fellow by the State of Michigan in 1998. Lapchick was the winner of the 1997 Arthur Ashe Voice of Conscience Award. He also won the 1997 Women's Sports Foundation President's Award for work toward the development of women's sports and was named as the 1997 Boston Celtics "Man of the Year." In 1995, the National Association of Elementary School Principals gave him their first award as a "Distinguished American in Service of Our Children." He was a guest of President Bill Clinton at the White House for National Student-Athlete Day in 1996, 1997, 1998, and again in 1999.

He is listed in Who's Who in American Education, Who's Who in Finance and Industry, and Who's Who in American Business. Lapchick was named as "one of the 100 most powerful people in sport" for six consecutive years. He is widely known for bringing different racial groups together to create positive work force environments. In 2003–04 he served as the national spokesperson for VERB, the Center for Disease Control's program to combat preteen obesity.

Lapchick has received eight honorary degrees. In 1993, he was named as the outstanding alumnus at the University of Denver where he got his PhD in international race relations in 1973. Lapchick received a BA from St. John's University in 1967 and an honorary degree from St. John's in 2001.

Lapchick is a board member of the Open Doors Foundation, SchoolSports, the Team Harmony Foundation, and the Black Coaches Association and is on the advisory boards of the Women's Sports Foundation and the Giving Back Fund.

Under Lapchick's leadership, the DeVos Program launched the Institute for Diversity and Ethics in Sport in December 2002. The Institute focuses on two broad areas. In the area of Diversity, the Institute publishes the critically acclaimed *Racial and Gender Report Card*, long-authored by Lapchick in his former role as director of the Center for the Study of Sport in Society at Northeastern University. *The Report Card*, an annual study of the racial and gender hiring practices of major professional sports, Olympic sport, and college sport in the United States, shows long-term trends over a decade and highlights organizations that are notable for diversity in coaching and management staffs.

In another diversity initiative, the Institute partners with the NCAS to provide diversity management training to sports organizations, including athletic departments and professional leagues and teams. The Consortium has already conducted such training for the NBA, Major League Soccer, and more than 80 university athletic departments.

In the area of ethics, the Institute monitors some of the critical ethical issues in college and professional sport, including the potential for the exploitation of student-athletes, gambling, performance-enhancing drugs, and violence in sport. The Institute publishes annual studies on graduation rates for all teams in college football bowl games, comparing graduation rates for football players to rates for overall student-athletes and including a breakdown by race.

The Institute also publishes the graduation rates of the women's and men's basketball teams in the NCAA Tournament as March Madness heats up.

Richard is the son of Joe Lapchick, the famous Original Celtic center who became a legendary coach for St. John's and the Knicks. He is married to Ann Pasnak and has three children and two grandchildren.

Jessica Bartter

Jessica Bartter is currently the assistant director of communications and marketing for the National Consortium for Academics and Sports (NCAS) located at the University of Central Florida.

At the University of California, San Diego, Bartter was a member of the nationally ranked NCAA Division II volleyball team where she was elected team co-captain during her junior and senior years. The UC San Diego Tritons went to the playoffs every year, including a Final Four appearance her junior season. As an individual who values teamwork, Bartter considers her Best Team Player award one of her greatest accomplishments.

Bartter attributes many valuable lessons she has learned to her experiences in sport and works to apply them outside of the sports arena and into her professional life. Prior to moving to Orlando, Florida, to work for the NCAS, Bartter worked for the UC San Diego Recreation and Intercollegiate Athletic Departments while she earned her bachelor's degree in management science, with a minor in psychology.

Born and raised in Orange County, California, Bartter attended Valencia High School of Placentia before becoming a Triton. Bartter is grateful to her father, who first introduced her to sports and to her mother who taxied her to softball and volleyball practices and even dared to catch wild pitches in the backyard. Bartter is the eldest of four siblings including Jacqueline, Brian and Kyle, all of whom have proudly donned the jersey No. 13. Bartter currently resides in Los Angeles, California, and is engaged to her childhood sweetheart C. J. Duffaut.

Sara Jane Baker

Sara Jane Baker is currently a graduate student in the DeVos Sport Business Management Program at the University of Central Florida working toward master's degrees in business administration and sport business management. She also works as a graduate assistant for Dr. Richard Lapchick. Prior to the DeVos Program, Sara attended the University of Nebraska earning an undergraduate degree in marketing. While at Nebraska, she was a heptathlete on the track and field team. In addition to being a co-captain in her senior season, Sara was a two-time All-American and second team Academic

All-American. Her success in track earned her a spot on the USA Track and Field team and a chance to represent Team USA in the Netherlands.

Sara was born and raised in Kalamazoo, Michigan. She is especially grateful to her parents and older brother, Lee, who have been supportive in all her endeavors.

Catherine Lahey

Catherine Lahey, known to her friends as Kt, is a graduate of the DeVos Sport Business Management Program at the University of Central Florida where she earned master's degrees in business administration and sport business management. While completing her studies, Kt worked as a graduate assistant in the national office of the National Consortium for Academics and Sports (NCAS). Before entering the DeVos Program, she attended Stetson University on the J. Ollie Edmunds Distinguished Scholarship, earning her undergraduate degrees in English and sport management. In her years at Stetson, Kt spent time volunteering in the Sports Information Department, studying abroad at Oxford University, working as a sports reporter for the student newspaper, and hanging out with legendary English professor Michael W. Raymond. Kt has proudly served as a softball coach at DeLand High School for the past six years. Although she attended Bishop Moore High School in Orlando, Florida, she happily considers herself an honorary DeLand Bulldog. Outside of the academic and professional arenas, Kt enjoys going to the beach with her dogs, spending quality time with friends and family, reading anything John Irving writes, and drinking Riptide Rush Gatorade.

Regarding the writing of this text, Kt is extremely grateful to have had the opportunity to speak with some of the incredible women who bravely pioneered athletic equality. The experience was humbling, enlightening, and inspiring.

Stacy Martin-Tenney

Stacy A. Martin-Tenney grew up in Bloomington, Indiana, where she began her athletic career at a young age. She credits her success to her parents Maureen and Randy, both former coaches. Her mother, Maureen, has been especially inspirational as a woman involved in sport. Maureen graduated too late to benefit from the freedom Title

IX afforded many women, but self-taught the game of volleyball and became a successful coach instilling values of self worth and determination in many young women throughout the years including her daughter. Stacy won two state titles her senior year with record-breaking performances and she was named the Gatorade National Female Track & Field Athlete of 1999. Auburn University offered her a full athletic scholarship in track and field. As an Auburn athlete, Stacy set new school records in the shot put, discus, hammer, and weight throw. A condition called Compartment Syndrome had plagued her legs for eight years and finally required surgery and extensive rehab that began with learning how to walk again. In spite of this obstacle, her numerous collegiate career accomplishments included an SEC Championship, Academic as well as Athletic All-American honors, and competing in the Junior World Championships. The pinnacle of her athletic career was qualifying for the 2004 Olympic Trials in both shot put and discus. In 2007, Martin was inducted into the Indiana Track and Field Hall of Fame for her athletic career accomplishments. She was named to the SEC Good Works Team, was a NCAA Leadership Conference Representative, president of the Student Athletic Advisory Committee, as well as being named to the SEC Academic Honor Roll all of her years at Auburn. She graduated with honors from Auburn University with a bachelor's of science in education and health promotion, and a bachelor's of science in business administration and human resource management. She has passed the torch on to her younger brother, Cory, who won two NCAA championship titles in 2008, in the hammer and the shot put and will be continuing his track and field career professionally.

After Auburn, Stacy entered the sports industry to work for the NCAA Beyond the Game Tour presented by CBS Sports, a promotional tour for student-athletes, and for ESPN on a summer sporting event production. She then earned a master's of sports business management and a master's of business administration at the University of Central Florida's DeVos Sport Business Management Program. She served as a graduate assistant to Dr. Richard Lapchick and The Institute for Diversity and Ethics in Sport (TIDES) and worked for the Orlando Magic during graduate school. She has participated in Deliver the Dream weekends for families that suffer from terminal illnesses and other community service activities. Stacy was a co-author on TIDES' *2005 Racial and Gender Report Card*, and the National Consortium for Academics and Sports' *100 Heroes* and *100 Pioneers* with Lapchick and other graduate students. Stacy took an internship with Disney's Wide World of Sports Complex on the sports event management team after graduate school. She is currently a marketing manager for Disney Sports, specifically handling the marketing efforts for Marathon Weekend and Disney's Endurance Series accounts. She is also part of the team launching a women's half marathon, Disney's Princess Half Marathon, focused on attributes of princesses, such as courage, bravery, and strength that all women possess. Stacy Martin-Tenney resides near Orlando, Florida, with her husband Anthony Tenney.

Horacio Ruiz

Horacio Ruiz is a graduate of the University of Central Florida's DeVos Sport Business Management Graduate Program, where he earned dual master's degrees in business administration and sport business management. He attended the University of Florida as an undergraduate where he received his degree in exercise and sport sciences. While at the University of Central Florida, Ruiz was a co-founder of the Hope for Stanley Foundation along with a group of his inspired peers. The purpose for establishing the Foundation was to create opportunities for people in sports to volunteer in New Orleans. Upon graduating from the University of Central Florida in December 2007, he accepted a position with the New Orleans Hornets as an inside sales consultant before accepting the Coordinator position for the Hope for Stanley Foundation. He now hopes to bring many people in sports to New Orleans to help rebuild the city. Ruiz's writing has appeared in ESPN.com, *The Miami Herald*, the *Independent Florida Alligator*, and GatorZone.com. He also was a contributing author to Dr. Richard Lapchick's 13th book, *100 Pioneers: African-Americans Who Broke Color Barriers in Sports*. Raised in Miami, Florida, Ruiz was born in Managua, Nicaragua. His father, mother, and sister currently reside in Miami.

Ryan Sleeper

Ryan Sleeper was born April 17, 1983, in Kansas City, Missouri, to his parents Pam Benton and Jeff Sleeper. He and his younger brother, Shane, were raised in the Kansas City suburb of Overland Park,

Kansas, with their mother, while spending the summer months in Central Florida with their father. Ryan credits having the opportunity to grow in two very different cultures as the reason for his openness to diversity, which has shaped everything he does.

Ryan is currently a graduate student at the University of Central Florida pursuing master's degrees in business administration and sport business management in the DeVos Sport Business Management Program. Ryan aspired to be in the DeVos program since the time he heard they were creating it in 2000 due to its well-rounded curriculum of business, diversity, and philanthropy. While in the program, he serves as Dr. Keith Harrison's graduate assistant. Ryan's work is for Scholar-Baller, a nonprofit organization that promotes a balance between academics and athletics. He has also made three trips to New Orleans, Louisiana, with the Hope for Stanley Foundation. Hope for Stanley is a nonprofit organization that assists sport business management programs around the country with making group trips to the Gulf Coast to help rebuild homes that were affected by Hurricane Katrina in 2005.

Before Ryan was accepted into the DeVos program, he earned a bachelor's of arts degree in psychology and a bachelor's of science degree in marketing from the University of Central Florida. Ryan's diversity courses for his degree in psychology were focused on women's studies. His previous experience in sports includes a marketing internship with the Kansas City T-Bones of minor league baseball's Northern League. He also worked a season for the Orlando Magic as a marketing research assistant.

Upon graduation, Ryan will return to Kansas City to work an internship in corporate partnerships for his hometown team, the Kansas City Chiefs. He is very excited to return home to join his favorite football team as well as to be near the rest of his dear family: Grandma Nancy, Grandpa Jack, Grandma Ruth, and girlfriend Brittain.

Catherine Elkins—Editor

Catherine Elkins is a student in the University of Central Florida's DeVos Sport Business Management Program. She grew up in Bernardsville, New Jersey, and is the oldest of three daughters born to Bob and Chris Elkins. She went to high school at Choate Rosemary Hall in Connecticut before heading to Middlebury College in Vermont, where she excelled in ice hockey, earning first team All-American status each of her four years. After graduation, she went to Division III rival, Manhattanville College in Purchase, New York, to be an assistant ice hockey coach while simultaneously earning her master's degree. She previously worked as a P. J. Boatwright intern with the Women's Metropolitan Golf Association, as a sales associate with CoSport—selling Olympic tickets and hospitality packages—and as a ticket intern with the Denver Outlaws. She is currently a graduate assistant for the National Consortium for Academics and Sports (NCAS) and The Institute for Diversity and Ethics in Sport (TIDES), where she co-authored the *Racial and Gender Report Card* for the National Basketball Association and the Collegiate Division I-A Diversity Study.